Themes in Comparative History

Themes in Comparative History

General Editor: CLIVE EMSLEY

PUBLISHED TITLES

Clive Emsley
POLICING AND ITS CONTEXT, 1750–1870

R. F. Holland
EUROPEAN DECOLONIZATION, 1918–1980

Ian Inkster
SCIENCE AND TECHNOLOGY IN HISTORY

Dominic Lieven
THE ARISTOCRACY IN EUROPE, 1815–1914

Pamela Pilbeam
THE MIDDLE CLASSES IN EUROPE, 1789–1914

Jane Rendall
THE ORIGINS OF MODERN FEMINISM: WOMEN IN BRITAIN, FRANCE AND THE UNITED STATES, 1780–1860

Ken Ward
MASS COMMUNICATIONS AND THE MODERN WORLD

FORTHCOMING

David Englander and Tony Mason
WAR AND POLITICS: THE EXPERIENCE OF THE SERVICEMAN IN TWO WORLD WARS

Joe Lee
PEASANT EUROPE IN THE EIGHTEENTH AND NINETEENTH CENTURIES

Rosemary O'Day
THE FAMILY IN FRANCE, ENGLAND AND THE UNITED STATES OF AMERICA, 1600–1850
Peter Rycraft
PEASANT REBELLIONS, 1400–1600

Series Standing Order

If you would like to receive future titles in this series as they are published, you can make use of our standing order facility. To place a standing order please contact your bookseller or, in case of difficulty, write to us at the address below with your name and address and the name of the series. Please state with which title you wish to begin your standing order. (If you live outside the UK we may not have the rights for your area, in which case we will forward your order to the publisher concerned.)

Standing Order Service, Macmillan Distribution Ltd,
Houndsmills, Basingstoke, Hampshire RG21 2XS, England.

THE ARISTOCRACY IN EUROPE, 1815–1914

Dominic Lieven

MACMILLAN

First published 1992 by
THE MACMILLAN PRESS LTD
Houndmills, Basingstoke, Hampshire RG21 2XS
and London
Companies and representatives
throughout the world

ISBN 0–333–38932–8 hardcover
ISBN 0–333–38933–6 paperback

A catalogue record for this book is available
from the British Library

Phototypeset by Intype, London
Printed in Hong Kong

In memory of my parents

Contents

List of Tables

List of Currencies and Measurements

1 desyatina (ds)	= 1.09 hectares (ha) = 2.7 acres
1 hectare	= 2.47 acres
1 pound sterling	= 6.6 Prussian taler
	= 9.58 Russian silver or (post-1896) gold roubles
	= 20 German marks (post-1871)
	= 11.8 South German florins (pre-1871)

General Editor's Preface

Since the Second World War there has been a massive expansion in the study of economic and social history generating, and fuelled by, new journals, new academic series and societies. The expansion of research has given rise to new debates and ferocious controversies. This series proposes to take up some of the current issues in historical debate and explore them in a comparative framework.

Historians, of course, are principally concerned with unique events, and they can be inclined to wrap themselves in the isolating greatcoats of their 'country' and their 'period'. It is at least arguable, however, that a comparison of events, or a comparison of the way in which different societies coped with a similar problem – war, industrialisation, population growth and so forth – can reveal new perspectives and new questions. The authors of the volumes in this series have each taken an issue to explore in such a comparative framework. The books are not designed to be path-breaking monographs, though most will contain a degree of new research. The intention is, by exploring problems across national boundaries, to encourage students in tertiary education, in sixth-forms, and hopefully also the more general reader, to think critically about aspects of past developments. No author can maintain strict objectivity; nor can he or she provide definitive answers to all the questions which they explore. If the authors generate discussion and increase perception, then their task is well done.

CLIVE EMSLEY

Introduction

Everyone knows what aristocracy means until they have to write a book on the subject. Then the problems of definition begin. In traditional English parlance aristocracy means the peerage, together with its brothers, sisters and children. It would not be difficult to write the history of so small and clearly defined a group. Before 1900 the peerage was homogeneous. England had been a unified nation-state for centuries. In the overwhelming majority of cases its peerage shared the same religion, education, culture and values.

But if a history of the English Victorian peerage would be easy it would also be boring. This is, apart from anything else, ground well trodden by historians. Moreover, the peerage was only one section of the traditional upper class. There was also the baronetage and the broader untitled landowning gentry, all of which would have been defined as noble on the European continent. Aristocracy and gentry were part of the same ruling class but although the two groups overlapped, their characteristics and functions were not precisely the same. Nor did the gentry have as many options as great landed magnates when faced with the challenges of the nineteenth century. To write a history purely of the peerage would therefore be to omit a key element in the story of how England's upper class confronted their rapidly changing society and what impact they had upon it. The most recent work on the eclipse of England's traditional ruling class, *The Decline and Fall of the British Aristocracy*, written by David Cannadine, therefore looks at the fate both of the peerage and of the untitled gentry. I have followed Cannadine's example, recognising as I do so that whereas the peerage is an easily defined group, drawing a clear dividing line between the gentry and some sections of the middle class is much more difficult.

Blurred definitions and unclear dividing lines are in any case inevitable when one moves from English aristocracy to that of the broader European continent. In no other European country, save perhaps Hungary, was there a precise equivalent of the English peerage. Certainly the titled aristocracy of Russia and Germany cannot be directly compared with members of the English House of Lords. Russia in 1900 did not have more titled families than England, especially when the differing sizes of the two countries' populations is taken into account. But the fact that in Russia all children shared their father's title and property meant that the automatic equation of title, status and wealth largely possible with respect to the English peerage certainly could not be made in the Tsarist Empire. Moreover, in Russia, the legal status of nobility, which had minimal political or social significance by 1900, was enjoyed by over one million people by the turn of the century.

In the German states and Austria the nobility was also enormous by English standards but even the titled aristocracy could not be compared to the English peerage. In the nineteenth century the legal distinction most commonly used in Germany was between so-called 'high' and 'low' nobility. All the former but also some of the latter had titles, including the most distinguished aristocratic titles of 'prince', 'duke' and 'count'. In theory the distinction between 'high' and 'low' nobility was between aristocrats, who had no sovereign other than the Holy Roman Emperor, and others who were the subjects of territorial princes such as the King of Prussia or the electors of Hanover, Saxony or Bavaria. This distinction, lovingly preserved in the *Almanach de Gotha*, never made much sense. Most of the 'high noble' families extant in the nineteenth century had not always enjoyed this status but had been promoted to it at some point in the history of the Holy Roman Empire. Other families – East Prussians and Balts – came from regions which were in practice beyond the Empire's borders. Above all, however, the historian of nineteenth-century German aristocracy is bound to see the distinction between 'high' and 'low' nobility as an anachronism. The Holy Roman Empire had, after all, disappeared in 1806. To confine a study of the German aristocracy to the 'high nobility' in other words to the so-called *Standesherren*, would be to ignore many of the most powerful, wealthy and interesting titled families of nineteenth-century Germany.

The titled nobility as a whole, however, was a group much larger and less homogeneous than the English peerage. In general, as in Russia, all children inherited their father's title but this rule differed from one German state to another and even between different categories of noble within a single state. In addition, as former theoretically sovereign rulers, the *Standesherren* were allowed even in the nineteenth century to set their own rules for inheriting titles within their families, which caused further diversity. Moreover, norms for inheriting property also differed. In England male primogeniture was the almost universal rule: in Russia it was a rare exception confined to some families of the magnate elite. In Germany, even indeed in the eastern Prussian provinces, practice differed greatly from family to family. For instance, strict primogeniture and entail prevailed in the Westphalian Catholic aristocracy, and indeed in most of the *Standesherren* families, but in very many Prussian noble families younger sons could expect to inherit part of their father's land. If the titled German aristocrat was less likely than many of his Russian counterparts to lack any wealth or status, he certainly could not be relied on to be rich and prominent in the manner of the English peerage.

Moreover, even more than in England, to limit a history of the Victorian Russian and German upper class to the titled aristocracy would be a gross error, for in both countries the untitled gentry was of great significance. In Russia, aristocratic magnates had dominated politics before 1800 and remained very important right down to 1917. But in the nineteenth century an increasingly professionalised military and civil bureaucracy, whose elite was largely recruited from the gentry, to a growing extent displaced the great aristocratic clans as leaders of Russia's government and armed forces. After 1861, the Empire's economic future to an ever greater degree rested on the efforts of state officials, industrialists and peasants. Unlike Russia, in Germany's most important state, Prussia, there never had been a magnate class. The Junkers were nineteenth-century continental Europe's most important traditional ruling elite. Their impact on the fate not only of Germany but of all Victorian and Edwardian Europe was of great significance. But the Junkers were a relatively poor, usually untitled gentry. Therefore a historian who wishes to say something significant about the relationship between modernity and aristocracy in Europe has to study not only titled magnates but also a broader traditional ruling class. The precise boundaries of this class will be difficult to draw. In Russia and the German states, for instance, the group will be wider than the titled families but much narrower than the entire nobility. In this book I will be studying the magnates and the richer elements of the provincial gentry, families with the wealth and status to 'live nobly' in the eyes of their peers. To avoid clumsiness and unnecessary verbiage I will describe this entire upper class as 'aristocracy'.

For both practical and theoretical reasons I intend to confine my study of European aristocracy largely to England, the various German states and Russia. To cover the whole of Europe is impossible, save in the most superficial manner which of necessity can never amount to much more than a repetition of received wisdom. In part also I chose Germany in order to force myself to learn the German language, without which in my view it is difficult to be a self-respecting scholar on Russian and Eastern European affairs, which are my speciality. Amidst the stresses of trying to study and teach contemporary – and since 1987 dramatically changing – Soviet and East European politics I reckoned that the only way to force myself to learn German was to tackle a book which could not be written without it.

But there are also good theoretical reasons for concentrating on the three countries which I have chosen. In the last 130 years Germany and Russia have been continental Europe's only two potential superpowers. Only they have had the population, resources, and economic and military might potentially to dominate the whole European continent. The two great wars of this century have above all revolved around the struggle between Russia and Germany to eliminate their great competitor, control the resources of all eastern and central Europe, and thereby acquire a power which would make them dominant throughout the continent. In pre-1914 Europe Britain too was a superpower, an actual and not merely a potential one. London's traditional policy was, however, not to dominate Europe but rather to protect her own back door by preserving a balance of power on the continent while using her resources to exercise world-wide maritime supremacy. Nevertheless when faced with the threat of a single dominant power on the continent the British Empire did intervene decisively in European affairs in 1793–1815, 1914–18 and 1939–45.

I chose to study England, Germany and Russia because in geopolitical terms these three countries more than any other have determined the fate of late-nineteenth and twentieth-century Europe. In addition, however, all three countries had powerful aristocracies which greatly influenced their societies and governments before 1914. Furthermore these aristocracies repay study not merely because of their importance but also because they represent widely contrasting variations on the European aristocratic theme. Aristocracy is best defined as an historical, hereditary ruling class and this term applies to the groups studied in Russia, Germany and England. But aristocracies can differ markedly in their overall wealth and its distribution within the ruling class; in the extent to which they directly control the apparatus of government and the means by which they do so; in their economic roles, cultures, religions, educations, career patterns, traditions and in much else besides. In these respects the contrasts both between and within English, German and Russian aristocracy were marked, and comparison therefore all the more useful and revealing.

This book aims to examine nineteenth-century German, Russian and English aristocracy as comprehensively as is possible in 80 000 words. It looks at these aristocracies' wealth and its sources, together with the economic roles of the three elites. It also studies the rules, norms and morals of upper-class society, together with everyday life and leisure in town and countryside. It covers education, culture and careers, in the latter case concentrating on aristocracy's traditionally foremost occupation, namely war. The book concludes by investigating the role of the traditional elites in government and politics. The study of Victorian and Edwardian aristocracy makes no sense, however, unless it is placed firmly within the context of the huge changes which were occurring in economy and society and the challenges these presented to traditional elites. The aim of this book is to explain both the challenges and aristocracy's response. It is to understand both what the nineteenth century did to European aristocracy and in turn how and why the upper classes' response to encroaching modernity influenced Europe's fate, not just before 1914 but in ways that cast a shadow to this day.

This book has many failings. Some of these are the inescapable consequence of trying to cover a vast and complicated subject in one small volume. Others stem from my own failings as an historian.

I am uneasily aware that this book is much more a study of male aristocracy than of its female relations. I do not think I have fully explained the influence of religion on aristocratic values and mentalities, or indeed explored sufficiently the fascinating contrasts in this respect between Lutheranism, Anglicanism, Russian Orthodoxy and Catholicism. I have in my time read Pushkin and Fontane, Turgenev, Trollope and Proust and perhaps unconsciously have gained from them some insights into aristocracy. But I have failed systematically to use nineteenth-century literature as a guide to aristocratic mentalities. Nor does this book discuss the thoughts on aristocracy of leading theorists of politics and society – Marx and Weber, Burke and Mill, de Tocqueville and Karamzin, the Slavophiles, or Lenin.

I am an historian of Russia who has lived most of his life in England. A German historian may feel that this explains some strange emphases and omissions in this book. Possibly he or she will believe that I have failed to grasp the significance of legal distinctions between noble and non-noble and the impact these had on the psychology and sense of exclusiveness of the noble estate. If so, this failing is no doubt rooted in the unimportance of such legal distinctions in Russia after 1861 and the fact that, with the exception of the peerage, no legal barriers divided the bulk of the English upper class from the rest of society in the nineteenth century.

I hope that some at least of these failings will be compensated by the advantages of the comparative approach I have attempted. I personally have gained enormously by rising above my own narrow area of late Imperial Russia, climbing like a balloonist away from the academic trench warfare about 'who lost Russia' and why Bolshevism triumphed. It is in my view worthwhile to ask fundamental questions about what options traditional European elites faced in confronting modernity and which factors influenced different elites to choose various strategies of survival. This book, I hope, says something useful about the relationship between economics and culture, politics and international relations, all of which were significant in determining aristocracy's fate. Timing, contingency, chance and miscalculation are always crucial in history. It mattered greatly, for instance, that England's aristocracy was faced with the issue of agricultural protection in the 1820s–1840s, and Prussia's not until the very different era of the 1870s–1890s. The fate of the aristocracy, and of all Europe, would have been very different had Russia's Revolution and disintegration occurred a little earlier, before the desperation and miscalculations of German military leaders caused the decision to launch unrestricted submarine warfare and thereby bring the United States into the war.

The comparative approach can change perspectives, ask new and relevant questions, shock historians locked in national assumptions or obsessively concerned with the supposedly 'great issues' of specific national histories. At its best it can be a liberating experience, a new dimension, the freedom and broad horizons of aerial warfare rather than the vast accumulation of material – not to mention sometimes bile – required for academic versions of the Somme or Passchendaele, in which sovereignty over inches of territory is fought for with vast ferocity. This book, however, also has a rather down-to-earth justification. No one has previously attempted an integrated study of nineteenth-century European aristocracy. Even the most determined academic enemy of the old upper classes would probably not deny that the subject is worthy of some study. In which case even an imperfect book is better than none at all.

A work of this nature is heavily dependent on secondary sources. My debt therefore to other historians is immense. I have tried in the bibliography to acknowledge this debt in part by noting the main sources from which I have drawn information and ideas. But given the scale of this book it is inevitable that I have not been able to produce a full bibliography nor indeed to read more than one-tenth of the sources necessary for a truly full and scholarly study of nineteenth-century aristocracy.

A major problem with the secondary literature is that, for all its often great virtues, it is overwhelmingly national in perspective. This means not only that it focuses on a single national, or even provincial, elite or issue but also that the approach and the questions raised are determined in large part by national historiographical traditions or obsessions. In Russia, 1917 dominates all. This means in part that the Soviet regime has barred free access to archives and influenced its own historians to adopt certain approaches and concentrate on specific areas of Russian history. Given these constraints it is astonishing how good some works by Soviet historians have been. But even among Western historians the shadow of 1917 often hangs over the nineteenth century, colouring both interpretations and the choice of subjects to study. The best, indeed only, examination of the nobility between 1800 and

1861 was, for instance, written well over a century ago and even that is a history of the nobles not just in the nineteenth century but throughout their existence.

Surprisingly, the situation is rather similar in Germany. Where Prussia is concerned, Soviet-style problems about access to archives and politically suitable areas for study remained relevant until very recently. In addition, Nazism often looms over German history as overpoweringly as 1917 does over Russian, determining many of the questions which Germans ask about their past. Nineteenth-century history becomes a battleground as to which group in German society bore responsibility for the country's tragedies in the twentieth century. An additional problem is that many German historians and social scientists share with some of their European and more of their North American peers the conviction that in the modern world aristocracy is an irrelevant and politically suspect area of study, to which only scholars tainted by social snobbery and attracted by a love for superficial glitter will dedicate themselves. Aristocrats and their progeny are dumb, wicked or, more likely, both. The curious result of these attitudes is that although many German historians attach huge importance to the Junkers, sometimes blaming them for the perversion of the whole of modern German history, no scholarly work has been written since 1945 providing a detailed, empirically based study of Junker economic, political or cultural life under the Empire.

The English case is very, almost indeed comically, different. Twentieth-century England has suffered no catastrophes such as 1917, Hitler or Stalin. Its nineteenth-century history has often, and not unjustifiably, been portrayed as a triumphantly peaceful and orderly process from aristocratic oligarchy to liberal democracy in which the traditional upper classes played an intelligent and decisive role. English aristocracy has had a far better press than its German or Russian counterparts. It has also been the subject of much more thorough recent scholarly work. I have relied greatly on the latter in writing the present book.

This book has had both friends and enemies. Among the latter the two most formidable were Mikhail Gorbachev and Alexandra Lieven – probably the only time these two names will be linked together in print. The year I committed myself to writing this book Mikhail Gorbachev came to power. His reign turned contemporary Soviet politics upside down, with dramatic implications for the workload of anyone like myself who was attempting to interpret and teach current Soviet developments. Three years after Gorbachev came to power, my baby daughter Alexandra arrived in this world, the most joyful but also the most disruptive event in my personal life.

Foremost among this book's friends were the Humboldt Foundation, which supported me so generously and efficiently during ten months of research in Germany. Enormous thanks are due to Professor Rudolph Vierhaus of the Max Planck Institute for History in Göttingen, who encouraged and guided my work, as well as to Professor Gerhard Ritter of Munich University. I benefited from a discussion with Dr Heinz Reif, from whose admirable work I learned a great deal, and both Dr Marion, Countess von Dönhoff and Dr Walter Demel very kindly sent me manuscripts or books which they had written. So did Professor F. M. L. Thompson, who also gave me much useful advice. John Barnes and Alan Beattie were good enough to read my manuscript and Mrs Marion Osborne laboured with great patience and efficiency to type successive versions of my text. My wife, Mikiko, bore with fortitude the combined burdens of a career in investment banking, first one and then two small children, and an increasingly exhausted and bad-tempered husband.

DOMINIC LIEVEN

The German Confederations in 1815

SWEDEN

BALTIC SEA

Danzig

East Prussia

West
Prussia

Pomerania

RUSSIAN

Berlin

Brandenburg

R. Vistula

POLAND

R. Elbe

Dresden

SAXONY

Silesia

Posen

Prague

Olmütz

Bohemia

Moravia

Vienna

R. Danube

Budapest

AUSTRIA

nich

Gastein

Carniola

HUNGARY

etia

nice

THE PROVINCES AND POPULATION OF EUROPEAN RUSSIA IN 1900

NORWAY

SWEDEN

GERMANY

AUSTRIA-HUNGARY

RUMANIA

TURKEY

PERSIA

White Sea

Baltic Sea

Black Sea

Caspian Sea

FINLAND

ARCHANGEL

OLONETS

VOLOGDA

PERM

ESTLAND

ST. PETERSBURG

NOVGOROD

KURLAND

LIVLAND

PSKOV

VITEBSK

KOVNO

VILNA

MOGILEV

SMOLENSK

GRODNO

MINSK

POLISH PROVINCES

VOLHYNIA

KIEV

PODOLIA

BESSARABIA

KHERSON

TVER

YAROSLAVL

KOSTROMA

VIATKA

MOSCOW

VLADIMIR

NIZHNI NOVGOROD

KAZAN

UFA

KALUGA

RIAZAN

TULA

PENZA

SIMBIRSK

OREL

TAMBOV

SARATOV

SAMARA

ORENBURG

KURSK

CHERNIGOV

POLTAVA

VORONEZH

KHARKOV

EKATERINOSLAV

DON

ASTRAKHAN

TAURIDA

KUBAN

STAVROPOL

TEREK

TRANS-CAUCASIAN PROVINCES

The first official Russian census was held in 1897. The total population was just over 129 million - nearly as large as the combined populations of Britain, France, and Germany. Over 80% of all Russians were peasants. Finland was an autonomous Duchy, and, like Poland, was subdivided into Provinces

MAIN NATIONAL & ETHNIC GROUPS IN EUROPEAN RUSSIA IN 1900	
Russians	55 million
Ukrainians	22 million
Poles	8 million
White Russians	6 million
Jews	5 million
Balts	4 million
Caucasians	3 million
Germans	2 million

Acknowledgements

Acknowledgement is due to Longman Group UK Ltd for permission to reproduce the map on pp. xxii–xxiii, taken from *The Origins of the Wars of German Unification* by William Carr; and to Martin Gilbert and George Weidenfeld & Nicolson for permission to reproduce the map on p. xxiv, taken from the *Russian History Atlas*.

1. The Nineteenth Century: Challenge and Response

THE nineteenth century was a good time to be an aristocrat. In comparison to ancestors who had lorded over society in aristocracy's heyday, the Victorian nobleman was likely to enjoy a longer, more comfortable and less dangerous existence. But as a ruling class aristocracy was in decline. Before 1917 in neither Britain, Germany nor Russia did this decline occur overnight. Because aristocracy entered the nineteenth century with immense wealth, power and status it would be a long time before noblemen became insignificant members of society. The decline of aristocracy did not occur at the same speed in Britain, Germany and Russia. It did not follow precisely similar patterns and there were times even when the process seemed to be moving in reverse. Nevertheless the history of European aristocracy between 1815 and 1914 is that of a class which was clearly and consciously on the defensive.

The assault on aristocracy began in the second half of the eighteenth century. The Enlightenment denied that earthly order reflected divine will. Man's goal was happiness on earth not salvation in the hereafter. Human misery was the product not of original sin but of the faulty ordering of government, society and economy. Rational men of goodwill must seek society's reform. Their merit and prestige should reflect their contribution as individuals to this cause. Traditional values, prescriptive rights and

1

corporate privileges were impeding the creation of the good society and should be destroyed. The aristocrat should forget his pride in birth and his overriding loyalty to family and class. He should become a citizen, cultivating the virtues of simplicity, kindness, rationality and hard work.

These doctrines undermined the principles on which the Old Regime rested. Their threat was, however, immensely increased by the outbreak of the French Revolution. France had been the greatest of Europe's absolute monarchies. Its court, aristocracy and culture had been looked up to by the rest of Europe's nobility. In the eighteenth century German and Russian aristocrats spoke French as their first language and regarded their native cultures and tongues as provincial and plebeian. The brutal overthrow of the Bourbons in the name of liberty, equality and fraternity was a shock. The rights of man were a threat in themselves; realised through terror and carried across Europe by the armies of the continent's most powerful country they were a nightmare.

It is true that Bonaparte destroyed much of the revolution's radical message. The militarised, service-orientated state he created in many ways brought French absolutism closer to the military-bureaucratic monarchies of Russia and Prussia.[1] Even Bonapartist 'enlightened' despotism, however, had aspects much disliked by traditional aristocracy: among them were fiscal and legal equality, and the centralisation and bureaucratisation of government. In addition, neither Bonaparte's tyranny nor the conservative powers' victory of 1814–15 could erase from men's minds the memories of 1789–94 or the myths, inspiration and models which these years bequeathed to later generations of European radicals.

The shadow of 1789 lay over Europe's nineteenth-century aristocracy. Never again would aristocratic politics be quite so carefree. Before the revolution France's aristocracy had absorbed many of the Enlightenment's values. This was particularly true among the aristocracy's plutocratic elite of courtiers. In these circles there was often ostentatious disdain for religion and for the traditional rituals that surrounded the throne and contributed to its prestige. A tendency towards 'radical chic' ensured powerful sympathisers for those who attacked government tyranny and religious obscurantism, or defended Rousseau's celebration of sensibility and simplicity. More seriously, many great aristocrats believed sincerely in the principle of constitutional government, while most provincial nobles supported meritocracy and careers open to talent in order to break the courtiers' hold on all senior posts in the armed forces. The great conservative 'interests' – monarchy, aristocracy, provincial gentry and church – were anything but united and it was their internal conflicts which were the initial cause of the Old Regime's demise.[2]

The French Revolution encouraged conservative consolidation in Europe, particularly in the years immediately following 1789 but in a more general way throughout the nineteenth century. Aristocratic liberalism was not dead. It was represented most famously by English Whiggery and reforming conservatism. It had its exponents among German nobles resentful of bureaucratic absolutism before 1848 and Russians who chafed under a similar regime until 1905. But the fact that moderate reform in France had quickly resulted in civil war and terror was a lesson often stressed by conservatives. Alexander II of Russia, contemplating cautious constitutional reform in 1881, could terrify himself by memories of Louis XVI and the Estates General.[3]

Even before 1789 conservative writers had begun to marshal their arguments against the ideas of the Enlightenment.[4] But it was in the years immediately after the revolution that seminal works of nineteenth-century conservatism were written. Most famous was Edmund Burke's *Reflections on the Revolution in France* but his defence of the ancient national constitution had its equivalents in both Germany and Russia. Common themes were the uniqueness of individual national traditions; the dangers of trying to transform society through rational blueprints; and the wisdom of custom, established institutions and religion as pillars of social stability and individual contentment. Nicholas Karamzin's *Memoir on Ancient and Modern Russia*, defending the ancient alliance of monarchy and gentry against the rising power of a rationalist, reformist bureaucracy, was the exact Russian equivalent of Burke's attempt to preserve English tradition from home-grown advocates of 'French' principles.[5]

So long as governmental, social and ecclesiastical elites were united there was little chance of successful revolution from below in societies where the great majority of the population were tradition-bound and semi-literate peasants. But the nineteenth-century revolutions in industry, communications and education transformed Europe, providing a mass base for the 'ideas of 1789' and creating a society over which it was impossible for aristocracy to rule in the traditional manner.

By 1851 more than half of the English population lived in towns and the same was true in Germany by 1900. Even in the vast and relatively backward Russian Empire one in five of the population had left the countryside by 1914. For the new urban labouring class living in towns meant escaping the supervision of aristocracy and established church at precisely the moment when workers were being subjected to the unprecedented disciplines and rigours of factory and slum: at the moment indeed when mentalities were being transformed. The urban working class might come under the sway of great entrepreneurs or of trade unionists and socialist politicians: whichever occurred, aristocratic control was gone.

A more serious challenge in anything but the long term was the new industrial, commercial and financial bourgeoisie. Quite quickly, industry, finance and commerce generated profits which agriculture could not match. This was abundantly clear in Britain, Germany and Russia by the last quarter of the nineteenth century. In any capitalist society, even under an absolute monarchy, wealth can buy patronage and influence. It can also purchase education and culture, together with the security, leisure and training useful to those who aspire to rule societies. It was not illogical for Marx to believe that the new bourgeoisie would supplant the aristocracy as Europe's ruling class. Why it had not completed this task by 1914 in England, Germany or Russia is one of the questions to be answered in this book.[6]

Although the rise of the bourgeoisie and of the working class were among the most obvious challenges to aristocratic domination of Victorian and Edwardian Europe, they were not the most fundamental threat. Society was becoming too complicated for aristocrats to manage.[7] The age of the professional and the expert – Burke's sophister, economist and calculator – was at hand. This was true even in armies, the most traditional field of aristocratic activity. The Industrial Revolution and the advent of the mass conscript army transformed the military art, greatly increasing the importance of the artillerist, engineer and expert in logistics. To organise, equip, mobilise, transport and direct the modern mass army required the skills of the professionally trained General Staff officer. By 1900 professionalism and, at least in principle, meritocracy ran the European military establishments. Even under the monarchies the aristocratic *beau sabreur* was relegated to a decorative role in a few Guards cavalry regiments and at the royal courts.[8]

If modernity threatened traditional aristocratic values with redundancy even in the army, the same was truer still in society as a whole. Industry, science, medicine, the law, engineering, even agriculture generated a host of experts whose opinions had to be listened to if a modern society was to be governed effectively. Government and politics themselves increasingly became a job for experts as State bureaucracies, especially in continental Europe, became far larger and more specialised, and as the arrival of a mass electorate made mobilising public opinion a grubby, time-consuming and increasingly professional occupation. Aristocracy lacked the numbers to fill all the posts of power and influence that an industrial society created. Aristocratic traditions, educations and cultures militated against occupying some of these positions, especially if the posts had to be fought for in open competition with members of the educated middle classes. But even if aristocracy had proved capable of dominating a wide range of industries and professions, it would in the process have lost much of the functional and cultural homogeneity which had always been a mark of the traditional European ruling class.

Faced by the modern world, a few key factors would determine aristocracy's ability to survive and to retain part at least of its old pre-eminence. Most important in a capitalist society was to preserve aristocratic wealth and property. This meant transforming agrarian estates into profitable capitalist enterprises and surviving the two great agricultural depressions of the nineteenth century. Even if this were achieved a gulf would open up between the rural bulk of the aristocracy and a narrow elite of magnates with industrial or urban property interests, or resources so vast that part of their wealth could be transferred into stocks and bonds. This gulf would divide the county gentry from the traditional core of the high aristocracy but it would also split the latter group, many of which would be left far behind in terms of wealth by the new financial and industrial elites.

Rich aristocrats ought in principle to be able to dominate high society. Wealth, inherited titles, social confidence and manners, together with domination of the royal courts, was a potent combination. The ability to control access to drawing rooms, clubs or enclosures at the racecourse was a form of social power and a means to impose aristocratic manners and even values on aspiring new elites. The effectiveness of this aristocratic power depended, however, on a number of factors. If high society was different ethnically to the new elites then it was likely in time to be pushed aside, as happened for instance in the Czech lands, the Baltic Provinces and Southern Ireland. If the aristocracy or royal court enjoyed little prestige among the new elites, if the latter had their own confident counter-culture or geographical base, then the result was likely to be the same. Instead of a single relatively homogeneous elite, inspired to a greater or lesser extent by aristocratic culture, a number of conflicting groupings with different values and bases were possible. This indeed was the pattern of late Imperial Russia.

Even where 'aristocratic' and 'bourgeois' culture strongly influenced each other, as was the case in both England and Germany, their mutual interaction was never simple. Moreover both aristocracy and bourgeoisie come in many shapes and sizes. A metropolitan court aristocracy has values and lifestyles very different from those of a rural landed elite or a service nobility, whether civilian or military. The 'bourgeoisie' can mean newly-rich industrialists of crude provincial origin but it can also denote an old, civilised and cosmopolitan commercial or financial elite, maybe Jewish, with its finger traditionally in politics and diplomacy. The 'bourgeoisie' can also encompass members of the free professions or senior state officials, whose mentality, values and skills will differ both from each other and from those of industrial, financial and commercial elites. The mingling of aristocratic and bourgeois values can lead to a kaleidoscope of possible combinations.

Traditionally, however, aristocracy meant not just wealth or social pre-eminence but also power. Even in the eighteenth-century absolute monarchies, where government was conducted by royal bureaucrats, aristocrats very often occupied top political and military positions and, if resident in the countryside, always exercised direct control over large numbers of peasants. Aristocracy meant ruling class. This became ever less true in the nineteenth and twentieth centuries as wealth and power became increasingly separate. However wealthy, the *rentier* aristocrat had lost his function in society. Though maybe no more idle than his grandfather, his self-esteem was likely to suffer from the fact that he lived in a society where an ability to be idle elegantly was not much respected. The prospect of vapid lives teetering towards degeneracy and scandal loomed. Meanwhile the less wealthy cousin who had donned the clothes of a state official or politician in order to continue a tradition of rulership was forced increasingly to shed his aristocratic style. These processes were far from complete in Russia, England or Germany by 1914 but they were very much in evidence.

In principle a variety of political strategies were available to nineteenth-century aristocracy. It could seek to emulate Pareto's lions by maintaining its dominion through force. Force, however, necessitated a police state which would in time not only keep the middle and lower classes in check but also infringe on the aristocracy's own civil, let alone political, rights. The Russian aristocracy experienced this truth in the Victorian era. Moreover, though a strategy of force might be effective in a relatively underdeveloped society, as modernisation took hold mere repression would leave a weakening aristocracy dangerously isolated. Though in theory efforts could be made to keep modernity at bay, in practice this was not possible for geopolitical reasons. In order to maintain their position as independent great powers in the wake of defeat at Jena and in the Crimea, first the Prussian and then the Russian Old Regimes were forced to embark on policies to transform backward economies, legal orders and societies. There was also a basic truth in Prince Evgeni Trubetskoy's comment, made in 1909, that 'it is impossible to govern against the people when it is necessary to turn to it for the defence of Russia'.[9]

The alternative strategy, perfected by the English, was that of accommodating the new elites. In economic terms assimilating the values of the capitalist era meant having an entrepreneurial attitude to one's estates and maybe even taking a hard-headed approach to the relative advantages of land as against stocks and bonds. Socially, modern attitudes might entail an overriding respect for money and a willingness to marry outside one's class when opportunity offered. Politically, accommodation meant allowing new elites a share in government and pursuing policies which reflected more than mere agrarian interests. As the socialist threat grew in the nineteenth century the attractions of an alliance of the propertied became ever greater.

But an alternative, anti-capitalist, strategy was also possible, at least up to a point. In alliance with the church, aristocracy could stress its Christian, paternalist and corporatist traditions. It could denounce unlimited individualism and the obsessive pursuit of profit. It could give substance to its words by adopting social welfare policies to aid the urban working classes. It could also seek to mobilise popular religious, xenophobic or patriotic sentiment against a liberal bourgeoisie. But there were limits to this strategy. The aristocracy were great owners of property, part of it urban and industrial; they were great employers of labour, which almost always earned less on agricultural estates than it did in factories; they were major beneficiaries of a very unequal society. Paternalism was fine so long as workers were willing to be patronised. An independent working-class movement was quite another matter.

Whatever strategy one adopted towards urban society the *sine qua non* for successful aristocratic politics was to retain control over one's rural base. This was true whether, as in England, one was merely trying to win parliamentary elections or, as in the Prussia of 1848, when counter-revolution was on the agenda. Neither the English nor the Prussian aristocracy lost control over the country-side. The Russians did, both in 1905 and in 1917. In the history of the nineteenth-century aristocracy no relationship is more impor-tant than that between nobles and the rural sub-elites, particularly the richer peasant and farmer.[10]

If one is to generalise about the whole of the nineteenth century and the entire European aristocracy then it is perhaps acceptable to isolate two key threats to the traditional ruling elite – namely the ideas of the French Revolution and Europe's economic trans-formation – and to point to a few basic strategies with which to counter these threats. Sometimes, however, these political strategies were not always mutually exclusive: under the Second Reich, for instance, Prussia's Junkers combined elements of all of them. In addition, especially before 1848, neither 'French' ideas nor the growth of towns and industry seemed the main threat even to the most politically active aristocrats in many societies. France had, after all, been defeated in 1814–15 and the Industrial Revolution seemed likely in the foreseeable future to remain a problem for the British. Rather it was the battle against the centralising, levelling bureaucratic state which remained top of the aristocratic political agenda.

This struggle always had local variations. In the 1820s and 1830s it was particularly fierce in southern Germany, where the traditional political order had been destroyed between 1797 and 1806. Forced under the sovereignty of Bavaria, Württemberg and Baden, whose dynasties they did not regard as being superior to themselves, the former South German imperial high aristocracy (*Standesherren*) raged at the destruction of their legal rights, their status and their political autonomy. In addition, especially in the short run, the loss of independence caused major financial loss as tax revenues were seized by the new governments and previously incurred 'public' debts left on the backs of the formerly sovereign aristocratic families. Where, as in Württemberg, religious objections to the secular state were added to particularist, legal and aristocratic resentments, the struggle could be very bitter. In combating their local Bonaparte, King Frederick I, and his rationalising bureaucracy Württemberg's newly acquired nobility were waging a campaign in nineteenth-century European aristocracy's war against not only modernity but also the overweaning powers of the state. But the details of that campaign, which were rooted in the nature of the old German Reich and the manner in which it had been destroyed, were unique to Germany and conditioned the mentality, goals and tactics of the *Standesherren*.

In Russia too in the first half of the nineteenth century the absolutist bureaucratic state was gaining power at the aristocracy's expense. Until 1785 the Russian nobility had never enjoyed corporate rights, let alone representative estate bodies of a European type. But in practice the eighteenth-century monarch had to tread warily where the interests of the court aristocracy were concerned. Effective government without the great aristocratic clans and their clients in the administration was difficult, in large part because a modern independent state bureaucracy was by no means yet fully formed. In addition, palace coups were frequent.

Under Paul (1796–1801), Alexander I (1801–25) and Nicholas I (1825–55) bureaucratic institutions of militarised type grew in scale and power. Though the coup which overthrew Paul in 1801 might have reversed this trend, the conspirators failed to impose constitutional limits on the new monarch, Paul's son, Alexander. In 1825 another aristocratic conspiracy, the famous Decembrist revolt, struck against Nicholas I, and this time the rebels had clear-cut and radical constitutional schemes. But Nicholas defeated the Decembrists, in the process confirming the suspicion of Russia's aristocracy, which was deeply rooted in Paul and all his sons. The centralised, thoroughly militarised state apparatus created by Nicholas helped to create a 'court versus country' divide within the

Russian upper classes. Slavophile doctrines, whose leading exponents were wealthy Moscow noblemen contemptuous of the court and bureaucracy, reflected part of the aristocracy's alienation from a St. Petersburg-based regime which they regarded not only as soulless and tyrannical but also as un-Russian. Instead the Slavophiles advanced doctrines which, though accepting the monarchy, claimed to be authentically national, popular and conservative, and for these very reasons hostile to the bureaucratic state.[11]

The frequent conflict in continental Europe between old regime state and nobility is of key importance to an understanding of aristocratic political strategies to master the challenge of threatening modernity. For an aristocracy to make effective, let alone wise, strategic choices it had to possess the political power to determine its own fate. This the British aristocracy had in abundance. A Parliament dominated by aristocrats controlled central government while local administration was monopolised by aristocratic Lords Lieutenant and gentry Justices of the Peace. In Prussia and, even more, Russia, monarchs and bureaucrats ruled, at least at the centre, and aristocracy exercised influence rather than direct power.

One can, for instance, see common, partly anti-capitalist, elements in the social welfare policies pursued by the English, Prussian and Russian Old Regimes. The reforms fitted in well with the proclaimed Christian and paternalist ideals of these regimes and were motivated in part by a desire to win workers' loyalty and maintain political stability. But the various forms taken by reform in the three states and, in particular, the very different biographies of the three individuals most prominent in social welfare policy tell one much about the contrasting natures of the Old Regimes they represented. Lord Shaftesbury was an independent aristocratic Member of Parliament; Otto von Bismarck, though the prince of Junkers, was the head of the Prussian government; Serge Zubatov was one of the chiefs of the Russian secret police.

Aristocracy's fate therefore by no means entirely rested in its own hands. Monarchs and bureaucrats could choose to ignore aristocratic interests or might defend them in incompetent, even suicidal, fashion. The ability to forge alliances with the bourgeoisie or with rural sub-elites depended on these groups as much as on the aristocracy. Stability in the countryside might have more to do with the structure and traditions of peasant society and the power of the church than with the activities of the aristocracy. The aristocracy's prestige among other classes, even its survival, could hang on the Old Regime's success or failure in war.

Ultimately the fate of Europe's aristocracy was decisively influenced by war and geopolitics, which sharpened and hastened aristocratic decline after 1914. In the second half of the twentieth century Europe came to be dominated by two superpowers, the USA and USSR, both of which were anti-aristocratic to the core. The Soviet regime exterminated the Russian aristocracy and, advancing into East – Central Europe after 1945, destroyed the nobility in its satellite states as well. These included the Prussian heartland of the German aristocracy.

Aristocracy's fate in the American-dominated western half of the continent was much kinder. The American occupation authorities did not for instance expropriate the west or south German aristocracy's land, in sharp contrast to their treatment of the Japanese landowning class after 1945. But American hegemony brought with it not only democratic political institutions but also the influence of a culture which was deeply anti-aristocratic and populist.

Joint American – Soviet hegemony in Europe was not inevitable. Nor was the triumph of anti-aristocratic principles in the United States and Russia. In the former, the first half of the nineteenth century witnessed the emergence of a potential independent nation in the southern states, rooted in slavery, agrarianism and links with the English cotton industry. The Confederacy's ruling class increasingly spoke of itself as an aristocracy. The fact that most Southern 'aristocrats' were freshly minted and that social mobility among Whites, by European Old Regime standards, was extremely easy, only strengthened the position of the planter elite. Mobilising the White population behind this elite was relatively simple given the call to racial solidarity and fear of the blacks. The Confederacy might well have emerged as a powerful aristocratic nation on American soil deeply rooted in populist racialism. For the North the political and military challenge of destroying and re-absorbing a country of this size was unprecedented and monumental. Had the Confederacy's bid for statehood succeeded, North America's ability to intervene decisively on the democratic side in twentieth-century Europe might well have been crucially undermined.[12]

In Europe the 1914–18 war was a major precipitant of aristocratic decline. It destroyed the Habsburg, Romanov and Hohenzollern empires. But the war's outcome was anything but inevitable; indeed virtually no one in 1914 could have predicted that, fighting on opposite sides, both imperial Germany and imperial Russia would end up among the ranks of the defeated. German victory was possible in 1914 and even more so in 1917, after the Russian Revolution. Even partial victory, bought at the expense of concessions to France and Britain, would have consolidated the Hohenzollern regime and by absorbing eastern Slavs directly or indirectly into the Reich would have strengthened nationalist and racialist trends already evident in pre-war Wilhelmine politics. The balance between 'old' and 'new' Right in a victorious Germany would have been neither that of pre-1914 nor that of the Nazi 1930s. The way 'forward' for the Right in a victorious Hohenzollern Reich would, however, have been in the direction of a more populist and racialist form of authoritarian nationalism.

To argue counter-factually in this way is useful. No more than the present or future was the course of the past fore-ordained. Aristocracy was bound to decline but the speed of its demise, the influences it stamped on its successors in power, and indeed the type of society and politics that followed aristocracy's era were by no means inevitable. It is important to reflect on this fact and to remember, when discussing societies' internal evolution, that broader geopolitical factors can exert a powerful influence.

Although aristocracy's fate depended in part on factors and forces outside its own control, the history of the traditional elite in the nineteenth century was also determined by its own characteristics, most of which were inherited from an earlier era. Of course all classes are to some extent prisoners of their past. The past shapes their instincts and values, partly determines their relationship to government and to other social forces, and often creates the institutions through which the group acts. What is true of other classes is doubly so of aristocracy since the latter is by definition long-established and very conscious of what separates it from the rest of mankind, and in general it possesses old corporate institutions and traditions. The roles and fates of Europe's various nineteenth-century aristocracies were determined to a very great extent by their history before 1815.

European pre-industrial society was simple by modern standards. Politics was largely a zero-sum game played by a small number of groups and individuals. If a country's aristocracy was very powerful then its monarchy, peasantry, towns and clergy probably would not be. Under a dominant absolute monarch, on the other hand, aristocratic pretensions would be held in check to some extent, peasant land protected from seizure and urban privileges probably upheld, for these policies best protected the crown's tax base. The church's position greatly affected the balance of power between other forces. If the church was still very rich then it mattered greatly whether juicy benefices were held by local aristocrats or 'professional' clergymen of humbler origin, often appointed by the Crown. If on the other hand the church had already been despoiled then it was of great significance whether its land had been bought by the aristocracy, held by the Crown or taken over by bourgeois or even peasants.

Seen in these terms the immense power of the English aristocracy is easily explained. By 1815, save in a few counties, the peasantry had long since been pushed off the land, roughly three-quarters of which belonged outright to the aristocracy and richer gentry. For over two centuries a system of land tenure unique in Europe had been in place. Agriculture was conducted by quite wealthy farmers without legal security of tenure and dependent on leases which reflected market prices. Aristocratic monopolisation of land and establishment of unrestricted property rights largely pre-dated the collapse of royal absolutism in the seventeenth century, though the Stuarts had made some not very effective efforts to check this process.

By 1815 royal power was very limited but, unlike in Poland, the rule of the magnates had proved compatible with effective government. A major factor in the consolidation of aristocratic power had been the Crown's inability to retain the huge estates it had seized from the church – roughly one-fifth of England at the time of the Reformation – almost all of which had fallen into the hands of the nobility and gentry. The remaining wealth of the Anglican church was enjoyed by the aristocracy and its clients, who monopolised the higher ecclesiastical posts in the eighteenth century. The largest towns, and especially London, were autonomous and powerful junior partners to the aristocracy in England's eighteenth-century governance. The alliance between the aristocracy and London's own oligarchy, operating through a parliamentary system of government, made the British state uniquely credit-worthy, itself a vital factor in Britain's rise by 1815 to maritime and commercial supremacy. The immense growth in Britain's wealth and power

after a century's rule by an aristocratic parliament gave great prestige both to the aristocracy and to the institutions through which
it governed.[13]

A striking contrast to English aristocratic power is provided by
the South German states of Württemberg and Bavaria. Württemberg was unique in having quite powerful estates in which towns-
men and clergy were represented but the nobility was not. There
was indeed some debate as to whether the Duchy of Württemberg
possessed an indigenous nobility at all. According to one estimate,
in the late eighteenth century only eleven noble families owned
land exclusively in Württemberg. Most 'Württemberg' nobles were
foreigners, often non-Germans, serving at the Duke's court: their
presence was at times loudly denounced by the local bourgeoisie.
Württemberg's traditions foreshadowed the country's nineteenth-
century political debates and culture. Between 1796 and 1812 the
duchy more than doubled in size and population and became a
kingdom, in the process absorbing some of the proudest families of
the South German imperial nobility. Conflict between the part-
democratic, part-despotic traditions of Württemberg on the one
hand and aristocratic *Standesherren* on the other was predictable.
On the whole the democratic tradition triumphed. Baroness von
Spitzemberg, born into one of the rare indigenous Württemberg
noble families but long resident in Berlin, bewailed the democratic
manners and values of her countrymen. Yuri Solovyov, a Russian
diplomat in Wilhelmine Germany, on the contrary gloried in the
bourgeois cosiness of Stuttgart society after over-exposure to aristocratic militarism in Berlin.[14]

In contrast to Württemberg, Bavaria did possess an indigenous
nobility, a few of whose families – notably the Törrings and Preysings – were very distinguished and had been established in the
electorate for many centuries. But the aristocracy had powerful
competition from both the monarchy and the church. At the end
of the eighteenth century nobles owned between a fifth and a quarter
of the land. This was rather more than the Elector's share but much
less than the 56 per cent of Bavarian land held by the church. The
monasteries in particular were far richer than any aristocratic
family. The eighteenth-century Bavarian church was run by high
clergy of mostly bourgeois origin, in this being quite unlike most of
the Reich's autonomous ecclesiastical states. When the church was
finally despoiled little of its land went to the aristocracy and the

nineteenth-century Bavarian countryside was largely owned by peasants. In Bavaria's case not only history but also geography con-
spired in this direction. Electoral Bavaria, a country of hills and
valleys in which soils vary greatly over a small area, is inherently
better suited to small-scale farming than to great estates. Strengthened by the absorption of many *Standesherren* and imperial knights
in the Napoleonic era, the Bavarian aristocracy was to play an
important role in their country's development up to 1914, but pre-
modern Bavarian history determined that this role was bound to be
more modest than was the case in England, or indeed in Prussia.[15]

In both Prussia and Russia before 1815 the aristocracy faced
little competition from either the towns or the clergy. It mattered
considerably, however, that whereas the Prussian church had been
despoiled in the mid-sixteenth century when the Crown was very
weak, a similar process did not occur in Russia until the mid-
eighteenth century, when Romanov autocracy was firmly established. In Brandenburg, of the 654 church estates taken over by the
Crown on the introduction of Lutheranism in 1540, 286 were held
by the nobility only a decade later. No similar process occurred in
Russia, which was one reason why the share of the land owned by
the Russian State in 1800 was very high by Prussian standards. In
eighteenth-century Russia the arbitrary and almost total power of
the serf-owner was exceptional by European standards but so too
was the proportion of the peasantry who lived on the Crown's
domains. Particularly in the north, nobles were few and far between,
and by the time emancipation finally came in 1861 less than half
of Russia's peasants were privately owned serfs. In Prussia the royal
domain was less extensive though its relative size differed greatly
from province to province: in 1800, 7 per cent of the Silesian peasantry were on royal estates and 55 per cent of the East Prussian;
Pomerania, with 30 per cent, stood closer to the norm. But the big
Prussian tenant farmer on the royal domain was a very different
figure from the Russian state peasant. In the nineteenth century he
would often not find it difficult to join the ranks of large-scale
capitalist estate-owners.

In both Russia and Prussia the aristocracy's great rival was the
absolute monarchy and the bureaucracy it had created to execute
its orders. By 1815 Russian autocracy and a quite formidable central
bureaucracy had existed for centuries. Prussian absolutism was a
creation of the late-seventeenth and eighteenth centuries. Both Peter

I of Russia (1689–1725) and Frederick William I of Prussia (1713–1740) succeeded in imposing compulsory State service on their nobles, whom they disciplined with a rod of iron. Up to 1815 neither in Russia nor in Prussia did any representative estate institutions exist at the centre. But, totally unlike Russia, Prussia did possess noble institutions in the provinces and a deeply rooted noble commitment to local government and provincial particularist traditions.[16]

The historical relationship in any state between monarchy, nobility, church, towns and peasantry to a considerable extent determined the role and fate of that country's aristocracy in the nineteenth century. But the relative size of a country's historical heartland and its outer periphery could matter greatly too. In some states the addition of new areas could actually strengthen the indigenous aristocracy. This was true, for instance, in Württemberg and Bavaria. It was definitely not true in England, Prussia or Russia.

Extremely powerful in England, aristocracy was less so in Scotland, not to mention Wales and Ireland, where it was an alien implant. After electoral reform in 1832 Conservatives had to reconcile themselves to being in a permanent minority in Scotland. In Wales and Ireland even the semi-democratic franchise of 1867 and 1884 meant the domination of local politics by anti-aristocratic forces. In Ireland it presaged expropriation. As late as 1910, in the great confrontation between the House of Lords and the democratically elected Liberal Government, the English electorate twice returned small Conservative majorities. The peers' fate was determined by Scottish, Welsh and Irish votes.

The Prussian aristocracy's dilemma was even worse, partly because its Conservative party was less successful than the English one in winning the support of bourgeoisie and workers in its own homeland. In addition, however, the rapid expansion of Prussia in the nineteenth century to encompass first the Rhineland and Westphalia, then Hanover, and finally in a sense the whole of Germany caused major difficulties for the Junkers. Even within the boundaries of post-1866 Prussia, let alone in the Reich as a whole, the Junker ascendancy faced opposition from forces which were not only alien but also often actively hostile to Old Prussian traditions. These forces might be particularist, Catholic, liberal, peasant or socialist: often in any locality they were a combination. Given the deeply rooted confessional and regional divisions in Germany, not to mention the fact that unity on Prussian terms had to some extent been imposed by force in 1866–71, it was evident that Prussian traditional elites would have an exceptionally hard task in preserving their domination over a country which in the nineteenth century had not only modernised but also expanded at extraordinary speed.

The Russian aristocracy's position was if anything even weaker. In the Black Earth Russian heartland south of Moscow the old aristocracy was well-rooted in 1800. But the rapid expansion of the Empire meant that new territories were constantly being absorbed. In Catherine II's famous Legislative Commission in the 1760s aristocratic voices from the central provinces calling, for instance, for much stricter controls over ennoblement were countered by delegates from the new nobility of the Ukrainian borderlands, often of Cossack origin and hostile to any whisper of oligarchy. The Russian aristocracy was diluted and made extremely heterogeneous as a result both of absorbing the nobility of adjacent territories and of the inflow of Western immigrants into the Tsar's service. Moreover, much of Russia itself, even in the nineteenth century, was a frontier society, fluid by definition and without old institutions or settled hierarchies. In some ways the Russian nobility was a cross between a European aristocracy and the planter elite of the *ante bellum* southern states of the USA, with its old landed gentry in Virginia and its new frontier in Alabama and Mississippi. By 1900 Russia's own new frontier was Siberia, where virtually no nobles lived and peasant colonists were arriving annually in droves. This was Russia's equivalent to Australia and Canada combined, with all that this implied in terms of populist and democratic values. The fact that Russia's Australia was attached to the mainland eased the country's problems of defence and made it likely that Russia would remain a great power long after the collapse of England's seaborne empire. But it did not bode well for aristocratic influence in Russian society.[17]

An aristocracy's structure also greatly influenced its character and its role. There was a big difference between an upper class dominated by a small group of immensely rich magnates and one consisting of a larger circle of only relatively wealthy provincial gentry families. Great magnates would be more cosmopolitan: in early-nineteenth-century Russia and Germany they would also be better educated and more cultured. A provincial gentry would have narrower horizons and would be more deeply rooted in a specific area. Its links with the population would be closer than those of a magnate, who would be forced to operate through officials and who would inevitably be an absentee landlord on many of his estates. On the whole the great aristocrat would find it easier to compromise with the modern world. His income would probably not be derived exclusively from agriculture and its diversity would protect him in times of agricultural crisis and enable him to reap the high returns on wealth invested in stocks, bonds and urban property. His wealth, titles and family fame would guarantee his status in bourgeois society in a way that was untrue of the mere landed gentleman. Great aristocrats could often therefore afford to be more liberal than the provincial gentry. This was to some extent the norm in the French aristocracy in the last years of the Old Regime and it was partially to recur in England, Russia and Germany in the nineteenth century.[18]

But even among the magnates there were sharp differences both between and within national elites. Great territorial magnates like the English, whose local pre-eminence was the basis for their power at the centre in Parliament, were likely to have mentalities rather different from those of aristocratic courtiers, however rich, in an absolute monarchy.[19] The courtier is to some extent always the creature of his master's whims and favour. Who could be more independent than an eighteenth-century Whig duke? Who less so than a Russian magnate at the court of the arbitrary and despotic Paul I (1796–1801), though in the Russian aristocracy's favour it has to be said that they responded to despotism by strangulation.[20] A family's individual history would condition many of its values. For a member of the House of Russell, constitutional limitation on monarchical power was his family's personal achievement. For a *Standesherr*, the violent rupture of a long-established legal order which had guaranteed his family political autonomy and social standing was an affront which often overhung the whole of the nineteenth century. It was easier for someone with the family history of a Russell to play a constructive role in Victorian Europe than was the case with an aristocrat still imbued with a sense of nostalgia for his family's lost status under the old Reich.

Prussia's Junkers were a provincial gentry *par excellence*. Their values were conditioned by provincial blinkers, a Lutheran tradition and the militarisation of the gentry in the service of the eighteenth-century Prussian state. The nineteenth-century confirmed rather than destroyed these values. The Junker's independent, *frondeur* spirit fed from the thought that his family had antedated the Hohenzollerns in Prussia and the reality that the Junker squire was more or less king in his tiny estate realm. His loyalty to the Crown was strengthened by his ancestors' communion in blood with Frederick II in the heroic days of the Seven Years' War when Prussia had stood alone against the three great powers of continental Europe. The fact that the Hohenzollern – Junker alliance had been so successful in raising Prussia from nothing to world power legitimised the militarist, authoritarian and aristocratic principles on which this alliance rested.

For the Russian aristocracy too military memories were very important. Memoirs are replete with mentions of ancestors' participation in battles stretching back to Muscovy's defeat of the Tartars at Kulikovo in 1380. A sense that aristocratic officers in the service of the autocratic Tsar had made Russia a force to be reckoned with in Europe was a major source of aristocratic self-esteem. The Russians had less of the *frondeur* spirit, and far fewer provincial loyalties than the Prussians. Many magnates came originally from royal houses older than the Romanovs but this fact meant little, for as courtiers they lived only in their master's sun. But the eighteenth century bequeathed to the Russian aristocracy a commitment to enlightenment and Westernisation. Culture, manners and excellence in foreign languages became the test of social status in a nobility in which access from below was simple, titles meant little and money was easily won and lost at court. Standing a little outside Europe, educated Russians became immersed in all its national cultures. The pull between national traditions and alien cultures created an elite more uncomfortable but also more creative than its English and German peers.[21]

England's too was a military aristocracy of a sort with its fair share of ancestral glories. But having suffered military despotism in its most unacceptable republican form in the mid-seventeenth century, England's elites created a uniquely aristocratic army whose officers purchased their way to high command. Only an island could have afforded such a method of running an army. The eighteenth-century English aristocratic youth was trained not for the disciplined subordination of army or bureaucracy but for a parliamentary world of rhetoric, debate and anarchy constrained by procedural rules. The landowner was powerful without being the serf-owning autocrat of Eastern Europe. The parliamentary and legal tradition was revered partly because it was England's and partly because it had served the country well at a time of unparalleled prosperity and power. In 1815 England's aristocracy was a ruling class in every sense of the word, in contrast to bureaucratic Prussia and Russia. For one and a quarter centuries it had directly governed the world's most successful country. It entered the nineteenth century with a storehouse of political experience which was to stand it in good stead as it faced the challenges of the Victorian and Edwardian eras.

2. Wealth

This chapter has three aims. Firstly, it seeks to discover in which regions of Germany, England and Russia great landowners were found. It will contrast aristocratic districts with ones whose land was owned for the most part by lesser gentry families or peasant farmers. Secondly, it will show who were the leading noble landowners in the three countries between 1815 and 1914. Thirdly, in the following pages an attempt will be made to gauge the wealth of the Russian, English and German aristocracy.

These three aims are the crucial foundation for any study of nineteenth-century aristocracy. Without knowing who the leading aristocratic families were, where they were based and how rich they were it is difficult to carry a study of Europe's nineteenth-century aristocracy beyond insubstantial generalisations. Information about the location, wealth and make-up of the three aristocracies allows comparisons to be made both within the societies and between them. It enables one to trace key shifts between 1815 and 1914. Vital issues such as mobility into and out of the top ranks of the aristocracy; the extent of the aristocracy's grip on the countryside; aristocratic wealth relative to that of other classes; the distribution of income within the aristocracy: these, and much else besides, should be illuminated by this chapter two.

Discovering where aristocratic landowning was concentrated and who the leading noble landowners were is at times difficult and tedious. Gauging aristocratic wealth is, however, far more troublesome. Especially in Russia and Germany, and particularly for the first half of the nineteenth century, statistics on aristocratic wealth are scarce, unreliable and sometimes even contradictory. It is not necessarily clear whether they reflect gross or net incomes – a distinction on which many Russian serf-owners themselves were often muddled.[1] Currencies play havoc with one's calculations. Before the 1870s many currencies existed in Germany and the precise exchange rates between them were by no means always clear. In Austria and Russia in theory there was only one currency but both states in practice had two: a stable metallic coinage and less valuable, but constantly oscillating, paper money. The rate of exchange between paper and metal not only rose and fell over time, it also differed, at least in Russia, from one region of the empire to another. In addition, both historians and contemporaries often cite statistics as to men's incomes without stating whether the sums in question were silver or paper.[2]

Even if one had precise and clear information on men's incomes difficulties would remain. The relative cost of living in the three countries has to be understood before real incomes can be compared. But even if one had a comparative cost-of-living index covering London, Berlin and St. Petersburg – which is to ask for the moon – it would still be wrong to assume that this reflected costs in, let us say, Bavaria or Tula province of Russia. Moreover, knowing men's real incomes requires that one also know their debts, but statistics on debt, even if available, can easily mislead. Great debts can reflect the extravagant desire to live beyond one's income. They can also be the means of profitable investment for the sake of enhanced later income. Particularly in Prussia and Russia, where nobles often had access to loans at preferential interest from the State, indebtedness could also simply result from the crafty desire to lend at a higher rate than one borrowed, or to splash out cash borrowed from the State in additional bonds or land whose value was rising much more quickly than the interest on one's loans.[3]

However difficult, attempts to estimate aristocratic wealth are, of course, vital. Moreover, though the statistics cited in this chapter may not always be precisely accurate, the broad picture they present of aristocratic incomes is almost certainly correct and allows meaningful comparisons to be made both across the three countries and within them. Nevertheless, more impressionistic comments, especially when made by individuals able to compare a number of societies, are an invaluable addition to the statistics on aristocratic wealth.

By European standards the English aristocracy and gentry owned an extraordinarily high proportion of their country's land. In 1873, when the first complete land register was made, more than one million people owned land in the United Kingdom. Four-fifths of this land was, however, possessed by less than 7000 individuals. In contrast to Germany or Russia, the English landowner's rights over his property were absolute even by 1815. They were, in other words, unencumbered by the peasant customary rights which, established either by law (Germany) or in practice (Russia), were to lead to the division of estates between lord and serf when emancipation came.[4]

The lack of peasant customary rights in nineteenth-century England reflects the almost complete non-existence of a continental-style English peasantry by 1815. In 1873 only one-tenth of England was farmed by owner-occupiers. In just one county, Middlesex, did owners of less than 100 acres possess more than 20 per cent of the land and in metropolitan Middlesex these men were Londoners rather than peasant farmers. Only in the far north-western counties of Cumberland and Westmorland and amidst the fens of Cambridgeshire and the plum-growers of Worcestershire were smallholders of any significance.

By contrast, the 363 individuals who owned over 10 000 acres each possessed just under a quarter of all English land. On the whole, these great estates were found at some distance from London, in the vicinity of which land prices were prohibitive. In nine counties great aristocrats with estates of over 10 000 acres owned 30 per cent or more of the land (excluding waste). Apart from tiny Rutland, Northumberland – whose Percy dukes owned vast properties – came top of the list. Wiltshire and Dorset in the West Country also scored highly (36 per cent each). The other great aristocratic counties stretched in a string across the north Midlands: Nottinghamshire, Cheshire, Derbyshire, Staffordshire, Northamptonshire – most of them, perhaps not incidentally, fine hunting country.

Below the 363 magnates but still rich by continental standards were roughly 1000 individuals who in 1873 owned between 3000 and 10 000 acres. These men came from the foremost county families, described in John Bateman's famous study of Britain's ruling class as the 'greater gentry'. In twelve counties men in this category owned 20 per cent or more of the land. These twelve counties were closer to London than the aristocratic nine, only Northumberland appearing on both lists. The foremost counties as regards the estates of the greater gentry were Shropshire, Huntingdonshire, Hereford-shire and Oxfordshire.

Where a family owned most land was not, however, necessarily where it lived or exercised most influence. In an attempt to define the most aristocratic counties in England, Michael Thompson combines the pattern of aristocratic landowning (that is, estates of more than 10 000 acres) with the distribution of great country houses. Though the guide is inevitably rough the North Midlands clearly emerges as the most aristocratic part of the country. Among the six 'most aristocratic' counties only Dorset falls squarely outside this region. Moreover, although Thompson stresses that this picture's accuracy can only be guaranteed for the years around 1873, he believes that it is unlikely to be much wrong for the whole period between 1790 and 1919.[5]

G. E. Mingay states that in 1790, roughly 400 landowners had incomes sufficient to maintain a large country house, a full London season and an aristocratic life-style. For this the minimum required was £5–6000 per year, though £10 000, the average income of the 400, was needed to live at this level in comfort. At the pinnacle of the aristocracy the Dukes of Bedford, Bridgewater, Devonshire and Northumberland, the Marquess of Rockingham and the Earls of Egremont and Shelburne probably had annual incomes of £50 000 or more. Beneath these magnates came the 700–800 wealthy gentry families, mainly baronets, who had £3–4000; the squires, roughly three to four thousand in number, who had between £1000 and £3000 per year; and the 10 000 to 20 000 gentlemen who lived on between £300 and £1000.

Between the mid-eighteenth century and 1790, landowners' incomes had increased by 40–50 per cent. From the late 1780s to the late 1820s rent-rolls roughly doubled, the war years in particular yielding immense profits. By 1819 the Dukes of Northumberland and Bridgewater, the Marquess of Stafford and Earl Grosvenor had incomes of over £100 000 a year. Not surprisingly, this was a period of massive aristocratic ostentation and expenditure. When, for instance, the Duke of Rutland came of age in 1799 roughly £10 000 was spent on celebrations and presents, a sum that was far greater than the annual incomes of many aristocrats deemed wealthy in other regions of Europe.

Mingay writes that in 1790 'the great landlords were far and

TABLE 2.1 Structure of English landowning incomes, 1790

	No. of families	Range of income £	Average income £	Proportion owned of cultivated land in England and Wales (%)
I Great landlords	400	5 000–50 000	10 000	20–25
II Gentry				50–60
(a) Wealthy gentry	700–800	3 000–5 000		
(b) Squires	3 000–4 000	1 000–3 000		
(c) Gentlemen	10 000–20 000	300–1 000		
III Freeholders				
(a) Better sort	25 000	150–700	300	
(b) Lesser sort	75 000	30–300	100	

Source: G. E. Mingay. *English Landed Society in the Eighteenth Century* (London, 1963).

away the wealthiest group in the country'. In the mid-eighteenth century to buy a big country house and 10 000 acres required an outlay of roughly £100 000, a sum vastly beyond the means of almost any non-aristocrat. This provides one explanation why movement in and out of the top ranks of the English aristocracy was very limited indeed in the eighteenth century, a point confirmed by John Cannon.[6]

Little had changed in this respect by the first decades of the nineteenth century despite the onset of the Industrial Revolution. High profits from land entailed rising prices for estates: by the early 1840s £100 000 was needed to buy a property of 3–4000 acres. At a time when most British industry was still small-scale with very little in the way of fixed capital, the purchase of estates of over 10 000 acres was open only to a minuscule number of, usually, financiers such as Alexander Baring and Samuel Lloyd. W. D. Rubinstein writes that 'during the first half of the nineteenth century – one or two full generations after the beginnings of the Industrial Revolution – the non-landed wealth holders were a virtually insignificant percentage of the entire wealthy class. An observer entering a room containing Britain's 200 wealthiest men in 1825 might be forgiven for thinking that the Industrial Revolution had not occurred.'[7]

A rather perceptive foreign observer of English society in the late 1820s was the German Prince Hermann von Pückler-Muskau. Pückler spent many months in England between 1825 and 1829 in search of an heiress. His comments on the relative cost of living in England and North Germany are of interest. In Pückler's view, strict necessities were not much more expensive in England than in his homeland but anything other than these was. To move in high society required a vast wardrobe. Posting around the country was four times as expensive as in Germany. So great was the luxury maintained in country houses that for the owners 'one hospitable month costs as much as a wealthy landed proprietor spends in a whole year with us'.[8]

It was, above all, England's great wealth that struck Pückler. He wrote in 1828 that 'what with us are called luxuries are looked upon as necessouries (sic) and are diffused over all classes'. The comfort and luxury of English life was above anything he had previously encountered. So too was 'the unbridled desire for and deference to wealth which characterises the bulk of Englishmen'. In particular, 'the great wealth of the landowners of England must always strike people from the continent'.[9]

Pückler admired the life-style of the county gentlemen whom he considered the best element in English society. These men were not interested in the pursuit of fashion in London but rather followed 'a domestic life polished by education and adorned by affluence, and in the observance of the strictest integrity'. Although 'with us they would be thought rich', there were 'perhaps not less than a hundred thousand persons in England [who] are in the enjoyment of such an existence . . . of such substantial and comfortable luxury in their peaceful homes, free monarchs in the bosoms of their families where they live in the security of their inviolable rights of property . . . it is precisely the extraordinary number of people of competent fortune . . . which makes England independent and happy'.[10]

Pückler was less enamoured of the aristocrats who made up London high society – in his view they were cold, arrogant and obsessively caste-conscious even by the standards of continental aristocracy. English aristocratic life breathed 'the long habit of great luxury'. The wealth of the nobility was 'vast . . . even our sovereign princes possess only fragments of what is here found united'. Some of the country houses were superb. Of Woburn Abbey, for instance, Pückler wrote that 'an accumulation of luxury and magnificence has been formed here, far exceeding the powers of any private person in our country'.[11]

Pückler's comments were informed by the sad awareness that his own revenues from Muskau were but a fraction of those received by Woburn's owner, the Duke of Bedford. In the years around 1820 Pückler's average annual income was 104 000 taler (£15 600). His debts in 1817 amounted to 400 000 taler (£60 000) and had risen to 600 000 taler (£90 000) by 1835. Pückler's disposable income in 1820 was a mere 30 000 taler (£4500). In contrast, the Duke of Bedford's annual income by 1840 was roughly £100 000, though he had inherited £551 940 of debts from his father. Bedford's disposable annual income was between £27 000 and £28 000 around 1840. The contrast between Bedford and Pückler did not therefore lie in the ratio between gross and disposable income, nor in the scale of their debts in proportion to their revenue. It rested simply on the fact that the Russells were far richer than the Pücklers. This made all the difference: Bedford had the means to survive and in time to reduce his debts. Hermann Pückler was ultimately forced to sell Muskau.[12]

It is possible to place Pückler rather precisely in the Prussian society to which his region of Saxony was annexed after the Treaty of Vienna in 1815. In the first years of the nineteenth century Muskau was valued for tax purposes at 500 000 taler (£75 000), though this sum represented less than half of its real market value in the opinion of the estate's historian. In the whole of Prussia at this time only two estates were worth more than one million taler (£150 000), another fourteen being valued at between 500 000 and one million taler, and a further twenty-nine at between 300 000 and half a million taler. Even if one accepts the declared tax value of Muskau or assumes that the Prussian estates were as under-valued for fiscal purposes as was Pückler's, the fact remains that the prince was one of Prussia's greatest landowners. This becomes doubly clear when one remembers that of the forty-four most valuable estates in Prussia in 1800, seventeen were in the Polish provinces of South Prussia and New East Prussia. These provinces, acquired after the Polish partitions, were forfeited in 1807 and not regained in 1815, becoming part of the Tsar's Polish kingdom. There is good reason to believe that, if one leaves aside the western provinces of Westphalia and the Rhineland, newly acquired by the Hohenzollerns in 1815, Pückler owned one of the fifteen greatest estates in the Kingdom of Prussia.[13]

Table 2.2 illustrates not only the gap between the wealth of the English and Prussian aristocracies but also the huge difference that existed from province to province within Prussia. With New East Prussia and South Prussia removed, Silesia's dominant position becomes clear. Of the twenty-seven estates valued at over 300 000 taler (£45 000), twenty (74 per cent) were Silesian. Among the 289 estates worth between 100 000 and 300 000 taler, 128 (44 per cent) were Silesian. To some extent these figures merely reflect the fact that there were far more noble estates in Silesia than in any other province but this is far from being the whole story, for Silesia's share of rich estates is much greater than is the case in the less valuable categories. There were, for instance, 2209 noble estates worth between 5000 and 20 000 taler (£750–3000). Of these, only 504 (22.8 per cent) were Silesian. None of the other provinces came close to matching Silesia. The Kurmark in Brandenburg had forty-eight estates worth over 100 000 taler and 465 of its 745 noble

29

TABLE 2.2 Prussia: Estates' value, 1800 (in £)

	1M+	500 000–1M	300–5000 000	100–300 000	50–100 000	20–50 000	5–20 000
East Prussia				31	86	244	403
West Prussia		1	1	22	76	183	321
Pomerania			1	24	76	235	430
Neumark (BDBG)			1	11	62	170	184
Silesia		7	12	128	363	784	504
Kurmark (BDBG)	1	2		46	154	311	232
Magdeburg } Halberstadt } Hohenheim }				27	63	121	135

Source: H. Schissler, Preussische Agrargesellschaft im Wandel (Göttingen, 1978).

estates (62.6 per cent) were worth between 20 and 100 000 taler. In the Neumark, also Brandenburg, most estates (54.2 per cent) were also in this 20–100 000-taler category. Elsewhere it was the smaller estates worth between 5000 and 20 000 taler which were in the majority.[14]

The statistics reflect the reality of a Prussian aristocracy split between Silesian magnate families – the Henckel von Donnersmarks, Hohenlohe-Öhringens, Ballestrems and Pless, to name but four – the leading county families of the other provinces and a mass of poorer nobles. Nineteenth-century Pomerania, for instance, had one truly aristocratic family, the princes Putbus, and their estates were not on the mainland but on the island of Rügen in the Baltic Sea. East Prussia had the Dohnas, Dönhoffs, Lehndorffs and Eulenbergs, though their wealth did not approach that of the Silesians. In 1800 East Prussia stood out among Hohenzollern provinces for its large number of wealthy free peasants, Silesia for its huge contrasts between wealth and poverty and the bitter social tensions these aroused. In contrast to England, regional differences not only were much greater but also mattered more. The two generations before 1815 had seen frequent frontier shifts and political uncertainty. The East Prussian nobility had sworn allegiance to the Russian Empress in the Seven Years' War and had shown further capacity for independent action in 1812–13. Silesia, only gained in the 1740s, was nearly lost in 1756–63. Provincialism was rampant throughout Prussia and no central parliament had ever existed. The radically different profile of the various provincial aristocracies is merely one reminder of the fact that even in the east the process of building a Prussian nation was far from complete by 1815.

The Treaty of Vienna imposed on Prussia the task of absorbing West German provinces whose religion, social structure and traditions were completely different from those of the Pomeranian and Brandenburg heartland of the Hohenzollerns' state. In geopolitical terms it made good sense to assign the Rhineland and Westphalia to Prussia, thus committing North Germany's only great power to the defence of the Rhine frontier against France. But the two western provinces were traditionally much more urbanised than the Prussian east and their peoples' communities and civic traditions were much more ancient and deeply rooted than was the case on the colonial plains of East Elbia. Moreover the Rhinelanders and Westphalians were mostly Catholics.

In 1815 even to talk of a Rhineland or Westphalia was a misnomer, for the two provinces under the Holy Roman Empire were a maze of small and intensely particularistic petty states. The region's nobility was divided both vertically and horizontally. At the top came the mediatised imperial aristocracy (that is, *Standesherren*). In Westphalia these included the Bentheims and Sayn-Wittgensteins, long established in the region, and the Hessen-Rotenburg, Croy, Arenburg, Salm and Looz-Corswarem families which had been compensated with Westphalian land for properties expropriated by the French elsewhere. The *Standesherren* families kept aloof from the local nobility and shunned intermarriage.[15]

Beneath the *Standesherren* there existed a number of fiercely parochial local nobilities, each of them rooted in a specific petty state of the former Holy Roman Empire. One such local nobility was that of the bishopric of Munster, the history of whose twenty-five leading families during the period between 1770 and 1860 has been studied in great detail by Heinz Reif. Before secularisation came in 1803 these families had dominated Munster, deriving between 20 per cent and 35 per cent of their income from their monopoly of rich pickings in the cathedral chapter. Linked by a dense net of marriages these families had partly maintained their monopoly on office by insisting that all candidates for profitable ecclesiastical positions must have impeccably noble ancestry in both the paternal and maternal line for four generations. The extremely narrow and cosy world of the Munster nobility, together with that of their peers in other sections of the Westphalian and Rhenish aristocracy, had been devastated by two decades of war, by secularisation, the end of the old Reich and incorporation into Prussia. Together with much of the rest of the German nobility, in 1815–30 they were still in a state of shock, struggling to come to terms both psychologically and financially with a new, uncertain and, at least initially, much poorer world.[16]

The Westphalian nobility was on the whole stronger than the Rhinelanders. In 1825, 533 (80.3 per cent) of the old noble estates (*Rittergüter*) remained in aristocratic hands. In the Rhineland this was the case with only 48.3 per cent of the *Rittergüter*. At this time the Prussian Oberpräsident von Vincke reckoned that between seventy and eighty Westphalian landowners had incomes of over

3000 taler (£450) a year. Even leaving aside the *Standesherren*, the local nobility included men of real wealth. Freiherr von Fürstenberg from the Arnsberg district was believed by Vincke to have an annual income of 100 000 taler (£15 000), Count Clemens von Westphalen one of 70 000 taler (£10 500) and Freiherr von Landsberg-Velen 50 000 (£7500). *Standesherren* apart, these were probably the richest nobles in Westphalia. Moreover, Vincke may well be exaggerating their incomes. Even so, the sums are striking.[17]

In the Rhineland the nobles' position differed enormously from district to district. They had held on to their estates much more successfully in the northern Rhineland, especially in the Kleve district, than in the more southern districts of Koblenz and Trier. In part this distinction stemmed from the different systems of land tenure existing in the various districts when the French arrived in the 1790s. Abolition of serfdom and feudal dues had a limited effect on North Rhenish nobles, whose lands were very often allodial or let to tenants on commercial leases. Overall, however, the Rhenish nobility only owned 6 per cent of the land, most of which was held by twenty families. Of these, the Salm-Dyck, Loe, Spee, Hatzfeldt and Nesselrode-Ehreshoven families were probably the best-known. Freiherr von Stein reckoned that the heads of these twenty families had annual incomes ranging from 10–40 000 taler (£1500–6000).[18]

The Rhenish – Westphalian picture of extreme local variety and parochialism within the nobility applies to other regions of Germany as well. The Ritterschaft of the 'electorate' of Hesse-Kassel was, like the Munster *Stiftsadel*, a small, ancient and exclusive noble order. It did not include either the handful of *Standesherren* incorporated into Hesse-Kassel after 1806, or a large section of the local 'lower' nobility. The great majority of *Ritterschaft* families could trace their origins to before 1400 and most had been members of the Hessian assembly, the Landtag, by the 1530s. Co-option of new families into the *Ritterschaft* was a rare and jealously guarded privilege bestowed by the corporation itself. The Hessian *Ritterschaft* were poorer than the Munster *Stiftsadel*. Hesse-Kassel's prince, the Landgrave, took a larger share of his country's wealth and offered many fewer fat sinecures to his nobles than was the case with Munster's bishop. Gregory Pedlow lists the annual incomes of seven *Ritterschaft* families at the turn of the century and of these the highest was the 5655 taler (£848) which the von Buttlar-Elberbergs averaged between 1781 and 1805. It is true both that the Buttlar-

Elberbergs were probably not the richest of the *Ritterschaft* families and that after 1810 their income from timber began to grow at great speed. Nevertheless, unlike in Munster, primogeniture did not apply in Hesse-Kassel and estate incomes were therefore divided among a number of male owners: as a result individual members of the Ritterschaft were generally poorer than their Westphalian peers.[19]

The Bavarian nobility was also seldom rich, though it is important to distinguish between the aristocracy of the old Wittelsbach electorate and the often much wealthier *Standesherren* and imperial knights from Schwabia and, especially Franconia, who were brought under the Bavarian Crown after the collapse of the Holy Roman Empire. In 'Old Bavaria' (that is, the electorate) a chance for the great expansion of noble landowning came with secularisation of church property in the Montgelas era. In fact, however, only thirty-one nobles were among the original buyers of church land, though this small group did pick up 23 per cent of the former ecclesiastical estates. To sit as a hereditary peer in the Bavarian nineteenth-century upper house one needed *inter alia* to own entailed estates worth over 240 000 florins (£24 820). According to Walter Demel, apart from the thirty-three actual hereditary peers, many of them Schwabians or Franconians, only a very few Bavarian families could meet this qualification though the annual income from a 240 000-florin estate was not much more than £1000. Of course a few individuals would have owned entailed estates of much greater value than the 240 000-florin minimum. Nor would all a family's estate be entailed. In the case of a tiny handful of old Bavarian aristocratic families – the Törrings, in particular – annual incomes would have been much larger than £1000. Nevertheless, the great majority of 'Old Bavarian' nobles in 1815 would have been poorer than the Hessian *Ritterschaft*, let alone the Munster *Stiftsadel*.[20]

Among the German *Standesherren* incomes differed greatly, but almost all the mediatised princes and counts were in financial difficulties in 1815. Loss of sovereignty had directly deprived them of part of their revenues and made it more difficult for them to squeeze dues and services from their peasants. The states, happy enough to confiscate *Standesherren* incomes, proved less anxious to take over their debts, some of which had been incurred for governmental purposes. In time, salvation lay in the large sums which flowed to *Standesherren* between the 1820s and the 1860s as redemption payments for the peasant dues and services which disappeared when serfdom was abolished. In addition, *Standesherren* incomes rose sharply in the nineteenth century as *demesnes* and above all forests were exploited commercially. But in the transitional period, at its most extreme between 1806 and 1830, the mediatised counts and princes faced great difficulties.

The history of the Hohenlohe family illustrates these points. In 1800 the Hohenlohe properties were split between the family's eight branches, which had established the principle of primogeniture only in the eighteenth century. Even together, the Hohenlohe lands were only one-fifth the size of the Duke of Württemberg's territories in the late eighteenth century. After mediatisation, seven of the Hohenlohe branches were incorporated into Württemberg; the eighth, Schillingfürst, came under the more generous rule of the Wittelsbachs. Even before mediatisation most of the Hohenlohe branches were not very rich and found it impossible to match income to expenditure. In 1804, for instance, Schillingfürst had an annual income of 64 000 florins (£6618) and expenditure of 87 649 florins (£9064), of which a disastrous 37 per cent was interest payment on the prince's massive debts. Bartenstein in 1797 had an income of 105 781 florins (£10 939) but debts of 449 000 florins (£46 432).

Given these debts, the steep decline in Hohenlohe incomes in the two decades after mediatisation was disastrous. In 1805 Langenburg had received 22 550 florins of his income from peasant dues but this had sunk to between 13 000 and 16 000 (£1344–£1655) in the years after 1815. For a time Bartenstein was forced to live on an allowance of only 2000 florins a year (£207). Even Öhringen, much the richest of the Hohenlohe branches, only drew net profits of 5166 florins from his Württemberg demesne land in 1828–29, though he did receive an extra 6500 florins in food and other goods. By now, however, Öhringen's main interests were elsewhere. That year his Saxon estates brought in a profit of 19 002 florins (£1965) and his Silesian ones 138 458 florins (£14 318). Öhringen was to use his Württemberg redemption money further to expand his Silesian holdings.[21]

By far the most thorough study of redemption payments and their impact on *Standesherr* incomes was made by Harold Winkel. The subject is a complicated one since different services, dues, tithes and taxes were redeemed individually. Nor did the various states act in unison as regards either timing or the terms on which redemption was carried out. Württemberg squeezed the nobles hardest, the Thurn and Taxis administration reckoning that if compensation for its Württemberg estates had been based on Bavarian redemption law they would have received 57 per cent more. The Prussian administration was particularly fierce in insisting that redemption payments for entailed estate (*fideikommissi*) be reinvested in land. Some redemption payments were made in cash but most took the form of interest-bearing bonds. As regards the adequacy of the compensation, much depended on whether indebtedness forced nobles to redeem the bonds before their expiry date. In the latter case bonds could fall to as low as 82 per cent of par value.[22]

Although nobles other than *Standesherren* received redemption payments, the lion's share went to the mediatised high nobility. The sums involved were great, Württemberg's *Standesherren* alone receiving 11 899 321 florins (£1 230 540) from the two redemption laws of 29 October 1836 and 17 June 1849. Payments generally wiped out *Standesherr* debts and allowed profitable investment in land purchases, stocks or industry. In the case, for instance, of the princes Öttingen-Spielberg, who received 1 483 830 (£153 447) from the Bavarian state, 588 900 florins went on paying off debts, 418 900 florins were used to purchase land and much of the rest went into government and railway bonds. With debts paid off, demesne farming underway and, much more important, the often huge tracts of noble forest becoming very profitable, the position of the average *Standesherr* in the second half of the nineteenth century was far stronger than it had been before 1850.[23]

The richest of the *Standesherren* were the Thurn und Taxis, who had estates in Bavaria, Württemberg, Hohenzollern-Sigmaringen, Prussia and Bohemia. In 1895 they owned 1 237 765 hectares. Even by the later 1850s Prince Thurn und Taxis had received 2 491 272 florins (£257 629) from Württemberg, 2 817 440 florins (£291 359) from Bavaria, 262 275 florins (£27 123) from Hohenzollern-Sigmaringen, 283 278 taler (£40 684) from Prussia and 556 000 Austrian florins (£55 600) from the Habsburg monarchy. In addition, in 1851 the family's postal monopoly in Württemberg was bought out for 1.3 million florins (£134 000). Even before redemption started, the vastly wealthy Thurn und Taxis had no debts to repay and a cash surplus of 477 000 florins. The huge sums entering the Thurn und Taxis treasury from redemption payments, craftily invested by the Rothschilds, made this family one of the very few in Europe whose wealth matched that of the richest members of the English aristocracy. But the Thurn und Taxis were not only German aristocrats but also Bohemian ones and it was in the top ranks of the Habsburg nobility that the English duke was likely to find his closest counterparts as regards wealth throughout the nineteenth century. In 1820, for instance, Prince Joseph II von Schwarzenberg, the head of his family's senior branch, had an income of 771 381 Austrian florins (£77 138), which if it did not quite yet match the Duke of Northumberland's revenues, nevertheless put the wealth even of a Silesian aristocrat in the shade.[24]

In the late eighteenth century the top level of the Russian aristocracy may have been as wealthy as its Austrian and English peers. Indeed, Ian Blanchard claims that 'in 1807 the average British citizen was barely richer than his Russian counterpart. The two nations – Britain and Russia – stood at the very top of the European national-income league table'.[25] Even English observers marvelled at the opulent life-styles of the Russian aristocracy, William Tooke commenting that many of the greatest nobles 'are owners of estates far more extensive than the territory of some sovereign princes in Germany'.[26] Certainly Elizabeth, Catherine II and Paul I (1741–1801) dispensed largesse to the court aristocracy on a princely scale. Between 1762 and 1783, for instance, the five Orlov brothers, favourites of Catherine II, received 45 000 male serfs and 17 million roubles (£1 770 000) in cash and valuables from the Empress. In the course of just two years Grigori Potemkin received 37 000 serfs and 9 million roubles (£937 500). The wife of Ivan Chernyshev, Catherine's ambassador in London, had jewels worth £40 000 and Count Nikolai Petrovich Rumyantsev spent 2 million roubles (£208 000) just on his museum in Moscow. When Napoleon invaded Russia a number of magnates – Count P. I. Saltykov, Prince N. S. Gagarin and N. N. Demidov for instance – formed and equipped whole regiments at their own expense.[27]

The great wealth of the late-eighteenth-century Russian magnates was a recent phenomenon. Pre-Petrine Russia had not been fertile soil for the consolidation of massive personal fortunes, though the Stroganovs had become rich through their commercial operations in Northern Russia and Siberia and all the leading court families had grown increasingly wealthy in the seventeenth century. The two main pillars of magnate wealth in 1800 were, however, the crown's huge land-grants to court families and the growth of the Russian economy in the previous century.

Jerome Blun writes that 'in the reigns of Catherine II and Paul, lucky courtiers received a total of 385 700 male peasants'. Imperial largesse was, however, very unevenly divided even within this lucky group, a fact which was to have a big impact on the distribution of wealth within the aristocratic elite down to the end of the empire. Between 1762 and 1801, seventy-nine individuals, each receiving between 1000 and 3000 serfs, amassed 120 400 in all. But eighteen people, averaging between 5000 and 10 000 serfs each, received 43 000. At the very top, the eight men who received over 10 000 serfs each amassed 154 200 male serfs, in other words almost 40 per cent of the total.[28]

In the eighteenth century, Russian aristocrats were not squeamish or constrained by noble inhibitions as regards the sources of their income. Imperial largesse and corrupt milking of the state were favourite methods of enrichment, but commercial enterprise was another. Distilling, cloth manufacture for the army, mining and metallurgy were probably the greatest areas of noble industrial enterprise in the era of serfdom, but the aristocracy was in general ready to turn its hand to most activities promising enrichment. In 1813 nobles held 64 per cent of the mines, 78 per cent of wool cloth manufacture, 60 per cent of the paper mills, 66 per cent of the glassworks and 80 per cent of the potash concerns in Russia.[29]

Some great non-noble fortunes were also made in the eighteenth century but almost all of them ended up in aristocratic hands through the ennoblement of merchant families and the marriage of heiresses into the high nobility. The Demidov, Lazarev, Mal'tsev, Gurev and Goncharov families, for instance, were all ennobled in the eighteenth century and joined the court aristocracy. A handful of other merchant families did the same. In other cases – the Tverdydshevs, Myasnikovs and Volynskys for instance – multi-millionaire non-noble families died out in the male line, their entire fortunes going through heiresses into the pockets of the court aristocracy. Commenting on the traditional relationship between aristocratic and non-noble wealth in Russia, E. P. Karnovich wrote that 'almost all the wealth originally created in our country in the sphere of industrial and commercial activity became noble wealth . . . the holders of these fortunes formed without great difficulty family ties with old aristocratic families, and their children and grand-children occupied eminent position within our old and rich nobility'.[30]

In 1800 Russia was Europe's greatest iron producer and the Demidovs were the empire's leading family in the iron industry. Family incomes were correspondingly princely. Nikolai Nikitich, probably the richest Demidov, had an income of 596 000 roubles (£62 100) in 1795. But N. N. Demidov's expenditure that year was an extraordinary 1 435 800 roubles (£150 000). The Counts Sheremetev, Russia's richest noble family, were not quite so extravagant. In 1798 Count N. P. Sheremetev's income was 632 200 roubles and his expenditure 692 000. In the nineteenth century matters worsened, however. By 1838, N. P. Sheremetev's heir had an income of 2.2 million roubles (£64 919) and expenditure of 3.4 million (£110 330); by 1859 he owed 6 million roubles (c. £562 500). Such extravagance was in part the product of individual foolishness and part inefficient management. But it was also the habits of an aristocracy whose wealth had arrived at great speed, much of it in the form of imperial grants designed to create a superb court which would redound to Russia's glory throughout Europe. To live in this court, let alone to compete among its grandees, required an opulent life-style.[31]

Extravagance took its toll on noble fortunes. Still more damaging was the practice of dividing estates equally among male heirs, with women often getting land as well. In addition the Russian economy as a whole was falling behind its West European competitors in the first half of the nineteenth century. In 1800 Russia produced more iron than England, in 1860 less than one-tenth as much. An English visitor to St. Petersburg in 1820–30 commented that the aristocracy no longer lived in the style of Catherine II's times: 'we may see the spacious hotels which they once inhabited; but the windows are shut, the doors are closed, and the owners are either absent or living in economical retirement'. Looking back from the second half of Nicholas I's reign on a childhood and adolescence at the turn of the century, F. F. Vigel recalled that the St. Petersburg aristocracy had patterned itself on Viennese attitudes and caste-consciousness. The great majority of St. Petersburg high society belonged to it from birth, huge fortunes still existed and magnates were imbued with aristocratic pride. 'Rich fortunes were then not yet divided among heirs . . . they belonged for the most part to people whose titles and high rank, though sometimes new, gave one the sense of an aristocracy . . . Catherine's predecessors, like she herself and her son, raising someone to a high rank, gave him the means not just to support the prestige of the title granted to him, but even to pass this on to his descendants'.[32]

Assessing nobles' wealth under Nicholas I (1825–55) is not easy. The conventional measure of wealth and status was the number of a man's serfs. Serf labour was in general exploited in one of two ways. Peasants either paid a money rent (*obrok*) or performed labour services (*barshchina*). Average *obrok* payments were reckoned to have risen from 3.12 silver roubles per male peasant in the 1790s to 7.5 by the 1840s, and 10–15 by the late 1850s, but these rises probably did little more than keep in step with inflating prices. *Barshchina* was more profitable to landlords, some experts claiming by Nicholas I's reign that noble incomes per serf from *barshchina* estates were three times higher than on *obrok* properties. *Obrok*, however, required few administrative overheads, whereas a *barshchina* estate, operating on forced labour, was more brutal and required more supervision. In addition, since *barshchina* estates were usually geared to the pro-duction of large crop surpluses, the system really required relatively easy access to markets if it was to be effective.[33]

Calculating estate incomes from the size of the serf population and the use of *obrok* or *barshchina* would, however, be a gross error. In most regions, by the 1840s the price of uninhabited land was not much less than that of an estate with serfs. Estate profits depended on efficient management, good soil, access to markets and the extent to which an estate contained industrial enterprises. In the first three decades of the nineteenth century, for instance, between a quarter and a half of Prince B. N. Yusupov's income came from his factories. An English visitor to Russia in the late 1820s com-mented on the great profits that serf owners were then deriving from manufactures.[34]

In his travels around the Russian Empire, A. V. Hauxthausen records hugely different returns from estates with equal numbers of serfs. In his view, whereas an estate of 500 serfs near Kiev would bring in c. 20 000 roubles a year, near Odessa the sum would be 80 000. Nor was the vicinity of Kiev by any means either bad land or an inaccessible backwoods by Russian standards. Stephen Hoch, studying the estate of Prince N. N. Gagarin at Petrovskoe in Tambov, comments that it was 'very profitable' though roughly average for the region. Petrovskoe's profits averaged, however, only

61 000 paper roubles (£1815) between 1845 and 1860 which, for an estate with extensive valuable woodland containing just over 1800 male serfs in 1859, only worked out at a little more than one English pound of profit per year per serf. Hoch's statistics fit in quite well with the £3437 annual profit said to be received in the early 1820s from a 4108-serf estate of the Golovin family in less fertile Nizhniy Novgorod, although on this property there was a steam mill and fine fisheries. Less compatible are the returns of another Golovin estate, this time at Sergeevskoe in Orel, whose 286 male serfs are said to have generated profits of up to 20 000 roubles in good years. Prince Boris Kurakin's average annual income of 541 000 (presumably paper) roubles (c. £15 000) in the 1820s from an estate of roughly 5000 serfs fits in better with Golovin returns from Orel rather than Nizhniy Novgorod and it may be significant that the Kurakin's main estates were in fact in Orel.[35]

Tables 2.3, 2.4, 2.5 and 2.6 are an attempt to look statistically at the location and structure of the mid-century Russian aristocracy. The attempt is highly imperfect not only because the information on serf-owning given in the tables does not necessarily reflect the wealth of individuals, but also because the sources on which the tables are based have some weaknesses. The materials published by the Editorial Commission did not cover the whole Urals region, thus omitting major noble families such as the Demidovs and the Balashevs. Nor do they provide information on the provinces of Kiev, Volhynia and Podolia; Kiev being the centre of the very profitable noble sugar-beet industry and a region, for instance, of big Bobrinsky estates. The Baltic Provinces, where serfdom no longer existed, are excluded by definition. In some provinces, notably St. Petersburg, the gathering of information was inefficiently executed and in a few districts only landowners' surnames were given, which makes correlating lists of nobles across district and provincial boundaries very difficult. Nevertheless, for all its failings, the information provided by the Editorial Commission is incomparably the best overall picture of the Russian serf-owning nobility on the eve of emancipation.[36]

Tables 2.3 and 2.4 show that nobles owning over 2000 serfs in a single province were concentrated in the Central Agricultural and central industrial regions, the heartland of the Russian state, and in the three so-called 'left bank' Ukrainian provinces of Chernigov, Poltava and Kharkov. There were also twenty-four serf-owning

WEALTH 41

magnates in the Volga provinces of Penza and Saratov. Great serf-owners were much rarer in the 'New Russian', recently-colonised provinces of the far south and non-existent in the so-called lake provinces of Novgorod, Pskov and St. Petersburg, though the incompetence with which information was gathered in the capital's province makes definite conclusions about its serf-owners a little dangerous. Russian magnates were also rare in the Lithuanian and Belorussian borderlands, with the exception of Mogilev.[37]

TABLE 2.3 Regional distribution of nobles owning more than 2 000 serfs in one province

		No. of serf-owners
1	Central agricultural	55
2	Central industrial	59
3	Left bank	36
4	Volga	35
5	Byelorussia	13
6	New Russia	4
7	Lake	0

1. Tula, Kursk, Voronezh, Orel, Ryazan, Tambov.
2. Kaluga, Moscow, Nizhniy Novgorod, Tver, Yaroslav, Vladimir, Kostroma, Smolensk.
3. Kharkov, Chernigov, Poltava.
4. Simbirsk, Saratov, Penza, Samara, Kazan.
5. Vitebsk, Vilno, Minsk, Mogilev.
6. Ekaterinoslav, Kherson, Tauride.
7. Novgorod, Pskov, Petersburg.
Source: *Predlozhenie k trudam redaktsionnoy kommissii* (SPB, 1859).

TABLE 2.4 Provinces in which individuals owned more than 2000 serfs

Province	No. of serf-owners	Province	No. of serf-owners
1 Voronezh	16	10 Moscow	9
2 Poltava	14	11 Vladimir	9
3 Penza	13	12 Kursk	8
4 Chernigov	12	13 Tula	8
5 Nizhniy Novgorod	11	14 Mogilev	8
6 Saratov	11	15 Tambov	8
7 Smolensk	11	16 Ryazan	8
8 Kharkov	10	17 Orel	7
9 Perm	9		

Looked at broadly, the map of magnate serf-owning shows that it stretched south from Moscow all the way to the 'New Russian' border, west to Mogilev and east as far as Perm and the Urals. North of Moscow great magnates were rare and this vast region comprises not only the far north – Olonets and Archangel – where noble landowning did not exist, and the also purely peasant north-eastern province of Vyatka. It also takes in the Lake region – Petersburg, Pskov and Novgorod – whose nobility was in the overwhelming majority of cases small and economically vulnerable. In addition, the three Central Industrial provinces to the north of Moscow, namely Kostroma, Yaroslav and Tver, had relatively few serf-owning magnates. But although this basic distinction between 'north' on the one hand and 'centre' and 'south' on the other is true and important, it bears remembering that provinces were often enormous and that the balance between magnates, gentry and state peasants could differ totally from district to district. Even in Voronezh province, for instance, where magnates were numerous, Voronezh district had no nobles owning over 500 serfs; Korotyaksky and Nizhnedevitsky had one each; the Ostrogozh district had fifteen, some of them magnates; and the Biryuchi district had eleven, one of whom, Count D. N. Sheremetev, owned almost 40 000 serfs in this *uezd* alone.

To put Table 2.5 into perspective one needs to remember that in 1858, 78 per cent of all serf-owners owned less than 101 male peasants. Only 1382 individuals owned estates of over 1000 serfs. Table 2.5 is therefore looking at the ultimate, very small and untypical elite of the serf-owning class. Yet even within this narrow group of only 127 people, inequalities were immense. The three individuals who each owned over 50 000 male serfs together held more 'souls' than the sixty-four people who possessed between 3000 and 5000 each. This is a far greater degree of inequality within the aristocratic elite than one would find in the mid-nineteenth century in either England or Germany. Equally specific to Russia is the fact that of the country's 127 greatest serf-owners, thirty-six (28.3 per cent) were women.

Table 2.6 lists the sixty-three individuals who owned over 5000 serfs each. Despite the prominence of Germans, and particularly Balts, in Russian government in the eighteenth and nineteenth centuries, it is striking how overwhelmingly Russian the list is. The richest German was Prince Peter von Sayn-Wittgenstein-Berleberg, the son of a *Standesherr* who became a Russian field-marshal in the Napoleonic era and received huge land grants not in Russia but in the western Borderlands. The only other German name on the list is Countess Sophia Ivanovna Borch, who was in fact a Russian whose property was her own, the von der Borchs not possessing great estates in Russia proper. Even when one moves down to the sixty-four individuals owning between 3000 and 5000 serfs one finds only one German, this time a genuine Balt, Prince Paul Lieven. His Russian estates of 3429 serfs were dwarfed by those of the great ethnically Russian magnates, though admittedly his properties in Ekaterinoslav were very valuable because of the minerals beneath their soil.[38]

TABLE 2.5   Owners of more than 3000 serfs

No. of serfs	No. of owners
50 000+	3
20–50 000	3
10–20 000	16
5–10 000	41
3–5 000	64
TOTAL	127

Source: *Predlozhenie k trudam redaktsionnoy kommissii.*

Among the sixty-three greatest serf-owners in 1859 (see Table 2.6) one finds, as one would expect, many descendants of leading figures at the imperial court in the eighteenth century. The names Potemkin, Shuvalov, Menshikov, Vorontsov, Panin, Bezborodko, Ryumin, Chernyshev, Orlov and Zubov all recall favourites and statesmen of the eras of Peter I, Elizabeth, Catherine II and Paul. K. E. Lazarev and Praskovya Myatleva, on the other hand, were members of wealthy bourgeois families ennobled in the quite recent past. Together, these names are a reminder that mobility into the top ranks of the eighteenth-century Russian aristocracy was far greater than, for instance, was the case in England. In Russia a very wealthy and powerful monarchy could turn favourites into magnates without difficulty. In England titles also reflected political influence at the centre, but the latter sprang from local power in the provinces which was itself largely a function of landed wealth.

TABLE 2.6 Russia's greatest serf-owners

		No. of serfs
1	Count Serge Dm. Sheremetev	146 853
2	Prince Peter Wittgenstein	69 961
3	Countess Nathalie Pavl. Stroganov	64 853
4	Prince Nikolai Bor. Yusupov	30 809
5	Prince Semen Mikh. Vorontsov	23 011
6	Prince Fedor Ivan. Paskevich-Erivansky	20 380
7	Prince Mikhail Al. Golitsyn	18 381
8	Count Ilarion lv. Vorontsov-Dashkov	16 641
9	Count Vladimir Petr. Orlov-Davydov	15 952
10	Al. Mikh. Potemkin	15 479
11	Count Viktor Nikit. Panin	15 325
12	Prince Vladimir Ivan. Baryatinsky	14 814
13	Princess Varvara Petr. Butero-Radali	13 932
14	Al. Dm. Chertkov	13 888
15	Vasili Sem. Kanshin	13 585
16	Count Al. Pavl. Bobrinsky	12 763
17	Countess Sophia Lv. Shuvalov	11 892
18	Count Alexander Serg. Uvarov	11 564
19	Count Grigori Al. Kushelev-Bezborodko	11 437
20	Khristofor Eg. Lazarev	11 253
21	Emmanuel Dm. Naryshkin	10 584
22	Princess O. F. Trubetskoy	10 031
23	Prince Nikolai Iv. Trubetskoy	9 505
24	Countess Nathalie Pavl. Zubov	9 200
25	Ivan Iv. Neplyuev	8 830
26	Pavel Dm. Durnovo	8 803
27	Count Nikolai Al. Kushelev-Bezborodko	8 384
28	Viktor Vlad. Apraksin	8 156
29	Count ?? Zubov	8 113
30	Count Hippolyte Iv. Chernyshev-Kruglikov	8 039
31	Praskovya Iv. Myatlev	7 827
32	Count Alexander Nik. Tolstoy	7 632
33	Princess Alexandra Serg. Urusov	7 579
34	Serge Iv. Mal'tsev	7 582
35	Countess Sophia Iv. Borch	7 373
36	Princess S. A. Shcherbatov	7 327
37	Princess Aglaida Pavl. Golitsyn	7 081
38	Princess Eliz. S. Vorontsov	7 080
39	Count Serge Grig. Stroganov	6 995
40	Count Alexander Grig. Stroganov	6 879

TABLE 2.6   *Continued*

		No. of serfs
41	Ivan Dm. Chertkov	6 838
42	Countess Anna Georg. Tolstoy	6 661
43	Countess Sophia Mikh. Shuvalov	6 659
44	Princess Olga Al. Orlov	6 480
45	Prince Lev Viktor. Kochubei	6 447
46	Count Aleksei Grig. Stroganov	6 416
47	Prince Alexander Serg. Menshikov	6 203
48	Prince Serge Grig. Golitsyn	6 200
49	Prince Vladimir Dm. Golitsyn	6 173
50	Count Al. Iv. Musin-Pushkin	6 061
51	Nikolai Gavr. Ryumin	6 012
52	Count Mikhail Ir. Khreptovich	5 933
53	Prince Al. Al. Golitsyn	5 861
54	Serge Vas. Sheremetev	5 821
55	Count Al. Vas. Bobrinsky	5 797
56	Princess Maria Alxdr. Meshchersky	5 600
57	Prince Serge Vikt. Kochubei	5 548
58	Princess Sophia Al. Golitsyn	5 542
59	Ivan Fed. Bazilevsky	5 288
60	Count Nikolai Al. Kushelev-Bezborodko	5 273
61	Prince Serge Serg. Gagarin	5 174
62	Anastasia Ya. Naryshkin	5 090
63	Prince Nikolai Al. Lobanov-Rostovsky	5 050

Sources: *Predlozhenie k trudam redaktsionnoy kommissii*; N. Ikonnikov, *La Noblesse de Russie* (Paris 1958–66).

Nevertheless, mobility into the Russian court aristocracy should be noted but not exaggerated. Among the eighteenth-century favourites of non-aristocratic origin there were some, of whom Menshikov is the most famous example, who came from nowhere. Many were scions of, usually, upper-level provincial gentry families, however, and would never have come within range of imperial acquaintance and largesse had this not been the case. Moreover favourites were quick to marry into established aristocratic families, partly for social reasons but also because it was difficult to operate in eighteenth-century Russian politics and government without the support of these aristocratic networks. Tracing the history of the great fortunes distributed to favourites in the eighteenth century, it is remarkable how many of them ended ultimately through inheritance in the hands of the old aristocracy.[39]

Nor should one forget how many of the greatest recipients of imperial largesse in the eighteenth century were members of the traditional aristocracy. Of the empire's sixty-three leading serf-owners in 1859, eleven were princely descendants either of Gedymin, the medieval ruler of Lithuania, or of Rurik, the Viking who founded Russia's royal dynasty in the Dark Ages. Five more men came from very old princely families and four others from untitled boyar families which had played leading roles at the Muscovite court from its earliest origins in the fourteenth century. Many other individuals, including four Stroganovs, two Naryshkins and an Apraksin, came from families which, though not quite as ancient or distinguished, had nevertheless played prominent roles in the history of pre-Petrine Russia. Moreover when one moves down to the sixty-four individuals who owned between 3000 and 5000 serfs, one finds eighteen princely descendants of Rurik and Gedymin, three other princes from ancient families, five men descended from old Muscovite boyar houses, and a mass of names descended from the Pre-Petrine nobility.

The emancipation of the serfs in 1861 ushered in a time of crisis for the Russian nobility which hit hardest the northern gentry and nobles whose income derived from factory serfs. The great landowning magnates, however, survived emancipation and the following decades much better than the provincial gentry largely because their resources were so much greater and were less uniquely dependent on agriculture.[40]

In the late nineteenth and early twentieth centuries no greater expert on European high society existed than 'Count Paul Vassili', who wrote under a pseudonym about aristocracy in the major European states. Turning to Russia in 1890, she wrote that at that time Russia's two richest aristocrats were Prince Yusupov and Count Orlov-Davydov. Apart from these two, the leading families of the St. Petersburg aristocracy were, in her view, the Apraksins, Bobrinskys, Chernyshevs, Golitsyns, Kochubeis, Lievens, Naryshkins, Paskevichs, Repnin-Volkonskys, Saltykovs, Shakhovskoys, Sheremetevs, Shuvalovs, Streshnevs, Tolstoys, Vasil'chikovs and Vorontsov-Dashkovs. But although some members of these families lived 'in Saint Petersburg in beautiful palaces filled with works of art and objects of luxury and . . . possess huge landed estates and chateaux in the countryside, . . . one cannot compare their wealth and their string of houses to those of some of the English lords, or some of the Roman princes or some of the princely lords of Austria-Hungary. One can scarcely believe the descriptions of fairytale fêtes given by some of their ancestors which so astonished foreign diplomats in the reign of Paul; of this there remains but the memory'.[41]

The most thorough study of early-twentieth-century Russian aristocracy has been made by L. P. Minarik, who looked in detail at owners of over 50 000 desyatiny (ds) (135 000 acres). By 1905, however, the extent of an individual's land ownership was an even less adequate gauge of his wealth than serf ownership had been in 1859. Land values varied immensely from province to province, the two extremes in 1905 being 5.52 roubles per desyatina in Olonets and 199.65 roubles in Podolia. The biggest noble estates in 1905 were in the Urals region but land prices in the Urals provinces of Perm (43.69 roubles per ds), Ufa (45.04 roubles) and Orenburg (28.51 roubles) were very low. An estate of 50 000 desyatiny in one of these provinces would probably be less valuable than 18 000 desyatiny in Ekaterinoslav (161.32 roubles per ds), Kiev (156.14 roubles per ds), or Kharkov (168.09 roubles per ds), let alone in Moscow (191.24 roubles per ds), Poltava (182.91 roubles per ds) or Kherson (197.85 roubles per ds). Among Minarik's group of owners of over 50 000 desyatiny many of the 'smaller' landowners had estates of much greater value than those of the Urals magnates.[42]

In addition to variations in rural land prices it is important to remember that urban property and ownership of stocks and bonds were becoming key parts of many noble incomes. When, for instance, V. V. Apraksin, a former Master of the Horse (*Shtalmeister*) at the Imperial Court, died he left landed property worth 251 750 roubles (£26 224) and stocks and bonds worth 3.3 million (£343 750). Most of the latter were railway bonds which undoubtedly brought Apraksin a much larger and more secure income than, to take but one example, the 130 509-desyatiny estate of V. N. Okhotnikov, whose land, according to Minarik, was valued at only 2.3 million roubles. By the standards of Minarik's magnates, V. V. Apraksin's cousin, Count Anton Stepanovich Apraksin also had very little rural property. He did, however, own the 8.3-desyatiny Apraksin market in the middle of St. Petersburg, whose annual wholesale turnover was larger than that of any other market in Europe. No information exists as to Apraksin's profits from the market but it would be surprising if they did not exceed those of very many of the landowning magnates cited by Minarik.[43]

Minarik lists fifteen estates of over 250 000 desyatiny (675 000 acres), of which all but two were wholly or largely in the Urals. Most of these Urals grandees were still very rich men. Prince Demidov San-Donato, the greatest of the region's mine owners, still received 10 million roubles profit (£1 041 667) from his works between 1895 and 1901, but only at the cost of threatening the enterprises' viability. Most Urals mines and ironworks were in serious crisis by this time. Prince K. E. Belosel'sky Belozersky, for instance, owned 372 748 desyatiny but his Urals properties, far from bringing him rich profits, threatened him with bankruptcy, from which he was only saved by the State's help and the income from his urban estate in St. Petersburg. Some great Urals landowners, such as Count I. I. Vorontsov-Dashkov, also had big rural estates in the rest of Russia to fall back on, but it was symptomatic that the greatest of the region's landowners, Count S. A. Stroganov, had decided by 1909 to close down all his mining and metallurgical concerns and concentrate entirely on timber. Had Urals property been retained and revolution not intervened, the construction of an adequate railway network and industrial expansion would in time have restored the value of the great Perm, Urals and Ufa estates, but between 1900 and 1914 most of them were of limited value to their owners.[44]

The two 'estates' of over 250 000 desyatiny listed by Minarik which were not in the Urals belonged to the Counts Orlov-Davydov and Sheremetev, in both cases being held by two brothers. Both these estates, made up, of course, of many separate units, were of immense value. Among other members of the traditional court aristocracy who also owned vast and hugely valuable estates the 186 587 desyatiny of Prince A. V. Baryatinsky, the 108 300 desyatiny of Prince S. S. Gagarin, the 134 900 desyatiny of V. L. Naryshkin, the 71 930 desyatiny estate of the Bobrinskys at Smela, and the 246 400 desyatiny owned by the Yusupovs stand out.

Seventy-nine families are listed by Minarik as owning over 50 000 desyatiny of which only twenty-nine had possessed over 3000 serfs half a century before. In fact, however, this picture of rapid mobility in and out of the landowning elite is an illusion. Many of Minarik's

TABLE 2.7   Owners of more than 100 000 desyatina (ds), *c.* 1900

		Total landowning (ds)
1	Count Serge Alxd. Stroganov (U)	1 464 978
2	Prince Sem. Sem. Abamelek-Lazarev (U)	869 714
3	Demidov Family (Paul, Elim, Alxdr and Aurora) [N](U)	739 937
4	Count Pet. Pavl. Shuvalov (and wife)(U)	537 030
5	Balashov Family (Ivan and Nikol. Petr) [N] (U)	521 838
6	Vas. Alxdr. Pashkov [N] (U)	425 997
7	Prince Mikh. Andr. Vorontsov-Dashkov (U)	421 461
8	Counts Sheremetev (Alxdr. & Serge Dm)	390 390
9	Prince Serge Mikh. Golitsyn (U)	384 730
10	Yuri Vas. Popov [N] (?U)	382 773
11	Vsevolozhsky (Vsev. & Nikita) [N] (U)	378 323
12	Prince Konst. Esper. Belosel'sky-Belozersky (U)	372 748
13	Counts Serge & Anat. Orlov-Davydov	321 437
14	Count Il. Il. Vorontsov-Dashkov (U)	298 720
15	Poklevsky-Kozell family(Vikentii & Stanislas) [N] (U)	298 460
16	S. F. Agarkov	255 000
17	Princess Zin. Nik. Yusupov	246 400
18	Faltz-Fein family	237 558
19	Barons Vld. & Grig. Vladim. Meller-Zakomel'sky	214 000
20	Vlad. Fed. Luginin [N]	195 650
21	Yu. Step. Nechaev-Mal'tsev [N]	190 000
22	Prince Alxdr. Vlad. Baryatinsky (& wife)	186 587
23	Nikolai Petr. Pastukhov (U)	182 132
24	Count Alxdr. Alxdr. Mordvinov	164 800
25	Count Aleksei Alxdr. Stenbok-Fermor (U)	164 530
26	Rukavishnikov family [N]	163 000
27	Vas. Lvov. Naryshkin [N]	134 900
28	Vlad. Nik. Okhotnikov [N]	130 509
29	Count Aleksei Ivan. Musin-Pushkin (& wife)	131 761
30	Count Alxdr. Vlad. Stenbok-Fermor	129 280
31	Anton Nikol. Shikhobalov	125 339
32	Pav. Petr. Durnovo [N]	123 600
33	Vlad. Alxdr. Ratkov-Rozhnov [N] (U)	123 400
34	Serge Mikh. Chelishchev [N]	119 449
35	Kamensky family	115 120
36	Alxdr. Fed. Bobyansky [N]	110 165
37	Prince Serge Serg. Gagarin	108,300
38	Lavr. Sem. Arzhanov	108 231
39	Franz Vladisl. Puslovsky [N]	106 970
40	Olga Petr. Druzhinin [N]	106 780
41	Zotov family (Alxdr., Nikol., etc)	105 657
42	Count Aleksei Fed. Orlov-Denisov-Nikitin	100 207

(U) = Urals landowner
[N] = (untitled) noble
Source: L. P. Minarik, *Ekonomicheskaya kharakteristika krupneyshikh sobstvennikov Rossii kontsa XIX–nachala XX vek* (Moscow, 1971); N. Ikonnikov, *La Noblesse de Russie.*

Table 2.8   Owners of 50–100 000 ds, *c.* 1900

		Total landowning (ds)
1	Anisim Mikh. Mal'tsev [N]	98 345
2	Serge Pavl. von Derviz [N]	88 584
3	Vikjt. Ivan. Bazilevsky [N]	88 070
4	Count Ivan Ippol. Chernyshev-Kruglikov	86 115
5	Prince Fed. Iv. Paskevich-Erivansky	84 476
6	Mikh. Nik. Raevsky [N]	83 764
7	Ivan Artem. Tereshchenko [N]	78 000
8	Serge Appol. Uvarov [N]	77 963
9	Vikt. Fed. Gelmer'son [N]	75 600
10	Count Alxdr. Alxdr. Bobrinsky	71 930
11	Dmitri Fed. Samarin [N]	70 233
12	Pav. Vlad. Rodzyanko [N]	70 144
13	Prince Vld. Nik. Orlov	67 914
14	Countess Marie Ivan. Pahlen	67 420
15	Anani Petr. Strukov [N]	67 273
16	Prince Viktor Serg. Kochubei	67 034
17	Appolon Konst. Krivoshein [N] (& wife)	66 920
18	Baron Christian Karl. Osten-Sacken	66 727
19	Prince Nik. Nik. Gagarin	65 232
20	Count Konst. Petr. Kleinmichel	64 182
21	Prince Alxdr. Serg. Dolgoruky (& wife)	63 409
22	Pav. Ivan. Kharitonenko [N]	63 000
23	Emm. Ivan. Batashov [N]	62 700
24	Evg. Grig. Schwartz [N]	62 000
25	Fed. Artem. Tereshchenko [N]	61 880
26	Prince Alxdr. Konst. Lieven	61 830
27	Count Ivan Vikt. Kankrin (& wife)	59 870
28	Marie Grig. Ushkov [N]	59 549
29	Count Konst. App. Khreptovich-Butenev	59 070
30	Princess Marie Hohenlohe	58 300
31	Counts Bobrinsky (Alxdr., Lev., Vld., Peter Alekseevich)	57 420
32	N. N. Vasilevskaya [N]	57 360
33	Konst. Nik. Manzey [N]	57 000
34	A. G. Shomansky [N]	56 360
35	Prince Mikh. Serg. Volkonsky (& wife)	54 660
36	Prince Nikolai Ivan. Svyatopolk-Mirsky	53 200
37	Count Pavel Serg. Stroganov (& wife)	53 080
38	Pav. Vas. Antonovich [N]	52 765
39	Count Platon Alxdr. Zubov (& wife)	52 556
40	Count Georgi Ivan. Ribeaupierre	52 479
41	Countess Elena Ivan. Shuvalov	51 800
42	Prince Edwin Drutsky-Lyubestsky	51 530
43	Emm. Dmitr. Naryshkin (& wife) [N]	51 500
44	Prince Aleksei Grig. Shcherbatov (& wife)	50 730
45	Vas. Aleks. Sheremetev (& wife) [N]	50 000

[N] = (untitled) noble
Source: L. P. Minarik, *Ekonomicheskaya kharakteristika krupneyshikh sobsvennikov Rossii kontsa XIX–nachala XX vek*; N. Ikonnikov, *La Noblesse de Russie.*

families are from the Urals, precisely the area only very partially covered by the Editorial Commission's statistics. Other families cited by Minarik owned land in Kiev, Podolia and Volhynia provinces. By 1900 some of the families listed in 1859 had died out (for example, Wittgenstein, Kushelev-Bezborodko) but their heirs appear in Minarik's list. Count A. I. Musin-Pushkin, for instance, inherited the Kushelev-Bezborodko estates through his wife. In addition, many magnates listed by Minarik came from families which in 1859 had owned between 2000 and 3000 serfs.

The majority of Minarik's landowners were in fact from the traditional aristocracy. Nevertheless exceptions existed. The Fallz-Fein family, German colonists, had acquired huge estates in Southern Russia since 1861. The Tereshchenko and Kharitonenko families owned sugar estates even more valuable than the Bobrinskys' famous lands and sugar mills at Smela. Of the seventy-nine families listed by Minarik, roughly twenty-five had not belonged to the court aristocracy or top level of the provincial gentry in 1800.

Figures exist for the wealth and incomes of a few of the families covered by Minarik. Count S. D. Sheremetev's property was, for instance, valued at 11.8 million roubles (£1 229 167) in 1901. His brother Alexander's annual income in 1913 was 1 550 000 roubles (£161 458). Count Platon Zubov owned 52 556 desyatiny at the turn of the century. His estates were worth 2.7 million roubles (£282 250), his St. Petersburg property 1.3 million (£135 417), and he owned 2 million roubles (£208 333) of stocks and bonds. The Bobrinskys at Smela owned sugar mills with an annual turnover of 10 million roubles in 1900. Three years before, their possessions had been valued at 17.5 million roubles (£1 822 917), of which 9.3 million lay in the land, 3.1 million in the factories, 2.3 million in dead inventory and the rest in cash and bonds. The 215 200 desyatiny owned by Princess Yusupov were more valuable, their worth being estimated at 21.3 million roubles (£2 218 750). This did not include her husband's 31 200 desyatiny. In addition, the Princess owned 3.2 million roubles of stocks and bonds. With such resources the extravagances of her son, Felix, and the family's annual deficit of expenditure over income could be survived. In 1914 the Yusupovs' profits from agriculture, mines and factories were 730 100 roubles (£76 000). The Orlov-Davydovs seem to have been roughly as wealthy as the Yusupovs. Their immovable property was valued at 15 926 917 roubles in 1900 (£1 659 000), and three years later they had 5.2 million roubles (£541 667) on deposit at banks as well as shares in a string of companies.[45]

The great wealth of these men gives the lie to the idea that the Russian aristocracy was on the verge of bankruptcy by 1914. When seen against their resources, aristocratic debts appear much less of a problem than had been the case a century before.[46] In an industrialising country, aristocracy could not, however, hope to maintain its old dominance in all spheres of life. Even in agriculture, where nobles still predominated, total outsiders like the Fallz-Fein, who were graziers, or L. S. Arzhanov, owner of the empire's largest flour-mills, could thrust themselves into the front ranks of the country's landowners. In mining and metallurgy the aristocratic Urals were being overtaken by Southern Russia and the Ukraine, whose industry was dominated by large combines minting great profits. One leading Southern industrialist, A. K. Alchevsky, for instance, saw the value of his investment in the region's metallurgy leap from 3–4 million roubles in the mid-1870s to 30 million by the 1890s.

Great fortunes were now also being made in worlds wholly outside aristocratic control – namely finance, foreign trade, and manufacturing. No man on a salary could compete with aristocratic wealth. In 1913, P. L. Bark (in his post as president of the Volga-Kama Bank, one of the best paid men in Russia) earned only 120 000 roubles a year. But capitalists were another matter. Even by 1861 a handful of business fortunes of up to 7 million roubles existed. In the following half century numbers increased greatly. Between 1873 and 1896 S. Morozov's firm, for instance, saw its immovable capital increase from 2.2 to 14.6 million roubles, with annual net profits averaging 20 per cent. No landowners could hope to compete with this. The temptation to exchange land for stocks and bonds was great. The need to seek accommodation and amalgamation with new elites was pressing.[47]

Direct comparisons between Russian and English wealth and incomes are difficult to make, because whereas the Russian statistics date from the period 1900 to 1914, the English ones are largely derived from the famous census of landowners carried out in 1873. In the decade before the First World War, to take but three examples, the Demidovs, Sheremetevs and Yusupovs appear to be in the range of the top 15–20 English aristocratic incomes from land (more than £100 000 per annum) of thirty years before, though no Russian

TABLE 2.9 Gross landed incomes of £75,000 or more in 1883

		Income (£000s)
£200 000 or more		
1	Westminster, Duke of	c.290–325
2	Buccleuch and Queensberry, Duke of	232
3	Bedford, Duke of	c.225–250
£150 000–£200 000		
4	Devonshire, Duke of	181
5	Northumberland, Duke of	176
6	Derby, Earl of	163
7	Bute, Marquess of	153
£100 000–£200 000		
8	Sutherland, Duke of	142
9	Hamilton and Brandon, Duke of	141
10	Fitzwilliam, Earl	139
11	Dudley, Earl of	123
12	Ancaster, Earl of	121
13	Anglesey, Marquess of	111
14	Londonderry, Marquess of	110
15	Portland, Duke of	108
16	Hertford, Marquess of	104
17	Portman, Viscount	c.100
£75 000–£100 000		
18	Rutland, Duke of	98
19	Cleveland, Duke of	97
20	Downshire, Marquess of	97
21	Overstone, Baron (includes Sir L. Loyd-Lindsay and L. Loyd)	93
22	Boyne, Viscount	88
23	Leconfield, Baron	88
24	Brownlow, Earl	86
25	Yarborough, Earl of	85
26	Richmond and Gordon, Duke of	80
27	Seafield, Earl of	78
28	Pembroke, Earl of	78
29	Norfolk, Duke of	76

Source: W. D. Rubinstein, *Men of Property* (London, 1981).

noble probably reached the £295–325 000 which the Duke of
Westminster received annually even then. In the years between
1873 and 1914 the wealth of the richest English aristocrats grew
greatly, Westminster – admittedly a totally exceptional case –
having an annual income of £1m by the outbreak of the First World
War. Moreover, John Bateman's figures exclude income from
sources other than land. The gap between the wealth of the richest
English nobles and their Russian peers was considerable and Russian visitors marvelled at the luxury of London high society. Nevertheless £100–200 000 per annum, the income of the Yusupovs, Sheremetevs, Demidovs and of a few other Russian magnates, remained
a very great fortune even by English aristocratic standards in 1914.
Moreover, a Russian nobleman, seldom enjoying the right of entail
and primogeniture, lacked the Englishman's corresponding burden
of responsibility for younger brothers and sisters, not to mention
dowagers. The differences in the income of an Orlov-Davydov and
a Cavendish were certainly much smaller than the gap that had
existed between the Duke of Bedford and Prince Pückler in the
1820s.[48]

Differentiation within the English ruling class followed a pattern
similar to that visible in Russia, and indeed elsewhere in Europe.
By the end of the nineteenth century a comparatively small group
of magnates had drawn far ahead of the bulk of the aristocracy and
county gentry. In part this was simply the old story of superior
resources. In the face of agricultural depression or the mismanage-
ment of family property the magnate could stave off bankruptcy by
virtually unlimited access to credit or by selling off part of his lands.
This could be the price of survival, or at least of preserving an
aristocratic life-style, in the era of agricultural depression in the last
quarter of the nineteenth century.

Above all, however, a gap was opening between nobles dependent
on agriculture and those financed, at least in part, through shareholding, industry or, best of all, urban property. In many parts of
Russia poor soil, dreadful communications and absence of markets
had always made agriculture a doubtful source of wealth. Magnates
had generally been mine- or factory-owners rather than pure agriculturalists. In England land was very profitable until 1815, though
in an industrialising era it could never hope to compete with much
riskier investments in trade and industry.

In the second half of the nineteenth century, however, income from land fell below even that from rock-solid government bonds. When on top of this was added the collapse of agricultural rents – a drop of 41 per cent occurring in the arable south and east of England between the early 1870s and early 1890s – the plight of the rural landowner was obvious. W. D. Rubinstein traces through the probate records the declining fortunes of prominent but not very wealthy English aristocratic families, commenting that 'in the course of the nineteenth century . . . the percentage of the group of substantial landowners leaving very large personal estates actually declined and, when the total capital value of their land becomes valued for probate in this century, only a single title-holder among this group left more than £500 000'.[49]

The decline in agricultural incomes was all the more palpable because it occurred simultaneously with a surge in the number of wealthy businessmen. Harold Perkin notes that 'between 1850 and 1880 Schedule D incomes from business and other profits of over £3,000 a year had risen from under 2,000 to over 5,000 compared with the 2,500 landowners with rentals (excluding London property) of over £3,000 a year in the "New Doomsday" returns of the 1870s; business incomes of over £10,000 had grown from 338 to 987, compared with 866 landed rentals at that level; and those of over £50,000 from twenty-six to seventy-seven, compared with 76 such rental incomes. By 1914 landed incomes had scarcely grown at all, so that most of the 4,843 incomes over £10,000 were from business sources'.[50]

Pre-industrial sources of wealth could no longer compete. The noble had to have a stake in the profits of urban and industrial society. A great increase occurred from the 1870s in the extent of noble shareholding and in the number of aristocrats who held directorships. Above all, however, it was the urban landlord, particularly if his property was in London, who moved most comfortably in the world of an increasingly plutocratic British high society. The Duke of Westminster, for instance, according to Bateman, had in the 1870s an income of only £35 000 from agricultural rents: add his London rental and his annual income leaps to £300 000. The Marquesses of Salisbury had a gross income of £53 000 in 1868 and of £60 000 by 1902 but the sources of their wealth had shifted considerably in this period. Although the Cecils were far from being one of Britain's greatest urban landlord families, by the 1880s well over half the income of the Third Marquess of Salisbury was derived from his property in towns. Moreover, Salisbury's net income gained considerably from this shift since whereas rural profits were to a large extent ploughed back into estates, urban ones were not, representing something closer to a *rentier*'s pure profit.[51]

A major contrast between the British and Russian landowning elites remained the position of women. Minarik's list of Russians owning over 50 000 desyatiny included seven women, but this is undoubtedly an underestimate, since she counts married women with their husbands. In a few cases, of which the Yusupovs were the best-known, it was the woman who owned the overwhelming share of a married couple's fortune. Bateman's list, on the other hand, includes no women among the sixty-seven people who enjoyed annual landed incomes of over £50 000.

The Russian group of seventy-nine great landowning families contained roughly twenty-five newcomers who had acquired their fortunes in the nineteenth century. Bateman's group of sixty-seven includes just one newcomer, Lord Overstone, whose wealth derived from banking. Of the sixty-seven only eight were commoners, three of whom did not in reality have rentals approaching £50 000 and the other five of whom all came from very well-established gentry families. Of the peers, only Overstone was in any sense a newcomer. All the other families were well-established by 1700, about half having been knights or nobles in the medieval era and almost all the rest 'arriving' within the upper levels of the ruling class by 1642.

Comparisons between social mobility into the Russian and British aristocratic elite need, however, to be handled with care. Buying big estates in Russia was far easier and cheaper because in 1815 the provinces bordering on the Black Sea were still barely inhabited frontier territory. After 1861 massive sales of land made it easy for wealthy purchasers of estates to build up large properties. But whereas entry into the aristocracy – as distinct from simply the group of large landowners – was much more open in Russia than in Britain before the 1870s, subsequently the opposite may have become true. Increasing numbers of non-landed peers were created in England from this decade and full-scale membership of high society could no longer just be measured by one's acreage. By contrast, in Russia, by 1914 none of the financial, industrial or commercial elites had been granted titles though a few, the sugar-magnates Tereshchenko and Kharitonenko for instance, had been ennobled.

Nor should ennoblement be the only criterion of assimilation of new elites into the aristocracy. Inter-marriage is also significant. By 1914 the Russian aristocracy had not yet married the new wealth created since the industrial boom of the 1880s and 1890s – perhaps unsurprisingly given the short time involved. In contrast, by the outbreak of the First World War, London had seen many examples of the marriage of old and new wealth, of which the most spectacular were the alliances between British peers and American heiresses.[32]

The correspondence of Queen Victoria and her eldest daughter, the Princess Royal and future German Empress, contains interesting asides on the relative wealth of English and German aristocracy. In 1877, for instance, the Princess Royal wrote 'you know how small fortunes are in Germany and how little people are accustomed to luxury and *train du grand monde*'. As Prussian Crown Princess, Victoria did not think she could afford a London season unless she could live in her mother's house and the Queen agreed that 'the expense of a season in London . . . is ruinous to almost anyone who is not rich'. Justifying Princess Louise's marriage to the Marquess of Lorne, Queen Victoria noted that part of the British aristocracy, 'possess large fortunes and rank certainly equal to small German princes'.[33]

Another, later, English implant into Prussian society conveys a rather different picture. Admittedly Daisy Cornwallis-West's parents were not very wealthy and her husband, the Prince of Pless, was one of Germany's richest noblemen. Nevertheless Princess Daisy's sister married the Duke of Westminster and she was well placed to make direct comparisons between English and German life-styles. From her diaries one gets the sense that Silesian aristocratic life was stiff and pompous by English standards but certainly not poor. On the contrary, she stresses the cost and extravagance of life at Pless, noting that their annual disposable incomes varied between £35 000 and £120 000, depending above all on market prices for her husband's coal. Even in the 1890s 'Germany was primitive' by English standards but, in Princess Daisy's words, by 1910 it was racing ahead as regards all consumer products. It would indeed be very strange if the rapid economic advance of Germany had not narrowed the gap between aristocratic incomes in the two countries.[34]

As regards the wealth of the early-twentieth-century German nobility, by far the best sources of information are Rudolf Martin's

TABLE 2.10 Wealth in Bavaria: 1914

Property value (in millions of Marks)	Total	Non-noble	Noble		Counts & Princes		Royal	
			Bavarian	Foreign	Bavarian	Foreign	Bavarian	Foreign
+20	18	7	5	11	2	5	1	2
10M–20	48	16	21	32	6	10	4	4
5M–10	115	54	55	61	23	26	0	2

Source: R. Martin, Jahrbuch des Vermögens und Einkommens der Millionäre in Bayern (Berlin, 1914).

lists. Because these are based on tax records they may well at times underestimate the wealth of individuals. In addition, Martin's lists cover not the whole Reich but only its individual states. Nevertheless Prussia and Bavaria, the two kingdoms covered by my tables, included three-quarters of the empire's population. For all their problems, Martin's statistics and the detailed discussion in his appendices of many individual fortunes are invaluable to a student of the pre-1914 German nobility.[55]

In 1914 Bavaria was, by German standards, still a relatively poor country. It did not have great coal or iron deposits, nor an extensive heavy industry. Not surprisingly, Bavaria had fewer millionaires per thousand population than the heavily industrialised Kingdom of Saxony or the Prussian provinces of Silesia and the Rhineland, let alone Berlin. Nevertheless Martin lists eighteen inhabitants of Bavaria with fortunes of over 20 million Marks (£1 million), of whom two were royal and eleven noble.[56]

As a guide to the wealth of the richest elements of Bavaria's own nobility this figure is, however, a little misleading. A number of great nobles (Prince Guido Henckel von Donnersmarck, for instance) had summer residences in the Bavarian countryside but their estates and main houses were elsewhere. Though Prince Albert von Thurn und Taxis and Prince Adolf Josef zu Schwarzenberg had big estates in the kingdom these were dwarfed by their properties elsewhere and neither man was in any sense a Bavarian.[57] Of the eleven nobles owning property worth over 20 million Marks, six were in fact foreigners. Of the other five, three were from industrialist families (Maffei, Klett, Lotzbech) ennobled in the nineteenth century and only two, Prince Öttingen-Wallerstein and Count Törring, were from the old local nobility. Öttingen was a *Standesherr* from Schwabia, Törring from a very ancient family of the Bavarian electorate. Both men's landed wealth consisted largely of forest but although Öttingen had the more valuable property, 36 million Marks to Törring's 25 million, Törring's estates brought him an annual income of 1.2 million Marks (£60 000) whereas Öttingen only received 1 million (£50 000).[58]

Forty-eight inhabitants of Bavaria were 'worth' between 10 and 20 million Marks (£½million to £1 million). Of these, thirty-two were noble and four royal. Among this less wealthy group fewer were foreign, though defining what precisely constitutes 'Bavarian' and what is 'foreign' has its problems. Among the twenty-one Bava-

TABLE 2.11 Wealth in Prussia: 1912

Property value (in millions of Marks)	Total	Non-noble	Ordinary noble	Counts, princes, dukes	Rulers & Hohenzollern family*
100+	4	0	2	2	0
50–99.9	8	1	2	5	0
25–49.9	29	15	13	1	0
15–24.9	72	24	30	16	2
10–14.9	119	66	34	18	1

* Martin was tactful enough not to include the Kaiser, his sons or brother in his list.
Source: R. Martin, Jahrbuch des Vermögens und Einkommens der Millionäre in Preussen (Berlin, 1912).

TABLE 2.12 Prussian ordinary nobles: provincial residence: 1912

Property value (in millions of Marks)	Berlin	Frankfurt	Köln	Hesse (other)	Rhine (other)	Brandenburg	E. Prussia	W. Prussia	Posen	Silesia	Schleswig-Holstein	Saxony	Total
100+	1				1								2
50–99.9		2											2
25–49.9	4	2	1	2	1					2		1	13
15–24.9	7	7	6	3	3	3						1	30
10–14.9	5	7	1	2	6	3	1	1	1	6	1		34

Source: R. Martin, *Jahrbuch des Vermögens und Einkommens der Millionäre in Preussen.*

rian nobles, twelve individuals were from business families ennobled in the nineteenth century but the rest were older nobles. These included Schwabian (Függer von Babenhausen and Öttingen-Spielberg) and Franconian (Leiningen and Löwenstein-Wertheim-Freudenberg) *Standesherren* as well as Countess Faber-Castell, the product of a union between a junior branch of the *Standesherr* Castell dynasty and the Faber business family. The Tuckers, from the old Nuremberg patriciate, were one of the very rare old German noble families whose wealth was derived from urban property, while the Poschingers were industrialists ennobled in the eighteenth century. None of the old noble families of the Wittelsbach electorate are to be found in this group of thirty-two nobles. Although on average the old nobles had more valuable property than the twelve bourgeois members of the group, their incomes were less. They ranged from 900 000 Marks (£45 000) for Christoph Freiherr von Tucker, whose income was mostly non-agricultural, to 300 000 Marks (£15 000), which was all Prince Függer von Babenhausen drew as an annual income from assets valued at 15 million Marks (£750 000). On average the twelve bourgeois had incomes representing 6 per cent of their assets, the nine old Bavarian nobles having to make do with 4.5 per cent.

The profile of the 115 individuals who owned assets valued at between 5 and 10 million Marks (£250–500 000) is rather different from that of the two richer groups. The proportion of bourgeois is much higher and there are far fewer foreigners. Of the sixty-one nobles, thirty-six came from the old nobility of the Bavarian electorate, Schwabia and Franconia. Apart from the richer *Standesherren* families, it is in this group that one finds most of the best-known names of the nineteenth-century Bavarian aristocracy. From the old nobility of electoral Bavaria there are the Preysings, Arcos, Lerchenfelds and Gumppenbergs, for instance. From Franconia, alongside some of the less wealthy *Standesherren* (Löwenstein-Rosenberg, Ortenburg, Castell), come prominent old local noble families such as the Rotenhans, Crailsheims and Ingelheims. The old Schwabian contingent is smaller, but includes Függer von Glott and Pappenheim. By the standards of the British or Russian aristocratic elites these men were not wealthy. Count Joseph von Arco, for instance, had assets of 8 million Marks (£400 000) and an income of 320 000 (£16 000); Count Kaspar von Preysing received annually 280 000 Marks (£14 000) from assets of 7 million (£350 000). Preysing's income of £14 000 was roughly average for the thirty-six old nobles and represented a return of 4.54 per cent on their capital value. Once again the bourgeois 'worth' between 5 and 10 million Marks did much better than their noble peers, their incomes representing 6.6 per cent of their capital value.

As one would expect, Prussia had many more millionaires than Bavaria: sixty-four individuals had assets valued at over £1 million (20 million Marks) for tax purposes and if one was counting market rather than tax values the number would certainly be greater.[59] Of these sixty-four, twelve were princes, dukes and counts, twenty-eight were lesser nobles and twenty-four were bourgeois. The distinction between princes, dukes and counts on the one hand and lesser nobles on the other is important because it more or less precisely mirrors the gap between old and new nobility. By 1914 an old noble who was also a sterling millionaire would certainly have been raised into the higher ranks of nobility. All the twenty-eight *freiherren* or ordinary nobles (that is, simply carrying the predicate 'von') were from financial or business families ennobled in the previous half century. On the other hand, among the dukes, princes and counts, only Count Franz-Hubert Thiele-Winckler did not come from an old noble family.

Of the eleven 'old noble' millionaires, eight were Silesians. Among these the Hohenlohes, Ballestrems and Schaffgotsches were Catholics. So too, among the non-Silesian old noble millionaires, were the Duke of Arenberg and Prince von Thurn und Taxis, both of whom also had extensive assets outside Prussia which Martin did not include in his statistics. Thus in Prussia, standard-bearer of Protestantism, seven of the eleven richest old nobles were Catholics. Still more remarkable are the origins of the twenty-eight 'new nobles', thirteen of whom were Jews. Integrating the Prussian elite and making it tolerable to its own people was likely, simply on the basis of these figures, to present problems much more complex than those facing England's Anglican establishment. At least as regards the ennoblement of millionaires, the Prussian State seems to have showed no trace of anti-Semitism. All the Jewish millionaires were nobles, the twenty-four bourgeois millionaires being of Christian origin. The key distinction here was not, of course, that the Prussian State was deliberately discriminating in favour of Jews, rather it was that the Jewish millionaires were from financial families (Rothschild, Goldschmidt, Mendelsohn-Bartholdy, Friedländer-Fuld, Bleichröder) whereas many of the bourgeois Christian millionaires were from industrial and commercial ones (Henschel, Haniel, Thyssen, Stinnes). On the whole, governments came more into contact with and were more beholden to financiers than to traders or industrialists. The eleven old nobles had a return of 4.9 per cent on their assets, though the Henckel von Donnersmarcks, the Schaffgotsches and the Duke of Ujest did much better than this. The new nobles managed 5.96 per cent and the twenty-four bourgeois millionaires received 6.41 per cent. Of the twenty-eight new nobles, seven apiece came from Berlin and Frankfurt and three from Cologne, but the rest were scattered, though most were resident in towns. Only Eugen von Kulmitz, two of the von Stumm family and Herbert von Meister regarded a rural estate as their primary residence.

As one might expect, the group of Prussians whose wealth was valued at between 10 and 20 million Marks (£½ million to 1 million) was both more numerous and more bourgeois than the sixty-four sterling millionaires. A hundred and sixty-eight individuals fit into this 'less wealthy' category, of whom eighty-two were not noble. Thirty-three people were dukes, princes or counts or, in three cases, the ruling princes of other German states who also had big private properties in Prussia. Fifty-three individuals were either *Freiherren* or ordinary nobles. Once again the distinction between the dukes, princes and counts on the one hand and lesser nobles on the other reflects the distinction between old and new nobility, though not quite as precisely as was the case with the sterling millionaires. Count Hermann von Griebenow's title was dubious, recent and certainly not Prussian. Uniquely among very rich Prussians with the title of count or above, he cited not a country estate but a town as his main residence.[60] Equally anomalous was the case of C. F. von Bulow, the richest landowner in Schleswig-Holstein and the scion of an ancient family, who nevertheless contrived to remain a simple noble. Much more easily explicable are the situations of Albert von Burgsdorff and Freiherr Theodor von Flotow, both members of old provincial gentry families, whose fortunes were far greater than those of all other members of the eastern 'county nobility'. Burgsdorff had married into the very rich Poensgen family from Düsseldorf, where he himself now lived. Flotow had married a Grunelius from one of the wealthiest families in Frankfurt.[61]

Among the thirty-two titled 'old nobles', seventeen were Silesians.

Silesia's predominance thus remained very great, though not quite as overwhelming as among the very richest layer of Prussian aristocrats. Of the Silesians, a few were members of families whose names were also to be found among the sterling millionaires (Henckel von Donnersmarck, Hohenlohe) but most came from somewhat less wealthy dynasties (for example, Magnis, Biron von Courland, Maltzan, Oppersdorff, Lichnowsky). Many of the thirty-two were from rich *Standesherren* families, some based in Silesia (for example, Solms-Baruth, Hatzfeld-Trachenberg), others elsewhere. Much the greatest family in Prussian Saxony, for instance, were the Stolbergs, one branch of which (Wernigerode) had a fortune estimated at 27–28 million Marks, the other two branches (Rossla and Stolberg-Stolberg) being valued at 18–19 million and 10–11 million respectively.

The Prussian heartland, Pomerania and Brandenburg, contributed only two of the thirty-two families, the Putbus and the von Behr-Regendank. One branch of the Arnim family, always prominent among Prussian Junkerdom, had risen far above their peers in financial terms by acquiring Prince Puckler's estate at Muskau, which was being transformed into a great industrial centre.

The group of rich Westphalian landowners, second only to the Silesians at this level, is very interesting. By far the richest aristocrat in Westphalia was the Duke of Arenberg, but he was followed by three members of former *Stiftsadel* families, the counts von Westphalen, Fürstenberg-Herdringen and Droste zu Vischering. According to Martin, these three men were considerably richer than the two branches of the Sayn-Wittgenstein Westphalian *Standesherr* family, not to mention the best-known Bavarian, Hessian or, still more, eastern provincial gentry dynasties. Since nothing that occurred in the nineteenth century would explain a dramatically disproportionate increase in these Westphalian families' wealth, sources which by the 1820s stressed the prosperity of this section of the German provincial nobility were no doubt correct.

The fifty-three *Freiherren* and ordinary nobles were in the overwhelming majority of cases from financial or business families ennobled in the previous two generations. Nine individuals lived in Berlin, twelve in Frankfurt and five in Cologne. Two Eckardsteins, from a family ennobled in 1799, and two Carstanjens, ennobled in 1881, cited rural estates as their main residences. So did Karl Freiherr von Camp-Massaunen, who is recorded in the fiscal

TABLE 2.13 Prussian counts, princes and dukes: provincial residence: 1912

Property value (in millions of Marks)	Saxony	Silesia	Posen	Hesse	Brandenburg	Rhine	Pomerania	Hanover	Westphalia	Total
100+		2								2
50–99.9	1	4							1	5
25–49.9	1			1						1
15–24.9	1	10	2		1	1				16
10–14.9	1	8			1	1	2	1	4	18

Source: R. Martin, Jahrbuch des Vermögens und Einkommens der Millionäre in Preussen.

TABLE 2.14   Richest Prussian rural nobles (in millions of Marks)

		Wealth	Income	Province
1	Fürst Henckel v. Donnersmarck	177	12	Silesia
2	Christian-Kraft, Fürst zu Hohenlohe-Öhringen (Duke of Ujest)	151	7	Silesia
3	Hans-Heinrich, Fürst von Pless	84	1.9	Silesia
4	Hans-Ulrich, Count von Schaffgotsch	79	4–5	Silesia
5	Franz-Hubert, Count Tiele-Winckler	74	3–4	Silesia
6	Engelbert, Duke of Arenberg	59	2.6	Westphalia
7	Count Franz von Ballestrem	56	2–3	Silesia
8	Eugen von Kulmitz	32–33	1.0	Silesia
9	Freifrau von Stumm-Halberg	32–33	1–2	Rhineland
10	Christian-Ernst Fürst zu Stolberg-Wernigerode	27–28	0.4	Saxony
11	Herbert von Meister	27–28	1.8	Hesse
12	Freiherr Ferdinand von Stumm	23–24	1.8	Hesse
13	Albert, Fürst von Thurn und Taxis	20–21	0.67	Posen
14	Friedrich, Reichsgraf von Schaffgotsch	20–21	1.5	Silesia
15	Lazarus, Count Henckel v. Donnersmarck	20–21	1.5	Silesia
16	Viktor (Hohenlohe), Duke of Ratibor	20–21	0.78	Silesia
17	William, Grand Duke of Saxe-Weimar	19–20	0.79	Silesia
18	Jost Christian, Fürst zu Stolberg-Rossla	18–19	0.54	Saxony
19	Arthur, Count Henckel v. Donnersmarck	17–18	0.75	Silesia
20	King Friedrich August of Saxony	17–18	0.75	Silesia
21	Fürst zu Solms-Baruth	17–18	0.7	Silesia
22	Ferdinand Fürst Radziwill	16–17	0.6	Posen
23	Anton Count v. Magnis	16–17	0.68	Silesia
24	Gustav, Prince Biron v. Curland	16–17	0.68	Silesia
25	Ernst-Julius, Count v. Sedlitz	16–17	0.6	Silesia
26	Chlodwig,Landgraf v. Hessen-Phillipsthal	15–16	0.65	Hesse
27	Hermann, Fürst v. Hatzfeld, Duke of Trachenberg	15–16	0.56	Silesia

TABLE 2.14   *Continued*

		Wealth	*Income*	*Province*
28	Count Andreas v. Maltzan	15–16	0.56	Silesia
29	Prince and Duke Johann v. Arenberg	15–16	0.6	Rhine
30	Count v. Arnim-Muskau	14–15	0.6	Silesia
31	Hugo, Freiherr v. Stumm	14–15	1.1	Hesse
32	Franz, Fürst zu Putbus	14–15	0.5	Pomerania
33	August, Grand Duke of Oldenburg	14–15	0.41	Schleswig-H.
34	Edgar, Reichsgraf Henckel v. Donnersmarck	13–14	0.8	Silesia
35	Friedrich v. Martin	13–14	0.5	Silesia
36	Richard v. Hindersin	12–13	0.5	Silesia
37	Hans Georg, Reichsgraf v. Oppersdorff	12–13	0.5	Silesia
38	Prince Karl von Hohenlohe-Ingelfingen	12–13	0.4	Silesia
39	Karl, Fürst v. Lichnowsky	12–13	0.4	Silesia
40	Cai Friedrich v. Bulow	12–13	0.36	Schleswig-H.
41	Marie v. Kramsta	12–13	0.5	Silesia
42	Karl, Count v. Alten-Linsingen	11–12	0.13	Hanover
43	Karl, Freiherr v. Camp-Massauen	11–12	0.6	East Prussia
44	Moritz v. Carstanjen	11–12	0.45	Rhine
45	Robert v. Carstanjen	11–12	0.45	Rhine
46	Clemens, Count v. Westphalen zu Fürstenberg	11–12	0.45	Westphalia
47	Count Engelbert v. Fürstenberg-Herdringen	11–12	0.45	Westphalia
48	Heinrich v. Tiedemann-Seeheim	11–12	0.51	Posen
49	Emma v. Kramsta	11–12	0.5	Silesia
50	Marie, Fürstin zu Wied	10–11	0.33	Rhine
51	Klemens, Count Droste zu Vischering	10–11	0.47	Westphalia
52	Count August v. Behr-Regendank	10–11	0.21	Pomerania
53	Carl, Duke of Croy	10–11	0.35	Westphalia
54	Wolf-Heinrich, Fürst zu Stolberg-Stolberg	10–11	0.39	Saxony
55	Karl v. Naehrich	10–11	0.46	Silesia
56	Hugo, Count Henckel v. Donnersmarck	10–11	0.51	Silesia

TABLE 2.14   *Continued*

		Wealth	Income	Province
57	Wanda, Countess Henckel v. Donnersmarck	10–11	0.49	Silesia
58	Arnold, Freiherr v. Eckardstein	10–11	0.44	Brandenburg
59	Count Friedrich-Franz v. Brühl	10–11	0.39	Brandenburg
60	Karl, Count v. Brühl-Renard	10–11	0.35	Silesia
61	Richard, Freiherr v. Eckardstein	10–11	0.44	West Prussia

Source: R. Martin, *Jahrbuch des Vermögens und Einkommens der Millionäre in Preussen.*

statistics as much the wealthiest taxpayer in rural East Prussia. Camp-Massaunen was, however, anything but an old Junker. A successful civil servant, his wealth stemmed from his marriage to a member of the Bayer textile dynasty. In the pre-war years his income was double that of the second richest man in East Prussia, Prince Richard zu Dohna-Schlobitten, for Dohna's agriculturalprofits could never hope to match the dividends of a major industrial firm.[62] The new nobles' return on their assets was 5.46 per cent whereas old noble annual incomes represented only 3.83 per cent of their estimated wealth. Once again it was the rich bourgeois who did best, the eighty-two individuals concerned netting an average annual return of 5.66 per cent.

It could be argued that the statistics on noble millionaires omit precisely that section of the Prussian nobility which was most significant, namely the eastern provincial gentry; it was, after all, these gentry families, not *Standesherren* or Silesian magnates, who had created Prussia. It was also they, and not the wealthy aristocracy, whose agrarian politics were such a significant factor in Wilhelmine life. Table 2.15 represents an attempt to meet this criticism by profiling all landowning nobles in the Kingdom of Prussia whose property was valued at over one million Marks (£50 000) in 1912.[63]

The differences between Prussia's provinces emerge strikingly from the table. In 1912, as in 1806, the Silesians were most numerous at every level, but proportionately they predominated in the richer rather than the poorer categories. In old Prussia's two core provinces, Brandenburg and Pomerania, landowning magnates barely existed and the overwhelming majority of nobles owned property valued between 1 million and 5 million Marks, if, that is,

TABLE 2.15 Prussian noble rural millionaires by province

Wealth (in millions of Reichsmarks)	E. Prussia	W. Prussia	Brandenburg	Pomerania	Posen	Silesia	Schleswig-Holstein	Saxony	Hanover	Westphalia	Hesse	Rhine	Total
50+						6				1			7
20–49.9					1	4		1			2	1	9
15–19.9					1	9		1			1		12
10–14.9	1	1	2	2	1	14	2	1	1	4	1	3	33
5–9.9	5	2	16	1	14	35	9	12	6	11	2	15	128
2–4.9	12	11	32	38	42	99	28	44	22	23	18	40	409
1–1.9	35	30	71	99	60	133	22	76	38	18	18	36	636
TOTAL	53	44	121	140	119	300	61	135	67	57	42	95	1234

Source: R. Martin, Jahrbuch des Vermögens und Einkommens der Millionäre in Preussen.

they met even this minimum qualification. There were, however, far fewer Pomeranian nobles 'worth' over 5 million Marks than was the case in Brandenburg. The pattern of wealth in Prussian Saxony and Posen was similar to that in Brandenburg, though in Posen a major difference was that many of these noble landowners were Poles. East and West Prussia had much weaker nobilities than the other eastern provinces.

Major distinctions emerge from Table 2.15 as regards all the eastern provinces on the one hand, and Schleswig-Holstein, Westphalia and the Rhineland on the other. In the latter three provinces there were actually fewer nobles with property valued at between 1 and 2 million Marks than there were between 2 and 5 million. A large, relatively poor provincial gentry did not exist. Instead one had a much smaller but also distinctly richer rural nobility.

The difference between the structure and wealth of the Rhineland, Westphalia and Schleswig-Holstein nobility on the one hand, and the Junkers on the other was of great political and cultural significance in nineteenth-century Germany. Freiherr vom Stein, speaking as a member of a wealthy Rhineland noble family, commented about the Junkers that,

> The nobility of Prussia is a burden for the nation because it is numerous, largely poor and greedy for offices, salaries, privileges and preferments of all kinds. The consequence of its poverty is lack of education, the necessity to be brought up in poorly equipped cadet schools, incapability to fill the higher posts . . . this large number of semi-educated men exercise their pretensions at the expense of their fellow citizens in their dual capacity of noblemen and officials.[64]

The Catholicism of the Westphalian and Rhineland nobility would have sharply differentiated them from the Junkers whatever the socioeconomic similarities or differences between the two groups. But the nobility of Schleswig-Holstein was Protestant but also in many ways unlike its Prussian peers. Joachim von Dissow states that

> among the Schleswig-Holstein nobles one came across completely provincial backwoods Junkers less frequently than in our other

North German agricultural areas. This was partly to do with these families' historical links to the Kingdom of Denmark, and partly to their better economic position. The heirs to the big entailed estates (Fideikommissii) in their youth had visited foreign lands and had done their military service not in small garrison towns but for the most part in the regiments of the Guards cavalry, especially in Berlin and Potsdam. Cultural traditions were also often stronger than in the neighbouring areas, the estate libraries often richer, the furniture more valuable, the family portraits painted by better artists.[65]

From a complex and sometimes perhaps bewildering chapter, packed with statistics, four main conclusions emerge.

Firstly, though the geographical spread of the aristocracy within a society can be pinpointed and differentiation of incomes within this aristocracy measured, precise cross-national comparisons are difficult. Statistics are neither equally reliable from country to country nor do they always have the same date. Comparing Prussian tax statistics from 1912, for instance, with Russian nobles' own private accounts from roughly the same era and English estimates for four decades before has its dangers.

Nevertheless, some basic comparative points do emerge. If the Russian and English aristocratic elites had roughly similar incomes in 1800, by 1850 the English had drawn well ahead and they retained their lead up to 1914. The Germans, with the exception of the Bohemian magnates, were far poorer in 1815 than either the English or the Russians. By 1914 the richest Germans had caught up with the Russians and were within range of the English. Prince Henckel von Donnersmarck's 12 million Marks per annum (£600 000) would probably only have been exceeded in England by the annual income of the Duke of Westminster. Seventeen British peers had incomes of over £100 000 a year in 1883, however, and since most of these men had urban or industrial property their wealth would undoubtedly have increased three decades later. In contrast, only six Prussian titled landowners had annual incomes of over £100 000 in 1912. The English magnate still outclassed his Prussian counterpart.

As regards the bulk of the aristocracy and the richer families of the country gentry, however, the picture is much less clear. In 1873, 2500 British landowners, not counting holders of London property, had rental incomes of over £3000. The number must surely have declined by 1912 given the collapse of rents in the arable south of England and the steep decline of the Irish gentry. In Prussia, a less populous country, 493 noble landowners had property valued for tax purposes in 1912 at over 2 million Marks (£100 000), even the very poorest of them having annual incomes of £4000. Many of the 636 noble landowners with property valued at between 1 and 2 million Marks also had incomes at or above this level. Fair comparisons with Britain would, however, require inclusion both of Prussian non-noble landowners and also the many landowners, noble and bourgeois, with annual incomes of between £3000 and £4000. Add these groups together and take into account the differences in size and population between Great Britain and Prussia and the gap between the two aristocracies' incomes disappears. In total contrast to the situation prevailing in 1815, a century later the English non-plutocratic aristocrat or leading county family did not out-class its Prussian counterparts.

However, in Germany, Britain and Russia, aristocratic wealth could no longer dominate society as it had in the pre-industrial era. Returns on commercial industry or urban investment, or even indeed on state bonds, produced larger incomes. Most of the rich were neither aristocrats nor agrarians. Logically enough therefore in all three countries aristocrats able to hold their own among the very wealthy had to have non-agricultural sources of income.

3. Sources of Wealth: Agriculture

DEFINED in economic terms, European aristocrats were, first and foremost, landowners. This does not mean that their incomes were derived exclusively from agriculture; even in 1800 urban property brought healthy profits to a few English nobles. Some great Russian aristocrats at that time derived much of their wealth from factories. Forests were important in Russia and Germany, and mines in all three countries. Russian and German nobles in 1800 were still serf-owners and though most of the income they squeezed from their peasants ultimately derived from agriculture, some did not. In the infertile northern districts of Russia, for instance, a peasant might well pay his dues (*obrok*) from the proceeds of rural handicrafts or work in a town. Huge incomes were also sometimes won from the spoils of political office or favour, particularly in Russia and England.

Nevertheless it is a true generalisation that for most European aristocrats between 1815 and 1914 the single greatest source of income was agriculture. This did not mean that aristocrats necessarily involved themselves in agriculture or the management of their estates. Even in 1914 very few had any formal training to fit them for such a role. Whether or not they took an interest in agriculture was a matter of personal choice for richer noblemen able to hire and rely on efficient stewards. But the extent to which an aristocrat could become directly involved in farming also depended on the system by which the land was tenanted and exploited in his region or country.

In most of Germany west of the Elbe and most estates in the more northerly Russian non-Black-Earth (that is, northern) Russia, the noble landowner in 1800 was part *rentier*, part judge and part policeman. His role as a farmer was minimal, though a very small demesne might be preserved to meet his personal needs. In these regions a landowner's income derived from dues, tithes and services paid by serfs. The nature and burden of these charges differed greatly from region to region in Germany, according to the varying legal rights of the peasants concerned. In Russia too the *obrok*, or money rent, was by no means uniform from family to family or estate to estate. The key distinction between the serfs of a German or Russian '*rentier*' noble in 1800 was that whereas the former's obligations were enshrined in law and enforced by the State, the latter had few real rights against their masters. A Russian noble in search of a higher income could, and frequently did, transfer serfs from money rents (*obrok*) to forced labour services (*barshchina*).

The distinction between a West German *rentier* landlord (*Grundherr*) and an East Elbian demesne farmer (*Gutsherr*) went back to the late Middle Ages. Previously demesnes in the east had also been small, but the rise of an international grain trade linked to the growth of West European cities made it very profitable to produce grain surpluses on the plains of eastern Germany. To this end peasants were tied to the soil and forced to perform labour services, for in this part of Germany, especially after the Black Death, rural workers were in short supply. In Russia, too, inadequate labour supply was a major cause of serfdom's tightening hold in the sixteenth and seventeenth centuries but large-scale demesne farming did not exist in the pre-Petrine era. Only in the eighteenth century, as markets and transport developed, did the production of large grain surpluses bring profits, and even then only if estates were not too far removed from adequate communications.

Even in eighteenth-century eastern Germany, let alone Russia, estates were anything but modern capitalist enterprises run by noble entrepreneurs. Especially in Russia, properties were messily divided among heirs, and noble and peasant land was intermingled. In both Russia and Germany not only labour but also animals and tools were peasant, as were methods of cultivation. In both countries a basically military service gentry often had little time to devote to agriculture or estate management. Many Prussian estates were let. The great landowners of both countries, owning many estates, could not in any case run them all directly and were forced to rely on managers. If this was particularly true of the Russian court aristocracy, their lands scattered the length and breadth of a vast country, it was also the case among the grander nobles even in a single Prussian province. In East Prussia, for instance, at the end of the eighteenth century, Prince Leopold of Anhalt-Dessau owned thirty-nine estates, Count Carl Finck von Finckenstein, fifty-five; Count Carl von Dönhoff, thirty-three; and Counts Leopold von Schlieben and Friedrich von Dohna, twenty-nine each.[1]

The unique English system of land tenure stood between the two poles of noble *rentier* and noble farmer. Though the overwhelming majority of land was owned by the aristocracy and gentry, virtually none of it was directly farmed by them. By the end of the Middle Ages land was generally let to tenant farmers whose holdings were already very large by continental peasant standards. Initially many of these tenants held various types of customary and protected leaseholds but by 1800 in the overwhelming majority of cases tenancies-at-will prevailed. Leases and rents were determined on an annual basis in line with the movement of agricultural prices and prosperity. Although in principle the tenant had no security of tenure and no compensation for any improvements he might make to his farm, in practice eviction of good farmers who paid their rent very seldom occurred. Almost all the decisions and risks of agricultural entrepreneurship were taken by the tenant. He decided what to cultivate, owned the livestock and working capital and faced bankruptcy if agricultural prices collapsed. The landowner collected his low (3–4 per cent) rent, combining the ease of a *rentier* with the prestige of owning an estate.

Nevertheless, the landowner did play some role in agriculture. He was responsible for investing in fixed capital. At a time of enclosures, when fields had to be hedged, land cleared, roads built and new buildings erected this was an expensive but ultimately very profitable burden. Far less profitable was the often huge investment by landowners in drainage in the mid-nineteenth century, part of which was entirely wasted and none of which brought in profits remotely comparable even to government stock, let alone industrial shares. In addition to responsibility for fixed capital, the landowner in practice also had to reduce rents in bad times, sharing the burdens of agricultural depression, if he wished to retain efficient tenants. On some estates, even by 1800 tenancy agreements had mandatory covenants spelling out required rotations, though this was exceptional.

More generally, many aristocrats patronised and publicised new farming methods, established agricultural societies and shows, prided themselves on breeding high quality livestock and sometimes used their home farms as model experimental units. Since these home farms were often unprofitable, their educational value for tenant-farmers who could not afford to indulge in aristocratic farming games is debatable. The other aristocratic methods of advancing agricultural progress in the eighteenth and nineteenth centuries were important, however, and if the noble landowner was by no means usually the guiding hero of rural change portrayed by the Victorian panegyrist he did take an intelligent and effective interest in the 'new agriculture' much earlier than did his continental counterpart. In this, as in much else, the English aristocracy was to provide a model for their continental peers in the nineteenth century.[2]

In 1800 England's agriculture was far more modern than was the case in Germany or Russia. Indeed much of the history of European agriculture up to the 1870s was the attempt to assimilate changes introduced in parts of England in the eighteenth century. The key to these changes were improved crop rotations. Grass and root crops improved the quality of the soil, avoided the old need to leave one-third of the cultivated area fallow every year, and by providing fodder for animals allowed much larger herds and therefore more manure. New rotations, stall-fed cattle and improved animal breeds required that farms be enclosed, and the old agriculture of strip-farming and common land had largely gone by 1815. Although threshing-machines made their mark during the Napoleonic Wars in Scotland and north-eastern England, where labour was short, mechanisation was not a very important contributor to agricultural change before the late nineteenth century. In England, artificial fertilisers began to be used widely in the mid-nineteenth century but the great age of the agricultural chemist also lay well in the future. Mingay comments that between 1700 and 1850 'the major part of the increase in output was obtained by a large expansion in the cultivated acreage . . . improvements in yields and in average weight of livestock accounted for perhaps only about a third of the total increase'.[3]

Knowledge of the English agricultural revolution travelled fast in eighteenth-century Europe. The term 'new agriculture' entered the Russian language and Jethro Tull had his circle of devoted propagandists by the 1770s, many of them linked to the Free Economic Society. Outside the Baltic provinces, however, new agricultural practices had made progress almost nowhere in Russia by 1800. This was not true in Germany: Schleswig-Holstein and Mecklenburg were in the lead in introducing new grass crops and rotations, though by the late eighteenth century, East Prussian landowners also often preferred to employ free labour and some of the Silesian magnates were moving towards a more intensive agriculture. Although in 1800 three-field agriculture still reigned throughout Germany, in some areas the fallow fields were beginning to be sown with clover and other forage crops.[4]

Agricultural techniques were, however, linked to the way rural society was governed and organised: they could not be changed in isolation. Sometimes this evident truth is reduced to the formula that serfdom made agricultural modernisation impossible. Here caution is required, for serfdom meant many different things in different regions. These could include a peasant's lack of personal freedom, for instance, his inability to marry without his lord's consent. Serfdom might entail forced labour or the payment of dues or tithes or possibly both. It is also sometimes equated by historians with the whole old rural order, including joint and ill-defined rights to commons and forests, strip-farming, and the intermingling of noble and peasant land. Taken together these elements undoubtedly made modern agriculture impossible, but not all of these features of the old order impeded modernisation and some of them long survived emancipation. In Prussia, for instance, right up to 1918, the *Gesindeordnung* bound so-called 'farm servants' to a regime which was very far from that of free labour. In Russia's Central Agricultural region, for decades after 1861 many peasants continued to labour on their lord's demesne in return for land he allowed them to use for their own needs, thus perpetuating the methods by which *barshchina* estates had been run under serfdom.

Equally illusory is the idea that serfdom's abolition in any way guaranteed agricultural progress. Michel Confino explains very clearly, for instance, the impediments to agricultural progress on

Russian noble estates before 1861. He makes due mention of many landowners' lack of interest in agriculture and their ignorance, not to mention sometimes their dislike of borrowing foreign models. Other factors were, however, more important. As A. T. Bolotov, that most enthusiastic of aristocratic improvers, had admitted in 1771, 'useful and necessary as these inventions and experiments are, one must however avow that they are linked to enormous difficulties'.[5]

The Russian climate made the introduction of foreign cattle, seeds and crop rotations more difficult and risky. The very short agricultural season left little room for the error that was implicit in the introduction of new techniques and crops in an alien climate in an era when trial and error was the only possible method of scientific experiment. Given the very small urban population, huge distances and poor communications, access to profitable markets was a major problem. So too in a sparsely populated land was labour. Unlike England or Prussia, Russia had no pool of landless rural labourers. Because the commune redistributed village land periodically according to a family's size, the sharp differentiation of the German peasantry did not exist in Russia. If forced labour was abolished it was hard to see whence free labour would come at acceptable prices. But serf labour also presented problems for noble agricultural innovators. The new rotations and animal husbandry required much more numerous and more skilled workers. Serf labour was generally careless and needed close supervision on *barshchina* estates even when using time-honoured methods and its own implements. Cultivation of fodder crops and wheat rather than rye required that landlords buy much stronger ploughs and horses than the ones customarily used by peasants. Not only did these cost ten times more, but for the noble in traditional Russian agriculture the equipment and draught animals, provided by the peasants themselves, were free.[6]

Liberals claimed that the profits to be made from improved agriculture with free labour would recompense landowners for the trials and expense of innovation. This was not the experience of some innovators, moreover Steven Hoch argues quite persuasively that traditional *barshchina* estates under Nicholas I brought in respectable profits. Long ago August Hauxthausen argued that serf agriculture was more viable than any alternative system in Nicholas I's Russia. George Pavlovsky comments that 'monstrous as Russian serfdom was in the middle of the nineteenth century, considered from the moral and social view-point, economically it was the only system under which progressive large farming could exist in Russia in those days'.[7]

When emancipation came, the very existence of a rural nobility, both in central and western Germany and in northern non-Black Earth Russia was called into question. Nobles lost their police and judicial powers to the state. They exchanged their dues and services for interest-bearing bonds, becoming *rentiers* in the full sense of the word. With one's links to rural society cut, the temptation to move to the town could be overwhelming. Lesser nobles, often unable to live decently off their bonds and their remaining land, were particularly likely to seek urban employment. The towns of northern Russia filled up with noble *rentiers*, as a gentry already much poorer than their southern peers before emancipation increasingly abandoned the countryside. The Tyrtov family, established in their Tver estate since the fifteenth century, were a good example of provincial upper-crust nobles who retained some property as a rural retreat and for sentimental reasons but whose basic activity and source of income became the State's armed forces. Memoirs and contemporary articles testify to a plethora of Cherry Orchards among the northern gentry.[8]

Northern nobles who survived as landowners depended in general on forestry or cattle, not cereal production. In St. Petersburg province at the turn of the century, for instance, only 5 per cent of the land belonging to the big estates was arable and the overwhelming majority was forest. Near Moscow, dairy-farming was well-developed. In the Central Industrial Region as a whole the proportion of private land dropped from 37.3 per cent of the total land fund in 1877 to 30.6 per cent in 1905. But whereas the nobles had owned two-thirds of all private land (that is, land not owned by peasant communities) in the mid-1870s, their share was only 34.3 per cent three decades later.[9]

A. N. Kulomzin, himself a Kostroma landowner, recorded in his memoirs that the bulk of the province's gentry from the southern districts was bankrupted by emancipation. He himself prospered by exploiting phosphate deposits on his estate, but for the bulk of his peers, he records, survival was achieved, if at all, through forestry. This was to bear out Hauxthausen's gloomy prediction of the 1840s. He wrote that 'in these northern districts agriculture cannot be pursued on large estates as a profitable speculation . . . large proprietary farms can only exist in these districts in two ways; either as *corvée* establishments, where the landowner has not himself to maintain labourers etc (in other words to pay none of the farming expenses), or as ordinary farms with hired workmen and cattle, but united with manufacturing industry, by means of which the labour not required for agriculture might be constantly and profitably employed'.[10]

Emancipation usually left west, central and south German nobles much less land than was the case among Russian estate-owners in the non-Black Earth region. In 1905, for instance, nobles owned 13.7 per cent of land in the seven provinces of the Central Industrial Region around Moscow. This was far below the figure for most Russian regions but much above the level of noble landowning in most provinces of central, west or southern Germany.[11]

West of the Elbe, the German noble was in general left with his forest, whatever demesne and rented land he had possessed before emancipation, and redemption bonds to compensate him for lost dues and services. As in Russia, it was the poorer provincial gentry who were most often driven from the land. In Bavaria, for instance, most noble estates were small and indebted by 1815. Whatever farming they carried out was wholly dependent on peasant cattle, labour and tools. Many of their 'feudal dues' were paid in kind. The redemption bonds were no substitute for this and these nobles lacked the capital to set themselves up as farmers or the desire to sink into the peasantry. The city beckoned. Even in Middle Franconia, whose nobility was on the whole better off than that of the Bavarian electorate, many nobles had moved to the city of Nuremberg by mid-century. In 1815, roughly half of the Bavarian nobility owned land but by 1921 the figure was down to a third.[12]

Among the richer German nobles the picture was different. Here great efforts were made to use redemption bonds to buy new land, which was almost always regarded as the most desirable form of investment. In 1854, for instance, Prince Hugo zu Hohenlohe-Öhringen, the head of the Hohenlohe family and himself a great Silesian industrial magnate, stated that 'the re-investment of liquid capital in land is an essential condition for the nobility's existence'. None of the other Hohenlohes who heard Prince Hugo's words at the 1854 family conference disagreed with him, for in Germany, in partial contrast to Russia, noble family and caste spirit was not only very strong but also rooted in the belief that nobility without land was impossible.[13]

Spurred on by such values and by the traditional sense that land represented a safe investment, wealthy nobles searched for properties to buy, preferably whole estates, but where necessary, also peasant farms. The Fürstenbergs invested most of their redemption money in the Black Forest. In 1806 they had owned 22 791 hectares of demesne land, of which 62 per cent was woodland. By 1919 they possessed 42 000 hectares in Schwabia alone, three-quarters of it forest. Few nobles had the means to invest on such a princely scale, but the size of estates grew after the initial financial shock of emancipation had worn off and redemption funds began to come in. The Leiningen family, for instance, made themselves thoroughly unpopular in Baden by purchasing many woods, meadows and bankrupted peasant farms at auction, a policy which contributed to the bitterness of the 1848 revolution in the Odenwald. Undeterred, the family spent another 474 000 florins on land between 1849 and 1853. Below the *Standesherr* level the Westphalian, Hessian and richest Bavarian families were also very active in the land market. According to Heinz Reif, the Munster aristocracy in Westphalia made most of their purchases between 1830 and 1860, the average size of *Rittergüter* trebling.[14]

For many nobles in western, southern and central Germany the turn towards agriculture and the forging of local loyalties was the conscious policy of a class whose status was under challenge and which was threatened, if not by poverty, then at least by redundancy. Freiherr von Rotenhan, a leader of the Franconian nobility, wrote that his class's only chance of survival was to run their estates in an efficient, scientific and modern manner, forge links with the local peasantry, and use their superior wealth and education in a way that benefited local agriculture and the rural population. In 1849 the Oberpräsident of Westphalia, von Vincke, took a similar line, urging the local nobles to shed their excessive caste-consciousness and their reactionary longings for privileges held under the Old Reich. Instead they must become the first farmers of the village, creating a firm alliance with other agriculturalists.[15]

The strategy was correct but it had its pitfalls. In Westphalia as elsewhere in Europe, rich aristocrats anxious to justify their class's position by taking a leading role in progressive agriculture could lose a lot of money, for neither their motivations nor their instincts were businesslike. Count Joseph von Westphalen, for instance, tried in the 1820s to stop leasing out his land and to run his farms himself. The Westphalian nobility, however, had no experience of agriculture and the 1820s depression was not the best time to learn. Great expense was incurred through the investments needed to build up Westphalen's cattle and farm equipment, and debts rapidly mounted to 180 000 talers.[16]

The biggest problem facing rich nobles anxious to rebuild estates in west, south and central Germany was simply the lack of available land. This theme recurs constantly in estate records. In the 1850s Prince Függer von Babenhausen concluded that 'an immediate acquisition of land is not at present possible without great loss because of its high price in relation to its profitability'. Demands for estates far exceeded supply and, as Winkel notes, 'complete estates demanded too high prices because the sellers knew how earnestly landowners with redemption money were in search of such property'. Some nobles, of whom the Hohenlohes were the best examples, bought land far from their ancestral estates. A few with industrial connections invested in firms and factories. Most spare cash ended in state and railway bonds, however, and this turned out very much to German aristocrats' benefit. Had they succeeded in buying up huge tracts of land in the southern, western and central provinces not only would their incomes have been less secure but they would also have made themselves much more visible and unpopular. As it was, with one foot in local agriculture but with other sources of income too, they could ride out depression far more comfortably than the east German rye producers and they never again faced the unpopularity which surrounded so much of the west and south German aristocracy in 1848.[17]

Though information exists on the noble share of land in some nineteenth-century German provinces[18] the best overall guide is Theodor Häbich's work published in 1930. Prussia's loss to Poland of part of its eastern borderlands certainly affects the picture as regards East-Elbian landowning but there is no reason to believe that the situation in central, western and southern Germany had changed much since 1914.[19]

Tables 3.1, 3.2 and 3.3 are based on Häbich's statistics for regions of western, southern and central Germany. They show that on average noble estates of 500 hectares or more[20] made up roughly 5 per cent of the total area. In two provinces, Schleswig-Holstein and

TABLE 3.1 Noble share of land in western, southern and central Germany

	Baden	Württemberg	Bavaria	Rhine	Westphalia	Hesse (-Nassau)	Saxony (Prov)	Saxony (KGD)	Hanover	Schleswig-Holstein
Total (*hectares*)	1 261 078	1 750 202	6 655 066	1 908 747	1 761 549	1 385 718	2 244 564	1 349 167	3 270 638	1 332 374
Noble estates (500+HA)	30 625	121 322	154 274	86 135	190 594	64 280	205 042	67 979	98 350	145 198
	2.4%	6.9%	2.3%	4.5%	10.8%	4.6%	9.1%	5%	3%	10.9%
Noble estates (2300+HA)	24 499	84 964	46 064	25 039	115 026	31 154	70 820	26 995	44 186	97 415
	1.94%	2.06%	0.69%	1.3%	6.5%	2.2%	3.2%	2%	1.35%	7.3%

Total land: 22 929 103 HA
Noble land: 1 163 799 HA = 5.1%

Source: T. Häbich, *Deutsche Latifundien* (Konigsberg, 1930).

TABLE 3.2 Noble share of agricultural land in western, southern and central Germany

	Baden	Württemberg	Bavaria	Rhine	Westphalia	Hesse-Nassau	Saxony (province)	Saxony (kingdom)	Hanover	Schleswig-Holstein
Total (hectares)	637 790	1 128 692	3 948 395	1 137 029	992 709	700 901	1 608 372	927 901	1 779 519	1 038 053
Noble estates (500+ HA)	8 461	24 371	52 629	40 539	83 174	14 623	95 994	32 442	43 481	106 206
	1.3%	2.2%	1.3%	3.6%	8.4%	2.1%	6%	3.5%	2.4%	10.2%
Noble estates (2 500+ HA)	3 546	15 005	13 640	6 087	46 675	3 818	20 424	9 584	10 854	70 271
	0.56%	1.3%	0.3%	0.5%	4.7%	0.5%	1.3%	1%	0.6%	6.8%

Total agricultural land: 13 899 361 HA
Noble agricultural land: 493 459 HA = 3.6%

Source: T. Häbich, *Deutsche Latifundien.*

TABLE 3.3 Noble share of forest land in central, southern and western Germany

	Baden	Württemberg	Bavaria	Rhine	Westphalia	Hesse-Nassau	Saxony (province)	Saxony (kingdom)	Hanover	Schleswig-Holstein
Total (hectares)	567 825	634 907	2 187 033	611 376	518 632	617 205	522 376	362 431	671 345	107 217
Noble estates (300+ HA)	21 908	87 605	91 532	43 588	101 952	46 342	102 293	33 375	37 265	28 155
	3.8%	13.8%	4.2%	7.1%	19.7%	7.5%	19.6%	9.2%	5.6%	26.3%
Noble estates (2 500+ HA)	20 914	55 954	26 031	18 602	64 904	27 196	48 897	16 859	18 198	21 229
	3.7%	8.8%	1.2%	3%	12.4%	4.4%	9.4%	4.7%	2.7%	19.8%

Total forest land: 6 800 347 HA
Noble forest land: 594 015 HA = 8.7%

Source: T. Häbich, Deutsche Latifundien.

Westphalia, the nobles' share was over 10 per cent. In two others, Baden and Bavaria, it was under 2.5 per cent. In Westphalia and Schleswig-Holstein big estates of over 2500 hectares were far more important than in the other eight provinces: in the two former provinces they occupied 6.5 per cent and 7.3 per cent respectively of the total area, much more than half the acreage of the noble group as a whole. Elsewhere the great estates never had more than 3.2 per cent of the total land fund and always constituted less than half of overall noble property.

Nobles owned a much higher proportion of German forests than of the country's agricultural land. In the ten provinces covered by the three tables 3.6 per cent of agricultural land and 8.7 per cent of the forests belonged to noble estates of over 500 hectares. Except for Schleswig-Holstein, Westphalia and the province of Saxony, noble agriculture was of peripheral importance. In all but two regions, however, nobles owned more than 5 per cent of the forests, Baden and Bavaria once again lying at the bottom of the list. But in Württemberg the noble share was 13.8 per cent, in Westphalia and the province of Saxony it was almost a fifth, and in sparsely forested Schleswig-Holstein it was over a quarter. In general, estates of over 2500 hectares had a higher proportion of forest (56.2 per cent) than properties of over 500 hectares (51 per cent).

The effects of emancipation deepened the differences between aristocracy in western and eastern Germany. With seigneurial courts abolished and dues redeemed, the power of the noble in most of the western countryside declined sharply. In the Prussian east, however, the nobles' judicial and police powers survived for decades and their landholdings actually increased as a result of emancipation. This was partly because certain categories of peasant tenants had to cede up to one half of their land in return for emancipation from labour services. Nobles also received the lion's share of the 4.3 million hectares of common land that was divided up as a result of the 1821 decree, peasants receiving only 14 per cent of this. In addition, however, many peasant farms went bankrupt in the 1820s and were absorbed by the great estates, since peasant land, unlike under serfdom, could now be purchased by other groups. 'In Pomerania (without the most western part) more peasant land was appropriated by the landlords in the years 1807–48 than during the previous two centuries'. In two of the Brandenburg marks (Uckermark and Mittelmark) noble estates grew in size by 18 per cent between 1800 and 1860. Nevertheless, the Prussian big estates even at their apogee never monopolised land ownership in the English fashion. Only in two provinces, Pomerania and Posen, did large estates ever account for more than half of the total land fund in nineteenth-century Prussia. Moreover, many Prussian 'large' estates would have been considered of paltry size by the English gentry.[21]

Between 1820 and the 1870s the Prussian great estates were in the forefront of the country's agriculture, which began its transformation in this period. German agricultural production grew much quicker than French, despite France's more fertile soils. German scholars, with Albrecht Thaer in the lead, publicised English agricultural methods. Thaer's impact on the eastern landowners, whom he regarded as the natural leaders of agricultural progress in Germany, was great. By 1852 there were 361 agricultural societies in Prussia, with 30 000 members. Division of commons, separation of noble and peasant land, and the end of strip-farming allowed the introduction of new crops, improved rotations and better breeds of cattle. Between 1800 and 1860 cereal production per hectare increased in Germany by 45 per cent. Potatoes were introduced and took well to the sandy soils of north-eastern Germany, as did the huge flocks of merino sheep which were built up on the eastern estates in this era. Still more a mark of the big estates, especially in Silesia and Saxony, was sugar production, which, as in Russia, took off in the 1830s. In Germany in 1834–35 twenty-one sugar mills produced 25 346 *zentner* of raw sugar. Sixteen years later, 185 mills produced close to one million *zentner*. Because, unlike cereals, potatoes and sugar demanded plentiful labour in the spring and autumn they were particularly valuable to the big landowners who had otherwise unemployed workers to spare in these seasons. Although Prussian estate agriculture became much more intensive in this period, however, the biggest source of increased cereal crops, as had been the case in England, came from the decline of fallowing and the massive spread of cultivation into previously unused land. With the Prussian population and international grain prices rising steeply from 1830, those landowners who had survived the agricultural crisis of the 1820s made great profits. By 1870 eastern estates were selling for three to four times the price of a half-century before.[22]

The success of the Prussian landowners was in stark contrast to the fate of the Russian nobility after 1861. In the 1870s the only

region of the Russian empire in which noble agriculture was prosperous, capitalist and efficient were the three Baltic provinces of
Estland, Livland and Courland. Here indeed the great estates were
richer and usually more technologically advanced than in eastern
Prussia. But the traditions, society and land-tenure in these provinces were totally different from those of the rest of the Romanov
empire, and their aristocracy was German. In Russia proper,
although individual noble estates were prosperous and well-run, the
overall level of the big estates was very backward by German or
English standards. Huge tracts of land were either let to peasants
in small lots or exploited by the peasantry on the landlords' behalf
on a labour-rent or share-cropping basis. Lands cultivated in this
way were likely to be even more wastefully farmed than the peasants' own holdings. The unprofitability of estate agriculture led to
massive sales of land by the nobility. After emancipation, nobles
still owned 87.2 million *desyatiny* but almost 20 per cent of this was
disposed of within two decades and a further 20 per cent by 1902.
By 1914 only 41.1 million *desyatiny* remained in noble hands.[23]

The contrast between Prussian nobles' success in capitalist agriculture and the failure of their Russian peers was not, however, as
stark as these comparisons might suggest. In the two decades after
emancipation a large proportion of the Prussian landowning nobility
proved unable to adapt itself to capitalist methods, went bankrupt
and was forced to sell its estates: 40 per cent of noble properties in
Silesia were in bourgeois hands within a few years of emancipation
and the turnover in East Prussia was still more rapid. By 1856, in
the seven eastern provinces only 7023 of 12 330 (56.9 per cent)
noble estates were still in the hands of the gentry and some even
of these were owned by recently ennobled bourgeois. As in Russia,
lack of entrepreneurial skill, extravagance, inadequate means to set
up one's own equipment and animals, and excessive debts were the
chief causes of nobles' ruin. Prussians bought and sold properties
at dizzying speed, and showed no more sentimental attachment to
old family estates than existed in Russia. Equally similar was the
pattern in which small landowners frequently went to the wall while
the magnates usually survived. In Russia, for instance, between
1900 and 1914 the greatest 155 landowners sold 3 per cent of their
property, the nobility as a whole over a fifth. In Prussia by 1885,
whereas 43.1 per cent of all *Rittergüter* were in bourgeois hands, this
was true of only 32 per cent of estates of over 1000 hectares. Of the

159 properties of over 5000 hectares in the seven eastern provinces, only ten were owned by bourgeois.[24]

In contrast to Russia there were already sizeable groups of bourgeois big farmers in the pre-reform Prussian countryside. Even though this was illegal, 10 per cent of *Rittergüter* were owned by non-nobles. Many more noble estates were let to bourgeois tenants. So too was part of the extensive royal demesne where, before the reform, nobles were not allowed to hold leases. In East Prussia in 1800 there were around 800 landowners and 250 rich tenants, and the proportion, according to Schissler, was similar in other provinces. The Baltic grain-exporting ports also contained prosperous bourgeois with close links to agriculture. After 1807 these groups, and particularly the tenants, bought many estates. They rather than the nobility were in the forefront of agricultural progress in the following years, partly because they had a more professional interest in agriculture and a greater awareness of English innovations, partly because they lived less extravagantly and ploughed more of their income back into their estates.

These bourgeois landowners, in general anxious for assimilation into noble society, made a big contribution to the Junkers' ability to confront the challenges – political as well as economic – of a changing world. The Nathusius family's history provides an example of this. After emancipation Gotthob Nathusius, a tobacco manufacturer, bought a former Alvensleben estate near Magdeburg. Not only did it develop into a model of capitalist farming but it also generated a number of agricultural processing industries including fruit, potato starch and oil factories and a distillery. All four sons of Nathusius were ennobled, two becoming famous stock-breeders and two playing a major role in politics.[25]

Both the structure of pre-reform rural society in Prussia and Russia and the terms of the two countries' emancipation settlements help to explain why large estates flourished in one but not in the other. Prussian peasant society before 1806 was highly differentiated and this process was accentuated after emancipation. Big peasant farmers quite soon joined nobles in the defence of private property and market-orientated agriculture, and in opposition to insubordinate or socialist labourers. In most eastern provinces even in 1806 more than half the population were landless or very small property-owners. They provided a pool of labourers on whom the Junkers could draw after emancipation. Moreover the Prussian reforms of

1807–19 encompassed only the richer peasants who could afford a horse-drawn plough. Peasants outside this category, of whom there were very many, continued to perform labour services until after the 1848 revolution. Prussian landowners, armed with local police and judicial powers until 1872 and with strict controls over living-in farm labourers until 1918, were well placed to control their work-force.

The situation in Russia was very different. No bourgeois tenants lived in the countryside before 1861. Merchants who bought estates subsequently almost always did so for speculative purposes, not in order to farm. The much greater equality within the peasantry, secured by the repartitional commune, deprived landowners of stalwart peasant supporters of order and property, thus contributing to the general sense of insecurity which encouraged noble land sales and discouraged investment in agriculture, especially in the twentieth century. Before 1900 landless permanent agricultural labourers were scarce and often represented the dregs of the village. Russia's patrimonial courts and police powers had been abolished in 1861 and there was no Tsarist equivalent of the *Gesindeordnung*. Nor were any sections of the peasantry excluded from the settlement and bound to continued labour services. Finally, in complete contrast to Prussia, Russian peasant land remained protected: it could neither be sold nor confiscated for non-payments of debts.[26]

Both the Russian and Prussian nobilities were unfortunate in that the costs and dislocation of emancipation were quickly followed by a collapse of international agricultural prices and many years of depression. In Prussia the impact of the 1820s depression was increased by the fact that in previous decades the nobles had become used to steeply rising prices for cereals and estates and had based their life-style and economic strategies upon them. Between 1797 and 1817 rye prices in the eastern provinces' ports had more than doubled. By 1801–5 the price of estates had more than trebled in Silesia and almost quintupled in Brandenburg in the previous fifty years. Massive speculation in land occurred since money could be borrowed by nobles from the state at rates of interest well below inflating estate values. When agricultural prices collapsed and with them the speculative booms in estates' value, many landowners found that their property was mortgaged at levels well above its market price.[27]

The collapse in grain prices after 1817 was dramatic. In 1825 bread grain prices in German ports were 28 per cent of the 1817 level; in the interior they were only 23 per cent. The government stepped in, banning foreclosures on mortgages and bailing out many nobles by direct financial support. Some of the more enterprising landowners switched from grain to sheep but for many the sale of estates was the only option. Above all it was provinces geared to grain exports – Pomerania and West and East Prussia – which were hardest hit, in large part because the previously lucrative English market was closed to them in the 1820s by the Corn Laws. According to Wilhelm Abel, wheat prices in German harbours were 28 per cent of the English level in 1825, and even if one included the price of transport and delivery to London merchants, German wheat was still 56.6 per cent cheaper than English. Though English farmers also complained loudly about depression in the 1820s and looked back with envy to the exceptionally prosperous war years, their position was much easier than that of their Prussian peers. So was that of the Russian landowners, far less involved in the international grain trade in this era than was the case in Prussia.[28]

When the great agricultural depression of the late nineteenth century struck in the 1870s, however, it affected landowners throughout Europe, for the market's tentacles had now spread to all corners of the continent. The basic cause of collapsing agricultural prices was Europe's integration into the world market. In the New World vast areas had been opened up to agriculture. Cereal production boomed in North America, cattle farming in South America and sheep in Australia. Costs of production on virgin colonial soil were lower than in Europe. Transport costs were plummeting, the usual figure cited being the 75 per cent reduction between the late 1860s and early 1900s in the cost of shipping wheat from Chicago to Liverpool. Meanwhile the development of refrigerator ships made long-distance meat transport possible.[29]

All of European agriculture was affected by the depression but the large estates were hardest hit for three main reasons. In the first place, noble agriculture was mostly geared to cereals and in the depression grain farming suffered the most. Between 1808 and 1866 the percentage of England and Wales given over to the cultivation of cereals rose from 40 per cent to 58 per cent. The huge grain lands of the Russian southern steppes were opened up in these decades. In Prussia's north-eastern provinces, the home of noble agriculture, the nineteenth century had also witnessed a massive expansion of grain production into previously untilled areas. As American grain began to pour into Europe in the 1870s gentry agriculture faced disaster. In the 1850s the annual average of US grain exports to Europe was 5 million bushels. By 1875–9 it was 107 million. Prices plummeted unless maintained by tariffs: at their lowest point in 1894 English wheat prices were only a third of the 1867–8 level. In Prussia, at their lowest point (1901–5) wheat prices were 20 per cent down on 1871–5, and rye prices had fallen by 25 per cent. The relative impact on England and Prussia of agricultural depression was thus the precise reverse of the 1820s, largely because this time it was the Prussian farmer who was protected and the Englishman who faced the full force of international competition.[30]

The second great problem of noble agriculture was rising labour costs. In Russia the daily wage rates of agricultural labourers rose by 40 per cent between 1882–91 and 1911–14, though regional differences were very great. The same was true in Germany. In the Kingdom of Saxony, for instance, agricultural wages rose 50 per cent between 1896 and 1911, luring away many labourers from the eastern estates – to the Junkers' fury. Even in the Prussian east, however, the cost of labour was rising sharply: as in England, this was largely because of easy access to the cities by railway, and industry's competition for scarce workers. In the first half of the nineteenth century rural southern England and eastern Prussia had experienced rapid population growth, a major labour surplus and very low wages. Northern England, like western Germany much more industrialised, had to pay agricultural workers considerably more. By the last quarter of the nineteenth century, however, labour was pouring out of rural southern England and eastern Prussia alike. Even where, as in Prussia, political and legal repression made unionisation impossible, changing market conditions gave labourers a sense of their own increasing value and scarcity. Even very conservative Protestant pastors in eastern Prussia welcomed the way in which the shifting balance of power resulted in better treatment of labnur, not only matdrially but also in terms of respect for the labourers' dignity. Symbolic was the Junkers' dropping of the tradition of addressing their workers by the familiar, and contemptuous 'du'.[31]

In comparison to peasant family farming, the landowners' overheads were both great and inelastic. Faced by depressed prices the landowner still had to pay wages but the peasant could work himself harder, reduce consumption and even retreat towards subsistence. Probably the biggest single overhead in noble agriculture was, however, the aristocrat himself. David Lloyd George's comment in 1911 that a duke cost more than a battleship had a point. A few great nobles were able, and for a time willing, to subsidise agriculture from other income but most took from the land much more than they gave it. Gentlemanly living, let alone a magnate's glory, were not easily sustained by an industry whose profits were declining absolutely, let alone relative to incomes derived from other sources. Faced by depression, aristocratic life-styles could be reduced. Roberta Manning describes a younger generation of Russian nobles in the 1890s who determined to preserve and develop their properties by living simply and ploughing back profits into farming. In England costs were cut and manor houses even let for much of the year in some cases during the depression. But no aristocrat could cut his costs to peasant levels without abandoning all claims to status and esteem, not to mention watching his property tumble down around his ears. Sooner than the peasant, the aristocrat would be forced to sell out and seek his fortune in the city.[32]

Although the depression hit British, German and Russian agriculture alike, the latter was a special case. Agriculture in Russia remained on the whole backward by German or English standards right up to 1914. At the same time the Russians did not face the German or British problem of seeking to stop the domination of their home market by cheap foreign grain. On the contrary, Russia was a great grain exporter, by 1914 the largest in the world.

In pushing through the emancipation settlement of 1861, the Russian government pursued a strategy which, in its broad outlines, was similar to the plans for agrarian reform advanced by the Decembrist rebel P. I. Pestel and other radicals in 1825. The land fund was divided more or less in half. Protected by the repartitional commune and the ban on the sale of their land, Russian peasants would, it was hoped, avoid the differentiation, impoverishment and proletarianisation of so many of their Prussian counterparts. They would be protected from the full force of the capitalist market for the time being. When the economy had developed sufficiently to provide jobs in industry for former peasants the commune could be dismantled without undue suffering or disorder. Meanwhile, in their half of the land, Russian nobles could emulate their Prussian peers by developing a modern capitalist agriculture.[33]

This strategy failed. The commune retarded peasant agriculture, and massive growth of the rural population caused intense land hunger in some areas. Meanwhile, most noble estates did not become modern capitalist enterprises. Efficient aristocratic farming faced many impediments. These included the perennial problems of Russian agriculture – poor northern soils, harsh and unpredictable climate, short growing seasons. In some regions access to markets long remained difficult. Most nobles had never been entrepreneurs and coped with difficulty with the rigours of capitalist agriculture.[34] Labour was often inadequate, unskilled, recalcitrant and impossible to discipline. Given the size of noble estates, capital per acre ratios were often very low and the administrative problems of trying to run huge *latifundia* great. Had they possessed the wit and patience to learn some of the lessons of late-nineteenth-century noble agriculture the Soviet leadership could indeed have avoided some of the pitfalls of large-scale collective farming.

Perhaps the greatest single impediment to the development of a Prussian-style gentry capitalism in Russia lay simply in the contrast between the great difficulties and risks facing the capitalist big farmer, especially during the depression, and the much easier avenues open to a Russian landowner who desired a secure and comfortable income. Even Serge Bekhteev, a leading noble agricultural expert who owned a comfortable estate in fertile Orel, found supporting a gentry life-style on the proceeds of capitalist agriculture very difficult in the late nineteenth century. By contrast, with the price of land rising at tremendous speed from 1861 to 1914 the temptation to sell all or part of one's estates and invest the proceeds in bonds or shares was very great. 'Between 1862 and 1912 noble land had increased in value by 443 per cent even while diminishing in extent by more than one half . . . in 1910, of the 137,825 nobles residing in St. Petersburg, 49 per cent lived on income from securities'.[35]

Alternatively, a noble could hold on to his estates, watching their value inflate and deriving a comfortable income from letting his land to the local peasants without any necessity himself to take on the risks and costs of capitalist farming. Contrasting stable land prices in Wales during the Great Depression with sharply declining ones in England, F. M. L. Thompson explains the distinction by 'the persistent land-hunger of a peasant society'. Peasants could rent lands for prices which would have made profitable capitalist farming impossible. In many regions of Russia and the Ukraine land-hunger forced them to do so. A political price was, however, paid by nobles for treating their land in this way. In a country whose peasants had never felt great respect for private property and where socialist sympathies were strong in the intelligentsia, a nobility which turned their estates into model agricultural enter-prises would have increased the legitimacy of their wealth. It was difficult, however, to see the exploitation of peasant land-hunger through rents as anything but parasitism. But the gentry's position in the countryside was not easy. With land in short supply the nobleman who refused to let and tried to farm intensively, person-ally supervising his labourers and attempting to secure disciplined hard work, was also likely to be unpopular. Rising class tensions and insecurity in the countryside, which exploded in 1902–6, were a further incentive to noblemen to sell their land. In the immediate aftermath of 1905, massive sales occurred in the areas worst affected by the disturbances.[36]

By the twentieth century the nobles' role in Russian agriculture was of secondary importance. By 1914 the great majority of cattle belonged to the peasants, and the latter also produced 78 per cent even of marketed grain. The future of the Russian countryside depended much less on the nobles than on the ability of peasant farmers to capitalise on the unprecedented opportunities provided by literacy, co-operatives, the growing urban market and the Stoly-pin land reforms. Nevertheless, the nobles' significance should not be written off. Where the very large forestry and sugar industries were concerned they were of paramount importance. Their herds of cattle were generally far superior in quality to peasant animals, and where they went in for cereal farming the big estates produced, at a very conservative average, 50 per cent more grain per hectare than did the peasants. Because peasant agriculture was still for the most part very backward, the educational role of the progressive Russian gentry estate remained far more important than was the case in either Germany or England.[37]

Compared to Russia, late Victorian Germany and England seem very similar, if only because both were predominantly industrial and urban societies. But the fate of the two countries' agriculture could not have been more different. Between 1870–76 and 1904–10 grain fell from 25.5 per cent to 13 per cent of gross agricultural output in Britain. Animal products rose from 58.6 per cent to 71.5

per cent. In Britain, wheat prices in 1894–98 averaged half their 1867–71 level, while in Germany the maximum decline was 20 per cent for wheat and 25 per cent for rye between 1871–75 and 1901–5. The percentage of the land devoted to arable farming actually increased in pre-war Germany and the value of Junker estates began to rise firmly again. In England, rents and land prices plummeted. Though the average fall was 26 per cent between 1874–78 and the mid 1890s, in the arable south-east the drop was 41 per cent and on the lightest and heaviest soils even greater.[38]

The light soils of East Anglia had been the heartland of innovation and entrepreneurship in the English agricultural revolution but they suffered very badly in the depression. Between 1873 and 1894 the value of land in Norfolk halved and rents fell by 43 per cent; two-thirds of the Norfolk gentry sold their estates. Not surprisingly, Prussian nobles, in general farming even lighter and sandier soils, looked with alarm at developments across the North Sea. S. B. Webb concludes that 'without tariffs . . . the large estates would not have collapsed, but would have shrunk in their labour force, revenue and capital value'. Many Prussian nobles would not have been even this optimistic. The fate of unprotected English agriculture was a weapon frequently deployed in their speeches for, as Freiherr von Heeremann once commented, 'it is the duty of the state . . . to prevent the deterioration of agriculture to English conditions, even if class legislation should be necessary'. Wilhelm von Kardorff, a Free Conservative leader, prophesied that if Prussia followed the English example the eastern estates would become mere hunting reserves for wealthy businessmen.[39]

The relative prosperity of German agriculture was bought at the price of protective tariffs and furious political controversy, which pervades the historical literature to this day. From the standpoint of 1990 some contemporary attacks on the Junkers seem unjustified. Farmers in modern liberal democracies have been as determined and successful as pre-1914 Junkers in securing protection for agriculture, and this in societies far more predominantly urban than was the case in Imperial Germany. Nor has generous protection for agriculture stopped contemporary Germany and Japan from standing at the very forefront of international trade and technology. Even Max Weber's harshly consistent nationalist critique of the Junkers, whom he correctly accused of encouraging Polish immigrant labour into the eastern borderlands, rings a little unpleasantly to modern ears less sympathetic to nationalism and attuned to movements of labour across frontiers according to the logic of the international capitalist economy. Of course the debate about protection in Imperial Germany was never wholly – or even primarily – economic. The tariffs were also hated because they protected a powerful Junker elite which many Germans loathed and wished to destroy. Disentangling the truth about noble agriculture's performance under the Kaiserreich from the barrage of propaganda generated by this conflict is not easy.[40]

On the one hand it seems certain that the great eastern estates lost their undisputed position as the spearhead of agricultural progress during the Great Depression. After the 1840s, rich peasants had shed part of the financial burdens of the immediate post-emancipation era, had become more educated and aware of scientific agricultural techniques, and were also usually less in debt than the eastern estate owners, who had indulged in a further bout of land speculation in the 1850s and 1860s. The biggest single concentration of advanced farms by 1900 were the Saxon sugar and root-crop medium-sized units, but even in the east it was claimed by supporters of small-scale agriculture that peasant colonists produced 266.2 Reichsmarks (RM) per hectare of animal products and cereals as against only 213.9 RM from the big estates. The colonists' farms were much more manageable in size, did not face high labour costs, were much better manured and, according to Erich Kemp, produced anything from 25 per cent to 90 per cent more grain per hectare than local big estates.[41]

Nevertheless, the Junkers' inefficiency was exaggerated by their critics, as was the possibility of easy transition to forms of large-scale agriculture other than grain cultivation. J. A. Perkins argues that 'the majority of farmers in the eastern territories were not in a position to fatten cattle or establish dairies on permanent pasture in consequence of the infertility of their land'. Between 1873 and 1910 German agriculture made great advances, leading the world in the application of science to farming and catching up with Great Britain as regards cereal yields per acre. The big estates played a worthy part in this advance. Between 1899–1903 and 1904–8 yields of wheat per hectare increased by 29 per cent and of rye (the Junker grain *par excellence*) by 36 per cent, partly because they were increasingly cultivated in rotations with root crops. The cultivation of potatoes for distilling and of sugar beet, both well developed on the great estates, remained very profitable. Perkins concludes that 'the sugar-beet and many of the potato-alcohol producing Junkers were far removed from the archetype of historical literature. They had made in fact a complete transition from the manorial lords of the XVIIIth century whose patrimonies had supported their provision of service to the Prussian state, to heads of "agribusiness" in which the most progressive capitalist farming was integrated with industrial enterprises based upon advanced technology and the principle of profit maximisation'.[42]

In both Germany and England the increasing size and prosperity of the towns pushed up demand for meat and dairy produce. In Germany this mostly came from peasant farms in central, western and southern regions. In England the regional division was even clearer, the ten leading wheat-growing counties lying in the east and the ten front-ranking dairy counties in the north and west. The average fall in rents of 26 per cent between the mid-1870s and mid-1890s concealed the difference between a 41 per cent fall in the arable south-east and a 12 per cent drop in the north-west, the latter no disaster at all at a time of generally falling prices. Between 1858 and 1881 the Duke of Sutherland spent £100 000 on new buildings and drainage on his Shropshire livestock estate but the investment paid off in the sense that he survived the depression without any overall rent reductions. The Duke of Bedford, who also spent tens of thousands of pounds fighting the depression by improvements on his Home Counties grain lands, discovered that investment was no solution, further expensive conversion from arable to pasture could not pay, and substantial reductions in rent were inevitable.[43]

Although the decline of British farming in the Great Depression was not uniform, agriculture's overall performance relative both to British industry and foreign farmers was poor. C. O'Grada concludes that 'British agriculture performed badly in the face of foreign competition, judged at least by its very slow total factor productivity growth'. A major factor here was protection: by the 1890s, for instance, German wheat tariffs were 30 per cent of the British price and French ones 40 per cent. Nevertheless, as Avner Offer shows, protection was not the only element involved: 'Britain was not the only open economy. Belgium, Holland and Denmark allowed grain free entry, but did not stop growing it themselves. The three countries reduced their proportion moderately, but more than compensated by a large growth of their livestock sectors. Denmark in particular won a share of the British market for cheese, butter, bacon and eggs, while the Belgians expanded livestock production for home consumption'.[44]

Searching for the causes of British agriculture's poor performance by international standards, Offer discusses transport, soils, consumer tastes and machinery, but in his opinion Britain's vital failing was probably its system of land tenure. The prestige of aristocratic landownership kept land prices at a level which did not reflect agricultural values. Above all, however, Britain's farms combined internationally high numbers of paid workers and low levels of family labour. In addition, they had to support not only an exceptionally rich and high-living aristocracy but also a class of large farmers who did no manual work themselves and expected to live a life of, by American or continental standards, relative ease and comfort. In Offer's view, the 'sod house' simply out-competed the manor house. O'Grada's conclusions certainly bear out Offer's thesis. He quotes with approval the explanation by one contemporary expert of why Scottish immigrant farmers could flourish in East Anglia where so many local tenants and landlords had gone bankrupt: 'they and their families work immensely hard. The Scotch women certainly undertake work which no Suffolk woman would dream of doing'. The Scottish farmers themselves 'practically take the position of working foremen or bailiffs, being up in the morning when their men arrive and occupied with work connected with the farm after they leave at night'.[45]

4. Sources of Wealth: Forestry

IN 1800 there were less than one million hectares of forest in Great Britain, half of which were in England. For the nineteenth-century English aristocracy, with few exceptions, forestry was of peripheral importance. In Germany and Russia this was far from true. Especially after the end of serfdom, many German and Russian aristocrats derived most of their income from their forests. This applied above all to landowners in western Germany and in the more northerly non-Black Earth Russian regions.[1]

In 1800, West European forests were largely deciduous, while coniferous wood predominated in the northern and eastern regions of the continent. The more gentle and moist western climate, warmed by the Gulf Stream, was more favourable to forestry than the harsh extremes of the continental climate of the eastern plains. On the latter, snow was often on the ground for four months of the year and, especially in north-eastern Europe, soils were poor and light. As a result trees grew more quickly in the west and forests were thicker. They were also therefore more valuable.

In Germany, the hard woods from the forests of Saxony, Württemberg and Baden were worth more than the produce of the (in any case more sparsely wooded) pine forests of the Prussian east. Particularly in Brandenburg, Lower Pomerania and East Prussia forests often contained bare patches and the volume of timber they generated per hectare was much lower than, for instance, the Austrian average. In the 1860s coppices (*Niederwald*) in the Rhineland could be cut every 6–12 years, but in the eastern provinces 40-year intervals were required if deforestation was to be avoided.[2]

The situation was often worse still in the Russian non-Black Earth region. The fiercer the climate and the poorer the soil, the more light was required by growing trees and the thinner forests became. Short growing seasons, strong winds and irregular rainfall were problems. Comparing natural conditions in Russia unfavourably with Western Europe, Friedrich Arnold commented that 'to get a certain quantity of wood, we require a bigger area of forest than the Germans, the French or the Italians; more important, in tending forests we need to apply more varied and numerous methods than abroad; above all, as regards cutting and harvesting our forests, or allowing cattle to graze, we have to be very careful'. In the early twentieth century the yield in wood of 20-year-old Baden spruce was greater than that of similar trees in St. Petersburg province which had been growing for four to six times as long.[3]

In post-emancipation Germany and Russia, forests belonged overwhelmingly to one of three groups: the State; large (and usually noble) landowners; and peasants. In Bavaria more than half of all woodland belonged to peasants. In European Russia, 68.6 per cent belonged to the State. In Prussia by contrast, in 1855, 13.9 million hectares of forest out of a total of 25.6 million were in the hands of private, usually large, landowners. However, aggregate statistics for entire countries often conceal more than they reveal. In East Prussia, for instance, the State owned most of the forests, while in Munster, the largely Polish district of Posen, and the Silesian districts of Oppeln and Liegnitz, private landowners almost monopolised the woodlands. In the Potsdam district of Brandenburg, State and private ownership was balanced.[4]

Still more important were regional variations in Russia. More than three-quarters of the State's forests were in the five northernmost provinces of European Russia. Most of Archangel, Vologda, Perm, Olonets and Viatka was, however, virgin territory in which vast distances and non-existent communications made commercial forestry unviable. Outside these five enormous provinces, private ownership of forests prevailed. The rest of European Russia contained 49 million desyatinas of forest, of which less than a quarter was owned by the State and most was in noble hands. In twenty-eight provinces out of forty-nine, private landowners held over half the forests.[5]

In Russia as in Germany, the largest estates tended to contain the highest proportion of forest. Perm province, home of the Urals magnates, had the greatest concentration of noble forest-owning in Russia. In Germany, noble estates of over 2500 hectares had a higher percentage of forest than the wider group of properties of over 500 hectares. The sixteen German estates of over 20 000 listed by Häbich were almost 70 per cent forest. Forests were very valuable. In 1910 the 26 517-hectare forest estate of Prince Stolberg-Wernigerode at Ottowald in Upper Silesia was sold, for example, for 17 million Marks. In Silesia, however, the great forest-owner might well also be a major industrialist. It was above all *Standesherren* with large properties in west, south and central Germany for whom forestry was the paramount source of income.[6]

Fortunately for the big landowners, wood prices soared during the nineteenth century. If coal replaced firewood as fuel, this was more than compensated for by vastly increased construction of wooden ships and houses, and from the 1840s demand for railway sleepers and pit-props also increased at great speed. German timber prices had been rising gently throughout the eighteenth century but they shot up between 1780 and 1810. From the 1830s prices rose again at increasing speed until the 1870s, when they fell by an average of 30 per cent in the course of six years. The 1880s, however, ushered in a new period of rising prices which lasted until 1914. In the 1850s the princes Fürstenberg reckoned that the value of their wood had doubled in just six years. Between the 1780s and 1860s the forest income of the Hessian von Buttlar-Elberberg and von Dörnberg families multiplied ten times.[7]

Particularly in the pre-railway age, profits from forestry differed enormously from place to place. Leaving aside a forest's natural quality, given wood's bulkiness, it mattered greatly whether local demand was high and communications easy. In the 1780s a hectare of forest in Cleves (Rhineland) brought in seven times more profit than in East Prussia. During the nineteenth century the gap narrowed, partly because the increasingly skilled managers of the eastern forests increased the latter's yields. Even so, in 1865–69 the income from a hectare of woodland in the Saxon kingdom was 2.5 times more than in Bavaria and four times more than in Prussia. In 1875–79 a cubic metre of oak was worth 32 Marks in Trier, in the heart of the industrial Rhineland, and only 20 Marks in far-away East Prussia. Only with the railways could Bavaria's huge potential income from forests be realised. Indeed, before 1850 a lot of wood simply rotted, since poor communications made its exploitation unviable.[8]

Regional variations were even sharper in Russia. In the late 1880s profits per desyatina in the state forests ranged from 3 kopecks in Kostroma, Perm, Vologda, Viatka, Archangel and Perm to 5 roubles in thickly populated and under-forested Tula and Kharkov. Among private landowners the differences were much greater. In the western provinces in the 1870s, areas near rivers were denuded of trees by the Baltic and Black Sea timber trade, while in more remote areas of Smolensk, Minsk and Mogilev commercial forestry remained unviable. Railways transformed forestry both by their demand for sleepers and the access to markets they entailed. Wood prices in the Bryansk forests of Orel province shot up in the 1860s as the railway line approached. By the twentieth century even the huge forests of the Urals magnates could be exploited. The Stroganovs averaged 168 600 roubles per year net profits for their timber in 1903–6 and 599 500 roubles in 1910. In such a remote area, however, profit margins per hectare were low, skilled supervisers were unobtainable and the price of exploiting forests was their devastation by timber merchants who could be lured into the region only by being given near *carte blanche*.[9]

The commercialisation of forestry increased tensions between noble and peasant in both Germany and Russia. Under serfdom, peasants had enjoyed access to the forests for building materials and fuel. They had also been allowed to graze their cattle there. Now forests became valuable private property, whose efficient exploitation, let alone profitability, required that the peasant and his animals be excluded. The resulting conflicts contributed both to endemic rural lawlessness and to the revolutions of 1848 and 1905.[10]

Commercialisation also, however, could lead to a more intensive and scientific forestry capable of greatly increasing wood production without damaging the forests and even, sometimes, increasing their area through artificial planting. The leaders here were the Germans, who pioneered intensive forestry as unequivocally as the English led in progressive agriculture. By carefully studying trees, soils and climate, intensive forestry could determine what sections of a forest, or even in time individual trees, should be cut, how long rotations should be, and where artificial re-afforestation was desirable. To know how much timber an estate could safely produce and which types of trees best suited its commercial exploitation was the road to profit. It was a road which only the bigger landowners could travel comfortably, because labour costs per hectare were much greater in small forests, while rich nobles were best able to contemplate regular incomes from the systematic cutting of 1–2 per cent of their trees rather than by seeking windfall profits from massive immediate felling. Since the most efficient and profitable method to run a forest was to fell the trees oneself and own one's own sawmills, huge reserves of timber and adequate capital were useful.[11]

During the nineteenth century the German forests were managed with increasing skill and care. In the first half of the century there may have been many landowners who, like Prince Pückler, ravaged their forests to pay for their debts. Even in the 1850s and 1860s, especially in the east, high agricultural prices encouraged the felling of forests and their transformation into arable land in some districts. In others, however, profits from forestry were so high that the temptation did not arise. Writing in 1862, the Prussian forestry expert E. W. Maron commented that great improvements had occurred in recent years. Efficient management, widespread replanting of seedlings, and scientific planning were rapidly gaining ground. The arbitrary felling of trees and leaving nature to repair the damage was a thing of the past. Descriptions of the great forest estates of the Arnims in Saxony and of the Fürstenbergs in the Black Forest support Maron's comment.[12]

In Russia, matters were very different though the situation was not entirely black. Rubner states, for instance, that although much wood was ravaged in the nineteenth century (a third of all the forest in central and southern Russia disappearing between 1804 and 1914), at least the Russian government had a forestry policy, unlike its United States' counterpart. According to Rubner, the 1888 forestry legislation, though much evaded, was of some use. Moreover, by the 1880s Russia was producing its own forestry experts, seed and equipment, which removed the need for the would-be innovator to import expensive German knowledge and goods. Both Arnold and Anfimov cite examples of private forests which were efficiently managed by modern methods, the former adding that some were to be found in every region. Nevertheless, although some improvements were occurring by 1914, even in the immediate pre-war period the two largest areas of private forest-owning, namely the

Urals and the western Dvina region, were still being ravaged. In the former, the collapse of the local metallurgical industry was encouraging some magnates to recoup their losses through forestry. In the latter, huge German and English demand for pulp, staves and pit props had resulted in the doubling of exports of young spruce and pine between 1901 and 1908 with potentially disastrous results for the region's forests.[13]

J. C. Brown, a Scottish forestry expert who visited western Russia in the two decades after emancipation wrote gloomily of his impressions. Although some of the private forests, in Kursk for instance, were 'very satisfactorily preserved' the pressures on nobles to achieve high profits at great speed were intense. The best that could be said of the Dnieper private forests was that they 'are not quite exhausted'. Thinking long-term had gone out of fashion with emancipation. As regards planting forests, for instance, 'during the time of serf labour many occupied themselves with this on private estates, but have given over doing so now, commercial calculations having put a stop for many years to the slow process of forest planting . . . A German land steward, from the neighbourhood of Kiev who had the charge of a number of estates in that locality . . . said . . . of the Russian landowners . . . that they were so improvident, and so reckless of the morrow, that it was difficult to induce them to plant trees which will not attain their full growth till some 170 years later'.[14]

One explanation for the wasteful and rapacious attitude of Russian nobles was that theirs was a frontier mentality rather similar to that prevailing in the United States. With a centuries-old tradition of expanding frontiers and vast empty lands a thrifty attitude to nature had never developed. In many cases, according to Friedrich Arnold, there was little awareness that forests could be irreparably damaged. Hauxthausen's oft-cited statement that families had little allegiance to estates and seldom held them for more than three generations could be cited as a further explanation for Russians' rape of their forests. Some of these explanations are more convincing than others. If long family tenure of an estate guaranteed careful stewardship one would expect a clear distinction to be made between forestry in the Muscovite heartland and the western and southern borderlands. There is no mention of anything like this in the literature. One would also need to ask why Prussian nobles, notoriously willing to sell and exchange properties before 1806, should have been more careful with their forests than Russians in the second half of the following century.

Arnold's explanation for the problems of Russian private forestry is simpler. In Russia, unlike Germany, few nobles directly exploited their own forests, though those who did so and kept an eye on market prices usually prospered. As in France, most landowners sold standing wood to contractors either by volume, area or as entire forests. Where whole forests were sold the result was always devastation of woodlands and great loss to the landowner. Even where specific areas were prescribed, this was often done without a clear sense of the wood's value or the conditions necessary for the forest's regrowth. Nor were contractors either adequately supervised or forced to carry out cutting in tightly prescribed periods: in many cases they wandered the forest for years, leaving mess and devastation in their wake on a scale that made the growth of young plants impossible.

The failure to enforce sensible contracts on the timber merchants had a number of causes, among them carelessness, a lack of trained foresters to advise landowners, and an absence of business acumen. But the main explanation was often that landowners were in such need for ready cash that they were forced to accept whatever terms the contractors offered and were unable to pay for adequate surveys of their timber prior to its sale.[15]

Arnold offers the traditional 'Cherry Orchard' interpretation of the decline of Russian noble forestry. As one looks at the forced and unprofitable contracts which he describes it is hard to deny that his argument carries conviction or that noble timber sales were not very often the product of desperation, incompetence or both. Yet perhaps even in some elements of the history of post-1861 forestry one can find hints of Becker-like rational calculation in noble minds. M. A. Tsvetkov may well be right in arguing that investment in forestry brought lower returns at greater risk and trouble than in other branches of industry. At which point selling one's timber and shifting one's capital elsewhere might make sense. Moving from forestry to agriculture in Volhynia between 1905 and 1914 was to follow a path trodden by many Prussian landowners for similar reasons in the nineteenth century and might well fit the landowners' interests, whatever its long-term impact on the province's countryside. The strategy of the Yusupovs and Sheremetevs in shifting the main source of their income from agricultural rents to timber on the one hand and stocks and bonds on the other also made long-term sense. In the short run, timber brought major profit, the Yusupovs netting 344 568 roubles by 1916 and the Sheremetevs 250 000 in 1909. Looking further ahead, shedding unprofitable and unpopular rented agricultural land and depending on anonymous stocks and bonds, forests and a few model farming estates was to follow the rather successful strategy for survival of the wealthy western and southern German nobility.[16]

5. Sources of Wealth: Urban Property

WHEN he visited England in the 1820s Prince Pückler was amazed to discover that the local aristocracy owned not only great rural estates and mansions but also, in his words, 'most of London', which it let to tenants for great sums while retaining its property rights. By the time of Pückler's visit the leading London aristocratic estates of the nineteenth century were already well established: on most of them development was decades old. In the lead were the 500-acre estate in Mayfair, Belgravia and Pimlico which had come to the Grosvenors through a lucky marriage in 1677; the Russells' 119 acres in Bloomsbury and Covent Garden; the Duke of Portland's manor of St. Marylebone; and Lord Portman's land near Oxford Street. This was, however, only the tip of the iceberg where aristocratic property in London was concerned. The income received from some of these estates even in the 1820s was very great. By 1830 the Duke of Bedford's Bloomsbury estate alone brought in £66 000 and the Duke of Portland, who also owned part of Soho, had a Marylebone rental of £43 326 in 1828. Between 1821 and 1835 the Grosvenors' annual income from their London property advanced from £20 000 to £60 000.[1]

During the nineteenth century, London rentals rose far more steeply than any other source of aristocratic wealth. At the same time aristocrats began to derive large incomes from urban property elsewhere in Britain. 'In 1800 only fifteen towns (apart from London) had populations exceeding 20,000, but a century later this

109

figure had risen to 185'.[2] Whether in London or in most provincial towns, aristocrats inherited their property. They were the beneficiaries of a growth in urban society to which they themselves had made only a limited contribution, though by making land available, retaining their property rights and controlling the layout of many city districts they were by no means mere parasitic hangers-on. In some cases, most but not all of which were seaside resorts, aristocrats actually created towns from scratch in the nineteenth century.

The most enthusiastic aristocratic entrepreneurs were the Cavendishes. The Seventh Duke of Devonshire attempted to turn Barrow-in-Furness from the village he inherited into a great city and port to outshine Liverpool. Developing the large local iron ore deposits, building a railway, docks, jute works and a steel mill, the Duke poured over £2 million into Barrow. He and his successor also created the seaside resort of Eastbourne. During the Seventh Duke's lifetime Eastbourne yielded only a small profit, though in the longer term the appreciation of land values in the town brought its reward to the Cavendishes. Barrow, on the other hand, was a spectacular success in the 1870s and an even more awful disaster in the 1880's, during which time the Duke of Devonshire moved from having probably the greatest income of any English aristocratic millionaire to a position of almost equally unparalleled indebtedness.[3]

No other landowner was as willing or as able as the Cavendishes to pour such huge sums into virgin urban development. Nevertheless a number of seaside resorts were developed in the second half of the nineteenth century by aristocratic landowners anxious to cash in on a holiday trade made possible by the railways. Alongside Eastbourne, Torquay and Bexhill, Skegness and Folkestone, Southport and Bournemouth were monuments to aristocratic seaside town-building. Creating a town from scratch with all its infrastructure and sea defences was an expensive undertaking, however, which quickly proved too great for most aristocrats singly to sustain. Nor were the rewards of seaside landowning usually equal to those derived from the easier task of developing urban estates around established provincial towns, or from London rentals.[4]

The only English town apart from the seaside resorts whose land was owned almost entirely by a single family was Huddersfield, built on the 4230-acre Ramsden estate. The Butes, however, 'created' Cardiff almost as surely as the Cavendishes called Eastbourne to life. The Second Marquess of Bute built the docks around which the city grew up from the 1830s and his descendants still owned half of Cardiff's land a century later. The Butes' income from the Welsh capital multiplied eight times from £3487 in 1850 to £28 348 by 1894 but it remained very small by the standards of the London magnates.[5]

Even where a single aristocratic family owned most of a town's land its ability to control civic affairs never survived into the twentieth century and had usually gone by the last quarter of the nineteenth. What remained by the Edwardian era was a handsome income and, quite often, great local prestige symbolised by the head of the family's election as a dignified but largely powerless mayor. In the great majority of cities, however, aristocratic families shared land ownership with other nobles or with a mass of freeholders.

The Calthorpes, for instance, owned and developed the suburb of Edgbaston, from which they derived £30 000 in 1880, but they never aspired to control Birmingham. The Marquesses of Salisbury and Earls of Derby and Sefton all owned sections of Liverpool, the Seftons, like the Calthorpes, possessing a compact suburban estate which they tried to turn into a comfortable, middle-class residential area. In other towns aristocrats derived large incomes not only from ground rents but also from ownership of public utilities and market rights. By the 1880s, for example, the Duke of Norfolk was netting £10 000 a year from Sheffield's markets.[6]

By this time, however, the leading London magnates were making colossal fortunes. Between 1828 and 1872 the Portlands' Marylebone rental leaped from £34 316 to £100 000. By 1880 the Bedfords' income from Bloomsbury was £104 880, to which a further £32 000 was added by the Covent Garden market. Over and above regular rentals, huge extra sums were sometimes netted from fines or when long leases expired: 'The Portmans were reckoned to have received £1¼ million in March 1888 when their long leases fell in'. On the Grosvenors' London estate, normal rentals had reached £179 000 by 1894 but fines and renewed leases raised the overall gross profits to £491 135 and £427 533 in 1893 and 1894 respectively. Even the Marquess of Salisbury, who was far from being a London magnate, made £200 000 in 1888 from the sale of two small streets off the Strand near his family's former town house.[7]

Where urban property was concerned, there was a complete contrast between English and German aristocracy. Even in 1883 more than half of the seventeen British peers with annual incomes of over £100 000 derived much of their wealth from urban land and the proportion of urban property-owners in the wealthiest aristocratic group would probably have been even greater by 1914. At that time no old aristocratic magnate in Prussia derived a significant income from urban property and nor did any count, prince or duke whose wealth was valued at over 5 million Marks (£250 000). Even among the more recently ennobled, owners of many urban dwellings, let alone whole streets, were rare. No noble owned a Prussian equivalent of Belgravia, Covent Garden or Sefton Park.[8]

Only two nobles owned considerable property in Berlin: one was Richard von Kaufmann, a professor of economics who had married into a wealthy Cologne business family and was also a noted archaeologist. Kaufmann, himself ennobled, was a major speculator in the North Berlin property market. The other urban landlord was Arnold Freiherr von Eckardstein, whose family was ennobled in 1799 and whose wealth, partly lying in Berlin housing and partly in rural estates, was estimated at 10–11 million Marks (c. £½ million). Among the old nobility there were a handful of individuals such as Captain (retired) Count Carl von Dönhoff, who owned six houses, in one of which he himself lived. Perhaps there were also a few old nobles who, like Elard von Oldenburg-Januschau, bought or inherited land near Berlin and hoped in time to cash in on the demand for residential housing of a growing urban population. By the standards of the Grosvenors and the Russells, however, even Oldenburg's speculations were relatively small beer.[9]

The only nobles with land on Berlin's outskirts who were rich enough for Rudolph Martin to mention were the Counts von Voss. They actually sold their estate of Buch to the city in 1898, purchasing instead the 3381-hectare property of Doelzig in rural Brandenburg. If Doelzig was all the von Voss family got for the sale of Buch they appear to have made an appallingly bad bargain, especially since Count Max von Voss already had other rural properties to which he could have retreated from Berlin's environs. The contrast with the Calthorpe family's strategy is interesting. When in the late eighteenth century Birmingham began to spread into their main estate of Edgbaston they abandoned Edgbaston Hall and took refuge on their other, purely rural, property in Suffolk. But the Calthorpes retained and developed Edgbaston, and by so doing moved out of the ranks of the provincial gentry and into those of aristocratic semi-plutocracy.[10]

Elsewhere in Prussia (apart from Berlin) the value of a few aristocratic estates did grow greatly from proximity to urban centres, but incomes generally remained small. An interesting case was that of Count Karl von Alten-Linsingen, whose land was valued at 10–11 million Marks (more than £½ million) in 1910 but whose annual income was a paltry 130 000 Marks (£6500). Count Karl's land was so valuable because part of it had been absorbed by the growing industrial town of Linden, itself a suburb of Hanover. Indeed, his rural mansion now had the address, No. 1, Old Garden Street, Linden. Since the estate had been in the family for over 600 years its sale was inconceivable. Because it must have been a *fideikommissus* (i.e. entailed estate), commercial exploitation through the sale or long leasing of plots of land for house building would also not have been an option. In similar fashion the big forest *fideikommissi* of the Bismarck family in the Sachsenwald and of the princes Stolberg-Rossla in the Harz mountains, both of vast potential value if sold in small lots as bourgeois villa property, brought in relatively small incomes.[11]

Outside Prussia the picture was no different, though the laws governing *fideikommissi* were rather less fiercely enforced. In the Old Reich a clear line had divided imperial cities, governed by their own oligarchies and guilds, and the rural nobility. The greatest non-Prussian nobles were in any case former sovereign princes, whose own home 'towns' were always small and who by definition were unlikely to own urban property in alien territory. Even the Thurn und Taxis, giants among *Standesherren*, owned only a collection of chateaux, gardens and greenhouses despite having run the imperial postal service from the town of Regensburg for centuries.[12]

In all southern Germany only one old noble family, the Tuckers, became wealthy because of ownership of urban property. The Tuckers had never, however, been great aristocratic magnates, nor were they traditionally members of the rural nobility. Instead, they belonged to the noble patriciate of the old imperial city of Nuremberg, which was absorbed into Bavaria in 1806. One of the sixteen old Nuremberg patrician families, the Tuckers were the only ones to be rich by the twentieth century, Freiherr Christian von Tucker having property worth 14 million Marks (£700 000) and an annual income of £45 000 by 1914. The Tuckers alone had held on to their land on the northern outskirts of Nuremberg until the second half of the nineteenth century, when the city's rapid growth made suburban estates extremely valuable. Land sold for building plots in these suburbs brought the Tuckers almost one million Marks between 1882 and 1910.[13]

Where urban property was concerned, the Russian aristocracy stood somewhere between the English and the Germans. In largely agrarian Russia cities were smaller and urban land less valuable than in England. On the other hand, unlike in divided Germany, the Russian aristocracy had always thronged to court and owned land in and around the Tsars' capitals. The greatest problem in defining the extent of Russian noble property in towns is simply lack of information. Where Russia is concerned we have an equivalent neither of David Cannadine's work on the English urban landlords nor of Rupert Martin's survey of the German tax statistics. Fragmentary evidence does exist as regards aristocratic property in Moscow and St. Petersburg. Elsewhere, however, we face a void.

Probably this does not matter too much, for Russian provincial towns were still for the most part very small, and noble property there was almost certainly neither great nor very valuable. An example of this is provided by the blooming textile town of Ivanovo-Voznesensk in Moscow Province. Before 1861 Ivanovo, all its inhabitants and the surrounding land belonged to the Counts Sheremetev. In the 1840s Hauxthausen described it as 'the Manchester of Russia, the village of Ivanovo; this place alone employs more than 42,000 persons in its cotton factories, which yield annually about 900,000 pieces of cotton cloth, of the value of 23,400,000 rubles' (£1,017,200). At emancipation, however, serf-owners received no compensation for the persons, houses and gardens of their former serfs and the Sheremetevs' stake in the town of Ivanovo therefore largely disappeared. The surrounding land, however, remained the count's property and in time Ivanovo's housing filled up the spaces in the old urban settlement and began to spread on to Sheremetev property. Even so in 1916 Count S. D. Sheremetev received only 42 500 roubles (£4 427) for suburban rents, 3,200 roubles for large buildings in Ivanovo which he rented for commercial purposes and 600 roubles for a branch-line running across his land. If such relatively small sums were all a landowner received in the suburbs of Russia's Manchester, urban rentals elsewhere in the provinces were unlikely to have been great.[14]

Moscow and St. Petersburg were different, though until detailed research is done on noble property in the two capitals its dimensions and rewards will remain unclear. Some nobles clearly exploited all available corners of their property. Count Serge Dmitrievich Sheremetev, for instance, let out not only the land adjacent to the famous orphanage founded by his family in Moscow but also the pavement in front of the house and one of its hallways.

By 1910 this brought in 46 800 roubles a year, all of which the Sheremetevs passed on to the orphanage. Count Alexander Grabbe, the commander of Nicholas II's Cossack escort, was poorer and less altruistic than the Sheremetevs. He inherited through his wife 'several old city properties' in St. Petersburg and embarked on a second, secret, career alongside his military one, a career that involved buying and redeveloping St. Petersburg properties to turn them into 'modern apartments for the rapidly growing sector of middle-income workers'. Beneath the romantic uniform of the Cossack guards there lurked the mind and talents of a capitalist property tycoon.[15]

Most nobles were not developers, however, but simply owners of urban property. Many, including a considerable number of aristocrats, owned a handful of houses in either Moscow or St. Petersburg. Especially in Moscow, the overwhelming majority of these urban landlords would have been like Carl Dönhoff in Berlin, in other words recipients of comfortable but by no means enormous rental incomes. But 'houses' could mean not family homes but rather great blocks of apartments, the form of housing that dominated St. Petersburg and was widespread in Moscow by the twentieth century.

Probably the most famous aristocratic apartment block was the Shcherbatov building in the heart of fashionable Moscow, whose owner, the Prince, had demolished his town house and built in its place a spectacular block of flats, the finest of which he reserved for himself. Buildings like this could be extremely profitable. One of the Counts Shuvalov, for instance, at the end of the nineteenth century invested most of his spare cash in six large residential buildings whose insurance value was 2 562 700 roubles (£266 948). A Count Zubov owned a single house on St. Petersburg's Nevsky Prospekt valued at 487 000 roubles (£50 729) in the early twentieth century. By 1910 the annual income from his house had reached 62 000 roubles (£6458), his net return on capital of 12.5 per cent far exceeding the rate a rural landowner could expect from his land. The most profitable single building owned by an aristocrat may well, however, have been Count S. D. Sheremetev's house on the corner of Nikol'sky Street and Cherkassky Lane in the heart of Moscow's business quarter. This was let out as shops and offices, bringing in 126 800 roubles (£13 208) in 1900 and 250 400 roubles (£26 083) by 1910.[16]

Serge Dmitrievich Sheremetev and his brother Alexander were probably the largest aristocratic landowners in Moscow, together possessing the estates of Marina Grove (Roshcha), Ostankino and Kuskovo. At Marina Roshcha even in 1899, 54 desyatiny (146 acres) were let and brought in 26 000 roubles profit. The Sheremet-evs also owned and let forty-six of their own buildings for commercial purposes, just four of which netted 2975 roubles (£310) in 1899. At Kuskovo in 1910, 363 plots for summer cottages brought in 27 800 roubles profit. Ostankino was less well managed, for the thousands of people living there on Sheremetev land were still paying customary rents far below the twentieth-century market rate. In 1912 Count Serge Sheremetev decided to exploit this land commercially by teaming up with French investors to build large apartment blocks. Since this would have entailed the clearance of the customary tenants, Moscow's administration reacted to Shere-metev's plans with alarm.[17]

In St. Petersburg, the biggest aristocratic landowners were the Princes Beloselsky-Belozersky. They owned a massive town house on the Fontanka Canal opposite the palace of the heir apparent. This house was sold to the imperial family in the 1890s, Prince K. E. Beloselsky-Belozersky moving out permanently to his former summer house on Krestovsky Island in St. Petersburg's northern suburbs. The house on Krestovsky Island, prettier though a little smaller than the Fontanka Palace, had been in the family's possession since the reign of Paul I (1796–1801).

So had the whole of Krestovsky Island, approximately 2.65 square miles in area, which the Beloselsky-Belozersky family bought from Count Razumovsky at an absurdly low price, reckoned even at the time to be less than one-fifth of the value of the timber by which the island was covered. F. F. Vigel recalls sharing a rented summer house on the island in 1815, when 'Krestovsky Island was the most isolated spot in the environs of Petersburg, further out into the sea than all the other islands; its three verst area was surrounded on all sides by the wide channels of the Neva and covered by a thick impenetrable forest'. Even in 1815, however, the

Beloselsky-Belozerskys had not merely built and let some villas, but had also turned one small corner of the island into an entertainment centre to which much of St. Petersburg flocked in summer. Vigel records that the prince's inn had the worst and most expensive food in St. Petersburg. In the course of the nineteenth century the island retained its position as a leading centre of sports and entertainments. The river yacht club was there, as were the centre of pigeon shooting and other annual events in the capital. By 1890 Krestovsky Island had a permanent population of 1120 and a summer one of 6000. Between 1903 and 1908 plots of land amounting to less than one-tenth of the island's area were sold for between 1.3 and 1.5 million roubles and, as St. Petersburg expanded, the prince's property was bound to rise spectacularly in value. So too, as communications in the Urals improved, would the hundreds of thousands of acres of forest which he still owned in the region.[18]

In 1914, however, even Krestovsky Island was probably not yet as valuable as the 8.3-desyatiny (22.4 acre) market which Stepan Antonovich Apraksin owned in the heart of St. Petersburg. The Apraksin Dvor had the biggest wholesale turnover of any market in Europe, contained fruit, tea and wine exchanges, the headquarters of the Mutual Credit Society and a vast range of shops and stalls. Even in 1895 some individual shops had a turnover of more than 100 000 roubles and the profits from the market by 1914 must have been immense. No information exists as to the Apraksins' income but it was sufficient for Count Anton Stepanovich to buy out all the other heirs in 1873. Subsequently the scale of his family's expenditure on charities alone provides some evidence of their wealth.

The Count and his widow built the Church of the Resurrection of Christ on the Fontanka Canal between 1883 and 1894 at a cost of one million roubles (£104 167). They donated 130 000 roubles (£13 540) to provide a sufficient income to maintain the church and its clergy. In the late 1870s Count Apraksin built the Malyy Theatre on the Fontanka for some undisclosed but undoubtedly great sum. In 1901 the theatre burned down, only to be rebuilt by his widow within a year. In addition, the Apraksins donated a large house on the Fontanka as premises for a school and flats for its teachers. Between 1893 and 1901 they gave 68 500 roubles to support its pupils. Countess Apraksin donated the land for the Murzinka home for the blind, to which she also contributed 243 000 roubles

(£25 312) as a grant and an annual 7000 roubles for the home's upkeep. No doubt the Apraksins were unusually generous, but charity on this scale suggests a princely income and was certainly not based on the few thousand desyatiny of rural land possessed by the family. In the twentieth century the Apraksin family could only afford the kind of munificence practised by the richest of the pre-1861 serf-owners because they were tapping the wealth of urban and industrial Russia.[19]

6. Sources of Wealth: Industry

BEFORE the nineteenth century European industry was in general small-scale as regards both capital and labour. Much of it was rural and owned by aristocrats. Great nobles played a major role as both entrepreneurs and investors of capital. According to Lawrence Stone, this was true in England in the century before the Civil War. In the same era the high aristocracy dominated German metallurgy and mining, some of their enterprises, like the copper works of the Counts Mansfeld, being large and sophisticated. In the last decades of the French old regime, the court aristocracy was deeply involved in manufacturing, and the more technologically advanced and enterprising the concern the greater the level of aristocratic participation tended to be.[1]

The Industrial Revolution changed this, pushing aristocracy to the margins of industry in most of Europe. In the English textile sector, where the Industrial Revolution began, aristocrats played no role either as entrepreneurs or investors. In the iron industry they were more important, but given their extensive ore mines much less so than might have been expected. A handful of nobles operated ironworks in the first half of the nineteenth century but almost none thereafter. The great exception to this rule was the Seventh Duke of Devonshire, who founded the Barrow Haematite Steel Company, the largest Bessemer works in the country, in 1866.[2]

Even in the transformation of English communications the aristocracy was far from playing the leading role. According to Beckett, they were most involved in improving the roads, since this traditionally formed part of public service and local administration. Where canals and railways were concerned, these were seen as private money-making concerns, of most value to industrialists and merchants and therefore properly funded by them. The Duke of Bridgewater's famous role as planner and investor in the Worsley Canal was exceptional. Still less were aristocrats inclined to take the lead as railway entrepreneurs. Beckett cites figures showing that 23 per cent of investment in canals between 1755 and 1815 and 18 per cent of the nominal capital put into railways between 1820 and 1844 came from the aristocracy and gentry. In the earliest years of railway building the upper classes were inclined to play safe, however, and the percentage of aristocratic investment grew over time as railway bonds won public confidence.[3]

By far the biggest aristocratic stake in industry was in the mining sector. Because the aristocracy owned most of England's land they also possessed the lion's share of its mineral resources. These included Cornish tin and copper, whose most profitable decades ended in the late 1850s. The Great Consols copper mine on the Duke of Bedford's Cornish estate brought its owner £102 453 in dues in its first twelve years, at a cost to the Russells of minimal effort since the concern was let. Lead, mostly mined in northern England, also peaked in the 1850s, the Duke of Devonshire averaging £12 000–£15 000 a year from his lead mines in this decade. Thereafter foreign competition destroyed the profitability of lead, copper and tin mining. Devonshire's lead mines were shut in 1896 and Bedford's copper brought in no more royalties after 1884.[4]

Iron ore was more widespread and brought profits to more aristocrats than did lead, copper and tin combined. Even it, however, was insignificant in comparison to coal, Britain's chief source of energy in the century between 1815 and 1914. In 1800, roughly 10 million tons of coal were mined in Britain: even by 1885 the figure was 160 million tons. In Derek Spring's view 'it is unlikely . . . that more than a handful of estates in the first half of the nineteenth century derived a half or more of their gross incomes from (non-agricultural) sources', but by 1914 matters had changed radically. Of Rubinstein's twenty-nine super-rich aristocrats in 1883, most depended to a great extent on non-agricultural sources of income. Of these, coal ranked second only to London property and was much more widespread. Some lucky magnates, notably the Dukes of Devonshire, Portland and Norfolk, were great coal owners and urban landlords. But the wealth of the Dukes of Northumberland and Sutherland, the Marquesses of Bute and Londonderry, the Earl of Dudley and Earl Fitzwilliam was owed in large part to coal. And if this was true in 1883 it was still more the case by 1914 with agriculture in decline and coal as yet unchallenged by oil as the world's prime source of energy.[5]

In the eighteenth century most aristocrats had directly exploited their coalmines but this became ever more rare as the nineteenth century progressed. Beckett states that in 1890 'one-eighth of Yorkshire coal output was still worked by proprietors', implying that this was much more than the national average. By 1914 only a handful of the aristocratic coal-owning grandees still exploited their own mines despite the fact that the efficient owner – manager appears to have secured greater rewards than the mere lessor. Even the Lambtons, Earls of Durham, who had made £84 207 profit from their mines in 1856 and an extraordinary £380 000 in 1873, pulled out of mining in the 1890s, 'when they invested the large proceeds of the sale of their mines in stocks and bonds'.[6]

One reason for distancing oneself from coalmining, as from other direct involvement in industry, were the risks and costs involved. These had escalated tremendously in the nineteenth century as the scale, technological sophistication and capital requirements of the industrial economy had grown. Even in the late eighteenth century the Duke of Bridgewater's canal had put him into debt to the tune of £346 806 and though in the long run his scheme proved profitable, few aristocrats had the resources, nerve or incentive to risk such sums. Coal-mining was no less expensive. The Fitzwilliams' accounts appear to have been kept in a manner which defies assessment of investment costs but 'the Earl of Durham's six collieries had absorbed around £400,000 of his fortune by the 1830s . . . while Lord Londonderry put something over £1 million into pit improvements and expansion between 1819 and 1854'. Even this was only half what the Cavendishes were ultimately to invest in Barrow.[7]

Even where they had the means, it is not surprising that most aristocrats in Victorian England were averse to taking the risks that such huge investments entailed. Rich men, at least until the 1870s, with assured social status, they had fewer incentives to risk their fortunes than any other group in English society. Where others might gain comfortable living, acquire status or found a dynasty through risk and enterprise, an aristocrat already enjoyed all these benefits. In general full of family pride, he was likely to reflect that one false major speculation could destroy in months what his ancestors had taken centuries to build and had conveyed to him in trust. Aristocratic entrepreneurs – the Seventh Duke of Devonshire and the Third Marquess of Londonderry for instance – were likely to be men of exceptional temperament.[8]

English circumstances also favoured leases. Owners complained that managers were often unreliable. On the other hand, unlike in much of the continent, competent and controllable bourgeois tenants could be found from whom steady incomes from mining could be secured. Since the English aristocracy had a long tradition of letting its farms, it made sense to apply the same principles to the inherently riskier and more expensive world of mining.

On the continent, traditions were different and in the east favoured direct noble exploitation of estates. Within Germany it was the nobility of the southern and western regions who were most inclined to regard not only manual work but also all trade and industry as unaristocratic. The Junkers, with their long history of market-orientated demesne farming, were freer from such prejudice. Distilling was a case in point. This was one of the mainstays of noble incomes in the eastern provinces but although a few of the poorer Munster families opened distilleries in the 1820s, the majority of the Westphalian nobility regarded this as bourgeois, commercial and incompatible with noble status. Martin complained that the administration of *Standesherr* estates was notoriously top-heavy and inefficient, seldom exploiting the properties' potential to the full. Such criticism was truer of some *Standesherren* than of others. The Fürstenberg lands, for instance, appear to have been run on strictly no-nonsense capitalist lines after the appointment of Johann Prestinari as chief administrator in 1856. Indeed Prestinari seems to have made it a condition of his appointment that 'court' expenditure should be cut down sharply, economic rationality should reign, and the prince should refrain from interference in all business matters.[9]

In Russia, considerations of status seldom constrained aristocratic money-making. S. M. Troitsky, for instance, cites a range of activities, stretching in exceptional cases as far as money-lending and retailing, pursued by eighteenth-century nobles. If on the one hand this lack of constraint could be traced to the absence of an indigenous feudal tradition in Russia, on the other the eighteenth-century

French aristocracy, the Russians' major model, also freely engaged in a very wide range of business activities. Russian government legislation encouraged nobles to industrial enterprise. Nobles had a monopoly of serf-owning, distilling, salt mines, grain export and the production of tobacco and tallow. As important, the armed forces were the great consumers of woollen cloth and iron, and government contracts went, in the great majority of cases, to aristocrats. Not surprisingly, in 1800, 88 per cent of pig-iron, 85 per cent of copper and 46 per cent of cloth was produced in nobles' factories: 'As late as 1825 the overwhelming majority of labour employed in the metallurgical and textile industries belonged to the nobility either as manorial or possessional serfs'.[10]

After 1825 noble dominance began to weaken. Above all this was true in textiles, where by the 1850s peasant-owned cotton factories had thrust aside the old noble woollen mills. In Kaluga province, for instance, there had been fifteen woollen mills, eleven of them noble in 1839, but just nine years later only four remained, of which the merchant-owned Alexandrov factory far outweighed the rest. Meanwhile cotton production had increased fifty-fold between 1812 and 1860. Nevertheless, the decline of noble industry before 1861 should not be exaggerated. A. J. Rieber comments that on the eve of emancipation 'the nobility still clung to its control over the crucial, if decaying, sector of mining and metallurgy, and it monopolised the profitable agricultural industries – distilling, timber, wool, and especially sugar refining'. Noble distilleries alone employed between 70 000 and 100 000 peasants. Along with cotton, sugar mills were the most technologically advanced and rapidly growing sector of Russian industry. In 1830 there were twenty sugar mills, by 1861 there were 448, 85 per cent of which were driven by steam power and almost all of which were owned by nobles.[11]

By 1900 the situation had been transformed and the overwhelming majority of Russian industry was in non-noble hands. The emancipation settlement itself had destroyed many factories, which were only viable with serf labour. As communications improved after 1861 and urban industry attracted investment and modern technology, many small-scale and archaic noble factories became uncompetitive. In many branches of industry survivals of the old noble serf era were so rare that, like the famous Bakhmetev glassworks, they had acquired almost legendary status by 1914.[12]

The aristocracy only retained a major foothold in industries

linked to agriculture, forestry and mining, and even here noble
factories were in a minority. Only about 10 per cent of sawmills
and paper factories were owned by nobles in 1900. The aristocracy
possessed a much larger share of the distilleries but here the State
had intervened on the nobles' behalf in the 1890s by simply banning
the opening of further distilleries in the towns. Even, however, in
sugar refining, a traditional centre of aristocratic enterprise, twenty-
six years after emancipation half the mills belonged to nobles and
half to members of the Ukrainian and Jewish bourgeoisie: moreover
'the factories of the latter group were as a rule larger and better
equipped than the noble works'. As a result of the 1887 deal among
the leading sugar producers many noble mills in the Central Agricultural region were squeezed out of business. Moreover, though
the Counts Bobrinsky, who had originally introduced sugar production to Russia in the 1830s, remained one of the 'big four' among
Russian sugar magnates, they occupied fourth place behind the
Brodskys, Tereshchenkos and Kharitonenkos, the first Jewish and
the other two Ukrainian merchant families. Equally, though the
Mecklenburg-Strelitz estate at Karlovka was an exceptionally well-
run and profitable aristocratic enterprise, even its flour mills could
not compete in scale with those of L. S. Arzhanov, a non-noble. In
industry, even where aristocracy was strongest, it still occupied
second place.[13]

The most striking example of the decline of aristocratic industry
was the fate of the Urals metallurgical magnates. First in the world
in iron production in 1800, Russia's Urals metallurgy was dominated by the Stroganovs and Demidovs, ultimately of merchant
origin but now moving in the top ranks of the aristocracy, and
by branches of the Golitsyn, Shuvalov, Pashkov, Beloselsky and
Balashev families, all of which belonged to the court nobility. By
1850, Russia's iron production barely equalled Belgium's. Between
1887 and 1901 Urals metallurgy lost first place even within the
empire to the Ukraine, whose output of iron and steel was one-fifth
that of the Urals in 1887 and more than double it only fourteen
years later. Urals metallurgy remained noble, privately owned and
largely traditional in its technology and attitudes in the nineteenth
century. The new Ukrainian iron and coal industry, on the other
hand, was owned by limited companies linked to St. Petersburg
banks and foreign capital. It was run by a professional and cosmo-

politan elite, very few of whom were aristocrats and none of whom were magnates of the traditional Urals type.[14]

The decline of Urals metallurgy had many causes. In general in the nineteenth century a key to success in the metallurgical industry was to have iron ore and coal either in close proximity or tightly linked by railway. Urals ore deposits were far removed from coal mines and, until the 1890s when the railways began to arrive, transporting coal to iron works over vast distances was not an option. With huge forests nearby to tap for charcoal it seemed also barely worthwhile. An industry based on antiquated charcoal-based technology could not compete, however, with the modern ironworks springing up in Europe, especially since its produce had to reach even Russian markets by a slow and dangerous river passage. In addition, the legal status of the big so-called 'possessional factories' constrained their owners' ability to sell ore and timber at will. Management was also, however, partly to blame. When, for instance, in 1902 officials of the State Bank inspected the large but insolvent works of Prince K. E. Beloselsky-Belozersky they argued that geography favoured his factories since they were close to the new railway, generously supplied with ore and surrounded by rich forests. Beloselsky-Belozersky's troubles were in their view the result of inefficient planning and accounting, which had resulted in mistaken investments unsuited to market demands or local circumstances. No less damning was the conclusion of the Council of Ministers that 'the industrial enterprises of the Demidovs, at one time solidly established, are already long since in a state of full decline'.[15]

With even the Demidovs facing bankruptcy and the Stroganovs deciding in 1910 to close their factories, the future of the Urals appeared grim but in fact there was room for hope. The completion of the St. Petersburg – Viatka – Perm railway in 1906 reduced the region's isolation. The Urals had far greater ore deposits than the Ukraine and ample coal deposits existed in western Siberia. St. Petersburg finance was coming in to reorganise the Urals industry, building up the Krovlya sales cartel to challenge the giant Ukrainian monopoly 'Prodamet'. For the present, Prodamet was more powerful and the Krovlya cartel, of which the Demidovs, Stroganovs and Shuvalovs among others were founder members, could only hope to dominate the Urals, and Siberian and Central Asian markets. Given time, however, the great noble mines, factories and forests of the Urals might once again prove very profitable.[16]

For the moment the Ukraine ruled supreme in metallurgy and coal-mining. Until the 1880s much of the mineral wealth of the southern Ukraine was in noble hands but 'by the 1890s they were no longer able to maintain control over their mining properties. The big landowners who exploited the subsoil of their own properties, men like I. G. Ilovaisky, G. V. Depreradovich, Ia. I. Drevitskii, P. A. Karpov, V. N. Rutchenko, P. P. Rykovskii, and M. Shcherbatov, had begun to rent to Jewish entrepreneurs after the emancipation. Later, many sold out to the big foreign capitalists, who could afford to bring in the latest technology and hire the engineering specialists to apply it'.[17]

Ekaterinoslav province, and especially its southern districts, was the core of the Ukrainian metallurgical and coal industry. For most of the eighteenth century this was virgin land, thinly peopled since the reign of Elizabeth (1741–62) by refugees from the Balkans. 'Even in the second half of the nineteenth century,' commented one observer in 1916, 'foreigners were again the bearers of culture in this area. That is why there are so few estates here. You don't find a permanent well-rooted class of people in this area . . . if there were indeed in the past lands belonging to the best Russian families, the owners and their representatives never lived here and even had never visited their properties. Subsequently they began to sell the land on a big scale. As soon as the presence of coal and ore was discovered and industrialists offered them money . . . the owners immediately and willingly parted with their property. But they made an unprofitable bargain'.[18]

In the Donbass heart of the Ukrainian coal industry the most famous settlement was Yuzovka, founded in the 1870s by the Welsh ironmaster J. J. Hughes. His mines, containing the 'finest seam of coking coal in the Donbass' were part of a 20 000 desyatina estate belonging to Prince Paul Lieven, Lord Chamberlain to the Emperor Alexander II and Marshal of the far-distant provincial nobility of Livonia, where Lieven's roots and most of his estates were located. When Hughes rented the land 'there were two huts and a sheep pen, and around them, as far as the eye could see, the empty steppe, "a totally open area bare of any sort of growth".' Initially the Lievens let the mining rights to Hughes for ninety-nine years, but after the Prince's death in 1882 his widow finally sold the property.

The problems of creating from scratch a town and mining industry in a barren wilderness were beyond the competence of Princess Lieven and of any manager she might hire. Nor were an aristocratic lady and her steward capable of controlling the determined capitalist who had rented their far-distant land. Threats, accusations and litigation ensued. When the Princess visited the estate in 1887 the sight of rioting miners and Cossack detachments did nothing to calm her fears. Her son recalls that the unpleasantness created by Hughes and his constant infringements of the contract finally persuaded the Lievens to sell the property for 2.5 million roubles, which was used to buy a forest estate of equivalent size in Livonia and to invest in stocks and bonds. The deal was unheroic and vastly undervalued Yuzovka's potential worth, but in comparison to frontier lands, Welsh ironmasters and riotous miners, Baltic forests and Russian bonds were familiar, reliable and untroublesome sources of income.[19]

The role of the German aristocracy in industry differed vastly from region to region. In the Rhine – Ruhr – Westphalian heartland of German industry the aristocracy played no entrepreneurial role. Leadership in industry came from established commercial and financial families in the cities. Nevertheless, by 1914 two *Standesherren* were making great incomes from mining regalian rights inherited from their ancestors' position as sovereigns under the Old Reich. One was Engelbert, Duke of Arenberg and Croy, whose huge wealth in Germany was overshadowed by his still larger possessions in Belgium and France. The other was Alfred, Prince zu Salm-Salm.[20]

These princely owners of regalian rights made fortunes from mining with even less expenditure of effort than the English aristocrats who let their collieries. The precise terms on which they allowed mines to be opened and exploited depended on the contracts they made with specific companies and individual capitalists. At a minimum, however, they could expect to receive 1 per cent of all the coal mined. From just one of the many Westphalian coalmines over which he possessed regalian rights the Duke of Arenberg received 1.7 million Marks (£85 000) between 1893 and 1909 and as coal production boomed in the twentieth century the tendency was for his profits to rise steeply with every year that passed. Martin reckoned that by 1909 Arenberg's annual income from mining rights was more than half a million Marks and the Duke's overall income in Prussia had risen from 255 000 Marks in 1892 to 2.9 million Marks (£145 000) in 1909.[21]

For Prince zu Salm-Salm, on the other hand, mining rights were far more important sources of income than his quite small landed estates. Martin comments that 'The Prince is thus because of the wide extent of his regalian rights and the struggle among men to exploit the black diamond in the most pleasant position imaginable'. After acquiring from the Prince the rights to exploit six of his mines, the Essen Coalmining Company stated that 'the acquisition of this large and valuable area of mines ensures the existence and further expansion of the company into the distant future. This property is a reserve which the company can exploit at the time and to the extent desired when our Ruhr mines are exhausted'. How much Salm-Salm made from this deal is unknown but on two contracts with other companies for which information is available he seems to have made a minimum of 800 000 Marks (£40 000) on the one hand, and 120 000 Marks and 1 per cent of the coal's value on the other.[22]

In southern Germany, Bavarian nobles had never owned industrial concerns of any significance but in Baden the Fürstenbergs' ironworks were second in importance only to those owned by the State in the first half of the nineteenth century. In the early decades of the century only their forests brought the family more income. To some extent, however, the Furstenberg ironworks suffered from the same disadvantages as those of the Urals magnates. The factories were far distant from coal deposits, and communications were poor. Charcoal-based iron technology could not compete with coal, especially as the Ruhr's produce grew in quality after the mid-century. Huge sums, derived from redemption money, were invested from the 1830s, 1.2 million florins going into the ironworks between 1849 and 1860 alone. Johann Prestinari and other Fürstenberg administrators challenged this level of investment from the start, arguing that charcoal-based iron could never compete with the Ruhr in the long run, that the Fürstenbergs could never raise the sums needed to create large-scale competitive modern ironworks, and that valuable forests were being denuded by the industry's managers. After a period in the 1840s when large investments restored the ironworks' profits, the doubters were to be proved correct, though the closure of the factories was delayed beyond the economically rational moment by the Fürstenbergs' pride in their traditional industrial role and their desire not to leave 1500 workers and their families without a source of income. In the long term, however, Prestinari's strategy of dependence on forestry on the one hand and stocks and shares on the other was to prevail and prove successful. The Fürstenbergs were so rich that they could afford to pour money down their ironworks' drains and yet see their overall income grow steeply in the second half of the century.[23]

Prince Pückler's old estate at Muskau also witnessed the collapse in the second half of the nineteenth century of a long-established rural iron industry based on charcoal. Once again it was a combination of technological backwardness, lack of capital and defective communications which doomed the factory. In 1864 the estate's potash works, which had existed since the sixteenth century, also went under, although the factory had soap, vitriol and potash sections and was in principle a potentially flourishing basis for a modern chemical industry. Competition from the much larger and more advanced urban chemical plants, and the great costs of modernisation, persuaded Muskau's administrators to close the works, however, and in 1872 the Keula iron-tools factory was also sold to a Berlin businessman for similar reasons, though it proved its great potential profitability under the new owner. At this time Muskau, owned by the very rich Prince Frederick of the Netherlands, appears to have been run in a less than efficient and imaginative manner, its administrators seeking to retreat from the estate's old industrial traditions and to concentrate on forestry, which in this part of Germany could never hope to bring the kind of profits secured by the Fürstenbergs from the Black Forest woodlands.[24]

In 1883, however, Muskau was sold to Count Traugott Hermann von Arnim, who inherited both a good business sense and the Junker tradition of directly exploiting his estates. Arnim extended Muskau's forestry operations, building a light railway to overcome the transport problems by which they had been constrained in the past. He also reversed the estate's industrial decline. In 1883 he opened a steam-powered brick factory which, within easy range of the centre of the German glass industry, proved very profitable. So too did his coalmines, whose output under the Arnims increased from minimal levels in 1883 to 200 000 tons by 1915. His biggest industrial investment, however, was the very successful cardboard factory which, along with sawmills and pulpmills, he created as a spin-off of his timber business. Purchased for 6.6 million Marks in

1883, Muskau was (under) valued by Martin in 1913 at roughly 14 million.[25]

Arnim-Muskau's wealth and the size of his estate made him an untypical Junker but his establishment of rural industrial enterprises was not uncommon, especially where distilleries and sugar-mills were concerned. Werner Ludwig von Alvensleben, created a count in 1901, owned both a distillery and a mill, together with a coal-mine, a lime-kiln, a stone quarry and a gravel works. All Alvensleben's concerns were small-scale, the mine employing fifty-seven workers in 1916 and the Neugattersleben sugar-mill 155 men and women in 1879. Other marks of the Count's enterprises were low pay and the employment of many agricultural and female workers who would decamp to the fields for the harvest and other peak periods. By the 1890s the sugar mill, built in 1846, was out of date and Alvensleben could not afford to build a modern one from his own resources. He therefore teamed up with two noble neighbours, the three landowners establishing a new mill which they supplied with their own sugar beet and which netted them an annual average of 82 463 Marks between 1885 and 1916.[26]

By the standards of the Upper Silesian magnates, however, the industrial operations even of a 'big Junker' like Count Werner von Alvensleben were minuscule. Of the eleven richest Prussians in 1913, six were Upper Silesian aristocratic industrialists. As a mining and industrial centre Silesia stood second to the Ruhr in Germany. The world's greatest zinc producer, its coal deposits were exceeded in Europe only by those of the English Midlands. Of the leading Silesian magnates, many had interests not only in coal, their greatest source of wealth, but also in iron, zinc, lead and, sometimes, a number of other industries as well. The Prince of Pless alone employed over 8000 coalminers; Prince Christian Kraft zu Hohenlohe Öhringen, the Duke of Ujest, employed over 5000 coalminers and was simultaneously the world's greatest zinc producer. Among European aristocrats in 1914 the Silesians were unique.[27]

Upper Silesia's development depended on the existence there in close proximity of huge deposits of coal, iron ore, zinc, alum and a number of other minerals. The greatest consumer of the region's coal was always Silesia's own industries. Until the 1850s poor communications were the major check on development. Upper Silesia, rich in coal and other minerals, was positioned in the further south-eastern corner of Prussia and was cut off from its natural economic hinterland by Russian and Austrian tariffs. Not until the development of railways in the 1850s could Upper Silesian coal reach Berlin and north Germany at prices which undercut those of the Ruhr and England. Before 1850 zinc had been the key to Upper Silesian prosperity. From mid-century the railways allowed all the region's resources to be tapped and expansion occurred at extraordinary speed. In the two decades before 1914 incomes sometimes multiplied at dizzying rates as the profits from Silesian coal and zinc soared.[28]

The great aristocrats were crucial for Silesian development, especially before 1850. Their political weight in Berlin was valuable. Above all, in the absence of a wealthy bourgeoisie they were the only people who could supply both capital and entrepreneurship. Before the coming of the railways, transport difficulties shrank profits and surplus capital and made major investment risky. It took real enterprise to open up the zinc industry, the major achievement of the Hohenlohe-Öhringens, or to end the Silesian iron industry's technological lag, as Count Hugo Henckel von Donnersmarck did in 1837–40, by mortgaging his possessions up to the hilt in order to create, in the Laurahütte, Germany's most advanced ironworks, complete with blast furnaces, puddling and rolling mills.[29]

After 1850 Silesia's situation improved radically and profit-making became much easier. The aristocrats were joined, though never supplanted, by a handful of rich bourgeois, of whom Godulla, Winkler and the Borsig family were the best known. In time most of the aristocrats founded limited companies from their mines and factories, reserving for themselves the position of chairmen of the board. Count Andreas von Renard set the pattern in 1855 by creating the 'Minerva Forest, Works and Mining Company' but although most of his peers followed suit, some, the Pless and Ballestrems for instance, chose to go on running these concerns in traditional style.[30]

Whether mines and factories were still purely private or part of a limited company, the extent to which a magnate played a large personal role in their management depended on personal taste by the end of the century. Some of the Silesian aristocrats, Prince Hugo von Hohenlohe-Öhringen and Count Franz von Ballestrem for instance, were very active in politics. The heads of the Pless family seem to have played the minimum possible role in economic affairs, their estates in the twentieth century being the most conservatively managed among the magnates. But Prince Guido Henckel von

Donnersmarck, the richest of Prussia's aristocrats, played an exceptionally active and enterprising role, expanding into a number of new spheres (cellulose, wire, chrome, viscose, paper) and developing major interests in Russia, Austria, Hungary, France and Italy.[31]

The problem about enterprise, however, was that it entailed risks and these many aristocrats had neither the training nor the experience to judge. Prince Christian Kraft zu Hohenlohe-Öhringen attempted to match Guido Henckel von Donnersmarck and almost went bankrupt in the process. Together with Prince Fürstenberg he set up a corporation, the Handels-Vereinigung, whose interests included 'Berlin construction and transportation, coal and potash, banking, steamships, trade and expansion in Turkey, and one newspaper'. 'By 1909 collapse threatened on several fronts' and the result was 'the best-known bankruptcy in the Wilhelminian era, threatened litigation between Hohenlohe and Fürstenberg, the intervention of William II, and the need for Hohenlohe to sell part of his ancestral property'. The Austrian ambassador drew the moral that 'mere dilettantism was no longer sufficient to manage large estates in a capitalist world'. Baroness von Spitzemberg was more censorious, commenting that Hohenlohe's folly had resulted in hundreds of his dependants losing their jobs and that his activities would have horrified the older generation of his family.[32]

Fear of a disaster such as the one which struck Hohenlohe-Öhringen was a major disincentive to direct participation in industry by aristocratic magnates. Shareholding offered a means to tap industry's profits with less risk and personal involvement, which in turn allowed aristocrats the time to play the roles in politics and high society for which tradition and education best suited them.

In both England and Russia aristocrats were major shareholders by the twentieth century. Spring dates large-scale shareholding from the 1860s and Thompson adds that, although evidence is scanty, it is 'highly likely' that from the 1880s landowners were spreading their assets by moving into the stock market. Famous examples of this can be cited, such as the Russells' exchange of their London estate for stocks and bonds on the eve of the First World War. In this case fear of political risks to urban landlords as 'socialism' gained ground were paramount, but the more general cause of diversification was the collapse in agricultural rents, the declining political value of great estates and the increasingly plutocratic nature of high society.[33]

In Russia, land, especially after 1861, never possessed the status or guaranteed the income of the English gentleman's estate. In a partly frontier society with a court aristocracy and very little local politics land's social and political prestige was inevitably lower than in the English shires. Not surprisingly, a traditionally *rentier* and very often urban-based aristocracy took very comfortably to shareholding: 'In 1910, of the 137,825 nobles residing in St. Petersburg, 49 percent lived on income from securities'. Among the great magnates whose incomes have been investigated in detail shareholding was of great, and growing, importance. In 1913, 62 per cent of Count A. D. Sheremetev's annual income of 1 550 000 roubles came from stocks and shares: 'The Yusupovs owned only 41,000 rubles worth of securities in 1901, but after 1905 they sold and mortgaged many of their estates and increased their securities holdings to 5.1 million by 1915'.[34]

The most detailed breakdown of the forms taken by aristocratic shareholding is Harald Winkel's study of the uses to which the German high nobility put the redemption money which flowed into their pockets in the middle decades of the nineteenth century. Most aristocrats tried to buy land where the prices were not exorbitant. A few, generally with long family connections with industry, sought profitable investment in factories or industrial shareholdings. In the end, however, once they had paid off their debts and purchased whatever land was available at sensible prices most grandees were forced to turn to the stock market and, when they did so, in the overwhelming majority of cases they played safe by investing in government securities, initially usually German, but later foreign as well. The closest most of them got to investing in the industrial economy was in railway bonds. Deeply conservative for the most part, the managers of the *Standesherren*'s assets would have argued that their chief task was to secure the continued ability of ancient houses to live with dignity. They had not sold or leased their mines, iron works and factories only now to speculate in what was seen as inherently risky industrial paper.[35]

7. Life, Manners, Morals

In 1874 the Crown Princess of Prussia visited Russia for the first time, to attend her brother's marriage to the Tsar's daughter. Writing to her mother, Queen Victoria of England, the Crown Princess confessed herself enthralled by Moscow, a city whose like she had never encountered in Europe. The imperial capital, St. Petersburg, occupied less space in her letters. 'I do not talk of Petersburg,' she noted, 'as those who like to live in a whirl of excitement and frivolity can do so just the same as at Paris or Vienna, and have no time to observe anything beyond it or to reflect of the world beyond the brilliant salons, and the *luxe ecrasant* of the Palaces and frantic extravagance of so great a court'. Here spoke the favourite daughter of Albert, the Prince Consort, whose seriousness of purpose had made him many enemies among England's pleasure-loving aristocracy. But the young princess was right in believing that the pursuit of luxury and pleasure consumed more aristocratic time and energy than any other aspect of life. She was also correct in perceiving that high society operated on basically similar principles in most of the great European capitals.[1]

Where entertainments and life-style were concerned, a key distinction existed between the world of urban high society and aristocracy's life in the countryside. Still more basic were differences between the lives of men and women.

Victorian aristocracy was far from being a harem society, its women illiterate and largely excluded from male social life. If the club, the regimental mess and the smoking room in the country house were male preserves, the world of the court, the ballroom, the salon or the drawing room revolved around the mixing of the sexes. A key function of urban high society was to ensure the continuation of the aristocratic species by bringing young men and women together. One reason for society's exclusiveness, its elaborate rites of entrée and its strict controls over young women's activities was to ensure that the daughters of aristocracy married their social equals. With marriages now no longer simply arranged by dynastic-ally-inclined parents, but more dependent on young people's own choice, the need to exclude potential threats was all the greater. Married female aristocrats, elderly dowagers perhaps most of all, wielded great power in society and not only over younger women. More than their male counterparts they shaped society's rituals and opened or closed the gates to exclusive drawing rooms. Commenting on the position of Almack's in Regency society, Captain Gronow recalled that 'the female government of Almack's was a pure despotism . . . like every other despotism it was not innocent of abuses'.[2]

Nevertheless, though the sexes mixed in society, their roles and lives differed fundamentally. The education of boys tended to be much more thorough and purposeful. Even where boys' academic training was woefully inadequate and where families, as was par-ticularly often the case in Russia, put a heavy stress on educating their daughters, girls were still protected from the tough, competi-tive institutional life of the cadet corps, boarding school or univer-sity, which exposed children to the wider world and prepared aristo-cratic boys to play leading roles in society. Most aristocratic women were given the accomplishments necessary to attract future hus-bands but little in the way of rigorous intellectual training. Daisy Cornwallis-West, the future Princess of Pless, recalls that 'I received no education in the proper sense of the word', though she was despatched to Florence with her sister to learn Italian and singing.[3]

A male aristocrat, if tolerably rich, could live a life of pure leisure. He could, however, choose a military, diplomatic or political career. Active management of his estates provided another outlet for his energies. A woman had no chance of a career. Openings, even for well-educated daughters of the professional middle-classes, were few before 1914, and a young aristocrat generally had no financial motives to take the path of a career: there was formidable social disapproval to surmount and, in all probability, an inadquate edu-cation to boot. The Victorians' stress on the responsibility of aristocrats towards their dependants gave aristocratic women, particularly on rural estates, a legitimate role in charitable and educational work. Particularly in Russia, where rural health and education services barely existed before the 1890s, the school, hospital, orphanage and even old people's home provided by some great landowners could give aristocratic women a chance to display leadership and organisational talent in a worthwhile role. From this came effective aristocratic female patronage of peasant handicrafts.[4]

Throughout Europe the stress on warmer and less formal relations between parents and children gave maternity a greater prestige than it had enjoyed before 1815. The aristocratic mother could aim to be a source of love and warmth to her children, as well as being the individual who contributed most to their moral and religious values. Many women fulfilled this role but they had to contend, where their sons were concerned, with the tradition of military and boarding school education. They also faced criticism if their devotion to motherhood, let alone charity, took them away from their social duties. In society they could compete to be the most successful of hostesses, the most elegant members of the fashionable set, the arbiters of taste and manners. But the decline in importance of royal courts, the rise of bureaucratic and parliamentary institutions and aristocracy's need to preserve moral appearances deprived them of the role played in previous eras by a royal mistress. The last aristocratic woman to play the role of royal mistress in grand style was Catherine Dolgoruky, whose liaison with Alexander II in the 1870s had an impact on the rise and fall of ministers, the awarding of railway contracts, and relations between the Emperor and his heir.[5]

Prince Chlodwig zu Hohenlohe-Schillingfürst, the future German chancellor, commented on the unsatisfactory aimlessness of the life of the nineteenth-century south German great nobleman, whose chance of playing a meaningful role – political, military or economic – in the contemporary world was slim. He added that 'the happy people in this country, and in our class, are not the men but the women, provided that they appreciate their situation'. The implication was clear: since women could not play meaningful public roles, at least they were less subject to the disappointments of their male counterparts.[6]

Most aristocratic women accepted without question the life to which they were consigned by birth. Since this role was inescapable, generally privileged and comfortable, and sanctioned by very ancient and deeply held values, acceptance is not surprising. Baroness von Spitzemberg could agree with her sister that most German noblewomen had poor educations and few interests outside the home. But she herself believed that a wife had no right to influence her husband in key decisions concerning his career but should merely support him wholeheartedly in any choice he made. Princess Daisy of Pless, much less happily married and rather contemptuous of the submissiveness of German women, took a more independent line. She commented in her memoirs that 'every woman with a husband, children and houses is tied . . . Such a woman has to live according to the position she is almost paid to fill (And if the situation happens not to suit her she cannot give notice and change it). If the woman is content to appear nice to herself in the glass, and make friends of (mostly) fools, have furs and diamonds, and forget her soul, she may be happy, but not otherwise'.[7]

High society was governed by a plethora of rules and conventions, public flouting of which generally led to exclusion. Sometimes these rules were rooted, at least in theory, in moral principles. Baroness Spitzemberg was horrified by revelations of homosexuality in William II's entourage, which centred on the person of Prince Phillipp zu Eulenberg, the Kaiser's closest friend. The Baroness commented, 'these matters are immensely sad, because society's annihilation is so absolute . . . But morals and the consciousness of morality demand a boycott, the ostracisation of this kind of sinner'.[8]

Most rules were, however, linked less to morals than to a desire to maintain society's exclusiveness and force new entrants, whether young aristocrats or the upwardly mobile, to conform to its code. A key rule concerned who was or was not acceptable and on which occasions. Even at the end of the nineteenth century the relatively free-thinking Countess of Warwick believed that 'army or naval officers, diplomats or clergymen might be invited to lunch or dinner. The vicar might be invited regularly to Sunday lunch or supper if he was a gentleman. Doctors and solicitors might be invited to garden parties, though never, of course, to lunch or dinner. Anyone engaged in the arts, the stage, trade or commerce, no matter how well connected, could not be asked to the house at all'.[9]

An elaborate ritual surrounded morning calls, leaving one's card when visiting, invitations to dinner and even chance encounters on the street. According to Leonore Davidoff, these rituals allowed established members of society to signify acceptance or rejection of new aspirants. Books were written to guide the aspirant or the foreigner through the labyrinth. Murray's guides to Russia, for instance, warned those wishing to move in St. Petersburg's aristocratic society that fluent French was useful, letters of introduction and a full purse essential. 'Considerable expense, not to say extravagance, is unavoidable at St. Petersburgh, particularly if the visitor should desire to take any part in the gaieties and amusements which are unceasing during the winter months; the cost will be half as much again what it would be in Vienna or Rome'.[10]

In 1865 Murray reminded his readers that 'ladies wishing to pass a "season" at St. Petersburgh should recollect that Russian ladies dress very richly, though in great taste. The charges of dress-makers at St. Petersburgh being exorbitant, it is advisable to come prepared with all the necessary dresses. At balls, the only dance in which the stranger will not at first be able to join is the mazurka'. Like high society in all Europe's capitals, St. Petersburg had its timetable:

Winter is the season for gaieties in Russia. Travellers with letters of introduction will find the salons of St. Petersburgh as brilliant as those of Paris. Dinner parties, receptions, soirées and balls occur in such rapid succession that the man of fashion will find the winter too short, rather than too long. There is no dancing during the forty days that precede Easter. Christmas and the carnival are the gayest periods. Two or three Court balls are then given.

It is necessary to wear a uniform at court. French is the language of society but English is generally understood. Strangers are expected to make the first call, which is returned either in person or by card. In leaving cards on persons who are not at home, one of the edges of the card should be turned up. It is necessary to leave a card next day on any person to whom the stranger may have been introduced at a party. Those who are introduced to the stranger will observe the same politeness. Great punctuality is exacted in St. Petersburgh in the matter of leaving cards after entertainments and introductions . . . the hours for calling are 3 to 5 p.m.; dinner parties are generally convened for 6 or 6.30; and receptions commence at about 10 p.m., and last until very late.[11]

Free of the presence of the Imperial Court, Moscow was never quite as luxurious or punctilious as St. Petersburg, but even in the 1880s its rituals were still quite formidable. No lady could sit in the stalls at a theatre or travel in a cab. She must have a box and travel in her own carriage with a liveried footman in attendance. Much private entertainment, in the form of frequent dances and weekly receptions, was provided by families with eligible daughters. Anyone who danced with a young woman had to visit her home in the next couple of days to be introduced to her parents and thank her for the dance. With two or three major balls a week during the season this was a considerable obligation. Prince Evgeni Trubetskoy comments that 'this cumbersome apparatus of high society with its Chinese ceremonies was a burden to almost everyone. It left a feeling of oppressive emptiness in the soul and hit the pocket very hard'. Trubetskoy and his brother Serge, both outstandingly intelligent philosophy students at Moscow University, dropped out of Moscow aristocratic life, since being a socialite was a full-time occupation incompatible with serious work or academic studies.[12]

As elsewhere, however, Moscow aristocratic society fell victim to the encroachments of the industrial and bourgeois world. In the 1880s the social spheres of nobility and industry were still separate. Trubetskoy recalls that members of the industrial and commercial middle class never attended aristocratic receptions, though young male nobles were just beginning to put in an appearance in some merchant houses. By 1914 much had changed and the two worlds were far more mixed. Very many of the old aristocratic houses in the Prechistenka district of central Moscow were now in the hands of great merchants or industrialists. Others were hospitals, schools and military academies. Writing in November 1916, the society magazine *Stolitsa i Usad'ba*, Russia's answer to *Country Life*, spoke of the old Moscow world of noble palaces with their huge gardens and open house for visitors as part of an almost vanished world. On the eve of the First World War, the British Consul-General in Moscow commented that the city was 'Russia's commercial centre and the merchant is a characteristic type of its leading class ... At the present time there are very few aristocrats in Moscow, and such as there are so almost entirely owing to local official positions or to connection with the university'. One consequence of this was that the old rigid social rituals had become largely a thing of the past: 'If you are invited to a dinner in a Russian house, you will probably find that most of the men are in frock-coats, some in ordinary round morning coats, and but few in evening dress or a dinner jacket. Of the ladies also some may be very decolletées and hung over with gorgeous jewellery, whereas others will be in perfectly plain, as we should consider them, dark morning gowns'.[13]

United by rituals and convention, high society was divided into cliques and coteries. Some of these had clear political allegiances. In London, where politics was always one of aristocracy's most absorbing games, the political hostess could contribute significantly to the cohesion of a cabinet or a parliamentary faction. The Holland House set was early-nineteenth-century Europe's most famous family-cum-political clique, forming the core of the Whig parliamentary faction. Even in St. Petersburg, however, autocracy was very far from putting a stopper on political discussions and coteries in high society. An onlooker in the 1880s commented that St. Petersburg women were 'ambitious for their husbands and at the same time for themselves. They are all more or less tormented by the desire to play some sort of role, above all a political role . . . In this Empire, governed by a system of absolute autocracy, in this town where one would imagine that everyone is subject to police control, there reigns a freedom of conversation unknown elsewhere'. The semi-political salon, where individuals of similar political and cultural tendencies gathered, had long since been a feature of St. Petersburg life. In the 1840s and 1850s, for instance, the palace of the Grand Duchess Helen was the great meeting point for the men who were to devise and execute Alexander II's liberal reforms in the 1860s. The Grand Duchess spotted young liberal talent, brought it into contact with more senior reformist officials and cast her protection over the relatively free discussion of politics in her palace. Her role in uniting the reformers and encouraging the development of a concerted liberal strategy can scarcely be exaggerated.[14]

Many coteries might, however, have nothing whatever to do with politics and be little more than a racing set or a group of friends with other shared tastes or interests. In the 1890s the most fashionable and exclusive set in St. Petersburg society were the so-called 'Russian-bred lords', who prided themselves on their English accents and customs. Among the latter were opulent lifestyles, punctiliousness in dress and etiquette, and the cultivation of a cold and aloof aristocratic snobbery. In this world, a leading light was Princess Betsy Baryatinsky, 'one of those women whose entire life is devoted to the cares of being a power in society. She knows how to attract everyone who glistens by their beauty, their spirit, their birth, their wealth or their elegance. People go to her house because it's good form thus to affirm one's right to belong to the circle of her friends. People also go because one's sure to meet several members of the imperial family and many people of greater or less influence'.[15]

Rather arbitrarily, Arthur Ponsonby divided Edwardian aristocratic London into three main sets. The first, which he called reactionary, disliked almost all aspects of the modern world, though they accommodated those changes that contributed to their own comfort. The reactionaries, in Ponsonby's view, were distinguished by adherence to all the old conventions and by their expectation of unlimited deference from their social inferiors.

The second group was 'the sporting set, some merely happy-go-lucky, some frankly dissolute, devoting their lives to hunting, racing, shooting and other forms of sport; utterly uneducated, wildly extravagant, reckless, thoughtless and vaguely apprehensive that certain movements are on foot which seem designed to deprive them of some of their fun . . . they find the "lower orders" with whom they associate, i.e. jockeys, bookies, keepers, gillies, valets and grooms, are in no way discontented with their lot'.

Thirdly, there was a much brighter group, more in touch with public life. This group prided itself on its intelligence and its understanding of the cultural and the modern. Its members were 'accomplished conversationalists. Worldliness, superficial brilliance, and seemingly advanced ideas make them very prominent and much sought after. No one would dispute their social gifts or their attractive qualities. There is a dazzling aplomb about them which carries all before it. Critic and enemy alike, once within their orbit, come willingly under the spell'.[16]

At the centre of this third group, though rather long in the tooth by the time Ponsonby was writing, were the Souls. This was a coterie formed by a small group of friends in the 1880s, whose basic purpose was mutual entertainment. The main means to this was witty conversation laced with amateur theatricals, adultery and a shared belief in aesthetic values and passion. The Souls kept themselves apart from the dull conventional sobriety of Victorian aristocracy and from the philistine hedonism of the sporting set and of the Prince of Wales' Marlborough House circle. Arthur Balfour and

George Curzon were the most famous male Souls but it was in many ways the women, whose lives were more wholly confined to society and personal relationships, who formed the group's core. Good manners, lightness of touch and an arrogant but not unattractive independence bred of extreme social and intellectual self-confidence were their hallmarks.[17]

In a world in which, even in 1900, respectable ladies were only just beginning to enter restaurants and hotels, high society tended to revolve around the great aristocratic town houses. Even in Victorian London, Europe's richest city, there were never a great many of these, though the impact of two score of aristocratic palaces was augmented by the much more numerous smaller town houses owned or rented by lesser noblemen anxious to participate in the Season. Though the exteriors of many of the aristocratic palaces lacked distinction, the early nineteenth century saw restrained Adam interiors increasingly replaced by extraordinary displays of opulent decoration. Little distinguished these grand staircases, huge reception rooms and gilded ceilings from their St. Petersburg equivalents, though in the Tsar's capital the number of grand aristocratic mansions was even smaller than in London. Nevertheless, in 1914, the world of the great town palace was by no means dead in either city. Of the most famous London residences, only the Duke of Northumberland's palace had gone by the outbreak of war. Like Prince Beloselsky-Belozersky, however, he still owned a splendid suburban retreat at Syon House. In St. Petersburg, wastage had been greater than in London in the three decades before 1914 but there remained many more aristocratic palaces than in Moscow. The greatest houses – those of the Stroganovs on the Nevsky, the Shuvalovs and Sheremetevs on the Fontanka, and the Yusupovs on the Moika – were still in full flower.[18]

Berlin was always very different from either London or St. Petersburg. An English guide to the city of the 1840s warned that 'the society of the upper classes is on the whole not very accessible to strangers, nor is hospitality exercised to the same extent, chiefly because their fortunes are limited. The Hotels of the diplomatic corps are an exception and in them the most agreeable soirées are held in the winter seasons. That excessive military exclusiveness which originated at the court of Frederick the Great has not entirely disappeared – a uniform, especially if it is Russian, is still to a certain extent a passport to the fashionable circles of the Prussian

capital'. On the other hand, Berlin possessed 'an agreeable literary
society composed of the most talented men in Germany, whom the
government has the art of drawing around it in an official capacity,
or as professors of the university'.[19]

The style and ethos of Berlin society was strongly influenced by
the traditions of the Hohenzollern Court. Prussia's rulers had rooted
their claims to international status and prestige in a powerful army
and an austere and efficient bureaucracy. They had seldom tried
to compete with the Wettins or Wittelsbachs where display at Court
was concerned. The eighteenth century Romanovs, in any case far
richer than the Hohenzollerns, had asserted their claim to be a
European great power in part by building palaces and staging Court
spectacles on a scale to outshine anything else on the continent. By
contrast, Frederick II had barely possessed a Court and although
his nephew, Frederick William II, reversed this trend, from 1797
to 1888 Prussia was ruled by three monarchs whose shyness, aus-
terity and respect for family tradition encouraged them to maintain
the maximum degree of modesty in Court life compatible with their
status. Even after becoming first King and then Emperor, William
I continued to live in his old palace on the Unter den Linden, 'a
plain, entirely unpretentious house, of tasteful proportions and of
the simplest utilitarian style . . . the Imperial Palace is surpassed in
size and splendour by many private houses of men who are – or
would like to be – members of our Council of Commerce'. The
contrast between the austere, cost-conscious, dignified William I in
his simple house and the opulent mansions of the new, often Jewish,
financial oligarchy symbolised many of the anomalies and strains
inherent in old Prussia's promotion to the rank of world-class capitalist power.[20]

Aristocratic foreigners seldom thought much of Berlin. For 'Count
Vasili' in the 1880s it was 'essentially a little city. They gossip and
slander there more than anywhere else; besides, there is a quantity
of intrigues. The society has an excessively back-biting tongue, and
is constantly on the lookout for some scandal; it has no reading,
little education, and not the least interest outside of what concerns
it immediately . . . In general the Berlinese lady of the higher class
does not read, work or occupy herself. She passes her life in bab-
bling, dressing or undressing'.

By contrast, in the city's bourgeoisie 'one meets with honest souls,
elevated intellects, people with wholesome ideas and leading a life

of usefulness'. Only, however, in the drawing rooms of the Crown Princess and of Countess von Schleinitz would a member of high society meet literary, scholarly or artistic figures. Though Vasili thought the accumulation of immense wealth in the hands of the Jewish financial oligarchy had great political dangers, she found the wives and daughters of this oligarchy often very beautiful and polished: 'their minds are much more active and better developed than those of the ladies of the highest rank'.[21]

Hugh Vizetelly, an Englishman who studied Berlin in the 1870s, largely agreed with Vasili. In his view, Berlin

> altogether lacks the gay, kaleidoscopic life of a great metropolis . . . the aristocracy hold themselves as far aloof as possible from the untitled bureaucracy . . . the various circles of society in Berlin are mostly formed by the definite conditions of rank and office, and although rotating, rarely intersect one another . . . the stilted ceremonial etiquette of the past century is to-day *de rigueur* at Berlin receptions of any pretension . . . as a rule 'women of mind' are but little esteemed at Berlin . . . Society . . . is too absorbed in the worship of rank, the adulation of ancient descent, and decided reverence for the higher military element to trouble itself about encouraging intellect . . . the amalgamation of rank, wealth and intellect to be met within the leading London drawing-rooms is undreamt of in Berlin, where all the written or unwritten laws of etiquette and tradition would forbid anything approaching such a hetero-geneous assembly.[22]

How fully these criticisms of the 1870s and 1880s still applied to the Berlin of the 1900s is hard to say. Where, for instance, does Baroness Spitzemberg – intelligent, *au fait* with world affairs, well placed at court, involved in much philanthropic work, going to the theatre to see Gorky's plays – fit into the stereotype presented by Vasili or Vizetelly? Even William II tried at times to follow the example of the hated Edward VII by bringing together aristocracy and plutocracy into a new social elite. The Berlin Court was never exclusive by German standards and the last Kaiser loved the opu-lent wealth of Silesian magnates and financial oligarchs, rather despised reactionary Junker backwoodsmen, had a passion for modern technology, and was not too hidebound to deny his friendship to figures such as the Jewish shipping tycoon, Albert Ballinn.

Certainly Berlin was never aristocratic in the style of London or St. Petersburg. If the German aristocracy had a capital, at least before 1900, then it was Vienna, whose noble society was richer, larger and more exclusive than that of Berlin. Vizetelly commented that even in the streets anyone acquainted with great aristocratic cities would spot quickly that Berlin did not come up to scratch: 'Only a limited number amongst the wealthiest and noblest members of the Court circle keep their own equipages . . . well-matched pairs of thorough-bred high stepping, satin-skinned carriage horses are remarkably scarce in Berlin'.[23]

This was above all because

the larger landed proprietors have hitherto been poorly represented at Berlin, and are to be found in greater numbers in the provincial capitals, such as Breslau, Munster, Konigsberg, Stettin etc., where they hold solemn and exclusive high jinks amongst themselves. The noble families who come up in order that their head may occupy his bench in the Landtag or Reichstag during the season, generally accept invitations without giving entertainments in return, very few having houses or the requisite conveniences for receiving guests. The numerous petty princelets and dukelings moreover generally live in hotels, when summoned by duty or interest to Berlin, so that the obligation of entertaining all that is most noble . . . devolves upon the court, the various scions of the reigning house, the foreign ambassadors, the ministers, and those few nobles possessed of the wealth and the houseroom befitting the task.[24]

Among the latter, the Prince of Pless stood out because of his splendid palace in the Wilhelmstrasse. This was built in the 1870s, more or less in celebration of Berlin's promotion to be capital city of a great empire. Perhaps significantly, for a palace worthy of a *grand seigneur* it was deemed necessary to turn to French models, architects and even workmen. Baroness Spitzemberg attended a ball at the Palais Pless in 1895 whose 150 guests included, in her view, all the most beautiful women and best dancers in Berlin. The splendid house, lovely flowers, princely service and pleasant company added up, according to her, to a combination rare in

Berlin. By 1914, however, in Princess Daisy of Pless's words, 'the big ugly house on the Wilhelmstrasse was closed', partly because, in continental fashion, she and her husband had to share it with other members of his family, which they disliked. When visiting Berlin the Plesses preferred to stay at a hotel. In addition, the Berlin Court, in which precedence was traditionally given to top Prussian officials, grated on the aristocratic pride of the Prince of Pless and his wife. In 1903, for instance, Daisy of Pless wrote that she would not visit Berlin again until her husband had some grand official post, since it was humiliating to have to go in to dinner behind some bureaucrat's Frau. Not that, in her view, absence from the capital would be any great loss, for 'Berlin will never be a smart social centre'.[25]

Daisy of Pless's problems at the Hohenzollerns' Court were in part those of an English aristocrat in the rather different culture of the Prussian bureaucratic state. England's thoroughly aristocratic and unbureaucratic history was reflected in the fact that, until 1905, the rules of precedence might send the Prime Minister in to dinner behind a duke's son. In the Russian and Prussian military – bureaucratic regimes this was unthinkable. Such matters of precedence could obsess the Court nobility. This was a legacy of a process initiated by Louis XIV, who tamed the French high aristocracy by bringing them to Court, encouraging them to compete in the extravagance of their lifestyles and thus increasing their dependence on him for favours and pensions. Obsessive struggles for precedence which had some political significance in the eighteenth century looked increasingly bizarre in the industrial age but they nevertheless continued. Many nineteenth-century English aristocrats put great expense and effort into attempts to ensure their elevation in the peerage. In Germany the struggle for precedence was even more intense, entwined as it was in a mania for genealogy and a legalistic pedantry which had few equivalents in England, still less Russia. Germany's plethora of minor courts encouraged this obsessive concern with precedence and status. In addition, however, German aristocracy had inherited from the Old Reich a rather minutely regulated traditional pecking order which had been turned upside down in 1806–15, further disordered in 1866–71 and thrown into still more disarray by the differing impact on family fortunes of the Industrial Revolution. Plentiful fuel existed for conflicts over precedence and feelings of endangered status. The Reuss family withdrew from the Berlin Court because its females were not allowed to wear trains, thus denying them the status of semi-royalty. Most *Standesherren* were angered by William I's granting of the title of Royal Highness to collateral branches of the Hohenzollern family. Worst of all was the precedence granted over *Standesherren* to Knights of the Black Eagle, often Prussia's most senior statesmen and soldiers, a rule which caused such fury that William I tried to pacify indignation by decreeing that the precedence was not shared by the Knights' wives.[26]

The political significance of the royal Courts declined everywhere in the nineteenth century, though obviously more so in Britain than in the absolute monarchies of Eastern Europe. Even in Britain, however, Douglas Haig benefited in the First World War from his family links to George V's Court, and Edward VII had an important influence on key ambassadorial appointments. Regardless of their direct political importance, Courts remained places where powerful connections could be forged. When Baroness Spitzemberg returned to Court in 1884 after years of absence following her husband's death she did so, despite the cost, partly out of respect for the old emperor and partly because to do so would benefit her children's careers and marriage prospects.

A royal Court legitimised and glorified the workings of high society. It put the State's blessing, through the system of presentation, on the division between those who were 'in' and those who were 'out' of society. Its etiquette and precise ranking order strengthened hierarchy and formality within the social elite and provided a grand arena for displays of luxury and spectacular hospitality. Particularly in St. Petersburg, whose Court had been the most sumptuous in Europe and whose high society lacked London's wealth by 1914, the absence of a Court after 1905 was much resented. It contributed to the alienation of Nicholas II and his regime from St. Petersburg aristocratic society, a factor of real political importance in contributing to the elites' willingness to abandon the Romanovs in February 1917.[27]

Even in England, whose wealthy and politically powerful aristocrats were less dependent on the Court, the latter helped to shape society's values and habits. The Prince of Wales' extravagant tastes, a rejection of the simple values of his father, George III, chimed in well with the mood of an aristocracy whose opulence grew fast between the 1780s and 1815 as agricultural prices rocketed. Queen

Victoria's rejection of Regency morals and extravagance, on the other hand, fitted well an upper-class world whose members needed to display respect for the code of Christian dutiful leadership which they were preaching in opposition to the criticisms of the middle classes and the ideas of the French Revolution. In the Queen's own case the sense that aristocracy had to behave if it was to survive was deeply held and it contributed to her frustration at the loose morals and lack of seriousness displayed by her eldest son. But Edward VII's love of opulence, his concern for sparkling company and his relative lack of snobbery played a part in the transition from aristocracy to plutocracy in the English upper classes.

London, St. Petersburg and Berlin each had its aristocratic quarter. By 1900 the aristocracy had been moving steadily westwards in London for centuries, away from the city, industry, the port and the railway stations, away from grime and the poorest neighbourhoods, and towards the parks and the relatively fresh air of the West End. In the case of Berlin, as befitted a city which had been transformed from provincial town to world metropolis between 1850 and 1900, the Prussian aristocracy's move to the Tiergarten district was much more recent. In 1850 the district contained a few factories and pubs but it had 'a thoroughly rural, un-citified air'. By 1900 the Tiergarten was the fashionable residential area, abounding with 'shady drives and rides, more or less thronged during the season by the rank and fashion of Berlin'. For St. Petersburg, when revolution came, the most aristocratic part of the city was still the central district between the Winter Palace and the Tauride Gardens, but things were changing. According to *Stolitsa i Usad'ba*, this area, whose heartland lay around Sergeevskaya, Furstatskaya and Mokhovaya streets, was losing its chic and Kamenny Ostrov to the north, where space and fresh air was available and splendid new mansions were being constructed, was shortly to replace it.[28]

Within its fashionable enclaves the aristocracy ate, drank and made love. It visited the opera and the theatre, sometimes indulging in amateur theatricals itself. It read books, but more time was spent in playing cards, visiting one's peers and, above all, gossiping. Capital-city aristocratic society was, after all, a village, many of whose inhabitants were close relations and most of whom had at least a nodding acquaintance with one another since childhood. It had a village's self-absorption and interest in the affairs of one's neighbour. The aristocratic village, however, combined this with an exaggerated idea of its own importance. Its was to be the heroic part on the world's stage, with lesser mortals largely confined to subsidiary or non-speaking roles. Living in close proximity, with women often leading lives of considerable leisure, purposelessness and boredom, aristocratic society was a perfect breeding ground for gossip.

According to Captain Gronow, London society was much less drunken by the 1850s than had been the case two generations before: 'If the good society of 1815 could appear before their more moderate descendants in the state they were generally reduced to after dinner, the moderns would pronounce their ancestors fit for nothing but bed'. Massive drinking remained, however, a *rite de passage* for young officers, particularly in Russia in the most expensive Guards cavalry regiments. Food grew more complicated over the decades and the dividing line between aristocracy and gentry might often be defined according to whether or not a nobleman employed an expensive French chef. Russian aristocrats, always much influenced by the efforts of French high culture, seldom failed here, but Gronow describes the 'wonderfully solid, hot, and stimulating' meals of the English society of his youth, blessed by the 'ever-popular boiled potato', simple meats and 'very abortive attempts at continental cookery'. He emigrated to Paris in part, one may suspect, to please his stomach. It remained to that Parisian *manqué*, Edward VII, to spearhead England's introduction to the subtler arts of cookery, a process pursued by the prince with such erudite gluttony that he earned the title 'tum-tum'. Prussian royalty, for better or worse, lacked such a model and in 1880 the most exclusive club in Berlin was still dominated by 'respectable old Conservative country gentlemen' who 'demand that the Casino should be a genuine German institution, without the corrupting alloy of French cooking'.[29]

In Gronow's view, English women in the Regency era were no more virtuous than their French counterparts, but less inclined to hide their infidelities. A major cause of the latter was that their 'husbands spent their days in the hunting fields, or were entirely occupied with politics'. In the same era, Count Sollohub records, with some exaggeration, that in 'the High Society of Petersburg . . . only the rare person was actually the son of his nominal father', a fact which Sollohub, a Russian patriot, rather obscurely links to the point that 'some ladies were wholly unable to speak Russian'. Two generations later 'Count Vasili' had tactfully to warn the young aristocratic attaché to Berlin not to flirt with the beautiful daughters of the Jewish bourgeoisie for 'their manners are not those of the *grande monde* and . . . their principles . . . are solidly established'.[30]

Loose sexual morality in aristocratic circles is scarcely surprising. One is, after all, dealing with a class with plentiful leisure, for whom amusement was often life's major occupation. Marriages were made with at least one eye on their social and financial acceptability, while Christian ethics and publicly proclaimed sexual standards, though passionately believed in by some aristocrats, were regarded by others as necessary for the lower orders rather than as binding on themselves. The requirements of social order might increasingly demand that a veil be spread over infidelity lest what was spoken in the clubs might be printed in the press, but the upper class as a whole did not in general require more than this of its members.

Generalisations about classes or even families are, however, not easily sustained in this sphere. Charlotta Lieven, for instance, almost turned down the plum position of governess to the imperial children because of disapproval of the moral tone of Catherine II's Court. Her daughter-in-law was Dorothea, ambassadress in London, mistress of Metternich and Guizot and many others besides. Charlotta's granddaughter, Princess Marie Lieven, was also a society hostess in London though of a very different sort from her aunt Dorothea. Having abandoned Russia for political reasons she became the great patroness of German radicals fleeing after the 1848 revolution. According to one of her protegés, who later became a US senator, her moral character was 'perfectly spotless and unassailable' and 'for many of the refugees she was really a good fairy'. The next female generation would have regarded Dorothea Lieven's sexual escapades with as much distaste as their aunt Marie's political radicalism. They devoted their considerable energies to religion, and above all to rescuing prostitutes. The three daughters of Alexander II's Lord Chamberlain were never presented at Court because their mother believed that Court society was both a den of iniquity and a prime location for contracting venereal disease.[31]

At the beginning of the nineteenth century, small-town spas represented a half-way house between aristocratic life in the capitals and rural life-styles. In England, Bath was the most famous spa, though the Prince Regent made Brighton fashionable too. On the continent, French spas outnumbered German ones but the latter were more cosmopolitan and grander, with Carlsbad and Baden-Baden, the haunts of emperors and kings, in the lead. A British observer in the 1840s commented that in the summer months 'all that is distinguished in Germany' was to be found at the spas, where life was sociable but relaxed, etiquette was much reduced and many entertainments were to be found: 'State, and ceremony, and titled hauteur are in a great degree thrown aside in the easy intercourse of the bathing place'. Seeking to explain the extraordinary hold that the spas possessed in Germany, Murray's guide explained this in part by the absence in that country either of one great unequivocally capital city or of an English-style country-house culture. Without the relaxation or sporting habits of the latter or the universal meeting ground provided by the former, the Germans turned to the spa as a substitute.[32]

During the nineteenth century the leading German spas grew greatly in scale and comfort. Opulent hotels sprang up: by the 1860s there were twelve grand hotels in Baden-Baden alone, the most luxurious of all being the famous Cour de Bade. Great efforts were made to entertain visitors. A racecourse was built at Iffezheim near Baden-Baden so visiting aristocrats could indulge in their favourite pursuits, and great shoots were arranged in the neighbourhood. Berlioz conducted numerous concerts at Baden-Baden in the 1860s to an ever more cosmopolitan audience of the aristocratic and the rich. From the 1840s, Russian aristocrats began to flock to the great German resorts in large numbers, mingling there with their central and western European peers.[33]

The increasing sophistication and cosmopolitan air of the leading German spas was only possible because of the railway, which allowed the transportation, upkeep and entertainment of summer visitors on a hitherto unprecedented scale. Modern communications had other major effects on aristocratic life-styles. In England the gentleman resident in London could put his horse on the train and take a day off to hunt in the shires. The country house weekend, much beloved of the Edwardians, became a possibility. Horse-racing had been an English aristocratic pursuit since the seventeenth century, but the railway transformed it. Now huge crowds, which from the 1870s began to pay entrance fees, could attend the races, revelling in the performance of sleek race-horses generally owned by aristocrats. Intelligent peers could equate the thrill of winning the Derby with that of becoming prime minister. Racing became, like most other nineteenth-century activities, more organised over the decades and its ruling board, the Jockey Club, overwhelmingly aristocratic in membership, gave the traditional upper classes a new and potentially popular role. The sight of the nobleman leading his winning horse into the enclosure at the Derby amidst the crowd's plaudits could be seen, according to taste, as a new role and legitimacy for aristocracy in the modern age, or alternatively as the marginalisation, trivialisation and vulgarisation of what had been a ruling class. Certainly the physical drawing together of town and country made its mark on more than lifestyles. If the English public school helped to fuse the values of landed, professional and business elites through the creation of a single gentlemanly, sporting type, the railway and later the motor car allowed this man the physical possibility of combining city work with gentlemanly and sporting rural pursuits.[34]

For the first time in the history of Europe's nobility the English aristocracy became a model for others to follow, not only in politics or agricultural improvement but also in style and habits of leisure. The English country house combined opulence and comfort. Its owner was a relatively cultured and very self-assured man of the world but he was also deeply rooted in rural society, enjoying a deference in his locality which clothed him in dignity and ensured him political influence at Westminster. He bred the finest horses and trained the best hunting dogs in Europe. His fox hunts were trials of riding skill and courage which put the organised *battues* of animals by continental aristocrats in the shade as regards both excitement and risk. Throughout Europe the boredom, monotony and isolation of rural life had always oppressed some aristocrats and driven them towards the cities. In the past this had been true even in England: 'from the sixteenth century onwards the upper classes were spending more and more time in London ... Even when landowners were in the country they were often longing to get out of it'. By the nineteenth century, however, better communications, the development of rural sports and a sense that aristocracy, challenged in the cities, must fall back upon its country base had combined to reverse this trend. The English rural leisured class seemed to offer its European peers the answer to aristocracy's need for a role and a style with which to confront the modern world.[35]

Copying the English, however, had many difficulties, some of them severely practical. English style and habits were rooted in affluence: 'By 1800 English horses were the best in the world' but an English hunter, 'a horse that would gallop over distance and jump', might cost hundreds of guineas. Great English magnates who supported entire packs of hounds and horses, paid thousands of pounds annually for their upkeep, compensation to farmers for damage, and the other costs of the hunt.[36]

Sport on this scale – indeed the whole English country-house lifestyle – was well beyond the reach of most nineteenth-century Prussian nobles. Of the old Hohenzollern provinces, East Prussia had a handful of families – Dohnas, Dönhoffs, Lehndorffs, Eulenbergs – whose country houses rivalled those of the English nobility though even there one would look in vain for a Chatsworth, Alnwick or Woburn. The historian of country life and architecture in Mark Brandenburg comments that 'in general people didn't want to build *chateaux* or grandiose houses. They were too poor for this but also too dry, sober and uncivilised. Most manor houses in the Mark are relatively small buildings'. If Brandenburg nobles took enthusiastically to English gardens from the late eighteenth century, quickly destroying all traces of the old formal gardens, this 'didn't so much reflect the impact of Rousseauan ideas, or that Romanticism and sentimentality had gained the upper hand – in the countryside people were not much emasculated by such ideas – in many cases the simple cause was that maintaining the new lay-out seemed to cost less money'.[37]

The Brandenburg nobleman who wished to copy English ways needed to be much richer than most of his peers and yet to remain satisfied with the lifestyle of the British county family rather than of a magnate. Karl von Hertefeld, the wealthy scion of an old noble family who owned the fine house, library, park and estate of Liebenberg, was a model Prussian Anglophile. As a boy, Hertefeld had the typical rural noble's passion for hounds and horses. His Anglophilia stemmed from an extended visit to Britain in 1814, though it may have been encouraged by service alongside English regiments at the Battle of Waterloo. This Anglophilia took many forms, among them a great concern for agricultural improvement and liberal – conservative political views. Above all, however, Hertefeld became a passionate supporter of English-style hunting and horse-racing. He bred racehorses and, together with friends, established the Berlin racecourse. He rented the extra forests and heaths around his estate in order to indulge his hunting passion. After 1848 he was forced to abandon hunting in the English style, partly because his attention was now diverted to another English novelty, namely parliamentary politics, in which he played an active role, ultimately securing a seat in the Prussian House of Lords (*Herrenhaus*). Hertefeld died childless in 1867 and his estate went to his great-nephew, Count Phillipp zu Eulenberg. Under the latter's son, the last Kaiser's closest friend, Liebenberg became William II's favourite Brandenburg country estate.[38]

Copying English aristocratic life-styles might, however, require more than money, as the example of fox-hunting illustrates. The noble fox-hunter needed thousands of acres of flat land over which he and his peers could charge at top speed, flattening anything in their path. It also required foxes, whose lairs had therefore to be protected by game laws or social pressure, against farmers anxious to exterminate predators. With most English land in aristocratic hands and tenants deferential, compensated and sometimes enthusiastic hunters themselves, these conditions could be met, at least until the 1880s. On the continent, where peasant arable farming generally predominated, things were rather different. Efforts to hunt foxes in native style by the English expatriate community in northern France led to confrontations with peasants and police. Russian and German peasants were also unlikely, by the second half of the nineteenth century, to watch silently as their crops were trampled by noble huntsmen, and, like the French, by then they had the law on their side.

In Russia, according to the scandalised observation of one English visitor, 'no game-laws have ever as yet been enacted', though the shortage of game even by 1800 proved to the Englishman's view that this was a pressing necessity. 'It is never taken amiss,' commented William Tooke with surprise in 1799, 'when a sportsman with his friends, attendants and hounds, traverses his domains without first obtaining permission of the owner. Some few landlords forbid their boors to carry a gun; but this prohibition only produces a quite contrary effect, and the mischief clandestinely done is so much the greater'.[39]

Murray's guide-book even in 1865 warned English sportsmen not to expect large bags from *battue*-shooting in Russia since game was relatively scarce, especially near St. Petersburg. 'The winter shooting comprises bear, wolf, elk and lynx . . . Wolves are shot by hunting with dogs, by an ordinary battue, and sometimes by riding down; but this requires a peculiar condition of the snow, as well as rideable ground'. Even mounted hunting in Russia was seldom an English-style affair with organised packs and smart uniforms all paid for out of aristocratic pockets. To find such phenomena in Russia, especially by the twentieth century, one generally needed to look at rarities such as the hunts of the Grand Duke Nikolai Nikolaievich, or of the Officers Cavalry School – in other words, to members of the imperial family or to institutions.[40]

The only exception to this rule in the Russian Empire was the Baltic Provinces whose ethnically German landowners still owned large packs and staged English-style hunts, though by the twentieth century – as was indeed by then the case in England – a pack's upkeep was seldom the responsibility of a single aristocrat. *Stolitsa i Usad'ba* explained the Baltic gentry's unique ability to maintain old hunting traditions partly by the fact that, unlike their Russian peers, Baltic nobles lived on their estates all the year round. In addition, however, local law in the thoroughly feudal Baltic provinces still only gave owners of noble estates (*Rittergüter*) the right to hunt with dogs.[41]

In Germany proper the aristocracy conducted a very determined rearguard action to protect its hunting rights. Helmut von Gerlach writes of the Junkers that 'one cannot understand the conservative big landowners unless one realises that hunting took pride of place in their lives'. From spring to winter various animals were hunted with passionate seriousness. Noble hunting rights were widely detested by the rural population, partly because they included the peasants' obligation to provide beaters and other forms of labour to support the noble huntsmen. Still worse was the damage done to crops and cattle by wild beasts, against which the peasantry was traditionally forbidden not only to use weapons but even to build adequate defences to protect its own fields and animals. The French Revolution's abolition of hunting rights increased the tensions over this issue in the German countryside, and these burst forth in 1848. Nobles proved far more stubborn in the defence of hunting rights than over many other dues and services, whose redemption they often accepted without much struggle if compensation was adequate. This recalcitrance owed something to the fact that hunting was for some nobles the greatest enjoyment and time-filler in rural life. It was also an age-old and much regarded noble skill.

But H. W. Eckhardt is probably right in seeing here an element of defensive group psychology of a class which felt itself increasingly redundant and under attack and therefore sought to maintain inviolate from the modern world at least one traditional sphere of life which aristocracy had always monopolised and in which it remained pre-eminent.[42]

In 1848–50 the aristocracy largely lost the battle. In Prussia, Bavaria and some other states noble hunting rights were abolished for ever and without compensation. In Hanover, Saxony, Baden and Brunswick they were made redeemable. In 1848 a peasant war of extermination against wild animals took place and subsequently the remaining compact noble properties were unable to sustain anything like the previous level of wild animals. Adam Schwappach wrote in 1883 that 'with the change in the hunting laws, the diminution of game and the abolition of hunting labour services, there came a major change in the old methods of hunting. The former large-scale hunting and coursing with hounds, which had been the pride of the old hunt, has almost completely disappeared, with only a few exceptions which are becoming ever more rare.[43]

In its place came the shoot, which became the greatest rural pastime of European aristocracy by 1914 – indeed for some aristocrats something close to an obsession. *Battue* shooting required far less skill and courage than the fox-hunt or the pursuit on foot of big game. Modern firearms and cartridges, not to mention the artificial rearing of birds, allowed massive bags to be made which were counted with an obsessive competitiveness that earlier aristocratic generations had reserved for more important matters. Perhaps most unpleasant was the hunting of very rare wild animals, such as the Silesian auroch, or even of exotic beasts especially purchased from zoos and reserved for the guns of the most distinguished participants in a shoot. The junior aide-de-camp almost assaulted by a gamekeeper in 1913 for raising his gun towards – so he claimed – a kangaroo reserved for royal guests during entertainments surrounding the wedding of the Kaiser's daughter, witnessed the ultimate weird mingling of aristocratic hunting obsessions and modern transport and ballistic technology.[44]

Of all sections of the European aristocracy it was the Austrian high nobility who most successfully adopted English customs. In part this was simply because they came closest to matching English wealth. Perhaps too this exceptionally inter-bred, caste-conscious and narrow elite found it particularly easy to find a satisfying refuge from modernity in the world of the horse, ultra-elegant and exclusive social gatherings, and the unintellectual gentlemanly pursuit of leisure. The Liechtenstein and Schwarzenberg heirs, both of whom succeeded their fathers in the 1830s, had made long visits to England in early manhood and returned with many lessons learned. Leadership in agriculture, elegance and rural society seemed to promise a continuing role to noblemen displaced from government by the State and its officials. Anti-centralist and bureaucratic instincts fed greedily on the Romantic neo-feudalism of Sir Walter Scott, adored, for instance, by Princess Eleonore Schwarzenberg. The Liechtensteins' romantic gesture of buying back their ancestral principality in 1807 and the growing popularity of the 'natural' English garden were part of this trend. Dinner, usually commencing at 2 p.m. in the century's early years, was pushed further and further back in deference to English custom. The Schwarzenbergs even rebuilt Schloss Frauenberg in neo-Tudor style between 1840 and 1857. Nowhere, however, did Anglomania go further than in the worship of horses. The Jockey Club became 'the social centre of gravity of the nobility'. Prince Karl II Schwarzenberg spent a fortune on his racing stables. Prince Alois II Liechtenstein had a passion for English-style hunting. His stables, presided over by an Englishman, absorbed between 3 per cent and 5 per cent of his income. Hans Kudlich commented that Prince Liechtenstein 'imitated the high life of the old English aristocracy and sought to introduce its stiff style, its manners, horses, races, carriages and servants into the Austrian high nobility'.[45]

The Russian aristocracy also sometimes imitated the English, though less wholeheartedly than was the case in Austria. According to D. W. Wallace, Victorian England's greatest expert on Russia, only the St. Petersburg aristocratic elite adopted the cool, reserved exclusiveness of their English peers, in so doing going flatly contrary to the normal manners and instincts of Russian educated society. The dominant style of Russian country-house building remained 'empire' throughout the nineteenth century, though a Russian neo-medieval style did have its advocates, for all the gloomy half-light it shed in the house's interior. The English garden, on the other hand, patronised enthusiastically by Catherine II, had become popular by 1800. Manly sports were gaining an increasing hold on the aristocracy by 1914; Russia's tennis champion, for instance, was

Count Sumarokov-Elston. The only Russian school, however, even faintly to echo the English public schools' sports mania was the empire's most aristocratic civilian educational institution, namely the Alexander Lycée. Horse-breeding and racing, on the other hand, were widespread and long established. The first serious racing began in Moscow in 1785, a major patron being the empire's leading breeder, one of the counts Orlov. In the top ranks of the Russian aristocracy, ability to judge horse-flesh and secure huge shooting bags was as highly esteemed as anywhere else in late Victorian and Edwardian Europe. So too, by 1914, was the English nanny.[46]

Given Russian traditions, however, to turn its aristocracy into an English-style rural elite was exceptionally difficult. For centuries Russia's greatest nobles had formed a Court aristocracy. The Tsars had wished it so. Economic backwardness, poor communications and divided inheritance made the private accumulation of great wealth by estate-management impossible: imperial favour was necessary if magnate families were to sustain an aristocratic lifestyle. As the empire expanded in the seventeenth and eighteenth centuries the rewards handed out by the monarchs to Court families grew dizzyingly. But the westernisation of the aristocracy in the eighteenth century added a further cultural dimension to their desire to live in the capital city rather than sink in some rural backwoods hundreds, if not thousands, of kilometres from civilisation.

F. F. Vigel's recollections of late-eighteenth and early-nineteenth-century magnates forced to live on their rural estates illustrate graphically their isolation and alienation from their surroundings. Neither Prince S. F. Golitsyn nor Prince A. B. Kurakin wished to live in the countryside: both had fallen into imperial disfavour. Golitsyn in the Ukraine and Kurakin on the Saratov – Penza border, if not on the empire's frontiers, were nevertheless far from the centres of noble culture in the provinces around Moscow. The natural surroundings of the Golitsyn estate were beautiful, but from the owners' point of view they were living in a near desert. The local petty nobility, far their inferiors both socially and culturally, they regarded with scorn, but their nearest peers were scores of kilometres away. In this quite recently acquired region where the family had only been in residence for one year, the wooden house was neither palatial nor well-built and the gardens were only just being laid out. Prince Golitsyn passed whole days hunting hares, his position being not much dissimilar to that of an English peer exiled to a remoter American province in the 1760s. Prince Kurakin, on the other hand, living in a longer-settled area, adopted the life-style of a Polish magnate. Ensconced on his splendid estate of Nadezhdino he lived amidst strict etiquette in semi-regal style. A horde of local petty nobles swarmed to his 'court', serving him as chamberlains, stewards, secretaries and administrators. Kurakin, who adored Queen Marie Antoinette, amused himself by building and dedicating a church to her in his rural wilderness.[47]

In the more central provinces by the first half of the nineteenth century the cultured nobleman would have been far less isolated than Golitsyn or Kurakin. Hauxthausen describes the houses and life-styles of many cultured noblemen in the 1840s, and memoirs from this period emphasise the point that many provinces had quite a number of well-educated, quite wealthy and even relatively cosmopolitan landed families resident in the reign of Nicholas I. It was from this sphere, typically enough in the rich Black Earth provinces, that the leading Slavophile families came, for instance. Even in non-Black Earth Nizhniy Novgorod one could find, to take a not wholly untypical example, A. D. Ulibishev, whose estate was roughly thirty miles from the town. Like most of his peers, Ulibishev had served in the government for a number of years before retiring to his estate, whose library had a large collection of books on drama, philosophy, history and music. Ulibishev had his own small orchestra and also a circle of local landowner friends 'who were good and enthusiastic amateur musicians'. The years between 1812 and 1861 were the great era of Russian country house building; this was also the period when the Russian aristocracy was culturally most exciting and prolific. The cultured country house was still an oasis in the peasant desert and a contrast to the many philistine noble houses in the area, but the number of these oases was no longer small and the quality of their culture was often very high indeed.[48]

This culture grew thinner the further north or south one pro-gressed. In the far south, in provinces such as Kherson, Ekaterinos-lav, or northern Tauride, country houses were always few and far between. V. N. Kokovtsov was the nephew of the Marshal of the nobility of Novgorod province, in the infertile north-western region. His was an 1840s childhood in which apples were a luxury and cultured neighbours very few and far between. After 1861 cultured noble outposts in such regions became ever rarer and the country houses even of the richer central provinces were thinned out. On the other hand, the coming of the railway drastically reduced the isolation of rural life and the arrival of the *zemstvo* provided scope for noble participation in elected local self-government. A century after Prince A. B. Kurakin had lived in splendid isolation in the Penza-Saratov wilderness, Prince A. D. Obolensky could live a cultured life on his estate in the same region, helping as noble Marshal to turn Penza into a local centre of musical excellence, participating energetically in the *zemstvo*, and yet also able to reach St. Petersburg within a day in order to play his part in governmental committees and ultimately in the State Council, the upper house of Russia's legislature after 1905.[49]

8. Education and Culture

In education as in almost everything else, the English aristocracy was much more homogeneous than its German or Russian equivalent. In the eighteenth century a debate existed between the relative merits of a domestic and public school education. The advocates of the public school won, stressing above all that future rulers had to be brought up in a tougher and more sociable environment than the sheltered and isolated world of the young aristocrat tutored at home. Among eighteenth-century peers educated before 1700, 16.2 per cent had attended Eton, Westminster, Winchester or Harrow, but of those born after 1740 the proportion had leaped to 72.2 per cent, with Eton's pre-eminence already very clear. The nineteenth century confirmed this trend. By 1900 it was a rare peer who had not attended a leading public school, and Eton's position as educator of the aristocratic elite was unassailable. Moreover the public schools had become more homogeneous in their values and organisation during the Victorian era and were also much more systematic and effective in their control over boys' lives. No one knowledgeable about the English upper classes doubted the significance of the public school stamp on a man's personality and values. The Clarendon Commission, set up in the 1860s to investigate and to some extent reform the public schools, believed that the latter 'have had perhaps the largest share in moulding the character of an English gentleman'. Not surprisingly, 'the style and bearing of the governing elite was highly uniform'.[1]

A few basic factors shaped the schools' character. As boarding schools they were to some extent closed worlds, whose purpose was to mould not just the intellect but also the personalities, values and habits of the boys. Although, at least until the 1860s, most of the leading schools had contingents of poor scholars, the latter were thoroughly despised by the majority of boys and masters alike and played no part in determining the schools' values. They were removed in the 1860s thanks to the Clarendon Commission, which advocated social homogeneity among boys and achieved it by encouraging examinations for scholars which none but children of the elite could hope to pass. The leading public schools were defended with great determination by upper-class opinion. Their funds came largely from fees paid by wealthy parents, very many of whom were themselves Old Boys. This, combined with the fact that the leading schools were ancient foundations largely independent of any government control, ensured that the public schools were traditionalist to a degree but susceptible to shifting currents in upper class, and to an increasing degree, upper-middle class opinion. These currents they both shaped and reflected. From the tough, hedonist but genuinely freedom-loving Regency era the public schools passed into the Evangelical world of Thomas Arnold and thence to the rather stultifying conformism of the late Victorian period of organised games and empire worship.

Though public school values changed to some extent during the century it was always the case that 'the intellectual side of school life was relatively less interesting to most Englishmen than the moral'. Thomas Arnold, headmaster of Rugby from 1828 to 1842 and the major single influence on the Victorian public school, was a great moralist, a fine educator, not too much of a scholar and almost immune to sensual or aesthetic values. Edmund Warre, headmaster of Eton from 1884 to 1905, was not even much of a moralist or spiritual adviser in the Arnoldian sense. 'Boyishly enthusiastic' and wholly unintellectual, what counted for Warre were honesty, loyalty and courage. Organised games-playing bred all three virtues, in Warre's opinion: 'he thus made games frankly the centre of Eton life with the result that they dominated or crowded out all other activity'. Warre would not have disagreed with Tom Brown's father, who cared only that his son emerge from his public school 'a brave, helpful, truth-telling Englishman, and a gentleman, and a Christian'. The Clarendon Commission conceded that the intellectual attainments of the average public schoolboy could not 'by any stretch of indulgence be deemed satisfactory' but it too attached greater significance to the vital part played by the schools in forming the character of the British elite. 'It is not easy to estimate the degree in which the English people are indebted to these schools for the qualities on which they pique themselves most – for their capacity to govern others and control themselves, their aptitude for combining freedom with order, their public spirit, their vigour and manliness of character, their strong but not slavish respect for public opinion, their love of healthy sports and exercise'.[2]

Traditionally the public schools had allowed boys a great degree of freedom to run their own lives. If the very high ratio of boys to masters often made this inevitable before the 1830s, it was also something on which the British elite had always prided itself, contrasting its own independent and libertarian values to those of continental despotism. The antithesis of the public school was taken to be that old bogeyman, the Jesuit college. Here the authorities exercised, so it was said, strict and close control over the thoughts and words of their charges, on whom they spied, seeking to capture their hearts and minds, and thenceforth to manipulate the guilt-ridden subjects whose immature and defenceless persons they had conquered in childhood and adolescence. In contrast, the freedom-loving Englishman allowed boys room to breathe, thereby permitting the development of tough, self-reliant personalities. In the younger boys, conceit was banished by their seniors, while older boys learned the responsibilities of leadership in a community which checked arbitrary power through veneration of institutional traditions, the aristocratic schoolboy's respect for honour and courage, and the power of peer-group opinion. The school was, in other words, aristocratic Georgian society in miniature. It was a tough and rather anarchical world in which the possibility of wholesale chaos was partly checked by a brutal and repressive legal order. The weakling went to the wall but the eccentric tough enough to protect himself, the Byron, could flourish, was allowed the freedom at school to educate himself, and was even admired. For the rough and tumble of Georgian politics or the still greater test of the battlefield – and politics and war were aristocracy's major functions – the public school was not a bad training.

Thomas Arnold led the early Victorian effort to Christianise the public schools. He partly succeeded because his effort reflected changing values in upper-class society, which were symbolised in the transition from the Regency court to that of Victoria and Albert.

The power of his personality, of his religious belief and of his commitment was also vital. His basic technique was to win the older boys' sympathy and support and to use his prefects' example and power to spread his values throughout Rugby, exploiting in the process the deference felt by younger boys towards their seniors and the loyalty to the school to which the prefects could make effective appeal. Arnold did much to close the gap between masters and boys which had prevailed in the Georgian boarding school, uniting both sides in support of common values and endeavours. Interestingly, his principles found their most tenacious opposition in aristocratic Eton. The school's social prestige made it confident of its ability to hold out against 'progressive thinking'. Arnold's moralism, not to mention his glorification of the work ethic, often had little appeal to boys whose wealth guaranteed them against any need for employment and whose arrogance rebelled against a middle-class outsider influencing the hallowed privileges and customs of their school.

The Evangelical consensus on which Arnold's success was based weakened in the second half of the nineteenth century. Loyalty to school as an embodiment of religious and moral values, Arnold's ideal, became transformed into loyalty for its own sake to the community's traditions, ways and values. A military and imperialist spirit reigned, and nowhere more so than at Warre's Eton. This was a training ground for conformist, self-sacrificing patriotism – for a belief in 'my country right or wrong' tempered by the comfortable, uncritical instinct that one's own community could hardly wander too far from righteousness. E. C. Mack describes the virtues of the late-Victorian public schoolboy as 'good manners, stoicism, truthfulness and class loyalty'. Alfred Lyttelton believed that the schools created 'a sense of loyalty, of esprit de corps, a reverence derived from inspiring surroundings, an appreciation of corporate action, self-reliance, and a proper instinct for honourable dealing and for consideration of their fellows'. For all this, however, a price was paid. Comparing public school photographs of the mid-Victorian and Edwardian eras, Arthur Ponsonby noted the increased external smartness and above all the uniformity. 'And even the faces!,' he wrote, 'you can hardly tell one from another . . . it is, without doubt, an outward and visible sign not only of the love of the appearance of smartness but of the stereotyping and conventionalising effect of our modern educational system.'[3]

The failings of the late Victorian public school were to a great extent those of the rather smug elite of the world's largest empire at the seeming pinnacle of its power. They also, however, reflected the weakness of the academic education in most public schools throughout the nineteenth century. Though intellect was always more highly regarded at Winchester than at Eton or Harrow, most public schoolboys learned neither much useful knowledge nor the ability to think critically. Classics dominated the curriculum in 1815 and were still overwhelmingly pre-eminent a century later: 'In 1884 Eton employed twenty-eight classics masters, six mathematics masters, no modern language teachers, no scientists and one historian.' The position of classics was a pale reflection of Renaissance humanism and of the sense that Greece and Rome, together with Christianity, were the pillars of European civilisation.[4]

A minority of boys derived from their classical studies an admiration for Athens and for the cold, stoical, public-spirited qualities of the Roman ruling class, in Thomas Arnold's rather naïve judgement, men 'whose distinguishing quality was their love of institutions and order, and their reverence for law'. For this minority, classical lessons at public school were a mere introduction to the pursuit of 'Greats' at Oxford, easily the most prestigious course of university studies for Britain's Victorian ruling class. Plato and Aristotle legitimised the rule of elites and saw the art of politics as one of man's highest callings. This made them popular with England's ruling class, which found it easy to associate England and Athens, the British Empire and Rome. To a degree unequalled in Europe, government and politics had always been the *métier* of England's aristocracy, and with an empire now to be ruled as well there was plenty of room for middle-class recruits to join the ranks of would-be Platonic Guardians. A common belief in England's Empire as a second Rome helped to unite aristocratic and middle-class products of Oxford. In Richard Symonds's view, 'for a number of Oxford men' of the late Victorian era 'the stoicism of the classics and the mysticism of an Imperial faith were to replace the lost faith in Christianity'.[5]

If something of this filtered down even to the dimmest of public schoolboys, it is unlikely that this owed much to the way classics were drummed into adolescent heads at school. Most schoolboys were far too entangled in the undergrowth of Latin grammar to learn any lessons from the ideas of Plato, Aristotle or Thucydides.

Most public schools concentrated on drumming classical grammar and composition into boys' heads, in general making minimum effort, save with a minority of scholars, to convey a sense of ancient literature, society or history. Education's purpose was largely seen as teaching habits of memory, industry, systematic thinking and painstaking attention to detail. It was well understood that these qualities did not come naturally but, especially in the first half of the century, education's role was seen as disciplining and conquering human nature rather than, in the style of Rousseau, appealing to it. Though 'modern' subjects were increasingly taught after the Clarendon Commission's recommendations in the 1860s, the attempt to combine them with a still mostly classical curriculum jammed up the timetable and gave even intelligent pupils too little time to think. Since methods of teaching classics barely changed, games-playing was becoming an obsession, and even in 1906, 'our English secondary schools are . . . much more tolerant of cheerful and healthy-minded ignorance' than was the case abroad, the unthinking and complacent philistinism of most public schoolboys is scarcely remarkable. Arthur Ponsonby quite rightly stressed the uselessness of dry, badly taught classics from which no boy could grasp that Greek verse was actually poetry or see the remotest connection between what he was studying and the values and problems of his own era. In addition, history, unwanted for university examinations, was barely taught, while 'no Public Schoolboy of my time who had not been abroad could speak decent French'.[6]

Whereas in England the Catholic aristocracy was small and relatively unimportant, in Germany the confessional division was vital. On the whole the Catholic church gained in strength as a result of the events of 1789–1815. Persecution by the revolutionaries created martyrs. The Vendée became the great legend of conservative story-tellers, its armies filled with Catholic peasants led by local aristocrats and inspired by the clergy. Conservatives everywhere saw the roots of revolutionary ideology in the Enlightenment's worship of individualism and rationalism. It was not difficult to trace these back to the Reformation's revolt against ecclesiastical authority. The eighteenth-century German Lutheran church had, on the whole, shared the Enlightenment's rationalist faith, whereas the Catholic church had been a key enemy of Enlightenment and Revolution alike. Counter-revolutionary theorists looked back to the corporate and hierarchical society of the Middle Ages. For those who loathed the egoism and materialism which, in their view, liberalism unleashed, the church's defence of family and community solidarity was very attractive. So too was its belief in an absolute God-given order and moral values whose justification lay outside this world and beyond the grasp of reason. Even Protestant conservative thinkers praised many aspects of Catholicism and some (Carl Ludwig Haller in Germany and John Henry Newman in England, for instance) converted to the Roman religion.

If such trends existed within German Protestantism, it is scarcely surprising that most Catholic aristocrats should have been strengthened in their faith by the events of 1789 to 1815, not to mention the oppression to which Catholics were subject in the nineteenth century by the increasingly dominant Protestant states and communities in Germany. Commitment to the church differed from family to family, however, even indeed from individual to individual. So too did the willingness of Catholic German aristocrats to swallow the full range of anti-liberal papal pronouncements, up to and including Pius IX's Syllabus of Errors and doctrine of infallibility. Among the high nobility in particular, mixed marriages were quite frequent and often resulted in sons following their fathers' religion and daughters that of their mother. Sharp confessional antagonism was scarcely possible in such circumstances and loyalty to the Catholic church might retain much of the eighteenth-century combination of family tradition and a rational respect for the moral principles that underlay the social order.

This was, for instance, very much the attitude of Karl Egon II Fürstenberg, a free-thinker and mason born in the Age of Enlightenment and married to a Protestant. The prince had a great interest in science, technology and education. He was determined that his heir have the best schooling possible, to which end he engaged a Protestant governor for the boy and later despatched him to Heidelberg University for serious historical and legal studies. It was precisely family tradition and a sense that his religion bound him to his former subjects and gave him legitimacy in local eyes that kept Karl Egon II loyal to the church. His son, though himself married to a Protestant, was actually a much more enthusiastic Catholic than his father, but Karl Egon III numbered among his closest lifelong friends Prince Chlodwig zu Hohenlohe-Schillingfürst, the future imperial chancellor and the doyen of Catholic liberals, who was the most prominent of that small band of Catholic great aristocrats who sided with the Prussian liberal state even during the Kulturkampf.[7]

Hohenlohe was, however, exceptional, the great majority of Catholic aristocrats firmly disapproving of liberal policies, which in their view not only oppressed their own community but also were destructive of all political and moral order. Of all sections of the Catholic aristocracy, the Westphalians were probably the most consistent in their defence of conservative religious principles. Burghard von Schorlemer-Alst, admittedly not the most unbiased of observers, commented in 1866 that 'the Catholic nobility of Westphalia has, more loyally than the nobility of any other land, stood true to its church'.

In comparison to the Hohenlohes and Fürstenbergs, the Westphalian *Stiftsadel* was less grand and more provincial. The Munster nobility, for instance, married almost exclusively within its own narrow circle. In addition, in these former ecclesiastical territories the nobility's fate had always been very closely linked to that of the church. In Heinz Reif's view the Munster nobility responded to secularisation and the pressure of the Prussian liberal state by breathing new life into their Catholic commitment. In the eighteenth century many nobles had lived off ecclesiastical benefices but few had a deep or emotional religious faith. In the nineteenth century this changed and the church was often served selflessly and with great conviction, as were the charitable causes it sponsored. Though this faith and service was undoubtedly sincere, it is also true that Catholicism benefited the Westphalian aristocracy in many ways. Family solidarity, vital if the system of primogeniture was to be maintained, was threatened in the revolutionary era by the spirit of individualism spreading among younger sons and daughters. The impact of renewed Catholicism, linked to much deeper and more emotional relationships between parents and children, was to reverse this threat and cement family loyalty. In addition, the church provided the nobility with solid institutional support and a powerful anti-liberal ideology, whose aid helped the aristocracy partially to restore their position of leadership among the local Catholic population on the basis of a shared dislike of many aspects of Prussian statist liberalism.

As part of the process of preserving Catholic and family loyalty from the poisonous reach of liberalism and the Prussian state, the Westphalian and Rhenish nobility created the Bedburg Ritterakademie, where their sons could be provided with an academic education to match that of a Prussian gymnasium in an all-noble Catholic environment, where *noblesse oblige* could be taught alongside pride in family, religion and class. Similarly, some of the Schwabian Catholic *Standesherren*, incorporated into the Protestant, liberal Württemberg state after 1806, set up their own expensive private boarding school at Neutrauchburg to provide an educational equivalent to that of a gymnasium in a Catholic upper-class environment. At Neutrauchburg teachers did not, however, find it easy to inject any great enthusiasm for scholarly, religious or political effort into the rather lazy and easy-going scions of the South German high aristocracy. If Bedburg was more successful, even here faith and character always counted for more than intellect.[8]

For the Prussian Protestant aristocrat two main educational channels existed. The ordinary state high school, the gymnasium, was an all-class day-school attended by many upper-class boys but in which, even in the early nineteenth century, nobles were always a minority. 'The nobility are not ashamed to sit on the school bench side by side with the children of the trading classes' commented one British observer with admiration. As day schools, the gymnasiums concentrated on developing the minds rather than the whole personalities of their charges but their academic philosophy was far more enlightened than that of the public schools. As a State institution, the gymnasium was designed in part to create intelligent, cultured officials but its philosophy was explicitly non-utilitarian and was directed not to forcing information down boys' throats or imposing grammatical rules on them but rather towards encouraging what C. E. McClelland describes as 'the leisured, vaguely aristocratic ethos of self-development'. Through the neo-humanist course at the gymnasium and philosophical, legal and political studies at university 'Fichte and even Humboldt intended to produce, if not philosopher kings, philosopher-bureaucrats to rule Prussia'.[9]

Classics was the cornerstone of neo-humanist studies but it drew its inspiration from German academic research on the ancient world and sought to open boys' eyes not just to grammatical rules but also to the culture, philosophy and society of Greece and Rome. Matthew Arnold commented that by comparison with boys fed on a diet of pure grammar, 'in this way the student's interest in Greek and Latin becomes much more vital, and the hold of these languages upon him is much more likely to be permanent'. If the best Prussian schoolboy classicists had the edge on their English counterparts, the number of Prussians who derived something worthwhile from their classical studies was much greater than in England. In addition to classics, Prussian gymnasium boys were taught mathematics, German, French, history and natural science, but apart sometimes from gymnastics had no organised sports. Matthew Arnold concluded rather gloomily, 'in England the majority of public schoolboys work far less than the foreign schoolboy'.[10]

The Prussian nobleman who graduated from a gymnasium only encountered the type of socialisation existing at a public school if he joined a university corps. In contrast to Oxford or Cambridge, German university life was not collegiate and students lived separately in lodgings. For organised communal life the student looked to corps, associations and societies, membership of which was strictly voluntary. Of these various 'fraternities' it was the corps that were much the most exclusive, their members being drawn mostly from the noble and wealthy students of the law faculty, which itself had the justified reputation of being the laziest and richest section of the student community. It is, however, important to remember that by 1900 nobles were a small minority among university students and very many of them did not choose to join a corps. Indeed 'the overall proportion of nobles had sunk to 8 per cent in the Corps by the turn of the century'.[11]

The individual corps was always small, with often only ten active members enrolled at any time. It had a hierarchy, the newcomers (*Fuchse*) having to go through a series of initiation rites and perform a variety of services at the bequest of their seniors. A corps slang and ritual existed: 'elaborate rites governed the serious business of informal drinking'. Duelling was *de rigueur* and was designed to show courage, coolness and willingness to defend one's honour in the eyes of one's peers. Company, a sense of exclusiveness, and a love of ritual and dressing up united corps brethren. They prided themselves on their style, their self-control and their effortless superiority to other students. Old Boys, often passionately loyal to their corps, were a source of aid in future careers. Sentimental memories of youthful freedom, comradeship and debauchery bound them to the corps and the masonry of old corps brethren was exceptionally powerful, particularly in the more aristocratic sections of the civil and diplomatic service. In all of this there was much that was reminiscent of the public school, young men at both sets of institutions sporting a strange but symbolically powerful array of caps, uniforms, colours and such-like. Comparing upper-class youth across Europe in 1911, an intelligent Russian observer commented that English boys were the youngest for their age, for the most part combining innocence, love of sports and very limited views or understanding. Closest to them were the Germans, though the latter exceeded the English in their respect for authority. In the Russian's opinion, German boys – morally pure and physically strong – were often sentimental, dull, clumsy and obtuse. Like the English, they were far less dissolute than the French; much better-behaved and more uniform than the Russians. If the Russian was comparing the corps student and the product of one of the more exclusive public schools then he was not too far off the mark.[12]

For a Prussian nobleman, the major alternative to the gymnasium was the military cadet corps. In the nineteenth century these accepted boys aged 10, who then spent between six and eight years in the cadet corps before, if they graduated successfully, receiving their commission in the army. From the 1840s the cadet corps' academic course was close to that of a real gymnasium: in other words it was in theory equal to a gymnasium but put a heavier stress on mathematics and modern studies than on classics. Although military studies did not commence until the senior classes, a military atmosphere and values permeated the whole corps. Students knew that their chiefs cared more for 'character' and other military virtues than for academic brilliance. Boys who had chosen the army for their lives and who generally came from military families seldom needed much encouragement to adapt their values and behaviour accordingly.

Even by the standards of the late-Victorian public school the cadet corps was a tough, conformist and totalitarian institution. The cadet woke up at 5.30 a.m., went to bed at 10 p.m. and had every minute of the day regulated. His individuality was stripped away from him before he was even an adolescent. Discipline was strict, and absolute obedience was demanded. No concessions were made to weakness or temperament, for a Prussian officer was expected to live up to the honour of his uniform however exhausted he might be and whatever the tasks with which he was faced. Like the public school, the cadet corps had its formal hierarchy of boys, each level of which enjoyed certain privileges and the duty of enforcing conformity to communal rules and values. As in the public school, most socialisation was performed informally by the boys themselves. The aim was to produce tough, self-reliant cadets absolutely loyal to the officer corps and sharing its values. Young cadets were pummelled into conformity with these aims and most appear to have gloried in the experience. The prestige of the officer's calling was, after all, high, the rural backgrounds of most of the boys bred toughness and self-reliance, and the values enforced at the cadet corps were those of the Junker boy's father and home. The cadet corps was designed to steel the will and strengthen the body. It had limited time for intellect and none for sensitivity or aesthetics. In its defence it might be said that the corps' main purpose was to train regimental officers for the battlefield and that the qualities it bred were well-suited to this limited end.[13]

The eighteenth-century Russian nobility had no indigenous educational traditions or long-established schools. Educational principles were imported from the West and took shallow root in Russian soil. Often these principles were in conflict. By 1800, at one extreme one had the State's utilitarian desire for trained officials. At the other there were the principles inculcated into their charges by French émigré tutors, who sought to plant the manners, morals and ideas of the Parisian Old Regime salon in the Russian high aristocracy. Between these two schools stood the German bourgeois pedagogues who dominated teaching in eighteenth-century Russia and helped to develop ideas of cultural leadership and public service in the nobility. Ideas inspired by Rousseau were also making their mark. Foreign influences did not cease in the nineteenth century. A ferocious debate raged over the benefits or otherwise of classicism, a wholly Western import with no indigenous roots, and government support for the teaching of Greek and Latin rose and fell over the decades.[14]

Russia had no Prussian-style semi-autonomous universities, let alone independent English-style prestigious high schools. The State directly controlled education and its waverings on educational policy, the product generally of shifting political currents, meant that Russian educational institutions in the nineteenth century had a much less stable and consistent approach to teaching than existed in England or Germany. Both the latter countries were in any event very successful in the Victorian era and had limited reason to call into question the basic principles of how their elites were educated. Prussia had passed through its years of crisis between 1807 and

1815, radically reforming its educational system during this period. Matthew Arnold wrote of the Prussian gymnasium, 'the Prussians are satisifed with them, and are proud of them, and with good reason; the schools have been intelligently planned to meet their intelligent wants'. By contrast, Russia met its Jena in the Crimean War of 1854–56 and it was therefore in the mid-nineteenth century that she went through her era of radical reform, educational reform included.[15]

In addition, the Russian nobility was more heterogeneous than Prussian Junkerdom and the early nineteenth-century Russian State less efficiently organised and integrated than its Prussian counter-part. This was reflected in the education provided in Russian mili-tary cadet corps before 1861. Most Russian corps had the virtues and vices of their Prussian equivalents though their educational standards, for lack of adequate teachers, were often somewhat lower. As in Prussia, however, they were rather brutal, anti-intellec-tual establishments which nevertheless produced tough, courageous and loyal regimental officers who had at least some claims to edu-cation. But in Russia the various branches of the army always stood rather apart from each other, and education and culture, rare in the Russian backwoods, enjoyed greater prestige than in the West. Under Nicholas I, the artillery and military engineering schools had (by Western standards) surprisingly high status within the cadet corps and demanded much better educational standards of their boys than those existing in the ordinary corps.

Unlike Prussia, Silesia excepted, Russia had a magnate aristoc-racy and the two cadet corps which catered to this elite, namely the Corps des Pages and the School of Guards Sub-Ensigns, stood out sharply from the bulk of military schools. The Corps des Pages was Russia's closest equivalent to Eton and its senior classes despised bourgeois pedagogues and resented any trifling with the pages' traditions or authority over their juniors in a way reminiscent of Etonians' response to 'Arnoldism'. The pages' education reflected the concern for elegance, polished manners and flawless French which typified the Russian high aristocracy in this era. Indeed the major influence in the Corps under Nicholas I was a French émigré, Girardot. The School of Guards Sub-Ensigns was different, above all because its director, A. N. Suthof, had a high regard for the intellect. Since his aristocratic pupils came from much more cul-tured families than the average noble cadet and in addition paid expensive fees, Suthof could demand high educational standards from the boys, encourage cultural pursuits and hire the best teachers St. Petersburg had to offer.[16]

Nicholas I's regime devoted most of its energies to ensuring that Russia was a great military power. It derived much of its legitimacy from the fact that in the wake of 1812 the Tsar's empire was generally taken to be Europe's mightiest state. Defeat in the Crimea undermined this legitimacy and caused major soul-searching within the ruling elite as regards most areas of national life. Military education was transformed and, in a manner reminiscent of the Prussian reformers of 1807–12, the principle was established that the modern officer should have a complete high school education before being subjected to a military atmosphere or studies. The institutional incoherence of tsarist government also contributed to the peculiar but successful educational role of the military cadet schools in the 1860s and 1870s. The War Ministry controlled its own numerous educational institutions and its chief, Dimitri Milyu-tin, was a liberal strongly committed to high intellectual standards, to a 'modern' curriculum of mathematics and living languages, and to the training of first-class military teachers. Meanwhile the Ministry of Education, headed by the arch-conservative Dimitri Tolstoy, was attempting to thrust a classical curriculum down the unwilling throats of Russian boys in the ordinary gymnasiums. As a result the military schools became havens of relatively 'progressive' educational principles, good teaching, and friendly relations between teachers and students. Once again, however, politics was to intervene: the accession of Alexander III in 1881 led to Milyutin's dismissal and the re-imposition of a more conservative, military and anti-intellectual ethos in the army's cadet schools, though edu-cational standards never fell back to anything like the levels of pre-1861 days.[17]

Russian military education thus looked like its Prussian equiva-lent but was in practice often rather different. The same was even truer of the Russian gymnasium and university. Before the 1860s the Russian gymnasium suffered in comparison to Prussia because of its shortage of good teachers, its lack of a coherent educational philosophy to match neo-humanism, and because of political con-straints on what was taught. The curriculum was nevertheless broader and the teaching more thorough than at the average public school. In the 1860s Russia acquired a dominant educational philosophy in the form of Dimitri Tolstoy's classicism. As an antidote to growing nihilism among the young and the lack of self-discipline, order or consistency in Russian life, Tolstoy imposed a regime of classical grammar-teaching on the gymnasiums. The ideas or society of the ancient world were ignored, even feared, by the State's educators, who desired only that Russian boys should acquire trained memories and the habit of hard, logical and systematic thought. Tolstoy's efforts to depoliticise Russian youth backfired badly. The classical world and mental gymnastics meant even less to Russian schoolboys than to their English counterparts, who at least belonged to a society whose values derived ultimately from Greece and Rome and which in the Victorian era possessed an adequate number of trained classics teachers. Tormented by classical grammar and without the English boys' opportunity to take refuge from the classroom on the sports' field, the Russian pupils often came to loathe both their schools and the State which created them. Thomas Darlington, England's leading expert on Russian education, believed at the turn of the century that 'the Russian boy who has completed a course in the gymnasium or the *realschule* is undoubtedly better developed intellectually than an English public-school boy of the same age'. This was a compliment to Russian society's respect for the intellect and education, not to the methods of Tolstoy's gymnasium.[18]

The Russian university also suffered from political constraints imposed by the regime, as well as from the effects on teaching of the student body's politicisation. Nevertheless, from the 1840s, Moscow and, a little later, St. Petersburg were first-class universities, the match of any other higher educational institution in Europe. Thomas Darlington, not generally given to hyperbole, commented that 'seldom in the history of any country has so much intellectual power been concentrated within the walls of a single teaching institution as was to be found in the University of Moscow in the forties'. In Russia as in Germany most upper-class students attended the law faculty, which was notorious as a haven for lazy socialites. Moreover, the Russian university examinations were laxer than those that the Prussian State imposed on students attempting to enter its service. Nevertheless, in Russia as in Prussia, for the minority of students anxious to learn, the university had much to offer.[19]

The biggest difference between Russian education on the one

hand and English and German on the other lay not in curricula but in the student milieu. If the Prussian gymnasium and university was much more democratic in its intake than the public schools and Oxbridge, the same was true to an even greater degree in Russia. But it was not only that Russian schoolboys and students in general came from poorer and humbler backgrounds than their Prussian or English counterparts. They were also, particularly in the second half of the nineteenth century, likely to hold radical and anti-aristocratic views. Aristocrats who attended gymnasiums and universities often felt the hostility of students and teachers alike to the imperial regime and the social elite. Prince S. S. Volkonsky, for instance, recalls that ever since his schooldays he felt that his intellectual achievements and hard work were under-valued because he was an aristocrat. Prince Evgeni Trubetskoy remembers the hostility which initially surrounded him at his gymnasium, not to mention the bitterness aroused among pupils by Tolstoy's classical curriculum and his attempts to use schools as mechanisms of political control. The atmosphere of school was such as to turn even Trubetskoy, an aristocratic Slavophil by background and inclination, into a temporary nihilist. Indeed, Tolstoy's gymnasium was likely to breed boys with instincts exactly opposite to those of the English public schoolboy, with his strange trust in the justice and competence of umpires, judges and other figures of authority. By the time he entered Moscow University, Trubetskoy's idealist, religious and nationalist beliefs had again come to the fore but they marked him out as an oddity among students and staff alike and he was forced intellectually to confront the liberal, materialist and positivist ideas propounded by almost all the professors. For the intelligent young Russian aristocrat the educational path through gymnasium and university was far more challenging than the public school or the Imperial German university, where 'the student majority was unquestionably monarchist, anti-Semitic, anti-socialist and imperialist'. It is scarcely surprising that intelligent Russians subjected to this experience were more intellectually alive, less secure, less carefree and more adult than their Prussian or English peers.[20]

Classics in the gymnasiums and politics in the universities were an extra incentive for some parents to send their sons to one of the two all-noble civilian boarding schools established in the early nineteenth century to train upper-class boys for leading positions in government. Of these two institutions, the School of Law was a combination of a gymnasium course and, in the top classes, university legal studies. It was designed solely to produce educated, idealistic and incorruptible jurists. The Alexander Lycée was more interesting in that its history tells one something of the cultural aspirations of the Russian aristocracy and the frustrations these suffered under tsarist conditions.

The Lycée was established in 1811 in the initial liberal phase of Alexander I's reign. Under its first director, E. A. Engelhardt, it was thoroughly Rousseauist in its educational philosophy. Engelhardt was about as close to being friend and mentor of his pupils as any headmaster could be. He believed passionately that a teacher must win his pupils' hearts if he was to implant the vital principles of love, honour and duty. His major aim was to secure the trust, affection and confidence of the boys who, by English standards, lacked freedom but were treated with exceptional humanity and given a very broad, cultured and stimulating course of studies. The Lycée's curriculum centred around modern languages and literature, a popular choice in the midst of Russia's Romantic era. In addition, the legal–political senior courses taught about natural rights, justice, comparative political systems and the social contract.[21]

This extraordinary liberal idyll was bound to find existence difficult in tsarist conditions. In 1817 the political courses began to be slimmed down. Under Nicholas I a degree of militarisation crept in and close supervision over the boys at times verged on spying. But external pressure, never in any case applied as ruthlessly at the Lycée as elsewhere, did little to change the boys' spirit. The Lycée's first graduating class had produced both Alexander Pushkin, Russia's greatest poet, and Prince A. M. Gorchakov, who was to be foreign minister for most of Alexander II's reign. The institution's ethos and tradition were quickly established and it was, by the standards of the cadet corps or the public school, exceptionally cultured, liberal and cosmopolitan. The Lycéen, right up to 1917, spoke three foreign languages fluently and carried not a field-marshal's baton but a poet's pen in his knapsack. Even in the last repressive years of Nicholas I's reign, K. K. Arsenev, a student at the School of Law, commented that 'I knew well many boys of the same age as myself who were studying at the Lycée and clearly recall that they were much more interested in politics and literature than the *pravovedy* [that is, School of Law boys] . . . the traditions which came down still from Pushkin's time, even if having lost their strength, sustained among Lycée boys well beyond the period I am studying, an intellectual ferment which was entirely alien to those studying at the School of Law'. In the second half of the nineteenth century the Lycée suffered somewhat from trying to teach too much in too little time. Given the social origins of the boys and the exceptionally privileged and powerful position occupied by the Lycée in the tsarist establishment, the school was inevitably a basically conservative, patriotic and monarchist institution. It grew a little more complacent and self-satisfied than in its earlier years. But, true to its traditions, the Lycée was always one of the most liberal, cultured and cosmopolitan elements in the tsarist regime. Even in the post-Pushkin era it produced a number of leading cultural figures, the most famous of whom was the satirist M. E. Saltykov-Shchedrin. Former Lycéens also headed the foreign ministry for almost the entire period between the Crimean and First World Wars.[22]

A comparison between Russian, Prussian and English upper-class education in the nineteenth century provides some clues as to why the Russian aristocracy was in cultural terms much more interesting and creative than its German or English peers. The only German nobleman to leave a major mark on world literature in the nineteenth century was Heinrich von Kleist. Among the English there was Lord Byron and, closer to the edges of gentry life, Robert Shelley. By contrast, the Russian aristocracy, together with the top echelon of the provincial landowning gentry, produced Pushkin, Lermontov, Tolstoy, Tyutchev and Turgenev, together with a string of lesser lights. If the aristocratic contribution to literature had declined by 1900, Vladimir Nabokov was the grandson of a minister and a member of a very old and distinguished noble family.

If anything, the Russian aristocracy's contribution to music was even more impressive. It is difficult to imagine the upper ranks of the Victorian English or Prussian gentry producing a family to match the Taneevs, with two well-known composers and three private secretaries to monarchs in six decades. Like Russian authors, the composers were often obsessed with the task of creating a national music from the various European and Russian influences to which they were subjected. Sergei Rachmaninov, the last unequivocally great noble composer, came from the top rank of the Novgorod landowning gentry. The combination of Russia and Europe in him produced, on the one hand, classical music of immense power, technical excellence and international appeal, and on the other the deeply moving Vespers and Liturgy of Saint John. From its origins in Nicholas I's reign with Glinka, modern Russian music passed through the generation of the St. Petersburg 'mighty five' and Tchaikovsky to the world of Rachmaninov, Skryabin and Stravinsky. Like literature, its heroes included non-aristocrats (Stravinsky); those on the borderline between professional and noble such as Tchaikovsky, a product of the School of Law; and full-scale aristocrats such as Modest Mussorgsky. The latter, probably the most talented of the middle generation of Russian composers, was a cadet of the School of Guards Sub-Ensigns and an officer of the Preobrazhensky Guards, the senior regiment of the Russian army. It boggles the mind to conceive of the Prussian First Foot Guards or the English Grenadier Guards producing a phenomenon of this wildly creative and imaginative sort in the Victorian era.[23]

The Russian aristocrat was in cultural terms much less comfortable and insular than his English or Prussian peer. By 1800, in Europe but not quite of it, he was open to all the continent's national cultures, many of which he could appreciate in their original languages. Europe was a cultural unity to him in a way that could never be true of an Englishman or Prussian, whose perceptions were bound to be blinkered by the overwhelming influence of their own culture, which few of them could really see as but one part of a broader whole.

The Russian too had his own indigenous culture. He heard it in peasant folk music and in the liturgy, and read of it in medieval tales. But in the early nineteenth century the modernisation of this culture and language so that it could be used and valued by educated Russian Europeans was still underway. A great debate existed in educated circles as to the form that a Russian literary language should take and it was Pushkin more than anyone who settled this argument and established the elegant, clear and beautiful norms of later Russian literature. To be an educated Russian European and to possess patriotic self-esteem required the creation of a new cultural type. Otherwise it would be hard for the sensitive upper-class Russian to live with himself. In the early nineteenth century only the aristocratic elite had the wealth, leisure and education to meet this challenge. Unlike the English aristocracy they had no chance to develop a political genius through dominating the institutions of a parliamentary regime. Nor, isolated in the cultural desert of provincial Russia, could the civilised aristocrat of 1800 settle down to the farming life of the raw backwoods Junker. Their greatest challenge was a cultural one and it was a challenge to which they rose with distinction.

Their lives were not comfortable. Civilised and educated beings, they lived as islands in a noble world still often uncultured and obsessed with the traditional pursuit of rank and imperial favour. The peasantry and merchant classes were of a different cultural world. Brought up often in a civilised and free domestic environment, Westernised aristocrats confronted a rigid and oppressive political regime designed by and for people other than themselves. In many regions of Russia before 1850, provincial life had many of the freedoms of a frontier society. The serf-owner was unchallenged king on his estate. Russian life as a whole was less constrained than that lived in Central or Western Europe by tradition, convention, law or propriety. When the German and Russian student Corps at St. Petersburg University tried to hold joint sessions in the 1840s the Germans followed their solemn, ordered ceremonies and the Russian aristocrats clambered on to the table to make speeches. Not for nothing did the Russo-German senior official Fyodor Terner compare 'the narrowness and tightness of the conventions of life' in Germany to the 'so different freedom and openness in Russia and to the extended family life there'. For the young cultured aristocrat of Nicholas I's day the first shocking contrast between State and society might be the transition from the park and library of his father's house to the world of the cadet corps. Out of the contradictions, turmoil and difficulties of the Russian aristocracy's existence there emerged an upper class which, like its European peers, produced some statesmen and soldiers of distinction: but also, quite unlike most nineteenth-century European aristocracies, it was the seed-bed for writers and musicians of world fame and for Victorian Europe's two most famous anarchist leaders.[24]

9. The Noble as Warrior

WAR was aristocracy's oldest profession. The origins of the English and German aristocracy lay in medieval knighthood. Very many of the two countries' greatest families traced their origins back to this era and those that did not absorbed the corporate traditions of their class. In Russia too, surprisingly many old families survived over the centuries, maintaining their position within the aristocratic court elite from the Muscovite into the Imperial period. In its earliest origins the Muscovite aristocracy were the Grand Duke's comrades-in-arms in his *druzhina* (military household). As the Muscovite State's military needs and the size of its aristocracy grew in the fifteenth century, a lesser nobility developed, granted estates on conditional tenure in return for military service.[1]

The transition from the era of knights to that of the modern professional noble officer was not direct and smooth. In the sixteenth and seventeenth centuries the noble warrior on horseback was threatened with redundancy. Armoured knights were rendered useless by the cannon, pike and musket but the royal standing army had not yet emerged as an alternative channel for their military skills and instincts. Instead, leading aristocrats tended to be raised in the arts of the courtier and of the Renaissance humanist gentleman. Even in Prussia and Brandenburg the wealthy sixteenth- and early seventeenth-century nobleman was not a warrior but a gentleman–farmer–statesman whose sons were despatched on grand tours to learn the ways of Courts. The Russian nobleman of this era was uninfluenced by Renaissance humanism but he too was threatened with redundancy as the traditional noble militia cavalry was increasingly supplanted by professional foreign-officered units. According to John Keep, the seventeenth century was a time when a provincial gentry with strong local roots, potential farmers and local leaders rather than soldiers and servants of the State, appeared to be developing. It was Peter I who reversed this trend, dragooning the old nobility into the State's service and forcing them to become useful cogs in the machinery of absolutism.[2]

In the eighteenth and nineteenth centuries the armed forces were the favourite source of employment for English, Prussian and Russian aristocrats, though much less so for most of the German Catholic aristocracy, Bavarians and Westphalians included. In mid-nineteenth-century Britain roughly half the military and naval officers came from the aristocracy and gentry, though problems exist in defining the precise boundaries of the latter group. Granted that the officer son of a baronet or landed gentleman should be defined as 'gentry', is this landless officer's own son to be described as gentry, professional or simply middle class? David Cannadine believes that 'during the early 1870s the patricians were still the dominant element in the officer corps' but that the abolition of purchased commissions in 1870 contributed greatly in time to the declining weight of aristocracy in the officer corps. By the eve of the First World War only 35–40 per cent even of generals were of noble or gentry origin.[3]

Precise comparisons between England and Russia are bedevilled by problems of terminology. The Russian hereditary nobility, over one million strong in 1897, was made up for the most part of people who in England would have been considered professional middle class, petty clerks or, in many cases, semi-peasants. Nevertheless, the fact that nine Russian officers out of ten were nobles on the eve of the Crimean War and only one in two in 1913 tells one something striking about the shifting composition of the officer corps in the last decades of the Old Regime. As elsewhere but to a more dramatic extent, different sections of the army were colonised by different social groups. The high aristocracy monopolised above all three of the Guards cavalry regiments and two regiments of Guards infantry. The majority of the Guards was officered by less grand nobles, as was the artillery. The relative scarcity and prestige of education in Russia rubbed off on the artillery. Given the lack of a cultured middle class, artillerymen, who by definition required a superior education, had always been drawn either from relatively privileged sections of the nobility or from German–Russian families. Even in 1914 artillery officers shared with Guardsmen a considerable contempt for the officers of the infantry line regiments, about half of whom by then, even in peacetime, were the descendants of serfs.[4]

Prussia was like Russia in the fact that an officer corps which was predominantly noble until the 1860s was 70 per cent non-noble by 1913. As in Britain and Russia, aristocrats monopolised certain units, the most exclusive of all being the senior Guards heavy cavalry regiment in the three armies: Life Guards in England, Chevaliers Gardes in Russia and Garde du Corps in Prussia. In Prussia, however, the overwhelming majority of non-noble officers came from comfortable and educated professional or business families. Even in 1888, 28 per cent of Prussian officers had university degrees. The increasing unity of views and values of the Prussian upper and upper middle classes after 1870, not to mention the army's own socialisation of cadets, created in Prussia an officer corps much more homogeneous and much more aristocratic in tone than was the case in late imperial Russia.[5]

The relative decline in aristocratic control of the officer corps could reflect either that the armed forces had grown too big for aristocrats to monopolise or that the upper-class appetite for military service was waning. If the latter were true it might be a sign of modernity, as aristocrats ceased to be a narrow military caste and instead took advantage of the numerous new opportunities in the expanding civilian economy and society. Tracking the careers of tens of thousands of European aristocrats is beyond the reach of this author. Probably it is beyond anyone's reach since, particularly in Russia, the information does not exist from which confident generalisations and statistical conclusions could be drawn. Even in England and Germany the suspicion lingers that genealogical works are more inclined to list traditional, recognised and prestigious occupations than more mundane and modern ones. Nevertheless, the available evidence does suggest some shift in aristocratic and gentry career patterns before 1914, though not a dramatic or unequivocal one.

Michael Thompson argues that there was no decline in aristocratic or gentry willingness to serve in the British armed forces in the period before the 1880s: indeed, quite the opposite. Among the younger sons and grandsons of the peerage and baronetage born between 1750 and 1800 the armed forces were much the most popular career: 45.5 per cent of Thompson's cohort served in the army and navy; 25 per cent in the church; 13 per cent in India; and 7 per cent were lawyers. No other profession was significantly represented. By the time the cohort born between 1800 and 1850 were seeking employment there had been a further shift towards the armed forces, where 52 per cent of these aristocrats were now working. The church (23 per cent) and India (8.5 per cent) had both lost ground, the latter either because great fortunes were no longer to be made there or because, East India Company regiments no longer existing, the whole Indian army officer corps was now counted as part of the royal military service. A new category of employment, 'public service', had emerged, but this occupied only 4 per cent of the cohort, a tiny proportion in comparison to the number of Russian or Prussian aristocrats occupied in some branch or other of the civil service.

The younger sons and grandsons of the untitled gentry followed paths rather similar to those of the peerage and baronetcy. Among the gentry cohort born between 1750 and 1800, however, 48 per cent entered the church as against only 28 per cent in the armed forces. By the time the 1800–1850 cohort was in employment, the percentages had been reversed, with only 29 per cent in the church and 47 per cent now serving in the army and navy. Of the later gentry cohort, 11.5 per cent were lawyers and none appear to have been civil servants, the precise opposite of the Prussian or Russian gentry pattern.[6]

To gain a sense of the occupations of the English aristocratic elite, Table 9.1 looks at the families of the seventeen richest peers in 1883. It illustrates the careers of the younger sons in these families in the course of the nineteenth century. Though the sample of 109 is relatively small, it is homogeneous and the results are striking. In every cohort the armed forces were much the most usual form of employment, virtually the only others being politics, diplomacy and the church. As the century progressed the army became much more popular than the navy. Far from military service declining in prestige over the century, the proportion of younger sons in the army from the post-1850 cohort was higher than at any previous time. As one would expect under a system of strict primogeniture, heads of families were far less likely to make military careers, though a handful did so briefly. Much more common was a stint as MP in preparation for one's later position as an hereditary legislator. Politics was, with very few exceptions, the nearest any of these magnates came to having a professional occupation.[7]

TABLE 9.1 Careers of younger sons of English peerage

	Total	Army	Royal Navy
First cohort (born pre-1800)	26	7	7
Second cohort (born 1800–24)	27	9	5
Third cohort (born 1825–49)	28	10	2
Fourth cohort (born post-1850)	28	19	4
TOTAL	109	45	18

Source: J. B. Burke, A Genealogical and Heraldic Dictionary of the Peerage (London 1815–1914).

The evidence on Russian aristocratic and gentry careers presented in Tables 9.2 and 9.3 needs to be regarded with scepticism. N. I. Ikonnikov, on whose genealogical works these tables are based, cannot be relied on not to omit individuals or to pass over the careers of those he does include in silence. He provides fuller information on the generations before 1861 than on those living in the decades immediately prior to the Revolution and Tables 9.2 and 9.3 should not therefore be seen as proof that the Russian aristocracy and gentry were dying out. Table 9.2 covers the occupations of sixteen of the greatest Russian landowners listed in Table 2.7 (see page 49). It studies not only these men's occupations but also those of all brothers, ancestors and uncles in the male line born since 1760. Table 9.3 looks at the occupations of male members of eighteen of the most distinguished but untitled old Muscovite gentry families, confining itself to individuals born between 1775 and 1874.

TABLE 9.2 Russian magnates

	Total	Soldiers	
Cohort 1 (born 1760–99)	26	18	(69.2%)
Cohort 2 (born 1800–24)	34	24	(70.1%)
Cohort 3 (born 1825–74)	30	17	(56.6%)

Source: N. Ikonnikov, La Noblesse de Russie.

TABLE 9.3   Russian gentry

	Soldiers	Civil servants	Total
Cohort 1 (born 1775–99)	53 (65.4%)	32 (39.5%)	81 (100%)
Cohort 2 (born 1800–24)	35 (55.6%)	19 (30.2%)	63 (100%)
Cohort 3 (born 1825–74)	29 (29.9%)	49 (50.5%)	97 (100%)

Source: N. Ikonnikov, La Noblesse de Russie.

The main conclusion to be drawn from both tables is that military careers were becoming less popular for the Russian aristocracy and gentry. Among the great aristocrats roughly 70 per cent of those born before 1825 made military careers but only 56.6 per cent of those born subsequently followed their example. Moreover, the younger members of the latter cohort were the ones most disinclined to military careers. Among the gentry families the decline in the number of officers was even steeper: 65 per cent in the cohort born between 1775 and 1799, 55 per cent in the next cohort but only 30 per cent of those born after 1825. For all Ikonnikov's inaccuracies, the strength of this trend in both tables suggests that it reflects a real shift in career patterns. Among the gentry, declining popularity of military careers went alongside increased membership of the civil service. Again this probably reflects realities, since in Russia, as in Hungary, the sons of landowners hit by emancipation and agricultural depression frequently entered the ranks of a rapidly expanding civil service. Defining precisely what was or was not a civil servant in Imperial Russia can, however, be tricky; moreover, Ikonnikov is probably much more inclined to cite civil service ranks or jobs than the occupations of nobles employed in the free professions or business. Even so one does, for instance, find among members of the Arsenev family born after 1850 individuals working as land surveyors, doctors and insurance agents; jobs their ancestors would have scorned. Predictably, among the aristocrats one finds no examples of this kind of job. Nor was the civil service anything like as popular as among the gentry. Positions at Court, which were usually but not always merely honorary, in the diplomatic service and in membership of the State Council, the empire's highest legislative body, were far more frequent occupations among the magnates than were ordinary civil service jobs.[8]

No sensible observer could deny the existence of an aristocracy in nineteenth-century Russia or England. In Prussia a nobility existed, as did a landowning gentry, but a national aristocratic elite in the Russian or English sense did not. There were, of course, a number of great aristocratic families in nineteenth-century Prussia. These included *Standesherren* incorporated into the kingdom after 1800, and Silesian magnates. A handful of East Prussian families – Dohnas, Dönhoffs, Eulenbergs and Lehndorffs – were aristocrats, as were the Putbus in Pomerania. But it was a moot point whether the other leading noble families in Pomerania and Brandenburg – Arnims, Schulenbergs, Schwerins and a few others – really fitted into this category. Prussia's most prominent families were certainly not conscious of forming a single aristocratic elite group. Even leaving the Catholics aside, Protestant *Standesherren* would never have put themselves on a par with Silesian magnates, let alone with Eulenbergs and Arnims. In any event, by the time a Prussian aristocratic consciousness was forming, incorporation into the new Reich was again altering perspectives.

For this reason I have looked at *Standesherren* careers separately from those of other Prussian aristocrats. As one might expect, of all aristocratic groups, the exceptionally status-conscious *Standesherren* had the most predictable careers. In the overwhelming majority of cases Protestant aristocrats, even heads of families, served in the Prussian army. So too did a handful of Catholics, especially after 1871, though in these families Austrian, Bavarian or even Württemberg service was far more frequent. Apart from the army and hereditary membership of one or more German upper houses, the only occupation of *Standesherren* and their brothers appears to have been diplomacy. *Standesherren* marriages were also even more predictable than those of other European aristocrats, including great German families who were not formally members of the 'high nobility'. One searches in vain for a *Standesherren* equivalent to the Hatzfeld who married a Japanese, or indeed to Guido Henckel von Donnersmarck, Prussia's greatest aristocratic industrialist, who married two divorcées in succession, whose former husbands were Italian and Russian.[9]

Table 9.4 looks at seven aristocratic families from East Prussia, Brandenburg and Pomerania, namely the counts Dohna, Dönhoff, Kleist, Schulenberg, Finck von Finckenstein, Arnim and Lehndorff. In each cohort of those born between 1775 until 1875, roughly half the men served as army officers, a figure which does not include those who merely held commissions in the Landwehr or reserve.

Only among the Dohnas is there evidence of a marked decline in enthusiasm for military careers in the youngest cohort. Of those who were never professional soldiers, some were heads of families running large properties, though some *Fideikommissherren* did also hold regular commissions. Apart from the army, the most popular position was that of *Landrat*, though many Dönhoffs, Lehndorffs and Dohnas in particular held top positions at Court. Given the status of these families in Prussia, the absence of more than a handful of diplomats is worth noting.[10]

TABLE 9.4   Prussian counts

	Total	Soldiers	
Cohort 1 (born 1775–99)	17	9	(52.9%)
Cohort 2 (born 1800–24)	43	20	(46.5%)
Cohort 3 (born 1825–49)	48	28	(58.3%)
Cohort 4 (born 1850–74)	79	39	(49.4%)

Source: Gothaisches genealogisches Taschenbuch der gräflichen Haüser (Gotha, 1930–39).

TABLE 9.5   Prussian gentry

	Total	Soldiers	
Cohort 1 (born 1775–99)	38	21	(55.3%)
Cohort 2 (born 1800–24)	85	51	(60%)
Cohort 3 (born 1825–49)	125	80	(64%)
Cohort 4 (born 1850–74)	231	105	(45.4%)

Source: Gothaisches genealogisches Taschenbuch der uradeligen Haüser (Gotha, 1930–39).

In contrast to Prussia's aristocrats, there does seem to have been a decline in the popularity of military careers among the youngest cohort of the non-titled gentry families. If 45.4 per cent reflects by modern standards a remarkably uniform choice of career by members of a social group, a drop of almost 20 per cent from the previous cohort must surely be significant. As one would expect, the group of non-titled nobles is not only much larger but also more heterogeneous than the titled aristocrats. Some branches of these families had already dropped out of the upper classes by 1815, their members holding in general very lowly State positions. Along with a handful of emigrants there are also, in the younger two cohorts, a small number of men working in private business. Much larger is

the group of landowners pure and simple and – to a lesser extent
– of civil servants. Among the latter there are some *Landräte*, though
proportionally many fewer than among the titled aristocrats. There
are also relatively speaking many fewer middle and senior civil
servants than in the equivalent Russian group, and almost no diplomats at all.[11]

The wealthy aristocrats from great families who officered the most
exclusive Guards cavalry regiments seldom had a very professional
attitude to military service. In general they served for a few years
in the agreeable and sociable milieu of their peers before abandoning the officers' mess for the cares and pleasures of inheriting a
large fortune. For such men there was little incentive to master all
aspects of the military art or to contemplate the long haul up the
army's hierarchical ladder. Count A. A. Ignatev recalls that joining
the Chevaliers Gardes in the 1890s felt like entry into a fashionable
and comfortable club. Every officer knew that his expenses would
far exceed his salary. The club atmosphere was increased by the
fact that many officers' families had served in the regiment for
generations. Ignatev's own father, for instance, had formerly commanded the Chevaliers Gardes and he himself had been born in
the regimental barracks. Social rather than professional issues were
the general topic of conversation in the mess and an atmosphere of
polite, easy-going and tolerant well-being reigned – as indeed it
might given the Chevaliers Gardes' officers' rather small share of
life's burdens.[12]

Poorer and lesser nobles had greater incentive to take an
ambitious and professional attitude towards military careers. The
most famous aristocratic military class in Europe were Prussia's
Junkers, but Russia and England had their equivalents even if not
in quite the same numbers and style. Russia's two greatest generals,
Suvorov and Kutuzov, came from the ranks of the upper gentry,
not from the court aristocracy, and so did most of her nineteenth-
century military leaders. The eighteenth and early nineteenth-
century Russian State showered most of its blessings on the Court
noble elite, but provincial nobles could rise to the top of the military
and civil bureaucracy, in sharp distinction to the magnate-domi-
nated Polish republic or indeed the general practice in pre-Petrine
Russia. The possibilities of advancement open to the gentry were
indeed one of the keys to the success of post-Petrine tsarism and to
noble loyalty to the autocratic state.

Corelli Barnett describes the Anglo-Irish gentry as 'the nearest thing Britain ever possessed to the Prussian Junker class. Often poorer than their English brethren owing to Irish rural poverty and consequently low rents, the Anglo-Irish lived a horsey life particularly remote from the modern world of industry and towns. As with the Junker, son followed father into the army down the generations. Roberts, Wolseley and Kitchener were all sons of soldiers, none of them rich like many English officers, although possessing sufficient private income to live on; all therefore highly ambitious'. Barnett could have pushed his comparison with the Junkers further. The Anglo-Irish were, after all, a colonial aristocracy. Many of them had the rather tough attitudes to be expected of landowners living amidst a subjugated peasantry. Surrounded by a Catholic sea, Irish Protestantism could take on a somewhat Prussian hue and be quite far from the tolerant latitudinarianism often to be found in the English aristocracy. The Anglo-Irish gentry's contribution to the army's top ranks did not cease with Kitchener, Roberts and Wolseley. Even in the Second World War Britain's three most famous generals – Montgomery, Brooke and Alexander – were drawn from this group. Harold Alexander, the son of a peer and himself a Guardsman, came from the top rank of the Anglo-Irish gentry. In 1919, during the Russian civil war, he was seconded to command the militia of the Baltic German landowners. The latter, wealthier and more easy-going than most Prussian nobles, were in a sense super-Junkers and they and their 'super-Anglo-Irish' noble commander understood each other to perfection.[13]

The values of most aristocratic officers were those we have already encountered at the cadet corps. They included physical courage, toughness and endurance; the ability to bear pain and extremely stressful conditions without losing one's calm or one's resolve. Comradeship, loyalty and a willingness to subordinate one's individuality to the demands of group and institution were required. Leadership and example were highly valued. So too were certain practical skills such as horsemanship and, especially later in the century, marksmanship and an eye for ground. There was a symbiotic relationship between aristocratic and military values and qualities. Countess Dönhoff's recollections of childhood on an aristocratic Prussian estate are a catalogue of horses, outdoor pleasures and physical hardihood; uncomplaining endurance of painful accidents; acceptance of a world of hierarchy and paternalism; and subordination to the rules and rituals of an upper-class household. Country life tales from England and Russia tell a similar story. Apologists for the noble officer who stressed how well his home upbringing prepared him for regimental life were not far wrong. Nor is it surprising that, at a time when aristocracy was losing many of its functions, members of the upper classes should identify with and indeed glorify the qualities and world-view of the officer corps, a group whose role was still legitimate and honoured by society in the imperialist era.[14]

'Regimental values' left much to be desired. The mess was not the best breeding ground for intellectuals, aesthetes and eccentrics, nor indeed for members of a genuine political ruling class. The noble officer's conception of honour could be taken to ludicrous and dangerous lengths. Uneducated subalterns could look down on civilians as inherently dishonourable, in arrogant ignorance of the qualities that made bourgeois society so vibrant and creative. The need to preserve the special military conception of honour could be invoked to defend the duel, beloved of the bully through the ages, against the criticisms of those who sought to uphold the law and civilised norms of behaviour.[15]

It is, however, naïve simply to deride 'regimental values' or to imagine that officers can be trained as if in preparation to become professors or art critics. In his sensitive study of the battlefields of Waterloo and the Somme, John Keegan reminds one, if that is necessary, of the appalling carnage with which the young officer was surrounded, amidst which he was expected to display not merely personal courage but also leadership and a concern for the morale of his soldiers. To din such totally unnatural qualities into young men in a manner that would leave them intact at times of great trauma required methods other than those of a humane and liberal education.

Keegan's work also reminds one of the importance of intangibles such as the regimental flag or, above all, the officer's conception of honour:

In a way the most perceptive of all the comments about Waterloo is the best known and apparently the most banal; that it was 'won on the playing-fields of Eton'. The Duke, who was an Etonian, knew very well that few of his officers were schoolfellows and that football bears little relation to war. But he was not speaking of himself, nor was he suggesting that Waterloo had been a game. He was proposing a much more subtle idea: that the French had been beaten not by wiser generalship or better tactics or superior patriotism but by the coolness and endurance, the pursuit of excellence and of intangible objectives for their own sake which are learnt in game-playing – that game-playing which was already becoming the most important activity of the English gentleman's life.

Napoleon had been repulsed above all because English officers had been too jealous of their self-respect and too determined to maintain their reputations before their peers to show any sign of weakness, dismay or lack of calm despite the pressures to which they were being subjected. Regiments had held their ground, 'planted fast by the hold officers had over themselves and so over their men. Honour, in a very peculiar sense, had triumphed'.[16]

'Regimental values' were not those of capitalism or bourgeois society. The celebration of these values' superiority, often encountered in conservative nineteenth- and twentieth-century literature, was to have evil consequences when vulgarised and brutalised by Fascism. Yet in proclaiming the superiority of their own professional values over capitalism's worship of money and self-interest, officers were acting in ways common among modern professional groups, as any inhabitant of contemporary Britain must surely recognise. Nor were officers wrong in believing that the qualities and values that contributed to effective military leadership were not always easily squared with the world of the bank and the stock exchange. At the core of A. J. Hayek's thinking is the conception that the principles on which efficient capitalism is based are unnatural and run counter to the instincts and traditions of mankind. A world in which money was becoming the highest value and the crafty financier could, at least potentially, lord it over the courageous and patriotic warrior stuck in aristocratic gullets. But the new scale of values offended against the beliefs of almost every kind of traditional society and was thoroughly disliked by many Victorian non-aristocrats as well. Even today it is still found very hard to swallow by many members of Western society.

The nineteenth-century officer in general distrusted radical liberalism, let alone democracy or socialism. Radicals might preach unsavoury doctrines about the impending abolition of war or the need to replace standing armies by citizen militias. In any event the officer believed in authority, hierarchy and discipline. He himself in general held simple, clear-cut patriotic values and he wanted his soldiers to do the same. Democratic politics meant party conflict, class and ethnic strife, and political leaders inured to the compromises, manoeuvres and half-truths of parliamentary life. The noble officer had particular cause to dislike democracy. It might well threaten his own interests as landowner or *rentier* and would certainly endanger those of his brothers and cousins. It would replace his peers with rulers whose social origins and manners he probably despised and whom he suspected, sometimes rightly, of having risen to prominence by means considered unethical by aristocrats. Moreover these new rulers were unlikely to look as favourably on the interests and peculiarities of the officer corps as did the old aristocratic political elite.

Throughout the nineteenth century the British or Prussian officer could be relied on to support the existing political order. In early nineteenth-century Russia the situation was more equivocal, for St. Petersburg had witnessed a number of military coups since 1725. Most of these coups were little more than violent extensions of factional politics at Court, though at times they acted as a check on monarchs who trampled too heavily on the interests and self-esteem of the aristocracy. The so-called Decembrists of 1825, however, though like earlier conspirators drawn from the aristocratic officer corps of the Guards, did have a radical political programme and in a way were forerunners of some post-1945 Third World 'modernising' military regimes. The Decembrists drew part of their inspiration from the victories of their radical Spanish officer contemporaries and it is possible that success in 1825 might have had similar long-term consequences. These might have included the politicisation of the army and frequent subsequent coups. These would have de-stabilised and de-legitimised all dynastic or civilian authority. They would also have weakened the armed forces as purely military instruments of great power policy.

If Spanish-style military–political traditions had taken root in Russian soil the whole of modern Russian history could well have been transformed. In fact, however, the Decembrists were crushed and a Russian military tradition of conservative support for legitimate dynastic authority was established. Just as the Prussian officer corps was a key factor in the defeat of the 1848 revolution, so its Russian counterpart saved the Romanovs in 1905. The revolutions reinforced the determination of rulers, generals and conservative political leaders to keep the armed forces subordinate to the monarch alone and out of the clutches of suspect parliamentary institutions. The Prussian constitutional crisis of the early 1860s was partly rooted in this determination and many of its battles were to be re-fought in Russia between the Crown and the newly created parliament (that is, the *Duma*) after 1905.[17]

In Britain too the early-nineteenth-century army was a bulwark against social revolution. Its officers to some extent also became involved in domestic politics just before 1914, the so-called Curragh Mutiny reflecting their abhorrence of Liberal policies in Ireland, which threatened the integrity of the British Empire. Where the army was concerned, however, Britain was in most ways very different from Russia or Prussia.

This had much to do with England's early and unpleasant experience of standing armies. Unlike Russia or Prussia, which created modern armies above all to face foreign foes, England's regular forces were the product of civil war. The formidable New Model Army destroyed the Royalists, supplanted its own political leaders and imposed semi-military rule on the country between 1649 and 1660. After the Civil War Royalist aristocrats paid heavy fines. During the interregnum the House of Lords was abolished and even local elites were to some extent challenged in their control over county government. Oliver Cromwell's major-generals did not on the whole come from the top layer of the county gentry, let alone from the magnate class. No social revolution occurred in England in these years, but some extremely radical movements came to the surface and army rule did deprive the traditional ruling elites of their control over the nation's destiny by imposing a form of government which not only aristocrats but also most Englishmen regarded as illegitimate. Having acted in this way the army then split and collapsed, handing power back to its aristocratic enemies.

The result was to have a big influence on the army and its officers right up to the twentieth century. Tight parliamentary control over the army became an absolute principle of aristocratic politics. A professional officer corps dominated by non-aristocrats was seen as a threat to noble power and English liberty. Venality was viewed as a guarantee that officers would be aristocrats sufficiently independent to check the ambitions of any potential royal military tyrant. By continental standards the English officer corps was wealthy, aristocratic and amateur. Comparing meritocracy in the French army with the shameful treatment of Waterloo veterans in Britain, Gronow complained that 'under the cold shade of aristocracy, men who in France would have been promoted for their valour to the highest grades of the army, lived and died, twenty or thirty years after the battle, with the rank of lieutenant or captain'. These men were forced to watch while 'children held colonels' commissions in certain regiments'.[18]

Even in 1816, long after any conceivable military threat to aristocracy had passed, the Prime Minister, Lord Liverpool, reacted to plans to set up a United Services Club with the comment that 'a general military club with the Commander-in-Chief at its head is a most ill-advised measure, and so far from its being serviceable to the army it will inevitably create a prejudice against that branch of our military establishment, and we shall feel the effects of it in parliament'.[19]

In England a homogeneous, self-conscious officer corps sharply aware of a division between itself and civilian society never existed in the eighteenth or, to a slightly lesser extent, the nineteenth century. Quite contrary to the tradition later established in continental parliamentarism, British serving officers were frequently MPs and felt few inhibitions about criticising their own government. Off-duty officers wore civilian clothes, of all England's peculiarities the one that most staggered Prince Pückler in the 1820s. Significantly, this was not a custom followed in Ireland or the colonies, where the British army's position among the local population was similar to that of dynastic armies in Europe vis-à-vis their own middle and lower classes. The unique position of officers in British society is the main reason why duelling had disappeared from the United Kingdom by 1850 whereas it survived, admittedly in decline, in Prussia and Russia up to 1914. In the two continental States the army was the great protector of duelling. Its leaders claimed that preserving the duel was vital for the military concept of honour, a concept that no civilian could fully embody or grasp. Defenders of duelling used the army's independence of any civilian authority to ensure that their views were not overruled by some non-military source. In England, however, the army was subordinate to Parliament and the officer's sense of honour was that of the public schoolboy and indeed of the whole ruling class. When the latter's values and its sense of what was politically expedient condemned the duel as illegal and immoral in the 1830s the habit was quickly extinguished in the army as well.[20]

History conditioned the English aristocratic prejudice against a professional officer corps; geography and geopolitics made it possible to indulge this prejudice right up to the end of the nineteenth century. Because Britain was both an island and the world's economic and naval superpower she could afford to have an amateur army, whose main role was to police the Empire. By continental standards it was small and ill-organised. Tactics and weapons long outdated in Europe could be used to effect against non-white enemies. Regimental officers' qualities shone in colonial campaigns and were sufficient to ensure victory. In the Sikh Wars of the 1840s, one of the Victorian army's most serious colonial conflicts, 'the British Commander-in-Chief, General Gough, was an Irishman, impetuous, hardy and very brave; but his orders were seldom clear and his staff had a genial habit of not only keeping no record of the instructions they issued, but frequently of forgetting what they were. Gough's battles tended to be gallant but somewhat muddled affairs'. Because the nineteenth-century army confronted Sikhs rather than Prussians, it could get away with not thinking seriously about the problems of warfare in the industrial age. This, combined with Wellingtonian traditions of one-man leadership and a smug self-confidence born of British power meant that Victorian Britain lacked a military or naval general staff, capable of thinking systematically about the impact of socioeconomic change on war.[21]

By contrast, in the century before 1914 Russian and Prussian military leaders faced enormous challenges. Their armies had to adapt themselves to a world changing at great speed. Taking the century as a whole, four main themes emerge. Firstly, the size of populations and armies increased enormously, which greatly complicated both logistics and, above all, command and control in battle. Secondly, the railway, telegraph and telephone revolutionised communications, which was of vital importance for the mobilisation and control of military units. Thirdly, massive changes occurred in weapons technology, drastically increasing, for instance, the power of defensive firepower at the expense of mobile, offensive forces. Finally, soldiers in most mass armies were far more literate, thinking beings in 1914 than had been the case a century before.

The business of warfare was transformed and to master its new requirements required an unprecedented degree of thoughtful professionalism in military leaders.[22]

Clearly the Prussian army after 1850 met the challenges of modernity more efficiently than did the Russians. This was not, however, because the Russian army was more aristocratic in composition – if anything, it was quite the opposite. Nor were the Russian army's most glaring weaknesses in general the fault of its aristocratic officers. They stemmed first and foremost from the empire's poverty and backwardness relative to Central and Western Europe. This resulted in a relatively small pool from which to recruit adequate officers and NCOs and a lack of initiative and even literacy among the rank and file. Pay was very poor and much of a regiment's time was spent on providing itself with food, clothing and equipment. In this vast, multi-ethnic and sparsely populated empire an inordinate amount of officers' energy was spent on administration. In addition, promotion was very slow and senior officers often much too old, and in certain cases the patronage of the monarchs and their relations also resulted in unworthy candidates holding high positions. A specific difficulty was the presence of Romanov Grand Dukes in key posts. Even when competent, the Tsar's relations had a strong tendency to turn the branches they ran into independent empires beyond the war minister's control, further exacerbating the problems of an administration already given to excessive departmentalism.

In short, the army suffered much less from an excess of aristocracy than from too little money and education, too much bureaucracy and too many Romanovs. To anyone familiar with the history of the Russian empire this will come as no surprise.

Specific criticisms might be levelled against the aristocracy. Before 1861 the survival of serfdom made it impossible to introduce a modern military system based on conscription and the creation of adequate reserves. Even, however, if one accepts that the main rationale for serfdom was aristocratic rather than State interests, the fact remains that in autocratic Russia the impetus for reform could only come from the government, and Nicholas I's regime lacked the stomach to face this issue. When emancipation and military reform did come in the 1860s and 1870s the efforts of the liberal war minister, Dimitri Milyutin, were constantly under attack from a number of senior aristocratic officers, notably Prince A. I.

Baryatinsky and R. A. Fadeev. But neither Baryatinsky nor Fadeev could fairly be described as the leader of an aristocratic military party, nor in any event were they able to stop Milyutin's reforms.

In longer and more structural terms the obvious area of aristocratic privilege in the army was the Guards, whose officers, right up to the twentieth century, were promoted more rapidly than officers of the line infantry. On the eve of the First World War, most Russian generals were still drawn either from Guards backgrounds on the one hand or artillery and engineering ones on the other. Although the privileges of the Guards were unjust and caused bitterness they were not, however, as anomalous as is sometimes suggested. By the last three decades of the Old Regime former officers of the four or five genuinely exclusive and amateur Guards regiments, even when holding the rank of general, were very often serving in the civil administration or at Court. As regards other Guards officers, even by 1914 these were on the whole better educated and from more cultured backgrounds than the majority of the line infantry and in addition had been commissioned in the Guards as a reward for doing well in their cadet schools.

Nor in any case was service in the Guards after the 1870s the golden road to the army's upper ranks. On the contrary, from the war of 1877–78 up to 1914 it was General Staff officers who increasingly monopolised top positions. The General Staff was, however, a pure meritocracy, formed on the basis of highly competitive entrance examinations and a demanding course at the Staff Academy. In the complex and bewildering personal and factional battles which divided the pre-war army's high command most, though by no means all, of the leading participants – Sukhomlinov, Grand Duke Nicholas, Palitsyn and Roediger, to name but four – came from upper-class backgrounds. Though tensions between officers of differing social origins existed in the army the major battles did not divide officers along class lines and it is absolutely wrong to see aristocratic officers as belonging to a united, reactionary, inefficient or unprofessional camp. The Tsar's most successful general in the First World War was A. A. Brusilov, a former Guards cavalryman who later served under Trotsky. Tsar Nicholas's Chief of Staff was M. A. Alekseev, the effective commander of the army in 1915–17: he was the son of a peasant who later commanded the White army. Among Alekseev's comrades-in-arms in the White army were

Barons Mannerheim and Wrangel, aristocratic ex-Guards cavalry-men, and A. I. Denikin and L. G. Kornilov, the sons of peasants.[23]

If the Russian army was not inefficient because it was aristocratic, the Prussian one combined aristocracy and efficiency to a unique degree. This presents some problems to the historian as well as the sociologist and the political scientist. The nineteenth century is, after all, the era in which the bourgeoisie is supposed to have replaced the aristocracy as controller of Europe's destinies. The middle class's leading position stemmed, so it is said, from its superior industry, professionalism and education which better fitted it for a managerial role in an increasingly complex and technological world. But armies were by far the largest, most complicated and most technologically sophisticated organisations in pre-1914 Europe. And the continent's most efficient but also most aristocratic army was the Prusso-German one, the haven not only of the world's leading military intellectuals but also of an officer corps uniquely noble in ethos which insisted on its right to duel and its semi-feudal devotion to its supreme warlord, a semi-absolute hereditary emperor. Certainly the Prusso-Germans were more aristocratic and efficient than was Francis Joseph's army, its officer corps packed with men of lower middle class origin and, by Prussian standards, exceptionally generous in its treatment of Jews. The Prussian army had proved itself far superior in 1870–71 to Napoleon III's generals, the great majority of whom were hard-bitten professionals of bour-geois origin. Prussia's military–aristocratic elite represents a classic case of a traditional upper class's successful adaptation to the tech-nical and professional requirements of the modern world.

The bedrock of the army was its Junker officer corps. Together with the Hohenzollerns they created the army. They set its tra-ditions and moulded its ethos. The Junkers had the military quali-ties to be expected of a tough, poor rural upper class whose often huge numbers of sons had to find honourable employment. Military service was the obvious solution and once a tradition was estab-lished in the first half of the eighteenth century, boys had military virtues and pride drummed in to them by their fathers from an early age as a family heirloom. The Junker estate, its labourers directed by the noble owner himself, was in itself a training in command. Oldenburg-Januschau claims that 'at any time in any matter I would speak up for my people. Certainly I was never lenient but rather ensured than on my estate obedience remained the highest principle'. Here precisely was the Victorian officer's combination of authority, toughness and paternalism.

The Lutheran religion's sense of sin, its call to obedience to constituted authority and strict fulfilment of duty, helped to shape the values of Junker and labourer alike. Helmut von Gerlach's father gave a party for his labourers every Christmas Eve. Lest they get carried away by this gesture, however, he insisted that they kiss the hand of each member of his family, children included, before festivities began. Nor did he forget to make a speech before the party to the assembled company, outlining the sins of each of his 'people' over the past year. Lutheranism had little of Russian Orthodoxy's mysticism or its beautiful ritual. It had still less of the easy-going gentlemanly code of the broad Anglican church of the Augustan age, whose great monument, still very much alive in Victorian times, was the hunting parson.

The Junkers' country was for the most part neither rich nor beautiful. 'The Mark has in a real sense always been a colonial land. The political conquest of the land was completed in the thirteenth century but economic conquest is still in train in our time. This is because nature here makes few concessions to man. Sand, marsh and heath in all their bareness confront him as an enemy and must be mastered in long, hard work'. The Junker adapted well to his environment. His manor house was plumped down in the midst of estate administrative buildings, practical rather than aesthetic considerations dictating the layout. Helmut von Gerlach records that his aunt returned to their country estate from service at a minor court full of refined ideas, one of them being that his father should move the servants' quarters out of sight of the manor house. His father replied that he was a practical country-man and liked to keep his business under his eye. The same principle applied to the estate dung-pit, whose smell pervaded all approaches to the house.

Out of this world came the men who united Germany between 1866 and 1871, winning the sometimes exasperated admiration of Baroness Spitzemberg, a Würtemmberger, in the process. Men of 'tough, rugged wood', they were very often cold, hard, narrow-minded, provincial and stiff. But they were also, at their best, 'serious, honourable and brave men', with a 'Prussian sense of duty and Prussian efficiency'.[24]

For all the Junkers' virtues, however, on their own the Prussian

indigenous nobility would never have turned their country into a
great military power. The Hohenzollern State in the nineteenth
century added two key ingredients – willingness to accept foreigners
into its service and a great respect for education. Scharnhorst,
Gneisenau and the older Moltke all came from outside Prussia's
borders, from the ranks of the Protestant North German nobility
and educated bourgeoisie. The General Staff tradition they created
and embodied carried Prussia to greatness because it thought systematically about the impact of socioeconomic change on warfare.
Prussia did not defeat Austria and France in 1866–71 because it
was more populous, economically more developed or socially more
'modern'. It did so because its leading generals thought harder,
and by so doing mobilised more soldiers, moved them more rapidly,
armed them more appropriately and commanded them in battle
more effectively. If these generals were in a sense less humane than
their predecessors in the Reform Era, that was in part because they
were children of a Positivist age, not Romantics like their parents.
But the military revolutions they were confronting were also different. Napoleon's superiority over his enemies was rooted in the way
his armies were organised and motivated, and not at all in superior
technology. By creating a Prussian citizenry Scharnhorst and Gneisenau therefore intended to counter the French via themselves
mobilising the human factor. By the 1860s, however, the technology
of the Industrial Revolution was the novel element in warfare. It
was far easier to believe that this challenge could be mastered by
technocratic means, which to a great extent ignored the humanist
and even democratic conceptions of earlier reformers.[25]

In the First World War, which ended Victorian Europe, Britain
and Germany emerged as the pre-eminent forces in the rival
coalitions. The war provided an opportunity to evaluate their military systems, both deeply stamped by national aristocratic traditions. At the lowest level there was similarity. Young aristocrats
from both countries fought with a degree of courage and self-sacri-
fice exceptional even in wartime Britain and Prussia. In so doing
they were true to family traditions, but also unconsciously asserted
their class's claim to leadership in an area where aristocracy could
still make its mark. At other levels, however, the performance of
the two military systems was anything but uniform. The Prusso-
German system at tactical level was more professional, less rigid
and more imaginative. In March 1918 Ludendorff achieved the

breakthrough for which Haig had striven with such wooden resol-
ution in the two previous years. At this level the Prussian army not
only had a far larger pool of professional cadres but they encouraged
an initiative and thoughtfulness in warfare which was part and
parcel of the tradition handed down by Scharnhorst and Moltke
but alien to Wellington and the British regular army. But at the
highest strategic–political level the English aristocratic tradition of
strict military subordination to civilian government proved decisively superior to the Junker principle of keeping the armed forces
out of the clutches of the politicians. Technical military superiority
gave Germany the chance of victory in 1914 and 1917. The failure
to subordinate military strategy to political goals and realities threw
this chance away by bringing the United States into the war and
then attempting to achieve complete victory over the Western allies
by military offensives. The victory of Britain's War Cabinet over
Hindenburg and Ludendorff was precisely the triumph of the English military–aristocratic tradition over the Prussian one.[26]

10. Aristocracy in Politics

It is hard to imagine how an aristocracy could have been much more powerful than was England's in 1815. The deference granted to the aristocracy on its estates and in the neighbouring area was immense. The great nobleman was looked up to as the natural local leader and was expected to conform to public expectations of his position. He was not, in the style of the east European serf-owner, a despot. The law constrained him from arbitrary violence against his neighbours and dependents, though it protected his property, and above all his game, with great ferocity. But it was convention and, often, a tact born of generations of political leadership which largely guided and restrained the English aristocrat in the Victorian era.

In the nineteenth century in most of England one's peers or dependents did not consider it decent if tenants were evicted without good cause, which above all meant failure to pay rent without good excuse. Though in principle tenancies were held at will and, until 1882, no statutory right to compensation for improvements existed, in practice mutual trust beween landlord and tenant generally prevailed and a tenant's needs and interests were taken into account. Radical efforts to exploit farmers' possible resentment against the aristocracy failed largely because, where landlord–tenant relations were concerned, 'institutional arrangements which were theoretically objectionable did in fact work in practice'. Conventions differed between regions both as regards their details and the extent to which they were fully observed. 'Lincolnshire custom', for instance, grew up in the early nineteenth century in response to the

big investments required of tenants if advanced agricultural
methods were to prevail on the county's thin soils. This custom had
the force of law and guaranteed that compensation would be paid
for improvements and tenants not removed save in exceptional
circumstances. To follow this convention suited landlords' own
interests, which decreed that reliable and efficient tenants be
retained and farmers given the security without which agricultural
improvements were unthinkable. These tenant farmers were anything but peasants subservient to their master's whim. As R. J.
Olney states, well-dressed, well-horsed and in some cases enjoying
incomes of over £1000 a year in the 1830s, tenant farmers were not
easily coerced. Moreover, when times were bad the argument for
hanging on to good tenant farmers at all costs became particularly
strong.[1]

Landlord power had to be exercised with these realities in mind.
In Frank O'Gorman's view, 'deferential relationships and the values
that accompanied them, not merely legitimated the social and political authority of the elite but defined and limited that authority'.
Revolts were possible where the aristocracy was seen to be forfeiting
its trust and abandoning local interests. A Lincolnshire protectionist
farmer complained, for example, as early as 1843 that the Conservative Government's growing enthusiasm for free trade meant that
'we have been deserted by our natural leaders'. When Sir Robert
Peel abandoned protection entirely in 1846 a tenant farmers' revolt
did occur and a number of those who had voted for repeal of the
Corn Laws either lost their seats or retired from Parliament rather
than be forced to obey the dictates of their aroused farmer constituents.[2]

Landlords who squeezed tenants hard could easily face trouble
at elections. Political patronage was to some extent bought by an
open-handed attitude to voters of all descriptions, tenants included.
In county seats, of which there were 144 before the 1867 Reform
Act and 172 after, the electorate was usually too large for any single
patron to control. There were, however, exceptions: 'In Derbyshire
the influence of the dukes of Devonshire was concentrated in the
county's northern division after 1832, with the result that two Whigs
were returned at every election until 1867, and the western division
of the county – carved out in 1868 – remained a family fief down
to 1914 and even later'.[3]

The county election was, however, the traditional platform not just of great aristocrats but also of the independent untitled gentry. The smaller boroughs were the main keys to magnate power before 1832. In 1830, ninety-eight peers were believed to control the 'election' of 214 MPs. The latter were not only nominated by peers but also expected to resign should their views and those of their patrons diverge: in general, MPs conformed to this expectation. Even after the 1832 Reform Act swept away most of these rotten boroughs, up to 70 MPs were still the nominees of an aristocratic patron. Even in many of the smaller boroughs, however, the patron had to work to maintain his influence. In the early nineteenth century, for instance, 'those who voted for the fourth duke of Newcastle's nominee at Newark received a half ton of coal at Christmas and around 30 per cent lower rents than the prevailing price'. Between 1812 and 1815, on the contrary, the Second Marquis of Stafford raised rents and lost control of the two seats at Newcastle-under-Lyme.[4]

In the pre-reform Parliament the counties and, still more, the growing industrial towns were very under-represented while a swathe of tiny, or in certain cases even non-existent, electorates in small boroughs chose almost half the House of Commons. Not surprisingly, a lower house selected by these means was dominated by the aristocracy and gentry. Between 1734 and 1832, 30 per cent of all MPs were drawn from just 247 families. 'Even in 1868, 407 MPs came from families owning 2,000 acres or more', a figure which had dropped to 322 twelve years later. The decline of the aristocratic MP was palpable but scarcely precipitate: in 1895, 60 per cent of MPs were gentlemen of leisure, country squires, retired officers and lawyers, and there were still 23 eldest sons of peers in the House'. As successive reform bills enfranchised first the middle and then, in 1885, the bulk of the working class the old elites became more inclined to use the still entirely aristocratic upper house to check the reforms proposed by the House of Commons. Not until 1911 was the absolute veto of the Lords over legislation removed, which is remarkable given the fact that this purely hereditary body monopolised by the great old landowning families looked anachronistic even by the standards of Europe's other, and anything but democratic, upper chambers.[5]

Among Queen Victoria's Prime Ministers Peel, William Gladstone and Benjamin Disraeli came from outside the traditional upper class. None of the three were, however, self-made men. All had been brought up to be members of the ruling elite. Even so, they were exceptions to the rule that cabinets were dominated by the aristocracy and gentry. This rule prevailed until the Whig secession from the Liberal Party in 1885, after which the Liberal administrations had mostly middle-class cabinets with a healthy sprinkling of aristocrats. The last unequivocally Old Regime cabinet was Lord Salisbury's in the 1890s, the famous Hotel Cecil, in which Whig grandees sat alongside the usual Tory mix of aristocrats, members of the landed gentry and the odd member of the professional and business classes. David Cannadine comments of this cabinet that 'its tone was as aristocratic as its composition. Lord Randolph Churchill dismissed Richard Cross and W. H. Smith – both of whom had bought estates – as "Marshall and Snelgrove".'[6]

In Victorian times the British Parliament and cabinet presided over an administrative system which, by European standards, was so weird as to hardly seem to exist in some respects. Rural government and justice was amateur through and through. For almost the entire Victorian era it was dominated by the – exclusively aristocratic – Lords Lieutenant of the counties, who in turn exercised a decisive influence on the selection of JPs. The magistrates' bench traditionally controlled the county's life. The aristocracy and gentry, inclined to shirk their duty in the eighteenth century by avoiding service as JPs, returned to the bench in the Victorian era as part of the upper class's effort to be seen to be justifying its privileges by providing upright, unpaid service to the community. Not until the County Councils Act of 1888 was democracy introduced in local rural government. In most of Ireland and Wales this meant the end of aristocratic control over local administration, but this was much less true in England, though the picture differed from county to county. In many areas the aristocracy and gentry continued to dominate local government institutions because they had the leisure, a tradition of public service and a reputation for fairness. Since the rewards of local government service were few and much of the work not obviously attractive, competition could be scarce. In Wiltshire, admittedly an unusually deferential and aristocratic county, the Fourth Marquess of Bath chaired the new county council from 1889 to 1896, Lord Edmund Fitzmaurice for the next decade, and the Fifth Marquess from 1906 until after the Second World War.[7]

The Lords Lieutenant and the JPs were England's equivalent of the continent's ministries of internal affairs, in general the central and distinctly authoritarian pillars of domestic administration. By

European standards the central bureaux of the Home Office, which employed only thirty-six permanent officials in 1876, were absurdly small, as indeed were the other major ministries. So long as they remained that way, many of them were headed by offspring of gentry families, but when the great expansion of government began in the late nineteenth century the upper ranks of the civil service came very quickly to be dominated by a new elite, generally middle-class in origin and public-school and Oxbridge in education.[8]

As one would expect, given European traditions, the Foreign Office and Diplomatic Service were much more aristocratic than the domestic Civil Service. Writing of the period 1898 to 1914, Zara Steiner comments that 'all the clichés about the Foreign Office staff were true; it was indeed the stronghold of the landed classes and everything was done to preserve its character and clannish structure . . . between 1908 and 1913 nine out of sixteen candidates were Etonians . . . the landed bias in the Diplomatic Service was even more marked and the social circle narrowed rather than expanded in the pre-war period. The great families of England were well represented. Among the twenty-three secretaries appointed between 1908 and 1913, eight were the sons of lords and two were baronets'. Among successful candidates for diplomatic posts between 1908 and 1913, 'no fewer than 25 out of 37 came from Eton'.[9]

By contrast to the Diplomatic Service, neither the Colonial nor the Indian civil bureaucracies were very popular with the aristocracy or gentry. As regards the Indian Civil Service, 'during the early 1850s, when appointments were still by nomination, over one-quarter of the new recruits were from a genteel background. But after the introduction of open competition, between 1854 and 1856, the landed element dropped away very soon and very abruptly – to a mere one tenth by the 1860s, and to as little as 6 per cent by the 1890s'. The only areas of Indian and Colonial service which remained really popular with aristocrats were the courts and staffs of the various viceroys, governors and pro-consuls of Britain's Empire. These posts were educative, they were fun and they were a source of useful connections. They taught aristocrats about the British Empire and imbued them with a sense of imperial pride but they did not commit them to spending their whole lives overseas, in inhospitable climates and either in isolation or among people whom they regarded as distinctly their inferiors. To do the British aristocracy justice, the social elites of few countries provide many volunteers for semi-permanent exile. Moreover there was a great deal to be said for introducing the future rulers of empire to the colonies as young men before returning them to positions of power and influence in London. The impact of imperial thinking on the late Victorian and Edwardian elite was immense and when one recalls the colonial service of Winston Churchill, of Lord Milner's 'kindergarten' in South Africa, or indeed of many of the so-called Diehard Tory peers of 1911, it becomes clear that the sources of this thinking often lay in direct personal experience.[10]

In Russia and Germany aristocrats seldom matched English wealth and were challenged by peasant, bureaucrat and monarch for political power. On his own estates, however, the serf-owner's authority was less constrained than that of the English aristocrat. Even in southern and western Germany before 1848 the *Standesherr* combined the influence which derived from his wealth and social position with wide-ranging judicial and police powers. Only after the abolition of all elements of serfdom in that year did he become a landowner pure and simple.[11]

On the one hand 1848 sharply reduced the political significance of the west and south German nobility, particularly the *Standesherren*. From being possessors of many of the residual powers and trappings of sovereignty they became merely rich citizens in a society where wealth was soon to become quite widespread. On the other hand, for many Catholic nobles one result of 1848 was to make it easier for them to emerge as standard-bearers of their communities' religious and particularist values against the encroachments of industrialising capitalism and the modernising Protestant State.

Some of them had begun to take on this role in the period 1815 to 1848. A Catholicism more intense and emotional than that of their parents' generation was one key to this. Another was the anger of Rhineland, Westphalian and Schwabian noblemen at the Protestant liberal states which had annexed their territories, depriving them of both status and income in the process. The Westphalian aristocracy's biggest clash with the Prussian State centred around the issue of mixed marriages and reached its climax with the so-called Köln events of 1827 and the imprisonment of Archbishop (Count) Clemens August Droste zu Vischering. Similar battles raged in Württemberg in the 1830s and 1840s, the Catholic *Standesherren* in the upper house proving the biggest thorn in the side of the liberal but above all statist Württemberg bureaucracy. The *Standesherren* objected to the State's efforts to control ecclesiastical appointments, priests' legal activities, and the clergy's communications with Rome. They insisted on the church's right to demand that the children of mixed marriages be brought up in the faith. They resented the ban on a Catholic press and what they perceived as favouritism towards old Württemberg by the government at Schwabia's expense.

In both Prussia's western provinces and Schwabia some efforts were made to mobilise mass Catholic support behind the aristocracy's defence of the church. Most nobles, however, shuddered at the idea of appealing to peasants against legally constituted authority. Moreover, the sharp tensions between aristocracy and peasantry meant that such efforts were unlikely to succeed. The aristocracy's eyes were still largely directed backwards to rights lost since the fall of the Old Reich. They clung to remaining privileges, hunting rights for example, with great stubbornness. Clashes over access to forests, as well as over dues and services, remained fierce. The residual *Standesherr* police and legal institutions in particular seemed to peasants an unnecessary extra burden, given the existence of parallel State structures. In 1848 Karl Egon II fled from Fürstenberg in the face of revolution. The house of Count Clemens von Westphalen, the most outspoken of Westphalian Catholic patricians, was burned to the ground. In these circumstances the Schwabian *Standesherr*, Count Constantin von Waldburg-Zeil-Trauchburg, was exceptional in taking his Catholic and particularist commitments so seriously that he more-or-less joined the revolution and was elected to the National Assembly at Frankfurt on a democratic ticket. Caring above all else for the independence of the Catholic church and the interests of Schwabia, Waldburg-Zeil became convinced that if the aristocracy was to defend these causes against the Württemberg liberals it had to find common ground with the Catholic masses. To this end he became an advocate of universal equal suffrage, generous redemption terms and mediatisation of Württemberg in a Habsburg-led *Grossdeutschland*.[12]

The 1848 settlement, however, removed many of the causes of conflict between Catholic aristocrat and peasant. Incomes from stocks and bonds caused less tension than attempting to wring dues and services from the local peasantry. Increasing wealth made it easier for nobles to be generous and charitable local leaders, while the fact that many aristocrats had actually taken to farming their remaining lands created common interests between them and the peasantry. In the second half of the century all agrarians felt the increasing challenge of the industrial sector and their growing dependence on international market prices. Traditionalists – noble and peasant alike – disliked city values, which improved literacy and communications allowed to impinge more on the countryside than in the past. Above all, Catholics faced the growing domination of German government, culture and economy by Protestants, a process sealed by Prussia's conquest of Catholic Germany between 1866 and 1871. Catholics felt themselves to be despised and second-class citizens in the Protestant States. Matthew Arnold spoke for the Prussian liberal middle class he so much admired when he commented that 'the Romish party was in German countries the ignorant party also, the party untouched by the humanities and by culture'. The fact that there was some truth in this assertion made it more galling, particularly since it was used as an excuse to deny Catholics access to jobs in government service. When on top of this in the 1870s the Prussian liberal State attempted to impose its educational and cultural principles on the Catholic minority, in the process seeking to break the Church's links with Rome and gaoling most of the Prussian bishops, the reaction of most of the Catholic aristocracy was a furious one.[13]

The aristocracy played a big role in mobilising the Catholic community's opposition to the *Kulturkampf*. Among the notables who dominated the Catholic Centre Party in the 1870s and 1880s, aristocrats were often closer to the peasantry in interests and even values than was the case with many of the professional middle-class leaders from the cities. In part too, the often primitive and irrational outpourings of popular Catholicism jarred a bit less on rural anti-intellectual nobles than on the academically educated bourgeoisie. Burghard von Schorlemer-Alst founded the first important Peasant League, that of Westphalia, in 1862. The Rhineland and Silesian Peasant Leagues were created two decades later by Felix von Loë and Karl von Hoyningen-Huene respectively. The leading Bavarian Centrist was Count Konrad von Preysing; one of the best-known Silesian leaders was Count Franz von Ballestrem, who in the twentieth century served as President of the Reichstag. In Bavarian or Silesian terms, to be more aristocratic than this was scarcely possible. Some of these noblemen were a little surprised to find themselves under the leadership of the physically very unimposing Ludwig Windthorst, a bourgeois from Hanover. If, sometimes grudgingly, they accepted his primacy this had much to do with the need for unity during the *Kulturkampf*. It was also owed to Windthorst's outstanding skills as a parliamentarian.

The Centre Party was a strange mish-mash. The Catholic working class in the newly industrialising Rhineland stood alongside its often quite prosperous peasant co-religionists from the western provinces and their in general poorer south German peers. The growing Catholic bourgeoisie of the Rhineland and Westphalia were an important Centre constituency but so too were the Poles of Silesia. On top of this came the Catholic nobility, itself disunited and forced to take into account the different constituencies it led and represented, for by now politics revolved around an all-German Reichstag elected by universal male suffrage, and not the increasingly powerless upper houses of the various states. The Westphalian and Rhenish Peasant Leagues, with Schorlemer-Alst and Loë in the lead, might preach corporatist and anti-capitalist doctrines but the Silesian Catholic magnates, of whom Count Franz von Ballestrem was a worthy example, were among Germany's richest industrialists. Another variation on Catholic aristocracy was Count Georg von Hertling, the Centre's leader in the Reichstag from 1909, who came from a quite recently ennobled official family and was himself a university professor. Hertling had considerable sympathy for Catholic social theory but he was far too much the Victorian professor to believe that one could turn one's back on progress or doubt that its guiding principles were enshrined in capitalist economics and constitutionalist parliamentary politics. Between Hertling and the ultramontane, corporatist, reactionary, Prince Karl von Löwenstein, there was an abyss.

Inevitably Catholic aristocratic leaders differed in their political views and cannot be differentiated sharply from non-noble Catholic notables. Instead they mostly tended to share with the more oldfashioned bourgeois leaders a certain distaste and alarm at popular political demands and styles. In general close to the church's hierarchy, many aristocrats wished to heed Leo XIII's call for reconciliation with Bismarck in the 1880s. As the *Kulturkampf* wound down, most wished to ally themselves with other conservative forces and to be accepted as loyal and deserving citizens of the Reich. They disliked Windthorst's liberalism, expressed in opposition both to the repressive, authoritarian policies of the Prussian Government and to the latter's attempts to introduce old-age and invalid insurance in 1889–90: authoritarian paternalism was, after all, very much in the Catholic aristocratic tradition.

In the early 1890s the aristocrats' position came increasingly under threat as agricultural depression radicalised their rural constituency. As industrial capitalism developed, poorer peasants and parts of the lower middle class were threatened with extinction. Their response was frequently a violently anti-liberal, anti-government and anti-intellectual populism. It was very difficult for respectable aristocrats anxious to achieve compromises with the Imperial Government on issues such as defence and economic policy to satisfy an electorate hostile to all elites and primitively selfish in most of its demands for special privileges and subsidies to enable it to survive the modern age. Calls from Catholic populists for a progressive income tax contributed to aristocrats' discomfiture, which was confirmed in the disastrous showing of most noble Centre candidates in the 1893 elections, Wilhelm Loth commenting that 'when the Reichstag met again in 1893 . . . the aristocratic wing of the Centre possessed no power worth mentioning'.

But 1893 was not the end of the Catholic nobility's role in politics. When agricultural depression eased some of them staged a comeback. They remained powerful in Silesia and in the Centre's agrarian wing. The Conservative–Centre bloc of 1909 fulfilled their long-held ambitions for the Party's swing to the right, as indeed did the compromise the Centre achieved with the Government over naval policy. But after 1893 the aristocracy was never nearly as prominent in the Centre Party as had been the case during the *Kulturkampf*. Instead, the party was run by (mostly bourgeois) professional politicians, who were above all experts in gauging the moods of the Catholic mass electorate and balancing the demands of its various elements. By 1914 the power of Catholic aristocrats in the Centre Party was more akin to that of their British Liberal counterparts than to the major role still played by the traditional upper classes in the English or Prussian Conservative Parties.[14]

In comparison to the Junkers, German Catholic nobles lacked in the nineteenth century a great state of their own, whose army and civil service they could dominate and colonise with their sons. They were also simply much less numerous. Above all, though, their tradition of land- and serf-owning was different. The Junker tradition of themselves managing farms and their labour force, not to mention their custom of military service, stamped their personalities with a sense of their unique right and fitness to lead and command. In many ways these nobles of the eastern marches had much more in common with Russian serf-owners than with the west- and south-German aristocracy. In eastern Prussia, as in Russia, villages were scattered widely ove a land which, by Western standards, was sparsely populated and without strong urban traditions. Even in the late eighteenth century the rural community was semi-autarchic and very dependent on its lord. Travelling in the east for the first time in 1863, Baroness Spitzemberg commented that the villages there were not like in western Germany. The labourers' cottages huddled around the manor house and villages differed greatly in their order and prosperity, above all bearing the stamp of the noble family to which they belonged. On inheriting their farms before 1811 peasants swore fealty to the serf-owner, who in general regarded them as potentially unruly children in need of discipline. Whether discipline was accompanied by an element of paternal benevolence depended on the nobleman in question. On many late-eighteenth-century estates such paternalism appears unlikely since properties were bought, leased and let at dizzying speed. In Prussia as in Russia, however, it often paid the serf to play the role of a child.[15]

Admittedly, by the second half of the eighteenth century the Prussian serf-owner operated under more constraints than did his Russian counterpart. Prussian serfs often had rights, including property rights, and the Hohenzollern State was more or less able to ensure that these rights were not flagrantly violated. The sale of serfs without land, for instance, was successfully banned, save to some extent in Silesia. In Russia, on the other hand, the State lacked the resources to control its serfowners, at least before Nicholas I's reign. Given Russia's size and the scale and quality of its bureaucracy, the noble had the powers of a miniature king. These powers were generally not abused. On the bigger estates life was regulated by detailed rules and peasants lived under something akin to a regular system of government. Particularly on the big quit-rent (*obrok*) properties with absentee landlords, noble control was loose. The same was much less true where agriculture was conducted by serf forced labour (*barshchina*), a system that often demanded considerable coercion of 'lazy' and recalcitrant peasants. Moreover,

whether or not an individual lord ruled with justice and benevolence, the fact remained that neither the peasant's person nor his
property had any legal protection against his master's whim.[16]

When serfdom was abolished in 1861, however, the landowner
lost his rights over the local community. He now merely had the
influence of a relatively rich person living among rather poor ones.
Since most of the latter were largely self-sufficient and were organised in self-governing communes, this influence was not as great as
one might suppose. In Prussia, by contrast, the landowner retained
disciplinary powers over unmarried workers living on his premises
(*Gesindeordnung*) up to 1918. Until 1872, the *Rittergut* defined the
boundaries of the local community and its owners exercised police
and judicial power over all those living within it. He selected the
village's mayor and could veto all decisions of its assembly. When
in 1872 Bismarck and the National Liberals attempted to reduce
these and other rights of the *Rittergut* owners a rare revolt occurred
in the Prussian House of Lords (*Herrenhaus*). The wealthy nobles
who peopled this chamber believed the assault on the *Rittergüter*
would weaken their hold and prestige in the countryside, but the
reform also offended the principle, passionately believed in by old-
fashioned conservatives of Kleist-Retzow's stamp, that property and
wealth ought to be associated with the duties and responsibilities
of government. The swamping of the upper house by newly
appointed peers represented a further defeat for legitimist and old
Prussian principles, which had already taken a battering from
Bismarck's conquest of Germany and alliance with the National
Liberals.[17]

Above the level of the individual village and *Rittergut* local government in both Prussia and Russia was a curious mixture of State
and noble estate (*Stand*) principles and institutions. At least until
the second half of the nineteenth century the key difference between
the two countries was that Prussian noble local government officers
and institutions operated with far more efficiency and enthusiasm
than did Russian ones. This was in part because the Prussian
institutions mostly had deep roots which pre-dated Hohenzollern
absolutism. Though the Great Elector and Frederick William I had
established an absolutist state and cut back the power of noble
corporate institutions, the latter mostly survived, were subsequently
reinvigorated and were merged with the Crown's administrative
network from the reign of Frederick II. Unlike the Russian Court

and service aristocracy, the Prussian gentry had deep local and provincial loyalties and old traditions of public service in corporate institutions.

Even among old Russian gentry families in traditional Muscovite provinces such traditions did not exist. The Kulomzins, for instance, had been nobles in the Kineshma district of Kostroma Province for over 250 years by 1861 but the concept of service to the local community in elected office had to be learned by the young Anatol Kulomzin in the 1850s from his firsthand experience of the work of English JPs. This appears strange since a plethora of local government and noble corporate posts filled by election from the gentry had existed since 1775. These posts had, however, never been popular with nobles, in part because the State's bureaucracy burdened elected office-holders with numerous tasks, while allowing them no independence or status. In addition, the concept of office as public service rather than as a means to self-enrichment was a novelty which had only seized a small section of the aristocracy by 1800. These people, the educational and cultural elite of the nobility, gravitated to the St. Petersburg bureaucracy, not its provincial outposts, until the second half of the nineteenth century. Only then did service as provincial or district marshal of the nobility, or on the elected self-government councils (*zemstvos*), begin to enjoy popularity and prestige.[18]

Up to 1914 the key figure in local government in Prussia and Russia was the *Landrat* in the former and the District Marshal of nobility in the latter. The Marshal was in principle not a government official at all but rather the elected head of the district (*uezd*) nobility. Nevertheless, in the absence of any sort of State-appointed sub-prefect to co-ordinate government at this level the District Marshal filled the gap, an extraordinary anomaly by the twentieth century but one which lasted up to 1917. In Prussia the *Landrat* was a state official but one of a distinctly peculiar sort. Until 1872 he was selected by the king from candidates elected by local owners of knights' estates (*Rittergüter*) and the Government's proposal to make the somewhat more democratic district assembly the electoral college provoked further fury in the *Herrenhaus*.

Despite the change, however, the *Landrat* remained a peculiar, quintessentially noble, and in the eastern provinces generally Junker, figure who stood out from the rest of the State administration by his origins and the ethos he brought to his office. Hans-

Hugo von Kleist-Retzow, a Pietist reactionary of considerable intelligence and great honour, described his position as *Landrat* in the following terms in 1844: 'The office which God has entrusted to me is truly excellent and beautiful. Independent from above, from the government districts, as from the county residents below, the living contact that I establish with these residents is my responsibility alone. I can and must work with them more through my personality than through the administration of the laws'. The quotation expresses the values and prejudices but also the virtues of Junkerdom at its best: the sense of office as a responsibility which must be fulfilled according to the strictest dictates of the Lutheran conscience: the love of independence and personal relationships rather than the ordered, monotonous and inhuman rules by which bureaucracies and judiciaries operate. Even in 1914, 56.2 per cent of Prussia's *Landräte* were of noble birth.[19]

The Landrat or Marshal could often combine his official job with supervision of his estates. Like the army officer, he could serve for a number of years and then retire into private life. Many *Landräte* and Marshals followed this course, though some, on the contrary, continued with civil service careers, often rising far in the bureaucratic hierarchy. In general, to opt for a civil service career was to commit oneself to a full-time and life-time occupation. Nobles who took this path to some extent divorced themselves from their rural roots and took on another personality, that of the elite state official. Regardless of whether he was of noble or bourgeois origin, the official went through the same process of education and assimilation of the official's ethos. First there was the university, which always in Prussia and usually in Russia meant its law faculty for the future civil servant. Then there was the in-service schooling in the bureaucracy's disciplines, its style of work, its approach to problems. The independent nobleman must to some extent become a cog, a mere subordinate, a competitor for rank and office. Hans Rosenberg has traced the development of a highly cultured, rationalist, rather pragmatic bureaucratic elite in Prussia between 1660 and 1815. Here noble and bourgeois merged into a group of men who were in general liberal–conservative in their political sympathies, inspired by a sense of corporate identity and often possessed of the wide views required of those holding top positions in government. Figures such as Hardenburg, Humboldt and Schön in the Reform Era were the cream of this group.[20]

In the first half of the nineteenth century most of even the Russian central bureaucracy was far from matching Prussian standards of education, efficiency or honesty. The Prussian upper bureaucracy's corporate professional ethos, enshrined in the *Allgemeine Landrecht* of 1794, did not yet exist in Russia. The Prussian top official saw himself as the servant of the State, the guardian of the community's long-term interests. In Russia the sense of personal loyalty to, and dependence on, the monarch still prevailed. Nicholas I encouraged this by choosing most of his ministers from the army, the only branch of his government for which he had trust and affection.[21]

In the second half of the nineteenth century matters changed. First individual ministries, then the whole of the St. Petersburg bureaucracy and part of the provincial official elite came to match Prussia in their education, their level of professional competence and their ethos of public service and guardianship. Since in both Russia and Prussia the bureaucracy not only administered but also governed the State, its attitude to society, even noble society, could take on a distinctly avuncular, not to say arrogant, colouring. This was particularly true in Russia where the gap between ruler and ruled was sharper, partly for traditional reasons and partly because, unlike in post-1848 Prussia, Russia had no parliament through which society could exert an influence on government. The fact that a senior official and a noble landowner might be close relations did not mean there were no tensions between them. Faced with the Government's efforts to democratise but also bureaucratise local government, one indignant Russian noble landowner complained in 1909 that 'it's our brothers who, by the will of fate, have got themselves into the administration's feeding trough and are betraying us'.[22]

Right up to 1914 the social composition and ethos of the Prussian and Russian bureaucracies were affected by the different systems of training that prevailed within them. The Prussian administrative official required a complete education in gymnasium and university. He then faced a minimum of four years' unpaid probationary service and would not secure paid work until his late twenties at the earliest. The legal training required for either an administrative or judicial official cost 25 000 Marks by William II's reign, four times the price of educating a son at a military cadet corps. In addition, the officer would earn a salary at twenty-one. Not surprisingly, Junkers in the Prussian high administration were recruited only from the wealthier and more cultured sections of the nobility. Prussian officials were also much richer than most senior Russian civil servants, who required merely a university or equivalent-level education before taking up paid positions in the ministries. Russian civil service reformers envied Prussia, 'which beyond question enjoys an excellent officialdom and a model civil service system', but they knew that in much poorer Russia it would be impossible to expect parents of young officials to support their sons through years of unpaid in-service training. The only area of the Russian bureaucracy where formal probationary terms existed was the judicial department and even here the system did not really function until the 1890s. By the 1900s, however, senior Russian officials' inferiority complex *vis à vis* the Prussian bureaucracy was largely misplaced. It was a distinctly moot point whether years of largely legal education and training, together with the exclusion of all but the well-to-do that this entailed, were really the right preparation for future government leaders whose jobs required a grasp of contemporary economic and social realities. Senior Russian officials came from somewhat more diverse backgrounds than their Prussian peers and were socialised in a bureaucracy that was distinctly less law-abiding, systematic or uniform than Prussia's. To some extent the efficiency of Russian government suffered from this. On the other hand the entrepreneurial and political talents often required if one was to make one's way to the top of the more free-wheeling Russian bureaucracy could stand ministers in good stead as they fought to master the problems of governing and modernising a vast, chaotic and heterogeneous empire in the midst of great turmoil and conflict. The upper bureaucracy which produced a S. Yu. Witte, A. V. Krivoshein, P. N. Durnovo and P. A. Stolypin in a single generation was by no means merely the Gogolean–Rasputinesque farce familiar in much Western legend.[23]

The patterns of aristocratic service in the ministerial bureaucracy were roughly similar in Russia and Prussia. Technical jobs and the education ministry were shunned. The Court and foreign ministry were, above all, the homes of the wealthy aristocratic elites. Junkers were generally too poor, provincial and blunt to make good diplomats, though the eastern nobility very often held the ambassadorship in St. Petersburg. The Russian Foreign Ministry, sensitive to the prejudices of the host country, sent men with an abundance of aristocratic quarterings to Vienna, and wealthy noblemen to

London. The last Imperial ambassador in England, Alexander Benckendorff, was the son of a Croy, the cousin of the Prussian and Austrian ambassadors, and a comfortable member of Edward VII's circle. Still more at home was his counsellor, A. F. Poklevsky-Kozell, whose large private fortune enabled him to entertain 'Tum-Tum' and his friends in the required style.

The biggest difference between Prussia and Russia was that in the former nobles shunned the judiciary. In Russia, on the other hand, the extremely influential Imperial School of Law, entirely noble in its composition, existed precisely to send upper-class boys into the Ministry of Justice. If *pravovedy* seldom came from Russia's magnate class, they were nevertheless a distinctly privileged and well-educated stratum of the nobility. Russia was, however, similar to Prussia where top positions in the Ministry of Internal Affairs were concerned.

In the domestic administration of both countries the most aristocratic of all positions was that of provincial prefect – the Prussian *Oberpräsident* and the Russian Governor. Initially both the *Oberpräsident* and the Governor, rather like the *Landrat* or Marshal, were seen less as regular civil servants than as personal representatives of the monarch, viceroys of their provinces and supervisors of all institutions, State and noble, within it. By the late nineteenth century both the *Oberpräsident* and the Governor had, in practice, become parts of the administrative machine and subordinates of the Minister of Internal Affairs. Even so, their backgrounds set them apart from other officials. In Prussia, 83 per cent of the *Oberpräsidenten* were nobles by birth even in 1914, and the Russian governors were not merely more noble than most other senior officials but also much more likely to be landowners from old aristocratic families with, quite often, an education in elite military and civilian boarding schools. In both countries this prefectoral corps was in general professionally competent, experienced and well-trained but some of its members still had a very Old Regime style and flavour. In the 1870s, for instance, Pomerania, the heartland of Junkerdom, could still have an *Oberpräsident* drawn from one of the province's leading families whose previous qualification was confined to long service as a *Landrat* and who had avoided the stiff hurdle of civil service training by merely passing the rather easy *Landrat*'s exam. By the twentieth century, fewer such anomalies existed and the overwhelming majority even of Junker *Landräte* had passed through the full civil service education and training. Even so, William II's first two *Oberpräsidenten* in aristocratic Silesia were Hermann Prince von Hatzfeldt (1894–1903) and Robert Count von Zedlitz-Trützschler (1903–9), both members of great Silesian aristocratic families.[24]

The establishment of parliaments in Prussia and Russia after the 1848 and 1905 revolutions transformed noble politics. In the pre-constitutional era, nobles too energetic to do nothing but unenthusiastic about military careers had the choice between managing their estates in a provincial backwater or attempting the long climb up the bureaucratic ladder. Often neither appealed. N. V. Charykov, the scion of a distinguished gentry family who finally opted for diplomacy, commented that, 'had there been in Russia a constitutional government, I should certainly have tried to enter parliament'. Consitutional politics opened to Otto von Bismarck an avenue of escape from bureaucratic drudgery on the one hand or Pomeranian isolation on the other: too proud and independent to be a bureaucrat, too ambitious to live as a farmer and *Landrat*, Bismarck seized the chance of parliamentary politics.

So did Count Aleksei Bobrinsky, a Russian aristocratic magnate who, like many of his peers in absolutist Russia and Prussia hankered after the power, the independence and the fun that politics provided for English aristocrats. There was always a strong Whig element in Bobrinsky. Even in Alexander II's reign, when many constitutional schemes were in the air, Bobrinsky sought to use his position as St. Petersburg Marshal as a stepping stone to leadership of the Russian land-owning nobility, the class which he believed must take the lead in the constitutional and increasingly liberal Russian political system which would soon, in his view, develop. When at last a constitution was granted in 1905, Bobrinsky used the new freedom it brought to become the chairman of the United Nobility, the first nationwide noble association allowed in Russia. The United Nobility, an extremely powerful interest group in the constitutional era, acted as a stepping-stone to the Duma, State Council and ministerial rank for Bobrinsky.[25]

The arrival of parliamentarism not only removed the frustrations of intelligent and ambitious aristocrats chafing under the restrictions and, even for the social elite, humiliations of the absolutist police state. It also greatly enhanced the political power of the nobility as a whole. Under absolutism the monarch and senior officialdom

ruled, and even where the latter were largely drawn from the aristocracy they by no means necessarily pursued the interests of the
landowning nobility as the latter perceived them. In both Prussia
and Russia, however, parliaments created on the basis of limited
suffrage put most seats under the control of the landowners. The
latter's position was further enhanced by their domination of the
newly established upper houses, the Prussian *Herrenhaus* and the
elected half of the Russian State Council.

These institutions forced the nobility to organise on a nationwide
scale, to articulate its interests and programme and to discover its
own leaders and spokesmen. No longer could noble inexperience,
or lack of cohesion and institutions be exploited by the bureaucratic
elite to impose policies such as the Russian emancipation of the
serfs with land in 1861 or Witte's preference for industry over
agriculture in the 1890s. Even in pre-constitutional Prussia, whose
government was very solicitous of Junker interests, the policies
pursued in the Reform Era contributed to the bankruptcy of a
large proportion of the eastern nobility. Once nobles dominated
parliaments, governments had no option but to listen to their
demands. The Prussian agrarians were a thorn in the flesh of William II's Government. Piotr Stolypin could not impose the rational-
isation and democratisation of Russian local government that he
desired on chambers packed with landed noblemen. In 1815,
England's aristocracy had been the most parliamentary and politically the most powerful hereditary ruling class in the world. But by
1914 it had ceased to dominate the lower house and had lost its
veto in the upper one. By contrast, the previously weak Russian
aristocracy had acquired a parliament in 1906 and in the process
had gained unprecedented political power. Just as the English peers
were losing their veto, the Russian upper house, the State Council,
was torpedoing reformist legislation coming up to it from the Duma,
whose own composition and electoral base was roughly similar to
that of the House of Commons in the 1850s.[26]

The Prussian nobility's political experience in the years immediately after 1848 provides interesting similarities and contrasts with
Russian events in 1906–14. In both countries the pattern was the
same, in that after initially granting something close to universal
male suffrage, the governments then retreated to constitutions based
on a very unequal franchise. When it came to trying to control and
mobilise the rural population, the Prussian nobility, at least in

Pomerania and Mark Brandenburg, had the advantage of being thick on the ground and relatively prosperous by Russian standards. Local elected institutions, not to mention the overwhelmingly conservative and noble *Landräte*, could be used as organisational bases and means to persecute or dismiss from official posts local troublemakers. The numerous landless labourers depended for their incomes, homes and food on the Junkers, especially in an era of overpopulation and very limited job opportunities in the cities, let alone in the few towns of the eastern provinces. Liberals or radicals were not allowed on to the estates to canvass or pass around their ballot papers. Right up to 1914 the only ballot paper an estate labourer was likely to see was the Conservative one, handed to him by his foreman outside the polling booth. Open air rural meetings were illegal, which gave the landlord, his police and the *Landrat* the Heaven-sent opportunity to sabotage opponents by denying access to the village hall.

But tight control was by no means the only source of Conservative strength. Rural hostility to city liberals and their ways could be exploited. So too could class divisions within the rural population. Memories of serfdom and the inequitable terms on which emancipation had been based remained quite fresh in peasant minds. Particularly in some districts, noble–peasant hostility was strong and the later united front in favour of agriculture and against the towns could not yet be relied on. But the peasants shared with the nobles a desire to suppress any 'indiscipline' by their landless labourers and to keep wages to a minimum. They were stung by criticism from Pietist paternalist nobles of the old school who attacked peasant mistreatment of their workers and actually won some verbal support from Frederick William IV for so doing. If much of this propaganda was hypocritical, it certainly is true that the emerging 'Kulak' class in the villages had neither the means nor the inclination to emulate the genuinely benevolent paternalism of some of the Junker Pietists. By contrast with all this, the existence of the peasant commune, not to mention Russian peasant mentalities and class structure, meant that this option of divide and rule was not so open to the Russian gentry.[27]

How much similarity was there between the political positions of the Russian and Prussian nobilities? How much chance was there for the Russian elites to follow Prussia's lead to modernity and survival?

Looking at the Russian elites in 1900 through Prussian, let alone English, eyes it is their disunity which immediately springs to mind. In part this was institutional. The Russian government lacked even a German-style chancellor to co-ordinate its activities. The Emperor, unable to do this job himself, was in a position to stop anyone else from doing it for him. Ministerial empires were locked in conflict, the most famous battle being between the Ministry of Finance, linked to industrial development and the rising class of capitalists, and the Ministry of Internal Affairs, responsible for order and traditionally allied to the landed nobility, the main bulwarks of the rural administration.

But the picture was much more complex than this. The Ministry of Finance's great capitalist allies were the St. Petersburg financial and industrial oligarchy. Many talented financial officials moved into the banks and industries controlled by these oligarchs, on occasion returning subsequently to government service. Links with south Russian mining and metallurgy, as well as with the increasingly important Moscow business elite, were much weaker and more tension-ridden. K. A. Krivoshein comments that at the end of the nineteenth century so few contacts existed between the Moscow commerical–industrial elite and the St. Petersburg bureaucracy that they might as well have been living on 'different planets'. Nor was the Ministry of Internal Affairs' 'alliance' with the rural nobility a happy one. The Ministry saw landed nobles as pillars of stability and conservatism, but by 1900 much of the nobility was liberal in sympathy, resenting the repressive activity of the police state and deploring the Ministry of Internal Affairs' efforts to restrict the freedom of the noble-run local government councils (*zemstvos*). But while the nobility often resented the absolutist state's bureaucracy, its relations with industrial and financial elites were generally distant and its attitude to much of the intelligentsia was hostile. The dominant spirit in the intelligentsia meanwhile was one of hostility to government, capitalist and nobles alike.[28]

This was not a promising base from which to start on the Prussian road of modernity. Other, still greater, obstacles to this path also existed. Russia was not, unlike Britain and Germany, more or less a nation state. It was a vast multi-ethnic empire created by force and perhaps incapable of surviving on the basis of consent. In military, diplomatic and economic terms, Victorian Russia was also a failure by European standards, which made its elite unable to appeal to society in the German or English fashion, mobilising public pride at belonging to one of the world's most powerful, wealthy and admired countries. The yawning cultural gap between westernised elite and peasant mass, in Hauxthausen's words 'a much wider chasm than in the rest of Europe', is one of the great clichés of Russian history. Like most clichés it is largely true. The values and culture of elite and mass differed markedly, and this difference included conflicting views on justice, law and property. When Prussia embarked on its era of modernising reforms after 1807 liberal doctrines ruled supreme in Europe. That helps to explain how between 1807 and 1848 Berlin could pursue a liberal economic policy of great rigour and consistency despite the damage this did to many elite and mass interests. When Russia began its great era of economic modernisation in the 1880s not only did socialist doctrines already offer an alternative to liberal ones, but part of the intelligentsia was socialist and revolutionary in sympathy and had for twenty years been in search of a mass base with whose support not only Tsarism but also Victorian bourgeois civilisation in Russia could be overthrown.[29]

By Prussian standards the Russian nobility was both weak and vulnerable. It could be argued that its likeliest path to survival was not a Prussian but a Spanish one. Russia in 1900 was more like Spain than Prussia, let alone England. It was part of Europe but not at its core, geographically or culturally. In economic terms it was neither a colony nor one of Europe's real metropolises. Its traditions, like Spain's, were anything but liberal. Its political spectrum went from reactionaries still in revolt against the eighteenth century Enlightenment to anarchists and Communists. In the 1920s and 1930s Spain was sufficiently poor, radical and divided for the elites to fear that their property and values would be submerged under a political democracy. Forty years of Francoist authoritarianism protected the elites' position, spared them from most of the costs of modernisation, and created a developed capitalist economy and society in which the interests of the upper and upper-middle classes could survive the onset of democracy. The logic here is obvious enough and it leads back to the ideas of Peter Durnovo, the Minister of Internal Affairs responsible for crushing the 1905 revolution. Durnovo believed that from the elites' perspective it would be fatal to weaken the authoritarian state before socio-economic development had created a Russia in which large sectors of society shared the values and interests of the westernised property-owning minority. This was also the logic behind Stolypin's famous cry for twenty years of peace, after which Russia would not be recognisable.[30]

But although the Russian elites' position certainly was weak by Prussian or English standards, interesting changes were under way after 1905. The creation of the Council of Ministers and its chairman offered hope that ministerial co-ordination would improve, though Nicholas II's interventions weakened this possibility before 1914. Nicholas's death or removal, however, would give the throne either to his brother, aptly nicknamed Floppy, or to his invalid son. The chances of the monarchy being turned into a Thai or even Japanese symbol of sovereignty behind which others ruled would then be good.

More important, there were signs of growing cohesion within the elites. Nobles and industrialists were grouping themselves in the United Nobility on the one hand and the Congresses of Representatives of Trade and Industry on the other. The various sections of the elite were also organising themselves in the Dumas, whose establishment brought central government and the provincial *zemstvo* nobility close together. It would be naïve to expect all the conflicts between government, nobles, industrialists and intelligentsia to be resolved within seven years merely by the creation of a parliamentary system. But the first step to resolving these conflicts lay through the organisation of interest groups and parliamentary factions. Even in 1914 the form unity might take was shadowy but nevertheless discernible. It clearly lay in some form of liberal–conservative nationalism, as embodied in the 1915 Progressive Bloc.

The likeliest candidate to lead a government supported by the Bloc was Alexander Krivoshein, whose position tells one something about Russia's potential for Prussian-style development. As Minister of Agriculture, Krivoshein had built up good relations with the provincial nobility and the *zemstvo*, and had put into effect very radical agrarian reforms designed to undermine the communes and create a Prussian-style class of big peasants. Krivoshein's wife was the niece of Savva Morozov, most famous of Moscow's businessmen, so through her Krivoshein's links with the Muscovite industrial--commercial oligarchy were very strong. Krivoshein was also, however, in touch with liberal–conservative nationalist intellectuals, as too was Moscow big business. The major liberal–conservative publication on foreign policy, *Velikaya Rossiya*, was financed by the industrialist P. P. Ryabushinsky. Its leading contributors were Prince G. N. Trubetskoy, an important figure in Moscow liberal-- conservative intellectual circles who was also the head of the key Asiatic (that is, Balkan and Near Eastern) Department of the Foreign Ministry, and P. B. Struve.[31]

It was the latter who in 1909 had thrown the Russian intelligent- sia into frenzied debate by his contribution to the symposium *Vekhi*, in which a number of former leading radicals attacked the traditions of the Russian intelligentsia's leftism and announced their conver- sion to a combination of liberal, nationalist, religious and capitalist principles. The symposium was attacked ferociously, not least by V. I. Lenin, for whom its ideas were not merely poisonous in themselves and treasonable coming from such a source, but also a worrying sign of the times. Struve was quite consciously trying to move the Russian intelligentsia in the direction taken by Prussian national liberalism. And he was doing so at a time not only when much of the intellectual world was in revolt against utilitarian and materialist doctrines but also when Russian economic expansion was at last creating plentiful middle-class jobs. Was the age of the radical penniless journalist to be replaced by that of the liberal–con- servative lawyer or engineer?[32]

In 1914 it was still too early to say and old conflicts in the elite were far from dead. But it is worth reflecting on the fact that nine years after 1848, conflict between Crown and liberals in Prussia was sharpening, with the constitutional crisis that brought Bismarck to power still five years in the future. The military victories which solved this crisis and reconciled Crown and opposition came eight- een and twenty-two years after 1848. Given the speed with which the Russian armed forces were growing and improving after 1906, who can say how they might have performed in 1923 and 1927, or what the political effects of a Russian Sadowa or Sedan might have been? Knowledge of their own history and of Russian military and economic developments was a factor persuading the Prussian generals in 1914 that war was better not delayed. The German Foreign Minister, Gottlieb von Jagow, recollects a conversation with the younger Count von Moltke, chief of the General Staff, in May 1914: 'The prospects for the future weighed heavily upon him. In two to three years Russia would have finished arming. Our enemies' military power would then be so great that he did not know how he could deal with it. Now we were still more or less a match for it. In his view there was no alternative but to fight a preventive war so as to beat the enemy while we could still emerge fairly well from the struggle.'[33]

Looked at from the Russian perspective the position of the Prussian and English aristocracy in 1914 was on the whole both enviable and rather similar. It is true that, in the immediate pre-war years, both were under heavy attack. In 1905 the English Conservatives had suffered their biggest electoral defeat since 1832 and the new Liberal government had stripped the Lords of its veto, imposed extra taxation on the landowners and indulged in a great deal of anti-aristocratic rhetoric. In Germany the 'Blue–Black' Conservative–Centre coalition had collapsed and the Social Democrats had emerged from the 1912 elections as the largest and most popular party in the Reichstag.

But in key respects the English and Prussian aristocracies had surmounted problems which threatened the Russian nobility's existence. Britain and Germany were Europe's leading industrial states but in both countries traditional elites retained much of the power, prestige and wealth. Both aristocracies had held the support of their rural base, above all of the peasants and tenant farmers who were crucial sub-elites in the countryside, given their numbers and the control they could maintain over their labourers. If in England rural support was of limited use given the size of the non-urban electorate, in Germany it was crucial. The Russian aristocracy could only dream of an organisation such as the *Bund der Landwirte* in which the bulk of German farmers were mobilised in an agrarian lobby mostly led by noblemen and loyal on the whole to the Conservative Party, indeed to a considerable extent merged with it. In a country where, in 1905–6, peasants had first rioted and then voted in favour of the expropriation of noble estates, the dawn of a *Bund der Landwirte* still seemed some way off, though the Stolypin reforms offered some hope that it might come.

Equally important, and different from Russia, was the extent to which traditional elites, their values and their political ideals had captured middle-class support in Britain and Germany. The Russian nobleman who read *Vekhi* may have hoped that similar trends would unfold in his country but he knew that at present the rift between aristocracy and intelligentsia still ran deep. Of course the intelligent Russian aristocrat well understood that the English and

German aristocracies were far from identical and that the precise compromises they had achieved with their middle classes differed. From the Russian perspective, however, what mattered was that the compromise had been achieved and that, whether in the form of the public schoolboy or the reserve officer, the symbols, style and values of aristocracy had spread deep into the economic and professional elites of a modern, industrial society.

This Russian perspective of 1914, in which Germany and Britain seem rather similar, is not the one usually held by contemporary historians. Faced with the terrible experience of Nazism, it is Germany's differences, its special path (*Sonderweg*), which appear to require explanation. In moral terms it is asked how a country seen as a key constituent element in Victorian liberal and Christian civilisation could fall into the barbarities of Nazism. Politically, the issue becomes the divergence of Germany from the path of Anglo-American modernisation which the pre-1914 Whig interpretation of history celebrated as universal and which a good deal, at least of the more naïve, post-1945 scholarship has democratised, camouflaged in jargon, and deified as science in so-called modernisation theory. For many historians anxious to explain Germany's *Sonderweg*, the Junkers loom large. The survival of this pre-industrial elite into the modern age is regarded as a key to Germany's failure to take the democratic path to contemporary capitalism. Explicitly or otherwise a contrast is made between, on the one hand, a Junker class that put its agrarian interests above the public good and obstinately defended an un-democratic franchise; and on the other an English aristocracy which repealed the Corn Laws and conceded parliamentary reform, allowing a peaceful transition to democracy. The issue of agricultural protection in particular is worth pursuing in the context of an Anglo-Prussian comparison, for it tells one much about the two aristocracies and the political systems under which they operated.[34]

Protection encompassed not only agriculture. In many ways the key to its abolition in the England of the 1840s and its introduction in Imperial Germany depended less on the agrarian lobby than on the industrialists and the intellectuals. The interests of the English farmers and landowners in the 1840s and 1880s, and of their Prussian counterparts in the latter decade, were always Protectionist. In the 1840s, however, *laissez-faire* doctrines dominated the European intellectual world in a way which was much less true in the last quarter of the century. Most important, key sections of German heavy industry favoured protection in the 1870s and entered into alliance with the agrarians. In England in the 1840s, with a few maverick exceptions, industry was for free trade, with very good reason given its superior competitiveness to most of its international rivals. By the 1880s it was hopeless even to think of agricultural protection in England. 'The import economy of the south which generated so much of the mercantile, financial, rentier and professional incomes shared a free trade outlook with the textile, metal and machinery export industries of the north, with the shipowners of the great ports and the shipbuilders of the Tyne, the Mersey and the Clyde. Large imperial, military and naval interests relied indirectly on free trade, and investments in primary production and transport overseas were the mainstay of the late Victorian Stock exchange. Working-class electors stood firm against any attempt to exclude foreign grain'.[35]

The timing of the debate over protection is also very important. The 1840s and 1850s were, with a few exceptional years, a high-point of mid-Victorian agricultural prosperity between the depressions of the 1820s and 1870s. What really killed the cause of agricultural protection in England in the decade after 1846 was that farming remained in general rather prosperous. The indignation of tenants cooled and it was possible to argue that big investment in agricultural improvements, so-called high farming, would guarantee the industry's future. But even in the 1840s there was some wishful thinking here. 'High farming was an immensely costly business and profitable only in the very long run . . . only rich aristocrats . . . could invest heavily enough to make improvements comprehensive and thus worthwhile'. The Duke of Wellington congratulated himself on his scientific farming methods but he conceded that 'few other gentlemen are able by their circumstances to devote the income of their land to its improvement'.

From the 1870s critics of the Junkers also called for high farming and saw demands for protection as stemming from the inefficiency of the great estates. How true these arguments were can only be answered by a thorough modern survey of Prussian agriculture carried out by a scholar with no political axe to grind. English farmers in the 1880s would certainly not have believed these criticisms of their Prussian counterparts. 'Essex farmers had gained an enviable reputation as men of substance and active improvers. By

mid-century efficient drainage and widespread use of manures combined with good husbandry practices made Essex arable farming
among the best in the country'. Yet no county was worse devastated
by the agricultural depression of the late nineteenth century than
Essex. Farms were abandoned only to be taken up at much lower
levels of profitability by Scottish peasant-farmers willing to cut
overheads to the bone. But for a Junker to live as a Scottish peasant
was simply to abolish himself, destroying the characteristics which
defined his being.[36]

The timing of the English and German debates on protection
also had military and geopolitical implications. The Fifth Earl Fitzwilliam was to become one of the leading aristocratic opponents of
the Corn Laws. In the period immediately after 1815, however,
memories of the wartime continental blockade persuaded him that
the interests of defence required protection for agriculture and shipping. In the late Victorian era of imperialism, national security was
more of an issue than in the 1840s. A much more imperially-minded
aristocracy was increasingly obsessed, with good reason, by the
growing threat to the security of the British Empire. Protection, in
the guise of imperial preference, came back on the political agenda
as one means to meet this threat. After 1885 almost the whole
aristocracy was Conservative in principle. This increased upper-
class fury over three successive electoral defeats at the hands of the
Liberals between 1905 and 1911, not to mention the abolition of
the Lords' veto and assaults on aristocratic economic interests. The
awareness that it was Irish, Welsh and Scottish votes in 1911 which
had deprived the Conservatives of victory increased the bitterness.

But it was the Liberals' attempt at Home Rule, seen by many
Conservatives as heralding the break-up of the British Empire,
which caused the greatest outrage. G. D. Phillips, the historian of
the Diehards, concludes that the right wing of the Tories were much
less reactionaries defending a lost age than modern imperialists for
whom defence of Empire came before the aristocracy's traditional
regard for parliamentarism, legality and respect for freedom. There
was no element of bluff, in his opinion, in the Diehards' willingness
to resort to violence to avoid Home Rule, and much of the Tory
Party was with them. Phillips concludes that 'the outbreak of the
Great War, in which diehards participated with courage and much
sacrifice, diverted this potential revolutionary outburst from many
of England's oldest and supposedly most conservative families'.[37]

Even in the early twentieth century, Britain's island position and maritime supremacy, however, gave it a degree of security which no continental power could match. As German overseas trade boomed in the late nineteenth century, its vulnerability to British blockade became a serious threat. Among the barrage of arguments for protection put forward by German agrarians was the issue of national security, though it was neither their main plank nor, of course, the key motive for their platform. If Avner Offer is correct, however, in his study of agricultural aspects of the First World War the Prussian agrarians may, almost accidentally, have been dead right in their line on national security. Addressing the issue of German protectionism, Offer comments: 'What has to be asked, is whether production would have been larger with a lower tariff. The example of Britain suggests that it would have been much smaller'. Protection 'made available a larger domestic capacity in wartime'. Citing S. B. Webb's calculation that agricultural protection cost about 1 per cent of national income for grain and a bit less than 2 per cent for livestock, Offer argues that 'considered as an insurance premium, the subsidy for grain was not unreasonable'. Where livestock, a mostly peasant-run branch of German agriculture, was concerned, 'the hidden subsidy . . . might be regarded as excessive'.[38]

Questions of national security cannot be ignored in any comparison between British and German agricultural protectionism. But the key distinction, so it is argued, between the two countries is that whereas from the 1880s the Prussian Conservatives acted as an agrarian interest lobby, the English Victorian aristocracy operated in a manner befitting a ruling class sensitive to its national responsibility.

The argument is to some extent true and is rooted in the very different traditions of the aristocracies and in the nature of the political systems under which they lived. Through its parliamentary institutions the English aristocracy had been a ruling class in the fullest sense of the word since 1688. In Prussia, however, the King and his officials had always ruled, taking upon themselves the responsibilities of national leadership. The introduction of a parliament after 1848 did not fundamentally change matters. The Prussian, and later German, legislatures did not control the executive and their leaders were thereby encouraged to become (often irresponsible) defenders of sectional interests. As such the Prussian

Conservatives performed rather well, at least if the fate of German and British agriculture between 1880 and 1914 is compared. If the Conservatives pursued selfish concerns damaging to the national interest they were scarcely unique in this respect among modern parliamentary interest groups and parties. It is true that Conservative selfishness sat ill with the positions in State and army held by so many of their followers, let alone with their heart-wrenching propaganda about Prussian values. In covering interest in grandiose rhetorical visions and ignoring the claims of rival groups in society the Conservatives and Junkers were, however, following the general pattern in Imperial Germany. In comparison to some National Liberal attitudes to Catholics, Empire and lesser breeds, many Junkers actually appear rather charmingly bumbling and old-fashioned. Even the Social Democrats, who were admittedly defending the interests of the poorest sections of society, had a powerful and often passionately held vision of future Utopia in which, by happy chance, all the groups which they disliked – landowners, capitalists, Catholics and peasants – would have disappeared.

When Sir Robert Peel abandoned the Corn Laws in 1845–6 his party divided into two relatively clear groups. On the one hand there were the 'men of government'. Of the thirty-five Conservative MPs who had held cabinet or other senior public office, all but five voted for repeal. Of the remaining Tory MPs, 74 per cent opposed it. To understand the significance of this split one has to remember that, with the only major exception of the Whig 1830s, Conservatives had held office since the Younger Pitt came to power in 1784. The party had come to contain a group of more or less permanent ministers and their hopeful heirs. These men became Peelites in 1846. Their social origins were not uniform. Peel and Gladstone came from originally business families but had themselves been trained from birth to be members of the ruling classes. Other Peelites were born into gentry families, while some – the Duke of Buccleuch, the Earl of Lincoln and the Earl of Ripon, for instance – came from the top ranks of the aristocracy.[39]

What united most of these men was not their backgrounds but their ethos, particularly their attitude to government. They prided themselves on their sense of responsibility and their commitment to the public interest. They were efficient administrators, believers in the most modern ideas of *laissez-faire* economics, and wholly honest and incorruptible public servants – in total contrast to their ancestors, the eighteenth-century spoilsmen. In their political views they were liberal conservatives, enemies of democracy but believers that aristocracy must earn its position, rule efficiently in the general interest and reform abuses. They were for the most part deeply serious and committed Christians, not noted for their sense of humour or lightness of touch. This was a ruling aristocracy in an Evangelical era. Not surprisingly, Peel got on excellently with the Queen and Prince Consort. The Peelites disapproved of the Whig family clique, always happy (so the Peelites felt) to promote a cousin into a cosy niche rather than an efficient man of business.

Above all, many of them came to despise their landowning back-benchers, especially after 1846. The Corn Laws were not the only issue here, though the Peelites saw the Tory stand on this as prefer-ing selfish to national interests, in the process damaging the legit-imacy of the ruling class. The same backwoods aristocrats who forced Peel from office also in the same period threw out a bill granting equal rights for Jews. Above all the Tory landowners loathed Catholicism. Almost as much as repeal of the Corn Laws, it was this that turned them, along with their farmer supporters, against Peel's Government, which had made modest concessions to Irish Catholic opinion. By 1851 the Earl of Derby, Peel's successor as Tory leader, had come to the conclusion that agricultural pros-perity made protection impossible as a popular rallying cry. The only alternative was, in his view, anti-Catholicism. 'In my view,' he wrote, 'among all its evils and all its dangers, the evocation of the protestant spirit . . . is not without its use. Even the most Radical towns . . . are so furiously anti-Papal, that that feeling will neutral-ise the cheap bread cry'. To the Peelites it was precisely this sort of demagogic pandering to the bigotry and intolerance of the electorate which made Toryism objectionable.[40]

To the extent that the Peelites had equivalents in the Prussian ruling classes by 1914 they were to be found among the upper ranks of the civil service not in the political parties. Given the nature of German politics in the Wilhelmine era this is not surprising. Peel had trouble with his backbenchers and their farmer constituents in the 1840s but by the standards of the German electorate of the 1890s British politics in the early Victorian era was still very defer-ential and undemocratic. Most of the party leaders were peers, whose seats in the Lords were invulnerable to public pressure. One-tenth of the House of Commons were aristocratic nominees, while many other members sat for boroughs with small and relatively apolitical electorates. Peel did not have to cope with a massive socialist party committed in theory to the overthrow of monarchy and capitalism. Nor did he face peasant particularists whose response to the challenges of modernism was to demand that all margarine be coloured blue to deter potential consumers.

The German nobility of the 1890s had its share of 'responsible' liberal conservatives. In 1893 they faced, in Bavaria, a Peasant League whose slogan was 'No aristocrats, no priests, no doctors and no professors, only peasants for the representation of peasant interests'. Not surprisingly, noble moderate conservatives fared rather badly. In Prussia too the pressures on the Conservatives to indulge in demagogery were intense. Those who tried to resist the political style of the *Bund der Landwirte* with its radical, agrarian and often anti-Semitic demagogery found themselves squeezed out of politics for lack of electoral support. James Retallack is quite right to say that many Junkers were too arrogant, class-ridden and hostile to machine politics to make good modern politicians. In part they could afford to be so because traditional methods sufficed to get them re-elected in their dwindling number of rural eastern fast-nesses. But the overwhelming impression one gets from studying the potential conservative electorate in Imperial Germany is that only the aggressive agrarian demagogue had any chance of success. At this price the Junker Conservative leaders were remarkably successful at mobilising the rural vote on the basis of common agrarian interests and prejudices. Junker and peasant needed each other if votes were to be harvested, contacts with the ministries exploited, socialists and liberals held at bay, and agricultural labourers kept in their place.[41]

In these circumstances, quite apart from Prussian tradition, there were arguments for preserving government from the clutches of a divided and immature electorate and seeking to keep it in the independent, 'Peelite' hands of the senior civil service. Theobald von Bethmann-Hollweg, William II's last peace-time chancellor, was in many ways a model Peelite. A member of a rich bourgeois family assimilated into the Prussian ruling elite in the nineteenth century, Bethmann-Hollweg had a string of Peelite virtues. He was well educated, with a deep sense of duty and public service. An efficient administrator and totally incorruptible, Bethmann-Hollweg was a liberal conservative who had little faith in democracy but believed major reforms in Prussian political life were essential to maintain the ruling class's legitimacy and avert the threat of revolution. His attitude to the obscurantist and yet demagogic selfishness of the Conservatives was wholly Peelite.

But calling a senior Prussian official a Peelite has its flaws. However much of a professional administrator and permanent minister he might become, the English aristocratic MP had an independence which no Prussian official or ministerial servant of his king could enjoy. Moreover, since the introduction of parliament, first in Prussia and then in Germany, the politicisation of the upper civil service had become inevitable. Conservative supporters, albeit of an often rather milder form than the pure backwoods Junker, packed the senior ranks of the bureaucracy. Moreover, electoral arithmetic denied the chance of real independence from the Conservatives to a Wilhelmine chancellor. So long as socialists were pariahs and Catholic particularists a cause of uncertainty and suspicion, governments had to have Conservative support to get their bills through the Reichstag, let alone the Prussian House of Deputies.[42]

The repeal of the Corn Laws was not merely the product of Peelite virtue and the undemocratic nature of the British political system, however. Nor was it simply to do with agricultural prosperity in the 1840s and overwhelming support for repeal from non-agrarian MPs, important though both these factors were. The role of the Whigs was also essential. In part, the Whigs were playing party politics. John Vincent calls aristocratic English politicians in the nineteenth century 'the practitioners of an amateur sport', and there is truth in this. Playing the party political game was fun, winning it was better and the excitements of office was the icing on the cake. The manner in which the Second Reform Bill was passed in 1867 illustrates the possible radicalising effects when two basically aristocratic parties compete with each other for office and electoral sympathy. Subsequently some noblemen felt that England's aristocratic constitution had been sacrificed to the game of party politics.[43]

But Whiggery was more than mere party games-playing. To Prince Pückler it was one of England's many oddities, liberal and yet at the same time ultra-aristocratic: 'a certain vague general liberalism goes hand-in-hand with the narrowest pride, and most arrogant conceit of class . . . the haughtiest man in his own house possesses the reputation of the most liberal in public life'. 'The

Sacred Circle of the Great-Grandmotherhood' was at its core a tight aristocratic clique brought up to believe that its ancestors' successful struggle for the Protestant free constitution against Stuart absolutism was the key to England's subsequent rise to world supremacy. In his bones Lord John Russell believed that his family had invented the concept of liberty and donated it first to England and then to the world. If there was something faintly ridiculous and distinctly smug about this, it has to be remembered that obsessive family pride was a mark of aristocracy everywhere. If a Victorian aristocrat was bound to carry his family tradition close to his heart then liberty, reason and the rights of free-born Englishmen, the Russell motto, was not a bad tradition to which to cleave.[44]

The Whigs had absorbed Baron de Montesquieu's ideas about balanced constitutions and the role of the aristocracy as a vital intermediary between Crown and people. In 1883 the Marquess of Hartington, the Whig leader, summed up his party's contribution as follows: 'The Whigs have been able . . . to the great advantage of the country, to direct, and guide, and moderate . . . popular movements. They have formed a connecting link between the advanced party and those classes which, possessing property, power and influence, are naturally averse to change . . . it is greatly owing to their guidance and to their action that the great and beneficial changes, which have been made in the direction of popular change in this country, have been made not by the shock of revolutionary agitation, but by the calm and peaceful process of constitutional acts.[45]

The Whig magnate could in the most literal sense of the word afford to take a rather dispassionate and calm view of politics. John Vincent quite rightly praises the Marquess of Hartington's relaxed and fair-minded attitude to Irish agrarian issues in the early 1880s despite the troubles on his own family's estates, but it certainly helped that the Duke of Devonshire's heir need not fear that anything that happened in Ireland could reduce him to penury. Great incomes derived from many sources removed the temptation of a narrow agrarian approach to politics and encouraged broad views.

Nevertheless, David Spring is right to argue that counting a man's income and checking whether it derived in part from non-agrarian sources is a very unclear guide to an aristocrat's position on the Corn Laws, or indeed on politics in general. The Fifth Earl Fitzwilliam's support for repeal, for instance, stemmed from a general sense of the aristocracy's responsibility to take the national view. The interests of commerce and industry had to be upheld, for without them Britain would be another Poland. Fitzwilliam was possessed of an evangelical and utilitarian spirit, fascinated by modern science and convinced it could be used to improve the world. A man of 'wide systematic reading . . . intellectual sloth he took as verging on moral iniquity'. This was no owner of the Edwardian country house, its reading often confined to *Country Life* or its equivalents. Fitzwilliam was a member of an active, forward-looking ruling class. He concentrated on ancient classics, modern philosophy, history and political economy: novels were for ladies.[46]

The repeal of the Corn Laws was, however, owed to a spirit of liberal–conservatism in the English high aristocracy which spread well beyond the boundaries of the Whig Party. Of the 211 votes for repeal in the House of Lords, only 115, at a generous estimate, could be attributed to Whigs. Particularly between 1832 and 1905, the high aristocracy as a whole believed that liberal tendencies dominated the age in which they lived and that stubborn resistance to these tendencies could only lead to disaster. By English standards few men were more conservative than the third Marquess of Salisbury. In 1859 he defended the political status quo in terms which any continental conservative could have echoed: 'The classes that represent civilisation, the holders of accumulated capital and accumulated thought, have a right to require securities to protect them from being overwhelmed by hordes who have neither knowledge to guide them nor stake in the commonwealth to control them'. True to his belief that democracy would mean the use of State power to despoil the rich, Salisbury strongly opposed the Second Reform Bill. After the bill had passed, however, in line with the ethics of aristocratic sportsmanship and political pragmatism, he commented that 'it is the duty of every Englishman, and of every English party, to accept a political defeat cordially, and to bend their best endeavours to secure the success, or to neutralise the evil, of the principles to which they have been forced to succumb'. In terms of Conservative post-1867 policies this meant making democracy work as efficiently as possible and with as little detriment to a rational foreign policy and to the interests of the propertied as could be managed. Under Salisbury's cool, clear-headed but pessimistic guidance this exercise in damage-limitation was pretty successful. Pragmatism, realism, political skill, great intelligence and respect for the rules of the game were not, however, Salisbury's only qualities. He had a genuine love of freedom. Faced by Lord Milner, an imperial pro-consul with a belief in 'scientific administration' well-suited to the service of an enlightened despot, Salisbury noted disapprovingly that the man had an absolute disbelief in liberty.[47]

Nineteenth-century English history was a good advertisement for the role of the high aristocracy in politics. No doubt the magnates had their vices, among them often an extreme caste-consciousness and a disinclination to effort. Amateurism was also a frequent failing. It must have driven the very ambitious Disraeli crazy to see his boss, Lord Derby, shooting off down to his country house to get back to watching the races 'like a boy released from school' after resigning the prime ministership in 1852. Much more seriously, V. I. Gurko, an experienced Russian senior official, was infuriated by the easygoing amateurism of Prince P. D. Svyatopolk-Mirsky and Prince B. A. Vasil'chikov, aristocratic ministers in the years of revolution and crisis between 1904 and 1907. Both men lacked the professional experience and competence to run large and complex government departments. In addition, their lives had simply been too easy and undemanding to prepare them for the strains and responsibility of the job. Yet aristocracy was not always amateur and easygoing. The Plantagenet Pallisers existed in real life too, particularly in England, whose parliamentary constitution provided a much more accessible and congenial ground for aristocratic politicians than did Prussian or Russian bureaucratic absolutism. At their best, great aristocrats brought to politics a genuine breadth of public spirit and vision, and a lack of narrowness and egoism, which representatives of the landed gentry found it hard to match. The fact that, because of their wealth and status, modernity threatened magnates less than provincial nobles certainly contributed to this distinction.[48]

Walter Bagehot wrote in the 1850s that 'the grade of gentry who fill the country seats, and mostly compose the Conservative party in the Commons, are perhaps the least able and valuable part of English society. They have neither the responsibilities or the culture of great noblemen, and they have never felt the painful need of getting on, which sharpens the middle class. They have a moderate sort of wealth which teaches them little, and a steady sort of mind fit for common things, but they have no flexibility and no ideas'.[49]

Prussia had almost nothing in the way of a magnate class or tradition, as angry Junkers pointed out to Frederick William IV when he strove to create a House of Lords in the wake of the 1848 revolution.[50] On the whole its provincial backwoodsmen were unsophisticated even by the standards of Bagehot's Tory squires. A blunt and arrogant naïvety coloured many Junkers' views. For most of them there was no element of cynical self-awareness in their identification of the State's interests with their own. A rather dogmatic, simply held and unreflective religious feeling often contributed to an honest and direct truthfulness. Pietism, anything but an intellectual faith, could persuade already rather self-confident people that God had blessed their power and was speaking through their hearts.

In Baroness Spitzemberg's diary there are ironic references to 'truly Pomeranian refinement'. In 1894 she mentions Konrad von Falkenhausen, prone to denounce in the bluntest terms any fellow guest who had betrayed Junker interests and values by voting for the Russian trade treaty, a betrayal which in his eyes only a desire for favours at Court could explain. Fourteen years later the Baroness commented, 'in talking to these Junkers it always frightens me how little they even remotely guess of the difficulties and relationships in foreign affairs and therefore say and advise things which simply stagger anyone with an even remotely cosmopolitan upbringing. I am even more troubled by their faith in the monarchist feeling of the Prussian people; if it ever comes to a crash then I fear that very many of the supports on which people count today . . . will break'.

To put things mildly, this was not a group from which to expect attitudes suitable to the ruling elite of a world-class empire. Indeed, to a great extent the generation of Prussian nobles who had conquered first Germany and then France between 1866 and 1871 were not really attuned to the idea of a German empire at all. Elard von Oldenburg-Januschau, a leading Conservative right down to the empire's demise, commented that 'as soldiers we were much too Prussian not to find our models only in Prussian history. The founding of the Reich did not have the same impact on us as on the following generations. We saw in the German Reich of 1871 not the coming together of all branches of the German people but, following the words of the old Kaiser, only an enlarged Prussia'.[51]

Old Prussia – particularly the land of Frederick II – had in many ways been Europe's model enlightened despotism. All the

eighteenth-century absolutist states were variations on the theme of
royal–noble alliance but, as Perry Anderson writes, the Prussian
variation was in many ways the most comfortable and perfect fit.[52]
Unlike France, the Hohenzollern state was not hampered by venality or by a magnate class at Court yearning for an English oligar-
chical constitution. Prussian Junkers from the eighteenth century
never had the Moscow nobility's sense that the ruling dynasty,
Court and capital city were to some extent alien implants on native
soil. It had no wild but also often very cultured Russian-style
magnates resentful of a Germanic dynasty's efforts to enforce discipline, order and a respect for bureaucratic subordination on the
social elite. The Prussian marriage of centralised bureaucratic institutions and local noble government in the form of *Landräte* and
estate bodies had not been without serious initial conflict, but by
Frederick II's reign it was working well. In Russia, by contrast,
where no meaningful local noble institutions existed, the full weight
of the bureaucratic apparatus bore down directly on the nobility,
with no cushioning intermediary bodies, inspiring a degree of semi-
anarchical alienation from the State which had no counterpart in
Prussia. The Prussian Old Regime's neatness and sense of proportion was symbolised by its rulers and the palaces they built.
Few monarchs had such a clear-headed ability to match means and
ends as the Great Elector, Frederick William I, and Frederick II.
By Russian standards Sansouci and Potsdam are modest examples
of a restrained and austere good taste.[53]

Even in 1914 Prussia was uncomfortable in the clothes of empire.
Its fine austere classical architecture gave way to vast, pompous,
fussy vulgarity in the Wilhelmine era. William II himself was a
self-conscious and very uncomfortable amalgam of Junker King,
world-power Emperor and hi-tech tycoon.[54] All late Victorian aristocracies found it difficult to come to terms with the age of money.
Previously the aristocracy had been richer than anyone else and
noble elites had indulged in ostentatious display and competition.
But no aristocratic value-system saw money as the highest good.
Now suddenly non-aristocrats could out-compete their 'betters'.
Jibes at plutocracy and anti-Semitism were a frequent response,
especially from poorer aristocrats suffering a decline in not only
status but also in wealth.

On the whole, however, English and Russian aristocratic elites
found it easier to come to terms with the age of money than did

the Junkers. St. Petersburg and London aristocrats were richer, less provincial and rural, more cosmopolitan and worldly wise than the Prussian nobility. Both the English and the Russian ruling classes had been extremely corrupt in the eighteenth century and had done very well for themselves out of government. The English and, to a lesser extent, the Russians, mended their ways in the nineteenth century but neither approached the Prussian official culture of almost obsessive thrift, self-discipline and devotion to duty. When combined with relative poverty and declining religious faith, these were difficult values with which to confront the booming millionaire-infested country that Prussia became so suddenly after 1871. The strains and hypocrisy involved in adapting to this gilded age were likely to be greater than in the traditionally more corrupt, loose-living and opulent world of St. Petersburg or amidst the easy-going and wealthy English aristocracy, with its old links to financial and overseas trading interests.[55]

Coming to terms with the age of money was just one aspect of coping with a troubling modern world. The basic problem for aristocrats was simple and had no solution. A class which had dominated Europe since time immemorial was being displaced as a result of revolutionary changes in economy and society. There was, save in the short term, nothing that aristocracy could do to avert this fate. Aristocrats could not dominate an urban, industrial, technological and educated society, least of all one that had ambitions to be a leading world power. The speed with which these changes occurred compounded the problem, especially in Germany and Russia. In 1866 a young lieutenant of simple Junker origin called Paul von Hindenburg fought at the battle of Königgratz. In his youth he witnessed the triumph of the Prussian noble officer corps, its realisation – in the awful language of nineteenth-century academic nationalists – of Germany's historical national tasks. Almost as Hindenburg fought, the German industrial revolution and the agricultural depression were threatening to make Junker-dom redundant. In a single lifetime Hindenburg lived through old Prussia's triumph, transformation and extinction. Never exactly an intellectual eagle, it is not surprising that the old field marshal was a bit bewildered by 1933.

By the late nineteenth century, the aristocracy's future revolved around a number of questions. Did aristocrats understand the way the world was going, or were they too provincial, blinkered or uneducated to do so? Did their societies offer golden bridges over which the aristocracy could retreat into the modern world, preserving part at least of its wealth and status? What forms of modernity – democratic or otherwise – were on offer and in what ways did a particular aristocracy's traditions shape its choice of bridge? If all or part of an aristocracy had no golden bridge to cross, how powerful and destructive would its rearguard action be in the face of the modern era? *In extremis*, would aristocrats be sufficiently reactionary or civilised to remain constrained by traditional conceptions of religion and honour, or would insecurity, resentment of lost status and agnosticism lead them down the path towards totalitarian nationalism and its inevitable companion, barbaric anti-semitism?

Conclusion

In an influential book, Arno Meyer argued that the Europe of 1914 was still dominated by pre-industrial institutions, elites and values. For Meyer 'old regime' encompassed more than the aristocracy: for instance, kings, classical styles in literature and art, and small-scale traditional business also came within this rubric. Yet, for him, of all aspects of pre-industrial Europe aristocracy was the most significant. And the survival of pre-industrial elites and values in his view was a key to understanding Europe's descent into war in 1914.[1]

At least where the aristocracy is concerned, Meyer's argument about the economic pre-eminence of pre-industrial forms of wealth is unconvincing. In England and Germany a few aristocratic magnates were among the tiny set of multi-millionaires, but their wealth derived precisely from the modern, industrial era – in the form of mines, factories or urban property. If a much larger group of rural landowners, especially in Germany, had weathered the period 1880–1914 rather better than one might have expected, the fact remains that in the richer sections of German and British society aristocrats were now far outnumbered by individuals from middle-class backgrounds with non-agricultural sources of wealth. As explained in Chapter 2, Russian statistics do not enable one to be as categorical on this point where the Tsarist Empire is concerned, but the evidence nevertheless points to trends very similar to those documented for England and Germany.

In politics the picture is less clear-cut. By 1914 the political power of the British aristocracy was far smaller than it had been in 1815.

This was much less true in Prussia and Russia. Ironically, constitutionalism and parliamentary institutions in Russia and Prussia, whose introduction held out the prospect of development in an English-style democratic direction, very much increased the political influence of those social groups who had the most to lose from democracy. In some respects the decline of the English aristocracy by 1914 and the survival, even rejuvenation, of its Prussian and Russian peers is what modernisation theory would lead one to expect. The theory's basic tendency is to see change first in economics, which leads to sociocultural development and finally has its inevitable knock-on effect in politics. The English Industrial Revolution commencing around 1780 led to a decline in aristocratic power but this only became a steep one from about a century later. In Prussia and, still more, Russia, then decades behind Britain economically, old elites therefore could be expected to remain politically stronger even in 1914.

This is, however, to take an overly mechanistic and optimistic view. In 1914 Prussian and Russian aristocracy clung to political power partly from a clear-sighted presentiment that, as classes, they would not survive its disappearance. Magnates might flourish in a plutocratic era but how well would the Prussian gentry do without agricultural protection and the Junkers' traditional niche in the Hohenzollern State? Their days of glory and leadership would certainly be gone. Their landed estates might also soon be lost. In Russia the position was even starker. As the riots and elections of 1905–7 had shown, democracy would entail the expropriation of aristocratic property. It is unlikely that time alone would have guaranteed the old elites' acquiescence at their disappearance from the scene in peaceful English style. Apart from anything else that disappearance was, by English standards, likely to be extremely rapid and uncomfortable.

Aristocratic cultural hegemony is a still more difficult issue. If culture is taken to mean, above all, values, then it is clear that aristocratic influence in England and Germany was much greater than in Russia. The most obvious explanations for the Russian aristocracy's failure to impose its values on society are also the best ones. The elites' prestige suffered from Russia's relative failure in economy and war during the Victorian era, its overall backwardness by the standards of the world's leading States. The Tsarist State, with which the aristocracy was to a great extent associated, alienated educated society, including indeed many nobles, by denying it the rights and freedoms to which it felt entitled as a group of civilised Europeans.

The position was, however, rather more complicated than this. The key values and roles which the Russian aristocracy inherited from the eighteenth century were public service and cultural leadership. Aristocrats served the State and, to an increasing degree, Russia. They led the process of enlightenment in their country. To a considerable extent one could say that these aristocratic values – service and enlightenment – did continue to predominate in nineteenth-century Russia. But many educated Russians, including some nobles, came to see service to Russia – which some took to mean the peasant *volk*, as being incompatible with the traditional allegiance to Tsarism. As to respect for cultural leadership, this was sometimes debased into a crudely materialist and utilitarian concern to raise the population's living standards. But, on the whole, educated Russians, including the aristocracy, did contribute hugely to the world's literary and musical culture and retained a much greater aesthetic sensitivity than the English traditional elite, let alone Junkerdom.

The continued influence, even, as it is sometimes argued, preeminence, of aristocratic values in industrial England and Germany has been the cause of much debate. The survival of this 'cultural hegemony' has very often been noted with great surprise and blamed for many of the subsequent failings of German and British society. Both the surprise and the conclusions drawn from the influence of aristocratic values are, in my view, exaggerated.

Surprise at the survival of the aristocracy is linked to the correct idea that the Industrial Revolution marked a huge change in the history of mankind. A very different society came into being whose values and elites had to be fundamentally changed from traditional patterns. To expect the emergence of an industrial society in Victorian Europe to lead to the overnight disappearance of the traditional aristocratic elites is, however, a little naïve. These aristocracies had been around for a long time and were likely to take a generation or so to make their departure from the world scene. And from the German industrial take-off of the 1870s and 1880s to the world of 1914 was only one generation.

Particularly in England and Germany, it is by no means surprising that the aristocracy was often admired and its values emulated.

These were the elites in Europe's two most powerful and successful societies. Who could doubt, for instance, that the English aristocratic Parliament or the military skills of the Junkers had played key roles in their countries' rise to greatness, a greatness in which non-aristocratic citizens, of course, also took huge pride.

Nor should the extent to which these old elites adapted themselves to the requirements of the modern age be forgotten. This is most obvious in England. Well before 1815, land in England was a commodity to be traded on the market like any other goods. No legal restrictions barred access to the gentry. Money bought land – and time, together with the adoption of upper-class habits, secured acceptance. In politics, the English aristocracy developed parliamentary institutions which proved extremely effective at securing consensus and effective government in a modern society, far more effective than the efforts of absolute monarchs and their bureaucracies to mediate between conflicting groups and classes as complex industrial societies developed in continental Europe. All this has led some historians to describe the English aristocracy as being 'bourgeois' in 1815. This is an unfortunate term to use of a group which came closer to being an hereditary ruling class in the fullest sense of the word than any other European nobility. The English high aristocracy, meaning above all the peerage, was the richest, the most powerful, by no means the most open to new blood, and the most legally and constitutionally privileged of all Europe's noble elites in 1815. It was increasingly the model that other European aristocracies tried to emulate in the nineteenth century. To say that the English aristocracy adapted itself earlier and more successfully than any other to many of the requirements of the modern age is true. To describe it as bourgeois is absolutely to misunderstand its mentality, its virtues and vices, or its role in modern European history.

Nor should one underestimate the degree to which the Prussian aristocracy also adapted itself to the modern world. As a result of the reforms after 1807, purchase of land was opened to all classes and this included buying knights' estates (*Rittergüter*), with all the rights and powers associated with them. To the extent that coercive elements derived from the era of serfdom survived until 1848 and even beyond, these actually contributed to the development of agrarian capitalism on the great estates, just as their absence in Russia after 1861 retarded it. Given the massive influx of non-nobles into the class of eastern estate owners it is very hard indeed to argue that Junker society was a closed caste. Actually quite the opposite was true; the newcomers were very quickly assimilated into Junker society and contributed greatly to its strength and its adaptability to the modern era. In politics it is the case that the Junkers were for the most part thoroughgoing anti-democrats who disliked many aspects of modern political activity. They nevertheless succeeded in mobilising behind themselves the bulk of the German agrarian interest. The *Bund der Landwirte* was in many ways a very modern interest group in its organisational structure and complexity, its mass appeal and its ruthless selfishness. It was also exceptionally effective, as a comparison between the fate of the English and Prussian provincial gentries in the era of agricultural depression rather proves. Above all, though, the old Prussian elite proved themselves to be formidably professional technicians in the art of war, thereby satisfying the German thirst for national unity and power and coming in time to pose a threat to all Europe.

In terms of adaptability to the modern industrial world, however, it is the Russian case which is in a sense the strangest one. Public service and cultural leadership, the key aristocratic roles in 1815, are perfectly compatible with the modern world and its values. It is true that the meritocratic principles on which Russian State service was supposedly constructed were in practice much affected by socioeconomic differences between the classes and the informal advantages that personal connections, old-school links and suchlike gave to the traditional elite. Even in a modern capitalist society, however, this remains true to some extent, though not, of course, to the gross degree of early nineteenth-century Tsarist Russia. Even in Russia, however, modernisation and increasing meritocracy went together in the nineteenth century. Moreover, the Russian elites did not carry with them into the modern era the feudal baggage which made adaptation difficult for the English and Prussian aristocracies. Russia had no purely hereditary English-style aristocratic upper house with an absolute veto over legislation, an extraordinary affront to democracy. Mobility into and out of the aristocratic elite from 1700 to the 1880s was certainly much greater than in England. Nor by the 1870s did the Russian aristocracy come anywhere near matching the English upper class's percentage of national land-ownership.

Far less of a caste than the German high nobility, the Russians

also had no 'von' built into their names to distinguish them from
mere mortals. Once serfdom was abolished in 1861 nobility brought
virtually no meaningful privileges and was of increasingly trivial
importance. Moreover, traditional European aristocratic characteristics – obsessive family pride or a mania for genealogy, to take but
two examples – never had the same hold in Russia as elsewhere on
the continent. By far the Russian aristocracy's greatest affront to
the modern world was the persistence of serfdom, of a particularly
nasty sort, up to 1861. The shadow of this hung over events up to
1917. Yet if one looked at an aristocracy just in terms of its own
values and traditions one might very easily conclude that it was the
Russian one which offered fewest challenges to modernity and was
the most likely to survive. Certainly when one studies the intransi-
gent defence of its position by the nobility after 1905 it is important
to note that what nobles were above all defending were not 'feudal'
privileges but the very 'bourgeois' principle of private property in
land.

    In discussing aristocracy's survival in the modern era it is there-
fore necessary to remember the traditional elite's capacity to adapt,
together with its possession, even in 1815, of a number of values
and skills which are thoroughly suited to the industrial era. In
addition, one needs to reflect that the precise nature of successful
modernity is still a matter for debate. No one doubts that traditional
aristocracy – a hereditary, legally privileged, socially dominant
ruling class – is doomed to disappearance. But the liberal, individu-
alist values of nineteenth-century American capitalism may not
be the only ones compatible with a successful modern economy.
Wilhelmine Germany, whose capitalism was more statist, corporatist and authoritarian than the Anglo-American model, was defeated
militarily in 1918 rather than out-competed as an economic system.
Modern Japan, while anything but an aristocratic society, nevertheless combines some of the key principles of Old-Regime Europe –
a powerful and very prestigious State bureaucracy, strong family
loyalties, and a distinctly anti-individualist culture, to name but
three – with a very successful modern economy. It should not
therefore be taken absolutely for granted that all the values upheld
by nobles and conservatives in 1914 were out of date and that all
the principles of radicals and liberals were, by contrast, modern
and efficient.[2]

    In a post-war Britain increasingly concerned about economic

decline relative to its major competitors, the survival of aristocratic values in the industrial age has sometimes been blamed for the death of the entrepreneurial spirit. The most famous exponent of this view is Martin Wiener, who argued *inter alia* that the gentrification of the middle classes at the Victorian public school was a root cause of Britain's economic failures even in the 1960s and 1970s.[3]

Wiener's stimulating argument is not easily proved or disproved. Certainly, this book, which touches only tangentially on his thesis, can make no such claim either way. It does nevertheless shed some light on Wiener's arguments. Clearly, in the twentieth century, British aristocracy survived better than Russian or German, above all because Britain was victorious in two world wars. Particularly after the 1870s, a new plutocratic elite emerged, drawn from old agrarian and modern financial and industrial wealth. Like Britain itself, this elite was far more homogeneous than its pre-1914 German or Russian counterparts. Aristocratic values made an important contribution to this elite's make-up. Obviously, these aristocratic values were not entrepreneurial: rather they were those of a ruling class, a leisure class, and to an increasing extent in the Victorian era a public service class too. The public school was of vital importance in the formation of this elite. Its values were consciously non-entrepreneurial. They stressed character over intellect, classics over science, and were excessively amenable to the pursuit of leisure at the expense of hard work.

All this is grist to Wiener's mill, but a comparison between British, German and Russian aristocracy does cause his thesis some problems. The boom of the Russian economy in the Old Regime's last decades presents few difficulties. Russian elites were heterogeneous, the role of government and foreign capital considerable. In any case, ultimately the intelligentsia's anti-capitalist values, some of them inherited from the aristocracy, were to destroy entrepreneurship in spectacular fashion in 1917.

Germany is more of a problem for Wiener. Much of modern historiography is obsessed by the influence of 'Old Regime relics', above all aristocracy, in perverting German development along 'normal' liberal capitalist lines. But the Junkers certainly did not have a retarding influence on German capitalism, which boomed before 1914. It is true that both the Junker and the Silesian magnate were rather more entrepreneurial than their English *rentier* counterpart but, seen overall, the values of the German old elites were scarcely those of modern capitalism. Perhaps if the Hohenzollern regime had lasted for longer, the influence of its old elites would also have contributed to the decline of the German industrial spirit. It was one of the nightmares of Max Weber that the puritan entrepreneurial vigour of the German bourgeoisie – a key to German economic dynamism and world power – would be destroyed by the 'feudalisation' of the middle classes and their transformation into a class of *rentiers*-cum-Prussian reserve officers.[4] But one could also argue that the statist, corporatist and authoritarian forms taken by German capitalism perhaps married rather well with Prussian Lutheran, Old-Regime traditions and met the requirements of a competitive national economy.

Though Wiener's thesis undoubtedly has some force, in my view it is less interesting and less plausible than Harold Perkin's distinction between aristocratic, business and professional cultures in Victorian England and his careful analysis of how the struggle between the two latter groups has come to be a key factor underlying contemporary British politics. Since 1914 the professional middle class has been far more numerous and powerful than the old aristocracy and, at least on the surface, it is to its values rather than those of the old landed elites that one should look for the choking of the entrepreneurial ethos. Admittedly, in England, gentry and professional were historically harder to distinguish than was the case in most societies. In the 1860s, for instance, Matthew Arnold commented that 'in no country . . . do the professionals so naturally share the cast of ideas of the aristocracy as in England', something closely connected, one would presume, to the often-remarked downward mobility of the younger sons of the English nobility and gentry'.[5]

Even if Wiener's thesis was wholly true, however, it would still be an indictment of the British middle class rather than of the aristocracy. It is the case that the English magnates were less entrepreneurial than the Silesians and even the Junkers, just as their cultural achievements were small by the standards of the Russian aristocracy. But the English were above all a political ruling class and in this guise they managed with skill and realism the Victorian transition to democracy. In the Edwardian age some of them, it is true, began to harbour misgivings about their 'achievement', but even where the Diehard minority is concerned, intransigence was linked to conceptions which were by no means purely reactionary or selfish. The Duke of Bedford's comment that 'I cannot accept any other position in the world for Great Britain except that of first', reflected the arrogant patriotism of Victorian and Edwardian England, common to all classes of the globe's greatest imperial power. Holding these convictions, Conservative peers' near frenzy at Britain's military unpreparedness and her people's unwillingness to bear the burden of tariffs and conscription was not wholly misplaced. Lord Denbigh asked, 'were the people of this country prepared to stand calmly by and see the empire reduced to the two islands on which we lived and a few colonies scattered around the world'. If not, added the Earl of Selborne, then they must pay the necessary price for realising that 'if this country is to maintain herself in the years to come in the same rank with the US, Russia and Germany, the unit must be enlarged from the UK to the Empire'. Having invested much emotion and, in the two world wars, considerable blood in the cause of Empire, the cool realism with which Britain's elites managed the process of decolonisation was admirable and owned much to the pattern of pragmatic concession established by the Victorian aristocracy.[6]

The indictment against the Junkers is a good deal more serious than mere responsibility for declining economic growth rates. By some influential historians, the Prussian upper class is held primarily responsible for the defeat of democracy in the Second Reich, the outbreak of the First World War and the coming to power of the Nazis. There is some truth in these accusations. The Junker spirit was authoritarian and military through and through. The Prussian aristocracy were not the only anti-democrats and militarists in Imperial Germany nor the most convinced imperialists but they undoubtedly made a powerful contribution to blocking democratisation and creating the climate of opinion in which Germany's rulers chose war in 1914. By comparison with the English or West German aristocracies the Junkers were dangerous because they were too numerous, too tough and too deeply entrenched in 'their' Hohenzollern State to be easily marginalised. Moreover, the key ways in which the Junkers accommodated themselves to modernity – namely military professionalism and ruthless parliamentary interest group tactics – did not contribute to peace and stability in Germany or Europe.

Nevertheless, even leaving aside the contribution of other Germans, to lay the main blame on the Junkers for the collapse of peace in 1914 is to go too far. International relations in the imperialist age had their own unpleasant logic. This logic interacted with the domestic factors influencing governments but retained a considerable degree of autonomy. The empires against which Germany fought in 1914 had been acquired by force and were to a great degree maintained by the same means. As French activity in Morocco or the massive Anglo-French annexations after the First World War showed, their predatory instincts were far from dead. Given the way imperialist international relations were conducted, the Germans had reason before 1914 to fear growing Russian power or the potential British stranglehold on their increasingly vital overseas trade. Between 1900 and 1918 Germany acted both more stupidly and more brutally than most other powers, but the distinction was scarcely that between black and white.

Still less can the main responsibility for Nazism be pinned on the Junkers, or on the broader German aristocracy. The effects of war, Russian revolution, inflation and depression cannot simply be ignored. Some aspects of Wilhelmine Junkerdom were thoroughly unpleasant but for the Edwardian Russian upper class it would in the most literal sense of the word have been unthinkable to exterminate millions of civilians in concentration camps in a manner wholly unconnected to any kind of military rationale. The Junkers played their part in bringing Adolf Hitler to power but in this respect none of the German elites exactly covered themselves in glory. If the case of the industrialists was notorious, the Catholic hierarchy, uncommitted to democracy and hostile to liberalism, was very happy to sign concordats with the Fascists in Germany as in Italy. The Communists played a major role in easing Hitler's path, but even the Social Democratic leadership contributed, albeit less culpably, if only by the narrow ghetto mentality and the lack of imagination with which they responded to the crisis of the Depression in the 1930s.

Once Hitler had come to power his enemies among the old elite feared lest opposing him would give Germany to their socialist foes. More worthily and realistically, they also understood that a *putsch* would win them little sympathy among the nationalist masses. The evil doctrine of 'my country right or wrong' contributed to acquiescence in the rule of a man seen to be enhancing German power. Yet on the whole the aristocracy was less enamoured of

Nazism, with its racialist and *völkisch* theories, than was the case with the middle class. In part this reflected noble class consciousness and disdain for intellectuals, racialist ones included. But those aristocrats who opposed Hitler for many years and nearly destroyed him in 1944 were moved by higher motives too. Drawn very often from the cream of the Prussian upper class – Schulenbergs, Moltkes, Lehndorffs and their peers – more of the military conspirators came from the Ninth Infantry, successor regiment to the old First Foot Guards of the royal army, than from any other unit. These men shared a sense of responsibility for their country but also a physical courage and a genuine Christian conscience worthy of the old Conservative Pietists at their best.

To remember Claus von Stauffenberg or Heinrich von Lehndorff is not to whitewash the German aristocracy or to forget its fundamentally anti-democratic role in modern German history. But it is to seek a balance and to deny other groups the use of aristocracy as an alibi for their own misdeeds. This can be necessary. Neither Hitler nor his entourage were Junkers. Nor were the millions of people who voted for him and subsequently supported his rule. To blame the old aristocracy and its traditions for Nazism is extremely convenient. Aristocrats are a tiny minority of no relevance in the contemporary world, a group whose sins can easily be defined as those of a bygone era. To point the finger at the still very powerful professional middle class or, even worse, at the democratic electorate itself, is far more uncomfortable. The latter in particular raises questions about ourselves, about human nature and about the theoretical sovereign in contemporary politics, whose essential virtue is a necessary myth in any political system.

Notes

1. THE NINETEENTH CENTURY: CHALLENGE AND RESPONSE

1. See, for instance, Philip Mansel's comparison between the Russian and Prussian courts on the one hand and those of Louis XVI and Napoleon I on the other. *The Court of France. 1789–1830* (Cambridge, 1988), especially chs 1 and 3.

2. On the eighteenth-century French aristocracy, see G. Chaussinand-Nogaret, *The French Nobility in the Eighteenth Century. From Feudalism to Enlightenment*, translated by W. Doyle (Cambridge, 1985). Simon Schama summarises this book and adds some ideas of his own on pp. 112–21 of *Citizens. A Chronicle of the French Revolution* (London, 1989).

3. See W. E. Mosse, *Alexander II and the Modernisation of Russia* (New York, 1962), p. 112, for the Tsar's fears about constitutional concessions.

4. K. Epstein, *The Genesis of German Conservatism* (Princeton, NJ, 1966) chs 1–6.

5. Richard Pipes edited an English edition of the *Memoir*. See N. M. Karamzin, *Memoir on Ancient and Modern Russia*, translated and edited by R. Pipes (Cambridge, Mass., 1959).

6. An introduction to this theme is A. J. Mayer, *The Persistence of the Old Regime. Europe to the Great War* (New York, 1981).

7. At which point the whole debate and massive literature on modernisation becomes relevant. To put nineteenth-century changes in perspective, the place to start is E. Gellner, *Plough, Sword and Book* (London, 1988). S. P. Huntington, *Political Order in Changing Societies* (Newhaven, Conn., 1968) remains a classic work on the dilemmas of traditional elites in an era of modernisation.

8. For a rapid insight into this subject see the contrast between the Prussian General Staff professional and the aristocratic *Schlachtenbummler* at

Royal HQ in 1870 in M. Howard, *The Franco-Prussian War* (New York, 1969) pp. 57–63.

9. *Moskovskiy Ezhenedel'nik*, no. 1 (3 January 1909) p. 14.

10. Both Barrington Moore and Theda Skocpol have a good deal to say about this relationship and its implications for social stabilty. B. Moore, *Social Origins of Dictatorship and Democracy* (Harmondsworth, 1966) and T. Skocpol, *States and Social Revolutions* (Cambridge, 1979).

11. There is a big literature on the *Standesherren* and their integration into the South German states, especially Württemberg. The place to start is H. Gollwitzer, *Die Standesherren. Die politische und geselschaftliche Stellung der Mediatisierten 1815–1918* (Stuttgart, 1957). The best general survey of relations between crown and nobility in Württemberg is G. Herdt, *Der württemburgische Hof im 19 Jahrhundert. Studien über das Verhaltnis zwischen Königtum und Adel in der absoluten und konstitutionellen Monarchie* (Göttingen, 1970).

12. For a brief study of the military and political problems facing the Union see A. Jones, *The Art of War in the Western World* (Oxford, 1987) pp. 409–19; and an essay by H. S. Commager, 'How "the Lost Cause" was Lost', in *Readings in American History*, Bicentennial edn, vol. 1 (Guilford, 1975).

13. A small survey of English aristocratic history, useful because it places England in the European context, is M. L. Bush, *The English Aristocracy. A Comparative Synthesis* (Manchester, 1984). A narrower and more detailed work is J. V. Beckett, *The Aristocracy in England 1660–1914* (Oxford, 1986). On the eighteenth-century aristocracy a good place to start is a collection of essays by J. Cannon, entitled *The Peerage of Eighteenth-Century England* (Cambridge, 1984). L. Stone and J. C. F. Stone, *An Open Elite? England 1540–1880* (Oxford, 1984) provides impressive backing for the argument that easy mobility into the English elite is a myth.

14. Apart from Herdt, *Württemburgische Hof*, a number of works cover relations between Crown and nobility in Württemberg after 1806. Among them are: H. Weber, *Die Fürsten von Hohenlohe in Vormärz. Politische und soziale Verhaltensweisen württemburgischer Standesherren in der ersten Hälfte des 19 Jahrhunderts* (Stuttgart, 1977). W. S. Kircher, *Adel, Kirche und Politik in Württemburg 1830–1851. Kirchliche Bewegung, katholische Standesherren und Demokratie* (Stuttgart, 1973). For a study of the imperial Schwabian nobility on the eve of annexation by Württemberg see S. Bader, 'Zur Lage und Haltung des Schwäbischen Adels am Ende des alten Reiches', *Zeitschrift für Württemburgische Landesgeschichte*, V. Jahrgang (1941) pp. 335–89. For a typical comment by Baroness Spitzemberg, see, for example, her diary entry for 3 December 1861 (p. 46) where she writes that in Württemberg public life a noble name was a hindrance and not an asset. Württemberg democrats in her opinion disliked nobles much more than was the case in Bavaria. See R. Vierhaus (ed.) *Das Tagebuch der Baronin Spitzemberg* (Göttingen, 1960).

15. A short essay by Erwin Freiherr von Aretin is the place to start a study of the Bavarian nobility: 'Vom Adel in Bayern', *Suddeutsche Monatshefte*, 23/5 (Feb. 1926) pp. 385–91. The reader should then turn to an excellent survey by W. Demel, 'Der Bayerische Adel, 1750–1871', which

the author was kind enough to send me in MS. See also H. H. Hofmann, *Adelige Herrschaft und Souveräner Staat* (Munich, 1962).

16. F. L. Carsten, *A History of the Prussian Junkers* (Aldershot, 1989) is a useful short survey. For an older, more sentimental account, see W. Gorlitz, *Die Junker. Adel und Bauer im Deutschen Osten* (Limburg, 1964). For Russia, nothing has yet superseded A. Romanovich-Slavatinsky, *Dvoryanstvo v Rossii* (SPB, 1870). There is a huge historiography on the Russian autocracy, aristocracy and bureaucracy before 1815 which I attempted to summarise in Chapter 1 of my *Russia's Rulers under the Old Regime* (London, 1989). For a comparison between Russian and Prussian nobles' seizure of church lands see J. Blum, *Lord and Peasant in Russia from the Ninth to the Nineteenth Century* (Princeton, NJ, 1961) pp. 363–67 and R. Berdahl, *The Politics of the Prussian Nobility* (Princeton, NJ, 1988), p. 17.

17. All these issues will be tackled at greater length later in the book. On Catherine's Legislative Commission and the nobility good introductions are I. de Madariaga, *Russia In the Age of Catherine the Great* (London, 1981) pp. 140–4, 166–74; and P. Dukes, *Catherine the Great and the Russian Nobility. A Study Based on the Materials of the Legislative Commission of 1767* (Cambridge, 1967).

18. The distinctions between aristocratic magnates and provincial gentry is a major theme of Chaussinand-Nogaret, *Nobility*: see in particular chapters 3 and 5. Interesting comments on this theme can be found in F. M. L. Thompson, *English Landed Society in the Nineteenth Century* (London, 1963); see, for example, pp. 22–4, 134–6. Also in D. Higgs, *Nobles in Nineteenth Century France. The Practice of Inegalitarianism* (Baltimore, Md., 1987): see the contrast between three types of nobility on pp. 70ff. Otto Graf zu Stolberg-Wernigerode, *Deutschlands konservative Fuhrungsschichten am Vorabend des Ersten Weltkrieges* (Munich, 1968) pp. 141–52, 169–205.

19. On the courtier's world see N. Elias, *The Court Society* (Oxford, 1983).

20. J. J. Kenney, 'The Politics of Assassination' in H. Ragsdale (ed.), *Paul I: A Reassessment of His Life and Reign* (Pittsburg, Pa., 1979).

21. On the eighteenth-century nobility see M. Raeff, *The Origins of the Russian Intelligentsia* (New York, 1966). A short but useful introduction to the forces that shaped the North German nobility's structure and mentalities is R. von Thadden-Vahnerow, 'Der Adel in Norddeutschland', *Suddeutsche Monatshefte*, 23, 5, (February 1926) pp. 391–6.

2. WEALTH

1. The chaotic nature of accountancy on serf-owners' estates is a major theme of M. Confino, *Domaines et Seigneurs en Russie vers la fin du XVIIIe siecle. Etude de structures agraires et de mentalités economiques* (Paris, 1963).

2. On the German currencies, the English-speaking reader could start with two short extracts from S. Pollard and C. Holmes, *Documents of European Economic History*; vol. 1: *The Process of Industrialisation: 1750–1870* (London, 1968). They are found between pp. 450 and 455. The values of currencies

cited by Pollard and Holmes are the ones I have used in this book. On Russia, see the Appendix (pp. 256–63), 'The Problem of the "Popular Rates"'; W. M. Pintner, *Russian Economic Policy under Nicholas I* (Cornell University, 1967).

3. On English aristocratic indebtedness, the place to start is D. Cannadine, 'Aristocratic Indebtedness in the Nineteenth Century: The Case Re-Opened', *Economic History Review* (1977) XXV, no. 30, pp. 624–50. On Russia, see S. Becker, *Nobility and Privilege in Late Imperial Russia* (DeKalb, 1985) pp. 47–51. On Prussia, Berdahl, *The Politics of the Prussian Nobility* (Princeton, NJ 1988) pp. 78–80 summarises the situation in the early nineteenth century.

4. F. M. L. Thompson, *English Landed Society in the Nineteenth Century* (London, 1983), p. 27. Prince L. H. von Pückler-Muskau noted in the 1820s that 'when a man calls a village *his*, this does not mean, as with us, merely that he has the lordship over it, but that every house is his absolute property': *Tour in England, Ireland and France in the Years 1826, 1827, 1828 and 1829* (Zurich, 1940).

5. Thompson, *English Landed Society*, pp. 26–35; 111–18.

6. G. E. Mingay, *English Landed Society in the Eighteenth Century* (London, 1963) pp. 10–26; J. Cannon, *Peerage*, especially chs 1, 3 and 4.

7. Thompson, *English Landed Society*, pp. 36–40. W. D. Rubinstein, *Men of Property. The Very Wealthy in Britain since the Industrial Revolution* (London, 1981).

8. Pückler-Muskau, *Tour*, pp. 19, 34, 73, 155.

9. Pückler-Muskau, *Tour*, pp. 40, 48, 252–3.

10. Pückler-Muskau, *Tour*, p. 267.

11. Pückler-Muskau, *Tour*, pp. 67–8, 74–6.

12. H. Graf von Arnim-Muskau and W. A. Boelcke, *Muskau: Standesherrschaft zwischen Spree und Neisse* (Frankfurt, 1978) pp. 143, 162, 217–9. D. Spring, *The English Landed Estate in the Nineteenth Century: Its Administration* (Baltimore, Md., 1963) pp. 35–6.

13. Arnim-Muskau and Boelcke, *Muskau*, p. 143. H. Schissler, *Preussische Agrargesellschaft im Wandel* (Göttingen, 1978) pp. 79–80 and 225–6 (notes 45 and 46).

14. Note that these statistics record individual estates' values. Some nobles owned many such estates.

15. On the Westphalian *Standesherren* see pp. 240ff. of F. Keinemann, *Soziale und politische Geschichte des westfälischen Adels 1815–1945* (Hamm, 1975).

16. H. Reif, *Westfälische Adel 1770–1860* (Göttingen, 1979) is an outstanding study of the Munster Stiftsadel before, during and after this difficult era.

17. R. K. Weitz, *Der Niederrheinische und Westfälische Adel in ersten Preussischen Verfassungskampf 1815–1823/4* (Bonn, 1970) pp. 40–50. Keinemann, *Soziale*, p. 20 writes that Count Clemens von Westphalen was said to have an income of 45 964 taler in 1826.

18. Weitz, *Neiderrheinische*, pp. 14–39. See also F. Petri and G. Droege (eds), *Rheinische Geschichte*, 3 vols (Dusseldorf, 1976), vol. 2, pp. 489–91.

19. G. W. Pedlow, *The Survival of the Hessian Nobility 1770–1870* (Princeton, NJ, 1988) pp. 18–23, 126, 131–8.

20. W. Demel, 'Die Wirtschaftliche Lage des Bayerischen Adels in den ersten Jahrzehnten des 19 Jahrhunderts' in A. von Reden-Dohna (ed.), *Der Adel an der Schwelle des burgerlichen Zeitalters* (Stuttgart, 1988) pp. 239, 243, 258–9. Count Karl Arco, for instance, a member of a leading Bavarian family, had an annual income of c. £900 in the 1800s. One of the Preysings' Munich palaces was valued at 80 000 florins (£8273).

21. Weber, *Hohenlohe*, pp. 11–25, 37–8, 125, 174–6, 272–8.

22. H. Winkel, *Die Ablosungskapitalien aus der Bauernbefreiung in West und Suddeutschland* (Stuttgart, 1968) pp. 25–61, 109–11.

23. Winkel, *Ablosungskapitalien*, pp. 62–8.

24. H. Stekl, *Österreichs Aristokratie im Vormärz* (Munich, 1973) p. 35.

25. I. Blanchard, *Russia's Age of Silver* (Leningrad, 1989).

26. W. Tooke, *View of the Russian Empire during the Reign of Catherine the Second and to the Close of the Present Century* 3 vols, (London, 1799); here, vol. 2, p. 304.

27. E. P. Karnovich, *Zamechatel'nya bogatstva chastnykh lits v Rossii* (SPB, 1885) pp. 77, 130–5, 259, 265.

28. J. Blum, *Lord and Peasant in Russia from the Ninth to the Nineteenth Century* (Princeton, NJ, 1961) p. 357.

29. Cited in P. M. Pilbeam, *The Middle Classes in Europe 1789–1914* (London, 1990). See especially S. M. Troitsky, *Russkiy absolyutizm i dvoryanstvo v XVIIIv* (Moscow, 1974) pp. 318–62.

30. Karnovich, *Zamechatel'nya*, pp.12–13, 152–78.

31. Blum, *Lord and Peasant*, pp. 379–80. H. D. Hudson, *The Rise of the Demidov Family* (Newtonville, 1986). Karnovich, *Zamechatel'nya*, p. 217 for the comment of M. I. Vorontsov: 'my job forces me to live in the style of a minister, not of a philosopher'.

32. Blum, *Lord and Peasant*, p. 295. T. Raikes, *A Visit to Saint Petersburg in the Winter of 1829–30* (London, 1838) pp. 130–5; *Vospominaniya F. F. Vigelya* (Moscow 1864) 7 parts: here part 2, p. 17.

33. Blum, *Lord and Peasant*, pp. 450–1, 572.

34. W. L. Blackwell, *The Beginnings of Russian Industrialization 1800–1860* (Princeton, NJ, 1968) p. 204. Raikes, *A Visit to Saint Petersburg*, p. 132N.

35. A. V. Hauxthausen, *The Russian Empire. Its People, Institutions and Resources*, translated by R. Faire 2 vols, (London, 1968): see, for example, vol. 1, p. 370; vol. 2, p. 168; S. Hoch, *Serfdom and Social Control in Russia* (Chicago, 1986), p. 14; Karnovich, *Zamechatel'nya*, p. 102; Blackwell, *The Beginnings of Russian Industrialization*, p. 203.

36. The source for the following tables are the lists of serf-owners by district in the *Predlozhenie k trudam redaktsionnoy kommissii* of 1859. In addition to the problems outlined in the text, the mammoth task of correlating information on the many thousands of estates listed was beyond me. I therefore concentrated on estates of over 500 serfs (of which there were, even so, a few thousand) since I was intent only on creating lists of the biggest serf-owners (that is, owning over 3000 serfs). Having drawn up a list of all owners of over 2000 serfs I then checked back to see whether

these names occurred in the lists of owners of 100–500 serfs. It is possible that I may have missed one or two owners of over 3000 serfs whose properties consisted of very many small estates, but I doubt it.

37. I did not count Polish magnates in the Western provinces, where the Lubomirskis, Radzivills, Tyszkewiczs and Potockis owned very big estates. Nor do my statistics include members of the Romanov family.

38. This bears out Hauxthausen's comment about the Balts: 'scarcely any have acquired their fortunes in Russia. It would be easy to enumerate those who, like the Lievens and Pahlens, owe a part of them to the munificence of the czars', Hauxthausen, *The Russian Empire*, vol. 2, p. 199.

39. Karnovich, *Zamechatel'nya*, is a mine of information on the latter subject, though he does not always draw general conclusions from his own evidence. As regards the role of aristocratic networks, see J. P. LeDonne, 'Ruling families in the Russian Political Order 1689–1825' in *Cahiers du Monde Russe et Sovietique*, xxviii, 3–4 (July–December 1987).

40. On the widening gap between Russian aristocracy and gentry see, for example, the statistics on land sales produced by L. P. Minarik in *Ekonomicheskaya kharakteristika krupneyshikh sobstvennikov Rossii kontsa XIX–nachala xxv* (Moscow, 1971) p. 36.

41. Count P. Vasili, *La Sainte Russie* (Paris, 1890) pp. 249–52.

42. Minarik, *Ekonomicheskaya*. For land prices see *prilozhenie* 3 of N. A. Proskuryakova, 'Razmeshchenie i struktura dvoryanskogo zemlevladeniya Evropeyskoy Rossii v kontse XIX–nachale XX veka', *Istoriya CCCP* (1973) 1, pp. 55–75.

43. V. Ya. Laverychev, *Krupnaya burzhuaziya v poreformennoy Rossii 1861–1900* (Moscow, 1974) p. 69; V. R. Rubakhin, *Grafy Apraksiny i ikh Petrburgskaya votchina–Apraksin dvor* (SPB, 1912) p. 75, Brockgauz/Efron, *Entsiklopedicheskiy slovar'*, vol. 1a (SPB, 1890) p. 927.

44. I. F. Gindin, 'Pravitel'stvennaya podderzhka ural'skikh magnatov vo vtoroy polovine XIX–nachale XXv', *Istoricheskie zapiski* (1968) vol. 82, pp. 120–62. A. M. Anfimov, 'Chastnovladel'cheskoe lesnoe khozyaystvo v Rossii v kontse XIX–nachale XXv', *Istoricheskie zapiski* (1958) vol. 63, p. 25.

45. All the statistics come from Minarik, *Ekonomicheskaya*, and A. M. Anfimov, *Krupnoe pomeshchishchee khozyaystvo Evropeyskoy Rossii* (Moscow, 1969) pp. 296–315.

46. Count I. I. Vorontsov-Dashkov, for instance, in the early twentieth century had debts of 4.5 million roubles but the value of just half of his land was 7.5 million roubles. Yu. S. Nechaev-Mal'tsev had a mortgage of 8.7 million roubles in 1905 but his factory had a capital value of 12 million roubles even in 1894, and his agricultural land and forests were valued at 10.9 million even in 1900. Princess Yusupov owed 3.6 million roubles to the Noble Bank in 1900. All these statistics are from Minarik, *Ekonomicheskaya*.

47. Laverychev, Krupnaya, p. 73; P. L. Bark's memoirs were printed in the emigre journal *Vozrozhdenie*: see here, ch. 4, no. 157 (January 1965), pp. 58–60.

48. On the English, John Bateman is the essential source. I used primarily the 1883 edition: *The Great Landowners of Great Britain and Ireland* (London,

1883). A major gap in Bateman's figures is their failure to include London rents. This is corrected by Rubinstein, *Men*, pp. 194–6. See D. I. Abrikossow, *Revelations of a Russian Diplomat* (Seattle, 1964) for one Russian's glimpse of London high society.

49. W. D. Rubinstein, *Men of Property* (London, 1981) pp. 207–9. H. Perkin, *The Rise of Professional Society* (London, 1989) pp. 62–78.

50. Perkin, *The Rise*, p. 64.

51. On Salisbury, see F. M. L. Thompson, 'Private Property and Public Policy' in Lord Blake and H. Cecil (eds), *Salisbury. The Man and His Policies* (London, 1987) pp. 255–7. For a general survey of this period see ch. XI of Thompson, *English Landed Society*. There is a big difference between the Duke of Westminster's (non-London) rental in the 1876 (£59 241) and 1883 (£38 944) editions of Bateman. The change is explained by the rental income of the Dowager Marchioness, which was £5063 in the 1876 and £26 958 in the 1883 edition. No doubt Westminster's mother was an exceptionally expensive dowager but it is worth noting the dent that mothers could make on the supposedly princely incomes of their eldest sons. For 1883, see Bateman, *Great Landowners*; for 1873, J. Bateman, *The Acre-Ocracy of England*, London 1876.

52. Much of Thomas Leyland's estate belonged to his daughter-in-law. Both Sir John Ramsden and Sir John Saint Aubyn were assigned the entire gross rental of urban areas of which they were just ground landlords. As regards transatlantic marriages, see, for example, M. M. Montgomery, *Gilded Prostitution, Status, Money and Transatlantic Marriages, 1870–1914* (London, 1989).

53. R. Fulford (ed.), *Your Dear Letter. Private Correspondence of Queen Victoria and the Crown Princess of Prussia. 1865–1871* (London, 1971) p. 302; *Darling Child. Private Correspondence between Queen Victoria and the Crown Princess of Prussia 1871–1878* (London, 1976) pp. 171, 242.

54. *Daisy, Princess of Pless. By Herself* (London, 1928) pp. 12, 43, 58, 137, 256.

55. The two works on which the following discussion is based, both by Rudolf Martin, are: *Jahrbuch des Vermögens und Einkommens der Millionäre in Preussen* (Berlin, 1912) and *Jahrbuch des Vermögens und Einkommens der Millionäre in Bayern* (Berlin, 1914).

56. Martin, *Jahrbuch . . . Bayern*, p. 9.

57. This is obviously true of the Schwarzenbergs, less clearly so of the Thurn und Taxis, whose old headquarters in Oberpfalz, Regensburg, had been incorporated into Bavaria. But the greater part of the family's estate was now in Bohemia.

58. One is sometimes dealing with individuals owning a number of residences, and whose property could be scattered across a number of states – particularly of the smaller German principalities. Martin often defines an individual's main residence and describes the spread of their property. E. H. Kneschke, *Neues allgemeines Deutsches Adelslexicon*, 9 vols (Leipzig, 1859) is a very useful source as regards distinguishing old from new nobility and showing in which state a family was ennobled.

59. Martin, *Jahrbuch . . . Preussen* and Kneschke, *Neues allgemeines*, are the basic sources for my comments about Prussian millionaires.

60. Martin, *Jahrbuch . . . Preussen*, part 2, pp. 255–6.

61. Ibid., pp. 341, 348.

62. Ibid., pp. 353, 425.

63. The table was constructed by taking all Martin's noble millionaires for whom rural estates were cited as their main residence. With very few exceptions indeed, noble landowners, even if they owned urban property, cited their estates as their main homes, so the table is an accurate profile of the landowning class.

64. Carsten, *History*, p. 85.

65. J. von Dissow, *Adel im Übergang* (Stuttgart, 1961) pp. 147–8.

3. SOURCES OF WEALTH: AGRICULTURE

1. Chapter 1 of C. Dipper, *Die Bauernbefreiung in Deutschland*, gives a good introduction to the old German agrarian order and the distinctions that existed between east and west. For more detailed works on individual sections of the German nobility see, for example, Reif, *Westfälischer*; Pedlow, *Survival*; Demel, 'Wirtschaftliche Lage' on western aristocracy and Carsten, *Prussian Junkers*; Goerlitz, *Junker*; Schissler, *Preussische* on the eastern one. Confino, *Domaines et Seigneurs*, is the classic work on the late eighteenth-century Russian nobility and agriculture. Blum, *Lord and Peasant*, contains much information on the shifting relationship between *obrok* and *barshchina* estates and problems of transport (see the Bibliography for full details of titles quoted). J. Blum, *The End of the Old Order in Rural Europe* (Princeton, NJ, 1978) is an ambitious and excellent survey of rural conditions in Central and Eastern Europe in the last decades of serfdom.

2. Chapters 4 and 5 of J. V. Beckett, *The Aristocracy in England 1660–1914* (Oxford, 1986), summarise the literature on English estate-management and the aristocracy's role in the agrarian revolution. On the latter, the classic work remains J. D. Chambers and G. E. Mingay, *The Agricultural Revolution*, 1750–1880 (London, 1966). Its equivalent as regards estate management is D. Spring, *The English Landed Estate in the Nineteenth Century: Its Administration* (Baltimore, 1963).

3. G. E. Mingay (ed.), *The Agricultural Revolution. Changes in Agriculture 1650—1880* (London, 1977) p. 8. Two chapters in R. Floud and D. McCloskey (eds), *The Economic History of Britain since 1700* (Cambridge, 1981) vol. 1 are also very useful surveys of agricultural change; E. L. Jones, 'Agriculture 1700–80', pp. 66–86 and G. Hueckel, 'Agriculture during Industrialisation', pp. 182–203.

4. M. Confino, *Systèmes Agraires et Progrès Agricole. L'Assolement Triennal en Russie aux XVIIIe–XIXe Siècles* (Paris, 1969) pp. 143–6; Blum, *The End of the Old Order*, pp. 59, 129, 137; Goerlitz, *Junker*, pp. 117, 126–9, 134–5, 152–3. G. Franz, *Landwirtschaft, 1800–1850*, in H. Aubin and W. Zorn (eds), *Hand-*

buch der Deutschen Wirtschafts und Sozialgeschichte, vol. 2 (Stuttgart, 1976) pp. 276–320; here p. 285.

5. Confino, *Systèmes*, p. 275.

6. Confino, *Systèmes*, especially pp. 302–39.

7. Confino, *Systèmes*, pp. 316–7 for instance cites the case of S. S. Apraksin who invested a fortune in improved methods and tools only then to make a loss of 8000 to 9000 roubles per annum on his model farm. Hoch, *Serfdom*, on the Gagarin estate of Petrovskoe and P. Scheibert, *Die Russische Agrareform von 1861* (Cologne, 1973) are good places to start a survey of Russian agriculture in this period. Much of the Soviet literature is obsessed with ideologically related nostrums about the crisis of serf agriculture and the creation of a national market. A. V. von Hauxthausen, *The Russian Empire. Its People, Institutions and Resources* (trans. R. Faire) (London, 1968) (for example, vol. 1, p. 151) said that only big noble farms could at present promote improved agriculture but for estates to survive without serfdom was impossible.

8. On the Tyrtovs see D. C. B. Lieven, *Russia's Rulers Under the Old Regime* (Newhaven, Conn., 1989) pp. 17–18. On the Kaluga nobility, E. N. Trubetskoy, *Vospominaniya* (Sofia, 1922) pp. 47–9; on southern Vologda, *Stolitsa i Usad'ba*, nos. 81–2 (30 May 1917).

9. Proskuryakova, 'Razmeshchenie', tables 3 and 8, pp. 61 and 66. A. M. Anfimov, *Krupnoe pomeshchishchee khozyaystvo Evropeyskoy Rossii*, pp. 94–115.

10. Hauxthausen, *Russian Empire*, vol. 1, p. 151. For Kulomzin's (unpublished) memoirs, see ch. 7 (and footnotes) of Lieven, *Russia's Rulers*.

11. For the Russian figures see Proskuryakova, 'Razmeshchenie', table 8, p. 66.

12. W. Demel, 'Der Bayerische Adel 1750–1871', MS, pp. 20–1; H. H. Hofmann, *Adelige Herrschaft und Souveränes Staat* (Munich, 1972) pp. 377, 463–5, 502, 512–5.

13. H. Winkel, *Die Ablosungskapitalien aus der Bauernbefreiung im West and Suddeutschland* (Stuttgart, 1968).

14. Winkel, *Ablosungskapitalien*, pp. 53–5, 121–4. E. E. Eltz, *Die Modernisierung einer Standesherrschaft. Karl Egon III und das Haus Fürstenberg in den Jahren nach 1848/49* (Sigmaringen, 1980) p. 120. Dipper, *Bauernbefreiung*, p. 107. Reif, *Westfälischer*, pp. 222–7; Demel, 'Wirtschaftliche', p. 258.

15. Hofmann, *Adelige*, pp. 374, 504; Keinemann, *Soziale und politische Geschichte des westfälischen Adels 1815–1945* (Hamm, 1975) p. 100.

16. L. Graf von Westphalen, *Aus dem Leben des Grafen Clemens August v. Westphalen zu Fürstenberg* (Munster, 1979) pp. 121–6. Compare Westphalen, for example, with S. S. Apraksin (note 7 of this chapter) or with some of the English ducal investment in nineteenth-century drainage.

17. Winkel, *Ablosungskapitalien*, pp. 86, 139.

18. Dipper, *Bauernbefreiung*, p. 107 says 5.4 per cent of agricultural land and forests belonged to nobles in 1856. Reif writes (*Westfälischer*, pp. 223–4) that 6–8 per cent of Munster's land was in noble hands in the 1830s, and Keinemann, *Soziale*, that 5 per cent of Westphalia was still noble in 1900. Demel, 'Bayerische', p. 20 writes that 6.7 per cent of Bavaria was noble in

the first quarter of the nineteenth century and G. W. Pedlow, *The Survival of the Hessian Nobility 1770–1870* (Princeton, NJ, 1988), p. 95 says that 7 per cent of Hesse-Cassel was noble in the 1860s.

19. T. Häbich, *Deutsche Latifundien* (Konigsberg, 1930).

20. In fact Häbich's lists cover estates of over 500 hectares total land or 400 hectares of agricultural land.

21. Carsten, *Prussian Junkers*, p. 88; Berdahl, *Politics*, pp. 153–4; Schissler, *Preussische*, p. 109; Spring, *European*, p. 4 (see Bibliography for full details). In the 1850s c. 15000 Prussians owned 'large' estates of more than 375 acres which together made up 40 per cent of the country's land, though 62 per cent of Pomerania and 57 per cent of Posen.

22. The best short survey of German agricultural development in this period is by Franz, 'Landwirtschaft'. Most of the statistics in this paragraph are drawn from Franz (see especially pp. 281, 285–8, 307–14); W. Abel, *Agrarkrisen und Agrarkonjuktor. Eine Geschichte der Land-und-Ernährungswirtschaft Mitteleuropas seit dem hohen Mittelalter* (Hamburg, 1966) is a classic: part 3, pp. 182–242 is relevant here; Schissler, *Preussische*, pp. 145ff. summarises agricultural progress in this era.

23. For statistics on land sales see table 3, p. 32 of S. Becker, *Nobility and Privilege in Late Imperial Russia* (De Kalb, 1985). On the Balts, see ch. 4 of G. H. Schlingensiepen, *Der Strukturwandel des Baltischen Adels in der Zeit vor dem Ersten Weltkrieg* (Marburg, 1959) and (for example) G. P. Strod, 'K voprosu o vremeni pobedy kapitalisticheskogo sposoba proizvodstva v sel'skom khozyaystve Latvii', *Ezhegodnik po agrarnoy istorii Vostochnoi Evropy* (1963g) pp. 539–47.

24. Hans Rosenberg, 'Die Pseudodemokratisierung der Rittergutsbesitz-erklasse', in M. Sturmer (ed.), *Moderne deutsche Sozialgeschichte*, pp. 287–308, here especialy p. 293; Schissler, *Preussische*, pp. 165–7.

25. Goerlitz, *Junker*, pp. 214–5, 219–20; Schissler, *Preussische*, p. 87.

26. This summarises information gleaned from many sources. The best general survey of European emancipation is Blum *The End of the Old Order*.

27. Schissler, *Preussische*, p. 60; Berdahl, *Politics*, pp. 81, 266–7.

28. Abel, *Agrarkrisen*, pp. 210–25; Berdahl, *Politics*, pp. 264–86 is a useful summary in English of the problems of depression and agricultural modern-isation in the 1820s. According to Abel, in 1801–5, 50 per cent of English wheat imports came from Prussian and German ports, 19 per cent from Ireland, 11 per cent from the Netherlands and North America, and only 6 per cent from Russia (*Agrarkrisen*, p. 196). English wheat prices in the 1820s were on average two-thirds of the level in 1801–5: Thompson, *English Landed Society*, p. 232.

29. E. Jones, 'The Changing Basis of English Agricultural Prosperity 1853–1873', in P. J. Perry (ed.), *British Agriculture 1875–1914* (London, 1973) p. xiv.

30. Abel, *Agrarkrisen*, pp. 254–60; Franz, 'Landwirtschaft', pp. 305–10; M. Rolfes, 'Landwirtschaft 1850–1914', pp. 500–2.

31. G. Pavlovsky, *Agricultural Russia on the Eve of the Revolution* (London, 1930) p. 206; Rolfes, 'Landwirtschaft', pp. 508–9; Klaus Saul, 'Um die konservative Struktur Ostelbiens: Agrarische Interessen, Staatsverwaltung

und ländliche "Arbeiternot". Zur konservativen Landarbeiterpolitik in Pre-ussen-Deutschland 1889–1914', in D. Stegmann et al. (eds), *Deutscher Konservatismus im 19 and 20 Jahrhundert* (Bonn, 1982) pp. 129–98 (here p. 150); Perkin, *The Origins of Modern English Society* (London, 1969) p. 447; A. Offer, *The First World War: An Agrarian Interpretation* (Oxford, 1989) pp. 116–7.

32. Thompson, *English Landed Society*, p. 314; R. Manning, *The Crisis of the Old Order in Russia* (Princeton, NJ, 1982) pp. 11–17.

33. The best book on the government's agrarian strategy is by D. Macey, *Government and Peasant in Russia 1861–1906* (Dekalb, 1987).

34. Apart from the sources already cited, a useful picture of the Russian eighteenth-century rural nobility is given by W. R. Augustine, 'Notes towards a Portrait of the Eighteenth-Century Russian Nobility', *Canadian Slavic Studies* (1970) vol. 4, no. iii, pp. 373–425. Much of what Augustine says remains relevant to the nineteenth century. On post-1861 noble agri-culture the three major Soviet works are Anfimov, *Krupnoe*; Minarik, *Ekonomicheskaya* (see Bibliography); and I. D. Kovalchenko, N. B. Selunskaya and B. M. Litvakov, *Sotsial'no-ekonomicheskiy stroy pomeshchichego khozyaystva Evropeyskoy Rossii v epokhu kapitalizma* (Moscow, 1982). All are useful and Anfimov's, in particular, is extremely thorough and valuable. All three would, however, have benefited from rather less censorious a priori reason-ing about how gentry capitalist agriculture 'should' have developed and a greater attention to the actual problems of running profitable great estates in this period. Becker, *Nobility and Privilege*, is a sharp and valuable critique of much conventional thinking about the decline of the gentry.

35. Becker, *Nobility and Privilege*, pp. 44, 53; Lieven, *Russia's Rulers*, p. 314 (n. 63); A. P. Korelin, *Dvoryanstvo v poreformennoy Rossii 1861–1904* (Moscow, 1979) is a mine of information about the post-1861 nobility.

36. Thompson, *English Landed Society*, p. 318; Pavlovsky, *Agricultural Russia*, pp. 198–200, 208–9; Manning, *The Crisis of the Old Order*, pp. 162–3.

37. Pavlovsky, *Agricultural Russia*, pp. 213–21.

38. Thompson, *English Landed Society* pp. 308–12; C. O'Grada, 'Agricul-tural Decline 1860–1914', in R. Floud and D. McCloskey, *The Economic History of Britain since 1700*, vol. 2, pp. 175–97, here especially pp. 180–1; Rolfes, 'Landwirtschaft', pp. 501–2.

39. K. D. Barkin, *The Controversy over German Industrialisation 1890–1902* (Chicago, 1970) pp. 57–8, 78; M. L. Bush, *The English Aristocracy. A Comparative Synthesis* (Manchester, 1984), p. 66; S. B. Webb, 'Agricultural Protection in Wilhelminian Germany: Forging an Empire with Pork and Rye', *Journal of Economic History*, vol. XLII, no. 2 (1982) pp. 309–25, here p. 325.

40. On Weber and the Junkers see, for example, pp. 21–40 of W. J. Mommsen, *Max Weber and German Politics 1890–1920*, translated by M. S. Steinberg (Chicago, 1990); and K. Tribe, 'Prussian Agriculture in German Politics: Max Weber 1892–7' *Economy and Society* (1983) vol. 12, no. 2, pp. 181–226. Tribe reminds the reader that Weber did not object to Junker agriculture because it was inefficient but because it was anti-national: 'The advantage of peasant cultivation was not that it was efficient, but that it was insulated against fluctuations in the world market' (p. 210).

41. E. Kemp and R. Mührer, *Die volkswirtschaftliche Bedeutung von Gross und Kleinbetrieb in der Landwirtschaft* (Berlin, 1913) pp. ix–xxviii, 150–1.

42. J. A. Perkins, 'The Agricultural Revolution in Germany 1850–1914', *Journal of European Economic History*, vol. 10, no. 1 (Spring 1981) pp. 71–118, here pp. 78, 109, 117.

43. R. Perren, 'The Landlord and Agricultural Transformation, 1870–1900' in P. J. Percy (ed.), *British Agriculture 1873–1914* (London, 1973) here pp. 115–27; T. W. Fletcher, 'The Great Depression of English Agriculture 1873–1896', *Economic History Review*, vol. XIII (1960/1) here pp. 423–4; Thompson, *English Landed Society*, p. 311.

44. O'Grada, 'Agricultural Decline', pp. 175, 197; Offer, *The First World War*, pp. 96–97.

45. Offer, *The First World War*, ch. 8; O'Grada, 'Agricultural Decline', p. 191.

4. SOURCES OF WEALTH: FORESTRY

1. H. Rubner, *Forstgeschichte im Zeitalter der industriellen Revolution* (Berlin, 1967) pp. 78–88, 131–3. The Duke of Atholl was a rare example of an aristocrat who invested seriously in forestry. Friedrich von Arnold, *Russlands Wald* (Berlin, 1892) p. 23, after describing the division between State and private forest-owning in most of Europe, stated that Britain, the Low Countries and Denmark had too few forests to warrant serious attention.

2. Rubner, *Forstgeschichte*, pp. 67–9, 138; Arnold, *Russlands Wald*, pp. 26–7; E. W. Maron, *Forst-Statistik der sämtlichen Wälder Deutschlands einschliesslich Preussen* (Berlin, 1862) p. 217.

3. Arnold, *Russlands Wald*, p. 27; *Polnaya entsiklopediya russkogo sel'skogo khozyaystva i soprikasayushchikhsya s nim nauk*, 11 vols, (SPB, 1900–12) 'Lesnoe Khozyaystvo', pp. 297–301. Baden's superiority reflected not just a better soil and climate but also more skilled and careful management.

4. Maron, *Forst-Statistik*, pp. 4–10; Köstler, *Geschichte des Waldes in Bayern* (Munich, 1934) p. 4.

5. V. I. Denisov, *Lesa Rossii, ikh eksploatatsiya i lesnaya torgovlya* (SPB, 1911) pp. 3–6.

6. Denisov, *Lesa Rossii*, p. 6; Häbich, *Deutsche*, pp. 158–9, Eltz, *Modernisierung*, p. 116; Martin, *Handbuch . . . Preussen*, pt. 2, p. 11 (see Bibliography for full details).

7. Rubner, *Forstgeschichte*, pp. 58, 106–9, 152–5; Eltz, *Modernisierung*, p. 107; Pedlow, *Survival*, pp. 131–6 (see Bibliography for details).

8. Rubner, *Forstgeschichte*, pp. 71, 117, 139–41; Köstler, *Geschichte*, p. 65.

9. Arnold, *Russlands Wald*, pp. 31–2; A. M. Anfimov, 'Chastnovladel'cheskoe lesnoe khozyaystvo v Rossii v kontse XIX–nachale XXv', *Istoricheskie Zapiski* vol. 63 (Moscow, 1958) pp. 244–57, here p. 256; J. C. Brown, *Forests and Forestry in Poland, Lithuania, the Ukraine and the Baltic Provinces of Russia* (Edinburgh, 1885) pp. 124–30, 150–7; *Polnaya entsiklopediya*, 'Lesoupravlenie', pp. 353–9.

10. Arnold, *Russlands Wald*, pp. 209–10; see also, for example, Westphalen, *Leben*, p. 112.

11. Arnold, *Russlands Wald*, p. 173; Polnaya, 'Lesnoe Khozyaystvo', pp. 301–2.

12. H. Graf von Arnim-Muskau and W. A. Boelcke, *Muskau: Standesherrschaft zwischen Spree und Neisse* (Frankfurt, 1978) pp. 320, 352–7; Maron, *Forst-Statistik*, pp. 28–30, 38–9, 235. Eltz, *Modernisierung*, pp. 95–120.

13. Denisov, *Lesa Rossii*, pp. 27–36; Anfimov, 'Chastnovladel'cheskoe', pp. 246–7; Arnold, *Russlands Wald*, p. 227; Rubner, *Forstgeschichte*, pp. 176, 182.

14. J. C. Brown, *Forests and Forestry in Poland, Lithuania, the Ukraine and the Baltic Provinces of Russia* (Edinburgh, 1885) pp. 168, 176, 180, 233.

15. Arnold, *Russlands Wald*, chs 2 and 3, *passim*.

16. Anfimov, 'Chastnovladel'cheskoe', pp. 244, 250–2; M. A. Tsvetkov, *Izmenenie lesisosti Evropeyskoy Rossii s kontsa XVII stoletiya po 1914 god* (Moscow, 1957).

5.   SOURCES OF WEALTH: URBAN PROPERTY

1. Prince L. H. von Pückler-Muskau, *Tour in England, Ireland and France in the Years 1826, 1827, 1828 and 1829* (Zurich, 1940), pp. 40–1; Beckett, *The Aristocracy in England 1660–1914* (Oxford, 1986) pp. 267–72, 280–2.

2. Beckett, *Aristocracy in England*, p. 262.

3. D. Cannadine, 'The landowner as millionaire: the finances of the Dukes of Devonshire', *Agricultural Review* (1977) vol. 25, pp. 77–97; D. Cannadine, *Lords and Landlords. The Aristocracy and the Towns 1774–1967* (Leicester, 1980) especially pp. 285–98, 382–8. On the 7th Duke, see also ch. 12 of J. Pearson, *Stags and Serpents* (London, 1983).

4. Cannadine, *Lords and Landlords*, especially ch. 3; Beckett, *Aristocracy in England*, pp. 276–9, 283.

5. Cannadine, *Lords and Landlords*, especially pp. 41–2, 46–7, 415.

6. Cannadine, *Lords and Landlords*, pp. 43–60, 391–429; Beckett, *Aristocracy in England*, pp. 273–6, 283.

7. Beckett, *Aristocracy in England*, pp. 281–2; Thompson, 'Private Property', p. 278. Local history can tell one much about smaller-scale developments and the benefits they brought to more minor landowners. See, for example, S. Margetson, *St. John's Wood* (London, 1988) for a description (pp. 4–7) of the development of the Eyre estate by Henry Samuel Eyre, a colonel in the Guards.

8. Rudolph Martin, *Jahrbuch . . . Preussen*, lists meticulously every house owned in a town by one of Prussia's millionaires.

9. Martin, *Jahrbuch . . . Preussen*, part 1, p. 253; part 2, pp. 319–20, 380–1; E. von Oldenburg-Januschau, *Erinnerungen* (Leipzig, 1936) pp. 40–1. Oldenburg bought his property at Lichterfelde for one million Marks, 700 000 of which he borrowed.

10. Beckett, *Aristocracy in England*, p. 276; Cannadine, *Lords and Landlords*, pp. 218–25, 414–7; Martin, *Jahrbuch . . . Preussen*, pp. 497–8.

11. Martin, *Jahrbuch . . . Preussen*, part 2, pp. 214–6, 337, 437.

12. Martin, *Jahrbuch . . . Bayern*, pp. 116–22.

13. Martin, *Jahrbuch . . . Bayern*, p. 19; G. Hirschmann, *Das Nürnberger Patriziat im Königreich Bayern 1806–1918* (Nuremberg, 1971) pp. 14, 67, 80, 98–9.

14. A. V. von Hauxthausen, *The Russian Empire. Its People, Institutions and Resources* (London, 1968) vol. 1, p. 369; Anfimov, *Krupnoe pomeshchishchee khozyaystvo Evropeyskoy Rossii* (Moscow, 1969) p. 278.

15. Anfimov, *Krupnoe*, p. 277; Paul Grabbe, *Windows on the River Neva* (New York, 1977) pp. 15–19.

16. V. Ya. Laverychev, *Krupnaya burzhuaziya v poreformennoy Rossii 1861–1900* (Moscow, 1974) p. 69; Anfimov, *Krupnoe*, p. 277.

17. Anfimov, *Krupnoe*, pp. 275, 278.

18. I. F. Gindin, 'Pravitelstvennaya podderzhka ural'skikh magnatov vo vtoroy polovine XIX–nachale XXV', *Istoricheskie zapiski*, vol. 1, no. 82, p. 138; *Stolitsa i Usad'ba*, no. 76 (28 February 1917); F. F. Vigel, *Vospominaniya*, 7 parts (Moscow, 1864) p. 147; Brockhaus, *Entsikopedicheskiy*, vol. XVIa, p. 651.

19. V. R. Rubakin, *Grafy Apraksiny i ikh Peterburgskaya votchina – Apraskin Dvor* (SPB, 1912), *passim*; Brockhaus, *Entsiklopedicheskiy*, vol. 1a (1890) p. 927.

6. SOURCES OF WEALTH: INDUSTRY

1. Stone, *Crisis*, ch. 7; G. Chaussinand-Nogaret, *The French Nobility in the Eighteenth Century. From Feudalism to Enlightenment* (Cambridge, 1985) ch. 5; F. Redlich, *Der Unternehmer* (Göttingen, 1964) pp. 280–98.

2. J. V. Beckett, *The Aristocracy in England 1660–1914* (Oxford, 1986) pp. 221–3; D. Spring, 'English Landowners and Nineteenth-Century Industrialism', in J. T. Ward and R. G. Wilson (eds), *Land and Industry. The Landed Estate and the Industrial Revolution* (London, 1971) pp. 16–62. For a study of a rare English noble entrepreneur, see G. Mee, *Aristocratic Enterprise. The Fitzwilliam Industrial Undertakings 1795–1857* (Glasgow, 1975).

3. Beckett, *The Aristocracy in England*, ch. 7.

4. Spring, 'English Landowners', pp. 27–9.

5. Rubinstein, *Men of Property. The Very Wealthy in Britain Since the Industrial Revolution* (London, 1981), p. 194; Spring, 'English Landowners', pp. 30–7. Beckett, *The Aristocracy in England*, pp. 211–21.

6. Beckett, *The Aristocracy in England*, p. 215. Spring, 'English Landowners' p. 37.

7. Beckett, *The Aristocracy in England*, pp. 217, 260, 319; Mee lists the Fitzwilliams' colliery expenses up to 1856 as £1.95 million but deplores 'the limitations of the Wentworth accounts', *Aristocratic Enterprise*, pp. 200–2;

Cannadine, *Lords and Landlords. The Aristocracy and the Towns 1774–1967* (Leicester, 1980), p. 294.

8. Spring, 'English Landowners', pp. 45–51; Rubinstein, *Men of Property*, pp. 176–7 discusses motivations among British business entrepreneurs in a manner relevant to this paragraph. Even among businessmen, worship of unlimited wealth was far less common in Britain than in the USA.

9. J. Kocka, 'Entrepreneurs and Managers in German Industrialisation', pp. 482–589 in P. Mathias and M. M. Postan (eds) *The Cambridge Economic History of Europe*, vol. VII, part 1 (Cambridge, 1978), here p. 514; H. Reif, *Westfälischer Adel 1770–1860* (Göttingen, 1979) p. 230; E. E. Eltz, *Die Modernisierung einer Standesherrschaft. Karl Egon III und das Haus Fürstenberg in den Jahren nach 1848–9* (Sigmaringen, 1980) pp. 79–95 on the administration of the Fürstenberg properties; Martin, *Jahrbuch . . . Preussen*, p. 234.

10. S. M. Troitsky, *Russkiy absolyutizm i dvoryanstvo v XVIIIv* (Moscow, 1974), pp. 318 ff; A. J. Rieber, *Merchants and Entrepreneurs in Imperial Russia* (Chapel Hill, 1982) pp. 40–43; Chaussinand-Nogaret, *The French Nobility*, ch. 5.

11. Rieber, *Merchants*, p. 77; J. Blum, *Lord and Peasant in Russia from the Ninth to the Nineteenth Century* (Princeton, NJ, 1961) pp. 402–3; M. I. Tugan-Baranovsky, *The Russian Factory in the Nineteenth Century* (Illinois, 1970) pp. 23–4, 247–8; 'Sveklosakharnoe Proizvodstvo', *Polnaya Entsiklopediya*, vol. vii, pp. 841–9.

12. Tugan-Baranovsky,*The Russian Factory*, for example p. 249; D. C. B. Lieven, *Russia's Rulers Under the Old Regime* (London, 1989), pp. 259, 360 (notes 13 and 18).

13. A. P. Korelin, *Dvoryanstvo v poreformennoy Rossii, 1861–1914* (Moscow, 1979), pp. 106–22; A. M. Anfimov, *Krupnoe pomeshchishchee khozyaystvo Evrope-yskoy Rossii* (Moscow), pp. 255–71. M. Ya. Gefter, 'Iz istorii monopolistic-heskogo kapitalizma v Rossii, *Istoricheskie Zapiski* (1951) vol. 38, pp. 104–53 (the quote is on page 108).

14. R. Portal, 'The Industrialisation of Russia' in *The Cambridge Economic History of Europe*, vol. VI, part 2 (Cambridge, 1966) pp. 801–74; Rieber, *Merchants*, pp. 219–42; J. P. McKay, 'Elites in Conflict in Russia. The Briansk Company', pp. 179–201 in F. C. Jaher (ed.), *The Rich, the Well Born and the Powerful. Elites and Upper Classes in History* (Urbana, 1973).

15. Portal, 'Industrialisation', pp. 824–9; V. K. Yatsunsky, 'Geography of the Iron Market in Pre-Reform Russia', in W. L. Blackwell (ed.) *Russian Economic Development from Peter the Great to Stalin* (New York, 1974) especially pp. 83, 101; I. F. Gindin, 'Pravitel'stvennaya', pp. 122–23, 161.

16. Portal, 'Industrialisation', pp. 830, 847; Rieber, *Merchants*, p. 369.

17. Rieber, *Merchants*, p. 225; Korelin, *Dvoryanstvo*, p. 120.

18. *Stolitsa i Usad'ba*, no. 51 (1 February 1916).

19. T. H. Friedgut, *Iuzovka and Revolution*, vol. 1 (Princeton, NJ, 1989) especially pp. 42–6; Prince Paul Lieven, *Dela davno minuvshikh*, MS (1952) pp. 30–1.

20. P. M. Pilbeam, *The Middle Classes in Europe 1789–1914* (London, 1990) pp. 41–2; Martin, *Jahrbuch . . . Preussen*, pp. 49–54, 564–67.

21. Martin, *Jahrbuch . . . Preussen*, pp. 49–54.

22. Martin, *Jahrbuch . . . Preussen*, pp. 564–67.

23. Eltz, *Modernisierung*, pp. 123–32; Winkel, *Ablosungskapitalien*, pp. 87–92. There were, for example, no coalmines in Bavaria and no great aristocratic brewers. See Martin, *Jahrbuch . . . Bayern*, pp. 6–12, 108ff. Winkel, *Ablosungskapitalien*, provides other examples (for example, the Hohenzollern-Sigmaringen pp. 98–9) of magnates who sold or let industrial properties and bought forests and bonds.

24. Arnim, *Muskau*, pp. 227–8, 265–82.

25. Arnim, *Muskau*, pp. 352–63; Martin, *Jahrbuch . . . Preussen*, pp. 279–80, actually writes '14–15 million' but this includes three other small Arnim estates. Martin mentions the poor quality of the soil and the estate's geographical position but not its factories and mines.

26. H. Seffert, 'Die Entwicklung der familie von Alvensleben zu Junkerindustriellen', *Jahrbuch für Wirtschaftsgeschichte* (1963) part IV, pp. 209–43.

27. The key sources on the Silesian magnates are Martin's lengthy discussions of individuals and their assets in part 2 of *Jahrbuch . . . Preussen*, together with K. Fuchs, *Von Dirigismus zum Liberalismus. Die Entwicklung Oberschlesiens als preussisches Berg und Hüttenrevier* (Wiesbaden) and A. Perlick, *Oberschlesische Berg und Hüttenleute* (Frankfurt, 1953).

28. On incomes see, for example, Martin's table on p. 47 of Martin *Jahrbuch . . . Preussen*; Fuchs, *Dirigismus*, chs 4, 5, 6.

29. Perlick, *Oberschlesische*, pp. 41, 47–8; Fuchs, *Dirigismus*, pp. 143–4.

30. Perlick, *Oberschlesische*, p. 49; Fuchs, *Dirigismus*, ch. 6; Martin, *Jahrbuch . . . Preussen*, pp. 30, 55.

31. Perlick, *Oberschlesische*, pp. 42, 45, 50; Martin, *Jahrbuch . . . Preussen*, p. 30; Princess Daisy of Pless, *Daisy, Princess of Pless. By Herself* (London, 1928) p. 138.

32. Isabel Hull, *The Entourage of Kaiser Wilhem II 1888–1918* (Cambridge, 1982) p. 151; Spitzemberg, *Tagebuch*, p. 565.

33. F. M. L. Thompson, *English Landed Society in the Nineteenth Century* (London, 1973) p. 307; Spring, 'English Landowners', pp. 53–61; Cannadine, *Lords and Landlords*, pp. 419–21.

34. S. Becker, *Nobilty and Privilege in Late Imperial Russia*, (DeKalb, 1985).

35. Winkel, *Die Ablosungskapitalien aus der Bauernbefreiung im West und Suddeutschland* (Stuttgart, 1968). For example pp. 35–7, 66–8, 78, 82, 98.

7. LIFE, MANNERS, MORALS

1. R. Fulford (ed.), *Darling Child . . . Private Correspondence between Queen Victoria and the Crown Princess of Prussia . . . 1871–1878* (London, 1976) pp. 128–9.

2. Gronow, *The Reminiscences and Recollections of Captain Gronow* (London, 1900) 2 vols, here vol. 1, p. 32; L. Davidoff, *The Best Circles* (London, 1986) p. 49.

3. Princess Daisy of Pless, *Daisy, Princess of Pless. By Herself* (London, 1928) pp. 30, 37.

4. See, for example, Princess Anna Obolensky's activities on her husband's estate in Penza in D. C. B. Lieven, *Russia's Rulers under the Old Regime* (London, 1989) p. 260.

5. For example, Elard von Oldenburg-Januschau recalls in his memoirs (*Erinnerungen* (Leipzig, 1936) p. 11) that his mother directed their early education, gave them enormous love and developed their emotional life. His father taught them a strict sense of duty. Countless memoirs make rather similar comments.

6. Prince Chlodwig von Hohenlohe-Schillingfürst, *Memoirs of Prince Chlodwig of Hohenlohe-Schillingfürst* (London, 1906) 2 vols; here vol. 1, p. 30.

7. Vierhaus (ed.),Spitzemberg, *Tagebuch*, p. 103; *Daisy Princess*, p. 194.

8. Spitzemberg, *Tagebuch*, p. 472.

9. Cited in L. Davidoff, *The Best Circles* (London, 1986) p. 61.

10. J. Murray, *Handbook for Northern Europe including Denmark, Norway, Sweden, Finland and Russia* (London, 1848) p. 411.

11. J. Murray, *Handbook for Travellers in Russia, Poland and Finland* (London, 1865) pp. 46–7.

12. Prince E. N. Trubetskoy, *Vospominaniya* (Sofia, 1922) pp. 126–30.

13. Trubetskoy, *Vospominaniya*, p. 127; *Stolitsa i Usad'ba*, no. 69, (1 November 1916); H. M. Grove, *Moscow* (London, 1912) p. 123; G. Dobson, H. M. Grove and H. Stewart, *Russia* (London, 1913) pp. 95, 232.

14. P. Vasili, *La Société de St. Petersbourg* (Paris, 1886) pp. 208–10; on the Grand Duchess, see W. B. Lincoln, *In the Vanguard of Reform. Russia's Enlightened Bureaucrats 1825–1861* (De Kalb, 1982).

15. Vasili, *Société de St. Petersbourg*, p. 234; A. A. Ignatiev, *A Subaltern in Old Russia* (London, 1944).

16. A. Ponsonby, *The Decline of Aristocracy* (London, 1912) pp. 142–4.

17. This brief summary does little justice to the description of the Souls in Angela Lambert, *Unquiet Souls. The Indian Summer of the British Aristocracy* (London, 1984).

18. On London see C. S. Sykes, *Private Palaces. Life in the Great London Houses* (London, 1985); R. J. Olney, *Lincolnshire Politics 1832–1885* (Oxford, 1973), says most of the county's owners of 7000 acres or more had London houses (p. 2). As usual, there is no Russian equivalent to this synthesis. On the buildings themselves see *Pamyatniki arkhitektury Leningrada* (Leningrad, 1976); *Stolitsa i Usad'ba*, no. 74 (1 February 1917) describes the Yusupov palace and no. 45 (1 November 1915) that of Prince Abamelek-Lazarev.

19. J. Murray, *A Hand-Book for Travellers on the Continent: Being a Guide through Holland, Belgium, Prussia and Northern Germany* (London, 1843) p. 334.

20. K. Hammer, 'Die preussischen Könige und Königinnen im 19 Jahrhundert und ihr Hof', in K. F. Werner (ed.), *Hof, Kultur und Politik im 19 Jahrhundert* (Bonn, 1985). The quote comes from p. 183 of 'Unter den Linden' by P. Lindau, in R. H. Davies (ed.), *The Great Streets of the World* (London, 1892).

21. Count Paul Vasili, *Berlin Society* (New York, 1884) pp. 5–6, 140, 142, 152, 164.

22. H. Vizetelly, *Berlin Under the New Empire* (London, 1979) 2 vols; here vol. 1, pp. 80, 82, 85–6, 88.

NOTES 271

23. Vizetelly, *Berlin*, p. 95.

24. Vizetelly, *Berlin*, p. 84.

25. Princess Daisy of Pless, *From My Private Dairy* (London, 1931) p. 90; Anonymous, *Am Hofe des Kaisers* (Berlin, 1886) pp. 27–32; Spitzemberg, *Tagebuch*, p. 330; Pless, *Princess Daisy . . . by Herself*, p. 174.

26. Vasili, *Berlin*, for example, p. 122. For the background see N. Elias, *The Court Society* (Oxford, 1983).

27. For example, in Dobson (*et al.*), *Russia*, pp. 103–6 one reads 'Russian imperial ceremony and hospitality are provided on a lavish and gigantic scale, and in a setting of luxury and splendour such as cannot be surpassed, or perhaps even equalled, by any other Court in Europe . . . the prolonged absence of the Imperial Court from St. Petersburg has been a great loss to society and trade'.

28. D. Cannadine, *Lords and Landlords* (Leicester, 1980) pp. 396–400; Vizetelly, *Berlin*, vol. 1, ch. x; Lindau, 'Unter den Linden', p. 175; *Stolitsa i Usad'ba*, no. 74 (1 February 1917).

29. Gronow, *Reminiscences*, vol. 1, pp. 34, 37; Vizetelly, *Berlin*, vol. 1, p. 89; Murray's *Hand-Book* of 1865 recorded that 'to the Russian nobility of the higher class . . . no price is too great to be paid for some of the more rare and highly varied luxuries of the table' (p. 402).

30. Gronow, *Reminiscences*, vol. 1, p. 34; vol. 2, pp. 62–3; Vasili, *Berlin*, p. 140; Count V. A. Sollohub, *Vospominaniya* (SPB, 1877).

31. The quote is from C. Schurz, *The Reminiscences of Carl Schurz* (New York, 1907) 3 vols; here vol. 1, p. 391.

32. Murray, *Hand-Book* pp. 215–20.

33. Paul Gerbod, 'Le loisir aristocratique dans les villes d'eaux francaises et allemandes au XIXe siècle (1840–1870)' in Werner, *Hof*.

34. W. Vamplew, *A Social and Economic History of Horse Racing* (London, 1976, pp. 29–37 discusses the impact of railways on the sport.

35. M. Girouard, *Life in the English Country House* (London, 1978), p. 5.

36. R. Carr, *English Fox-Hunting* (London, 1987) for example, pp. 35, 120, 148.

38. Carl von Lorck, *Ostpreussische Gutshaüser* (Kitzingen, 1952); H. J. Helmigk, *Märkische Herrenhaüser aus Alter Zeit* (Berlin, n.d.) pp. 101, 168.

38. T. Fontane, *Wanderungen durch die Mark Brandenburg* (Frankfurt, 1984), *Funf Schlösser*, pp. 266–315. William von Kardorff was another hunting and racing squire who, unlike his Silesian magnate friends, could not afford this English lifestyle. S. von Kardorff, *Wilhelm von Kardorff. Ein nationaler Parliamentarier im Zeitalter Bismarcks und Wilhelm II (1828–1907)* (Berlin, 1936) pp. 22–25. Kardorff learned English and loved Carlyle and Trollope.

39. W. Tooke, *View of the Russian Empire during the Reign of Catherine the Second and to the Close of the Present Century* (London, 1799) 3 vols; here vol. 3, pp. 35–6.

40. Murray, *Handbook . . . Russia* (1865) pp. 43–6; 'Okhota', pp. 642–708 in *Polnaya Entsiklopediya*, vol. VI (1902); *Stolitsa i Usad'ba*, for example, no. 2 (15 January 1914); no. 3 (1 February 1914).

41. *Stolitsa i Usad'ba* no. 3 (1 February 1914) p. 14.

42. H. W. Eckardt, *Herrschaftliche Jagd, bäerliche Not und bürgerliche Kritik*

(Göttingen, 1976) *passim*; M. von Gerlach, *Von Rechts nach Links* (Zurich, 1937) pp. 35–6.

43. A. Schwappach, *Gundriss der Forst und Jagdgeschichte* (Berlin, 1883) pp. 180–1.

44. Anon., *Am Hofe des Kaisers*, pp. 38–40 describes a hunt on the Pless estate, 'The Eldorado of huntsmen', especially staged for one of the Hohenzollerns. My father was told the story of the 1913 shoot by the aide-de-camp in question. Perhaps it was apocryphal, though if it is, the caricature nevertheless expresses something of the unpleasant lunacy of the pre-war shoot.

45. Stekl, *Österreichs*, particularly pp. 112, 141, 154–5, 173–8; O. Brunner, *Adeliges Landleben und Europaischer Geist* (Salzburg, 1949) particularly pp. 330–7.

46. *Stolitsa i Usad'ba* is by far the best source on aristocratic leisure, particularly in the last years before the revolution, but also, in its historical pieces, on earlier periods as well: see for example, no. 22 (15 November 1914) on horse-racing; and nos 36–37 (1 July 1915) on country houses. Miraculously, there is a recent history of imperial and noble gardens: see A. P. Vergunov and V. A. Gorokhov, *Russkie sady i parki* (Moscow, 1988). H. M. Grove commented in 1912 that in aristocratic or wealthy Russian families, 'the person in charge of the children is generally an Englishman or Englishwoman'; Thomas Darlington, England's greatest expert on Russian education, commented in 1909 that 'games . . . occupy a larger place in the common life of the Lyceum than is usual in Russian schools', Board of Education, *Special Reports on Educational Subjects. Volume 23. Education in Russia* (London, 1909) p. 233.

47. F. F. Vigel, *Vospominaniya* (Moscow, 1864) part 1, pp. 124–32, 203–4.

48. A. V. von Hauxthausen, *The Russian Empire. Its People, Institutions and Resources* (London, 1968), for example, vol. 1, p. 363, 375–6, 394–6; V. I. Serov, *The Mighty Five. The Cradle of Russian National Music* (London, 1948) pp. 14–15; *Stolitsa i Usad'ba*, for example, no. 33 (1 May 1915). The first section of P. P. Semyonov's memoirs entitled *Detstvo i Yunost'* (SPB, 1915) gives a good sense of childhood in a cultured noble rural home under Nicholas I.

49. Lieven, *Russia's Rulers*, chs 3, 8.

8.   EDUCATION AND CULTURE

1. Cannon, *Aristocratic*, pp. 37–40; E. C. Mack, *Public Schools and British Opinion since 1860* (New York, 1941) p. 38; R. Wilkinson, *The Prefects. British Leadership and the Public School Tradition* (London, 1964) p. 104.

2. The quotes are from Mack, *Public Schools*, pp. 34, 36, 130 and E. C. Mack, *Public Schools and British Public Opinion 1780–1860* (London, 1938) pp. 172, 324.

3. On the Jesuit comparison see pp. 215–27 of Wilkinson, *Prefects*, or H. Reif's comments in *Westfälischer Adel 1770–1860* (Göttingen, 1979), pp. 148–9,

350–1; Mack, *Public Schools and British Opinion since 1860*, p. 125; A. Ponsonby, *The Decline of Aristocracy* (London, 1912) pp. 208, 217; G. D. Phillips, *The Diehards. Aristocratic Society and Politics in Edwardian England* (Cambridge, 1979) p. 15.

4. The quote is from Wilkinson, *Prefects*, p. 65.

5. C. Barnett, *The Collapse of British Power* (Gloucester, 1984) p. 25; R. Symonds, *Oxford and Empire* (Basingstoke, 1986) p. 25; see also chs 4 and 5 of R. M. Ogilvie, *Latin and Greek, A History of the Influence of the Classics on English Life from 1600 to 1918* (London, 1964).

6. Ponsonby, *The Decline*, pp. 247–56; page x of the introduction by Professor M. E. Sadler to F. Paulsen, *The German Universities and University Study* (London, 1906); C. Barnett, *The Collapse of British Power* (Gloucester, 1984) p. 25.

7. See E. E. Eltz, *Die Modernisierung einer Standesherrschaft* (Sigmaringen, 1980), pp. 24–37 on Karl Egon III's education. On religion and German conservatism see, for example, M. Greiffenhagen, *Das Dilemma des Konservatismus in Deutschland* (Frankfurt, 1986) ch. v.

8. Reif, *Westfälischer*, pp. 352–4; W. W. Kircher, *Adel, Kirche und Politik in Wu̇rttemburg 1830–1851* (Stuttgart, 1973) pp. 238–44.

9. C. E. McClelland, *State, Society and University in Germany 1700–1914* (Cambridge, 1980) pp. 106–21; Ponsonby, *The Decline*, p. 194.

10. M. Arnold, *Higher Schools and Universities in Germany* (London, 1892) pp. 110, 125.

11. K. H. Jarausch, *Students, Society and Politics in Imperial Germany. The Rise of Academic Illiberalism* (Princeton, 1982) p. 321.

12. Jarausch, *Students, Society and Politics* pp. 234–5, 310–21; Paulsen, *The German Universities* pp. 372–7; *Grazhdanin*, no. 15 (24 April 1911) p. 6; L. W. Muncy, *The Junker in the Prussian Administration under William II* (Providence, RI, 1944) pp. 105–7.

13. J. K. Zabel, *Das preussische Kadettenkorps* (Frankfurt, 1978) is the most recent survey on this subject. H. Vizetelly, *Berlin Under the New Empire* (London, 1979) pp. 386–406 is useful as a brief comment by an admiring foreigner of the 1870s.

14. See M. Raeff, *Origins of the Russian Intelligentsia* (New York, 1966) ch. 4.

15. Arnold, *Higher Schools*, p. 41.

16. I discuss these issues in D. C. B. Lieven, *Russia's Rulers Under the Old Regime* (London, 1989) pp. 91–6 and 98–102. On individual corps see, for example, D. M. Lyovshin *Pazheyskiy ego Imperatorskogo Velichestva korpus za sto let* (SPB, 1902); M. Maksimovsky, *Istoricheskiy ocherk razvitiya glavnogo inzhenernego uchilishcha 1819–1869* (SPB, 1869); V. Potto, *Istoricheskiy ocherk Nikolaevskogo Kavaleriyskogo Uchilishcha 1827–1873* (SPB, 1873); J. A. Armstrong, *The European Administrative Elite* (Princeton, NJ, 1973) is interesting on the relatively high prestige of technology in Old Russia.

17. Lieven, *Russia's Rulers*, pp. 96–8. See ch. 6 of P. A. Zayonchkovsky, *Samoderzhavie i russkaya armiya na rubezhe XIX–XX stoletiy* (Moscow, 1973).

18. T. Darlington, *Board of Education. Special Reports on Educational Subjects. Volume 23: Education in Russia* (London, 1909) p. 363. There are now a

number of good works on nineteenth-century Russian education in English. On Tolstoy, his principles and their effect on Russian education see A. Sinel, *The Classroom and the Chancellery. State Educational Reform under Count Dmitry Tolstoy* (Cambridge, 1973).

19. Lieven, *Russia's Rulers*, pp. 103–8; Darlington, *Board of Education*, p. 82.

20. Jarausch, *Students, Society and Politics*, p. 388; Prince Serge Volkonsky, *My Reminiscences* (London, 1924) vol. 1, p. 73; Prince E. N. Trubetskoy, *Vospominaniya* (Sofia, 1922) pp. 6–8, 38–44, 72–5.

21. I. Seleznev, *Istoricheskiy ocherk Imperatorskogo byvshego Tsarskosel'skogo nyne Aleksandrovskogo Litseya za pervoe ego pyatidesyatiletie s 1811 do 1861 god* (SPB, 1861) pp. 1–183 is a survey of the Lycée's early years. Many others exist. A. N. Kulomzin, 'Dmitri Nikolaevich Zamyatin', *Zhurnal Ministerstva Yustitsii*, no. 9 (November 1914) vol. 13, pp. 234–333 is a sensitive study of the impact of the Lycée on one of its earliest pupils, who subsequently became a liberal minister of justice under Alexander II.

22. K. K. Arsenev, 'Vospominaniya Konstantina Konstantinovicha Arseneva ob Uchilishche Pravovedeniya 1849–1855 gg', *Russkaya Starina*, vol. 50 (1886) pp. 201, 217–8. I discuss the Lycée in Lieven, *Russia's Rulers*, pp. 108–16. The best history of the Lycée (up to 1886) is by N. I. Kareev, 'Kratkiy ocherk istorii Litseya, sostavleniy professorom N. I. Kareevym', in *Pamyatnaya knizhka Imperatorskogo Aleksandrovskogo Litseya* (SPB, 1886) pp. 1–277.

23. See footnotes 105 and 106 of Lieven, *Russia's Rulers*; C. A. Moser (ed.), *The Cambridge History of Russian Literature* (Cambridge, 1989) is a useful survey of writers and the themes of their work, though it says little of the social or intellectual sources of Russian cultural creativity. V. I. Serov, *The Mighty Five. The Cradle of Russian National Music* (London, 1948) is a very easy introduction for the English speaker to nineteenth-century Russian music. *Stolitsa i Usad'ba* has some excellent articles on early nineteenth-century Russian culture. Two vital works for the English speaker are: Yu. M. Lotman, 'The Decembrist in Daily Life (Everyday Behaviour as a Historical–Psychological Category)' in A. D. and A. S. Nakhimovsky (eds), *The Semiotics of Russian Cultural History* (Ithaca, 1985) and C. H. Whittaker, *The Origins of Modern Russian Education. An Intellectual Biography of Count Serge Uvarov* (DeKalb, 1984).

24. Marc Raeff has come closest to tackling these issues in a comprehensive manner; see his *Origins*. The quote is from vol. 1, p. 49 of F. G. Terner, *Vospominaniya zhizni*, 2 vols (SPB, 1910).

9. THE NOBLE AS WARRIOR

1. On the Russian aristocracy see ch. 1 of D. C. B. Lieven, *Russia's Rulers Under the Old Regime* (London, 1989); P. Mikliss, *Deutscher und polnischer Adel im Vergleich* (Berlin, 1981) is a useful survey of the origins and history of the German nobility, within which the intricate legal distinctions separating

group from group are calculated to baffle the foreigner. Germans have, by Russian or even English standards, a passion for genealogy, and the medieval origins of most leading families are easily discovered in genealogical works. Even in the eastern provinces, whose aristocracy was in general of less distinguished and ancient origin than in the west, many families whose names were familiar from nineteenth-century history were well established in the twelfth and thirteenth centuries. See W. Gorlitz, *Die Junker. Adel und Bauer im Deutschen Osten* (Limburg, 1964), pp. 10–11, for example. On the English see my comments in Chapter 2 (pp. 56–7).

2. Gorlitz, *Die Junker*, pp. 57–9; F. L. Carsten, *A History of the Prussian Junkers* (Aldershot, 1989) pp. 10–11; J. L. H. Keep, 'The Muscovite Elite and the Approach to Pluralism', *Slavonic and East European Review*, vol. 48 (1970) pp. 201–31.

3. On the English, see F. M. L. Thompson, 'Aristocracy, Gentry and the Middle Class in Britain, 1750–1850', in A. M. Birke and L. Kettenacker (eds), *Bürgertum, Adel und Monarchie* (Munich, 1989), here pp. 31–2; D. Cannadine, *The Decline and Fall of the British Aristocracy* (Newhaven, Conn., 1990) pp. 264–80. The statistics for generals come from P. E. Razzell, 'Social Origins of Officers in the Indian and British Home Army', *British Journal of Sociology*, vol. xiv (1963) p. 253. Because definitions of 'gentry' do not tally, there is some conflict between these figures and those provided by C. B. Otley, 'Militarism and the Social Affiliations of the British Army Elite', in J. von Doorn (ed.), *Armed Forces and Society: Sociological Essays* (The Hague, 1960) p. 100; 'The native Bavarian nobility . . . showed little taste for active service', K. Demeter, *The German Officer Corps in Society and State 1650–1945* (London, 1965) p. 34. Above all, though, there were simply far fewer nobles in Bavaria than in Prussia or Russia. On the social structure of the Bavarian officer corps see pp. 61–96 of H. Rumschöttel, *Das bayerische Offizierkorps 1866–1914* (Berlin, 1973). The eyes of the Westphalian Stiftsadel were traditionally directed towards church careers.

4. J. L. H. Keep, *Soldiers of the Tsar. Army and Society in Russia 1462–1784* (Oxford, 1985); D. Beylau, *Militär und Gesellschaft im Vorrevolutionären Russland* (Cologne, 1984); P. A. Zayonchkovsky, *Samoderzhavie i russkaya armiya na rubezhe XIX–XX stoletiy* (Moscow, 1973) looks at the army from 1881 to 1903, and P. Kenez, 'A Profile of the Pre-revolutionary Officer Corps', *California Slavic Studies* vol. 7 (1973) pp. 121–58 takes the story up to 1914.

5. See Demeter, *The German Officer Corps* and M. Messerschmidt, 'Preussens Militär in seinem gesellschaftlichen Umfeld', pp. 43–88, in H. J. Puhle and H. U. Wehler (eds), *Preussen in Ruckblick* (Göttingen, 1980). On the officer corps in the reign of William II, see M. Kitchen, *The German Officer Corps* (Oxford, 1968).

6. Thompson, 'Aristocracy, Gentry', p. 34.

7. The statistics are drawn from Burke's *Peerage and Baronetage*, the editions of 1830, 1840, 1850, 1860, 1870, 1880, 1890 and 1900 being consulted. The 17 peers are those listed in J. V. Beckett, *The Aristocracy in England 1660–1914* (Oxford, 1986) p. 292. The table includes younger brothers of the heads of these families between 1815 and 1883. Where a magnate had made a career, it was usually because he was not born as direct heir but

succeeded a childless brother or cousin. The Fourth Duke of Northumberland, for instance, was a Vice-Admiral but only succeeded to the title in 1847 because his brother died without heirs.

8. N. I. Ikonnikov, *La Noblesse de Russia*, 2nd edn, vols. A1–Z2 (Paris 1958–66) was the source for these two tables. The aristocratic families covered were Beloselsky-Belozersky, Vorontsov-Dashkov, Stroganov, Demidov, Shuvalov, Golitsyn, Sheremetev, Balashov, Gagarin, Meller-Zakomelsky, Orlov-Denisov, Naryshkin, Kochubei, Bobrinsky. The gentry families were Pushkin, Khvostov, Novosiltsov, Velyaminov-Zernov, Musin-Pushkin, Neplyuev, Pleshchev, Saburov, Saltykov, Samarin, Kvashnin-Samarin, Arsenev, Zherebtsov, Velyaminov, Vorontsov-Velyaminov, Konovnitsyn, Kamensky and Kolychev.

9. The source for this paragraph is the *Almanach de Gotha* (Gotha 1816–1914).

10. The sources for this paragraph and Table 9.4 are various editions of *Gothaisches genealogisches Taschenbuch der gräflichen Häuser* (Gotha, 1930–39) and, for the Dohnas, the *Genealogisches Handbuch der gräflichen Häuser* (Marburg, 1981).

11. The source used is the *Gothaisches genealogisches Taschenbuch der uradeligen Häuser* (Gotha, 1930–39): the families covered were the Puttkamers, Bronsart von Schellendorffs, Kleists, Beneckendorff und Hindenburgs, Natzmers, Lettow-Vorbecks, Belows, Platens, Zitzewitzs and Burgsdorffs. The 1930s editions of the *Taschenbuch* contain these families' records.

12. A. A. Ignatiev, *A Subaltern in Old Russia* (London, 1944) pp. 66–78.

13. C. Barnett, *Britain and her Army. 1509–1970* (London, 1970) pp 314–5.

14. Marion Gräfin Dönhoff, *Kindheit in Ostpreussen* (Berlin, 1988).

15. V. G. Kiernan, *The Duel in European History. Honour and the Reign of Aristocracy* (Oxford, 1988) is an interesting though rather one-sided approach to this issue.

16. J. Keegan, *The Face of Battle* (London, 1978) p. 194.

17. On the Decembrists, the best book remains V. I. Semyovsky, *Politicheskie i obshchestvennye idei dekabristov* (SPB, 1909). See also ch. 11 of Keep, *Soldiers of the Tsar* and, for a later period, W. C. Fuller, *Civil–Military Conflict in Imperial Russia 1881–1914* (Princeton, NJ, 1985). On Spain, see, for example, P. Preston, *The Politics of Revenge. Fascism and the Military in 20th Century Spain* (London, 1990); R. B. Martinez and T. M. Barker, *Armed Forces and Society in Spain Past and Present* (Boulder, Col., 1988).

18. Captain Gronow, *The Reminiscences and Recollections of Captain Gronow* (London, 1900) vol. 1, p. 183; P. A. Warner, 'Peacetime Economy and the Crimean War' in P. Young and J. P. Lawford (eds), *History of the British Army* (Wallop, 1970) p. 152.

19. C. Barnett, *Britain and her Army 1509–1970* (London, 1970) p. 279.

20. Prince L. H. von Pückler-Muskau, *Tour in England, Ireland and France in the Years 1826, 1827, 1828 and 1829* (Zurich, 1940) pp. 158, 171 on uniforms. On duels, Kiernan, *The Duel in European History* is well supplemented by pp. 106–18 and by implication, pp. 408–20 of J. C. D. Clark, *English Society 1688–1832* (Cambridge, 1985). On late Imperial Russia and Germany see

Zayonchkovsky, *Samoderzhavie*, pp. 238–47; Demeter, *The German Officer Corps*, pp. 49ff.

21. J. P. Lawford, 'The Conquest of India', p. 141 in Young and Lawford (eds), *History of the British Army*. See also Brian Bond, 'Colonial Wars and Punitive Expeditions', ch. 18.

22. As an introduction to warfare in the nineteenth century see A. Jones, *The Art of War in the Western World* (Oxford, 1987), especially ch. 7; and M. van Creveld, *Command in War* (Cambridge, 1985) especially chs. 3 and 4.

23. For statistical information on military career patterns see Lieven, *Russia's Rulers*, pp. 64–7 and 163–7. Apart from the sources listed in note 4 of this chapter, see also M. Mayzel, 'The formation of the Russian General Staff 1800–1917. A Social Study', *Cahiers du Monde Russe et Sovietique* (1975) vol. xvi, nos 3–4, pp. 297–322; N. Stone, *The Eastern Front 1914–1917* (London, 1975); and J. Bushnell, *Mutiny and Repression. Russian Soldiers in the Revolution of 1905* (Indiana, 1985) also cast much light on the late Imperial army from different angles.

24. Helmigk, *Märkische*, pp. 100, 156; Spitzemberg, *Tagebuch*, especially pp. 368, 474; Oldenburg-Januschau, *Erinnerungen*, p. 44; H. von Gerlach, *Rechts*, pp. 22, 24; Fontane's *Wanderungen*, give one by far the best taste of Old Prussia, its traditions and values (see Bibliography for details).

25. On Moltke, the English-speaking reader should start with van Creveld, *Command*, ch. 4. The much-reviled Gerhard Ritter, *The Sword and the Sceptre, The Prussian Tradition 1740–1890*, vol. 1 (London, 1974) pp. 187–238 well repays study, partly because of its insight into traditional Prussian liberal–conservative views. Two excellent English-language studies of Moltke's key campaigns are G. Craig, *The Battle of Königgratz* (London, 1964) and M. Howard, *The Franco-Prussian War* (New York, 1969).

26. A. R. Millett and W. Murray, *Military Effectiveness: Volume 1: The First World War* (Boston, 1988) contains excellent essays by Paul Kennedy, Holger Herwig and David Jones on Britain, Germany and Russia respectively.

10.   ARISTOCRACY IN POLITICS

1. F. M. L. Thompson, 'The Second Agricultural Revolution', *Economic History Review*, vol. XXI (1968), p. 72; R. J. Olney, *Lincolnshire Politics 1832–1885* (Oxford, 1973) pp. 24–42.

2. Frank O'Gorman, 'Electoral Deference in "Unreformed" England: 1760–1832', *Journal of Modern History*, vol. 56, no. 3 (1984), p. 399; T. L. Crosby, *English Farmers and the Politics of Protection 1815–1852* (Hassocks, 1977) p. 129.

3. J. V. Beckett, *The Aristocracy of England 1660–1914* (Oxford, 1986), p. 430.

4. J. J. Sack, 'The House of Lords and Parliamentary Patronage in Great Britain, 1802–1832', *Historical Journal*, vol. 23, no. 4 (1980) pp. 914–5.

5. The statistics and quotes are from Beckett, *Aristocracy*, pp. 432–3. Ch.

iv of M. L. Bush, *The European Nobility*, vol. 1, *Noble Privilege* (Manchester, 1983) is a mine of information about nobles' parliamentary rights across Europe.

6. D. Cannadine, *The Decline and Fall of the British Aristocracy* (Newhaven, 1990) p. 208.

7. J. P. D. Dunbabin, 'Expectations of the New County Councils, and their Realization', *Historical Journal*, vol. VIII, no. 3 (1965) pp. 353–79; also ch. xi of Beckett, *The Aristocracy of England*.

8. See, for example, J. Pellew, *The Home Office 1848–1914* (London, 1982) pp. 5–10, 33–6; Cannadine, *Decline*, p. 240. Essential reading on comparative European bureaucracies is J. A. Armstrong, *The European Administrative Elite* (Princeton, NJ, 1973).

9. Z. S. Steiner, *Foreign*, pp. 16–20.

10. Cannadine, *Decline*, pp. 420–9; G. D. Phillips, *The Diehards. Aristocratic Society and Politics in Edwardian England* (Cambridge, 1979) ch. 5.

11. Gollwitzer, *Die Standesherren* (Stuttgart, 1957) ch. 2 is a good source on the high nobilty in this era. So too are E. E. Eltz, *Die Modernisierung einer Standesherrschaft* (Sigmaringen, 1980), pp. 15–73 and H. Weber, *Die Fürsten von Hohenlohe im Vormärz* (Stuttgart, 1977), *passim*.

12. The key sources here are H. Reif, *Westfälischer Adel 1770–1860* (Göttingen, 1979) and W. S. Kircher, *Adel, Kirche und Politik in Württemburg 1830–1851* (Stuttgart, 1973). Zeil is the key figure in the latter and his position in 1848 is discussed on pp. 180 ff.

13. M. Arnold, *Higher Schools and Universities in Germany* (London, 1892), p. 2.

14. My main sources here included W. Loth, *Katholiken in Kaiserreich* (Dusseldorf, 1984) (the quotation is from p. 51); R. J. Ross, *Beleaguered Tower: The Dilemma of Political Catholicism in Wilhelmine Germany* (Notre Dame, 1976); and D. Blackbourn, *Populists and Patricians* (London, 1987).

15. Berdahl, *The Politics of the Prussian Nobility* (Princeton, NJ, 1988) stresses the key significance of lordship, or in other words command, to Junker thinking. See also his 'Preussischer Adel. Paternalismus als Herrschaftssystem', in H.-J. Puhle and H.-J. Wehler (eds), *Preussen in Hinblick* (Göttingen, 1980), pp. 123–45; Spitzemberg, *Tagebuch*; D. Field, *Rebels in the Name of the Tsar* (Boston, 1976) is an excellent study of peasant attitudes to authority, admittedly in this case monarchical rather than noble.

16. The literature on Russian and Prussian serfdom is vast. J. Blum *Lord and Peasant in Russia from the Ninth to the Nineteenth Century* (Princeton, NJ, 1961), pp. 422–40 and S. Hoch, *Serfdom and Social Control in Russia* (Chicago, 1986), ch. 5 give rather different impressions of serfdom's brutality. A V. von Hauxthausen, *The Russian Empire* (London, 1986), vol. 1, p. 369, commented of Count Sheremetev that 'he has never oppressed his people, and takes less from them than the Crown does from its peasants; but I cannot say that some of his officials do not indulge in many kinds of exaction, and we heard that the rich inhabitants in his villages were very oppressive to the poor ones'. Ch. 4 of F. L. Carsten, *A History of the Prussian Junkers* (Aldershot, 1989), is a good summary of noble–peasant relations in eighteenth-century Prussia.

17. R. M. Berdahl, 'Conservative Politics and Aristocratic Landholders in Bismarckian Germany', *Journal of Modern History*, vol. 44, no. 1 (1972) pp. 1–20. The Kreisordnung bill is also discussed on pp. 406–10 of S. Wehking, 'Zum politischen und sozialen Selbstverständnis preussischer Junker, 1871–1914', *Blätter für deutsche Landesgeschichte*, vol. 121 (1985) pp. 295–447.

18. On Kulomzin, see D. C. B. Lieven, *Russia's Rulers under the Old Regime* (London, 1989) p. 237; Berdahl, *Politics*, pp. 198–220; R. Koselleck, *Preussen zwischen Reform und Revolution* (Stuttgart, 1989) pp. 448–86; S. F. Starr, *Decentralization and Self-Government in Russia 1830–1870* (Princeton, NJ, 1972) is the basic English-language work on Russian local government.

19. Berdahl, *Politics*, quotes Kleist-Retzow on p. 217; L. W. Muncy, *The Junker in the Prussian Administration Under William II, 1888–1914* (Providence, RI, 1944) pp. 175–96 discusses the *Landräte*. On the Marshals, see G. M. Hamburg, 'Portrait of an Elite: Russian Marshals of the Nobility 1881–1917', *Slavic Review*, vol. 40 (1981).

20. H. Rosenberg, *Bureaucracy, Aristocracy and Autocracy. The Prussian Experience 1600–1815* (Cambridge, 1958) is a classic study of the formation of the Prussian bureaucratic elite.

21. The fullest study of the Russian bureaucracy in this period is H. J. Torke, 'Das russische Beamtentum in der ersten Hälfte des 19 Jahrhunderts', *Forschungen zur Geschichte Osteuropas*, vol. 13 (1967) pp. 7–345. It is particularly valuable for its frequent comparisons between Prussia and Russia. Specifically on the Prussian bureaucracy in this epoch, see Koselleck, *Preussen* and J. R. Gillis, *The Prussian Bureaucracy in Crisis 1840–1860. Origins of an Adminsitrative Ethos* (Stanford, 1971). The line taken by Barbara Vogel, 'Reformpolitik in Preussen 1807–1820', in Puhle and Wehler (eds) *Preussen in Hinblick*, pp. 202–223 is refreshing.

22. *Trudy IV ogo s'ezda upol'nomochennykh dvoryanskikh obshchestv 32 guberniy* (SPB, 1909) p. 259. For the development of the Russian civil service over the centuries see ch. 1 (and the notes to it) of Lieven, *Russia's Rulers*.

23. Muncy, *Junker*, pp. 101–2, 119–21. Lieven, *Russia's Rulers* is a study of the Russian governmental elite under Nicholas II. Reinhard Hanf, 'Die Oberpräsidenten von Ost und Westpreussen 1871–1918' says that no administrative official could hope for a paid job until he was 29; see pp. 108–10 in K. Schwabe (ed.), *Die preussische Oberpräsidenten* (Boppard, 1985).

24. On the foreign ministries see L. Cecil, *The German Diplomatic Service 1871–1914* (Princeton, NJ 1976), I. V. Bestuzhev, *Bor'ba v Rossii po voprosam vneshney politiki* (Moscow, 1961) and D. C. B. Lieven, *Russia and the Origins of the First World War* (London, 1984) pp. 61–2 and 83–101. On the Russian civil service as a whole see P. A. Zayonchkovsky, *Pravitel'stvenniy apparat samoderzhavnoy Rossii v XIXv* (Moscow, 1978); and specifically on the governors, R. G. Robbins, *The Tsars' Viceroys* (Ithaca, NY, 1987). Muncy, *Junker*, is a mine of information but see also J. C. G. Rohl, 'Higher Civil Servants in Germany' in J. J. Sheehan (ed.), *Imperial Germany* (New York, 1976) pp. 129–51. On the *Oberpräsidenten*, see the essays in Schwabe (ed.), *Die preussische Oberpräsidenten*.

25. N. V. Tcharykow, *Glimpses of High Politics* (London, 1931) p. 90; L.

Gall, *Bismarck. The White Revolutionary* (London, 1986), 2 vols see vol. 1, chs. 1 and 2. On Bobrinsky, see Lievern, *Russia's Rulers*, pp. 155–9.

26. In my view many historians are too inclined to stress the benefits to the Junkers of reform and government–Junker collusion. The land-owning class was indeed strengthened but very many individual Junkers suffered and it is hard to imagine that a noble parliament would have been sufficiently unselfish or far-sighted to accept government policy. G. M. Hamburg, *The Politics of the Russian Nobility 1881–1905* (Rutgers, 1984) with its tale of noble political weakness is usefully contrasted to, for example, Roberta Manning, *The Crisis of the Old Regime in Russia* (Princeton, NJ, 1982) which documents aristocratic opposition to Stolypin's reforms.

27. On the Prussian noble response to 1848, see for example, R. Schutt, 'Partei wider Willen. Kalküle und Potentiale konservativer Parteigründer in Preussen zwischen Ersten Vereinigten Landtag und National Versammlung', and H. Fischer, 'Konservatismus von unten. Wahlen in ländlichen Preussen 1849/52: Organisation, Agitation, Manipulation': Both articles are in D. Stegmann, B. J. Wendt and P. C. Witt (eds), *Deutscher Konservatismus im 19 and 20 Jahrhundert* (Bonn, 1983). Older but still valuable works on the transformation of Prussian noble conservatism in this era include S. Neumann, *Die Stufen des preussischen Konservatismus* (Berlin, 1930) and E. Jordan, *Die Entstehung der konservativen Partei und die preussischen Agrarverhaltnissen von 1848* (Munich, 1914).

28. K. A. Krivoshein, *A. V. Krivoshein 1857–1921. Ego znachenie v istorii Rossii nachala XX veka* (Paris, 1973) p. 13. There is no study of Russian elites as a whole in this era and very little conceptual thinking about their inter-relationships. S. Becker, *Nobility and Privilege in Late Imperial Russia* (DeKalb, 1985) is a most interesting book, a little stronger however, on assertion than documentation. Manning, *Crisis*, is fuller but also more geared to preconceived viewpoints. Korelin, *Dvoryanstvo* is a mine of information, and the works of Laverychev, Chermensky and Dyakin though often rather dogmatic and narrowly political, have much of value in them. The best single-volume Soviet summary of Tsarism and its elites in the Empire's last decades is Akademiya Nauk CCCP's *Krizis Samoderzhaviya v Rossii 1895–1917*, which was published in Leningrad in 1984 and contains sections by B. V. Ananich, P. Sh. Ganelin and V. S. Dyakin. The best English-language work on Russian industrialists is A. J. Rieber, *Merchants and Entrepreneurs in Imperial Russia* (Chapel Hill, 1982) but there are a plethora of works recently published on the Moscow business elite and none on any other sector of the industrial bourgeoisie. G. L. Yaney, *The Systematization of Russian Government: Social Evolution in the Domestic Administration of Imperial Russia 1711–1905* (Urbana, 1973) is the great source on inter-ministerial conflict.

29. Hauxthausen, *Russian*, vol. 2, p. 185.

30. I have discussed these themes at greater length in chs 6 and 9 of Lieven, *Russia's Rulers*. On Spain, see, for example, R. Carr, *Spain 1808–1975* (Oxford, 1989); A. Shubert, *A Social History of Modern Spain* (London, 1990); F. Lannon and P. Preston, *Elites and Power in Twentieth-Century Spain* (Oxford,

1990); R. Carr and J. P. Fusi, *Spain. Dictatorship to Democracy* (London, 1979).

31. On Krivoshein see the biography, *A. V. Krivoshein*, by his son. I have discussed this liberal–conservative and nationalist movement in pp. 91–101 and 118–38 in Lieven, *Russian and the Origins*.

32. On Struve and *Vekhi* see R. Pipes, *Struve. Liberal on the Right, 1905–1944* (Cambridge, 1980).

33. Quoted on p. 9 of H. H. Herwig (ed.), *The Outbreak of World War I. Causes and Responsibilities* (Lexington, Ky, 1991). I discuss Russian military and political developments and their implications for the question of a German preventive war in Lieven, *Russia and the Origins*, pp. 101–38.

34. Hanna Schissler, 'The Junkers: Notes on the Social and Historical Significance of the Agrarian Elite in Prussia' in R. G. Moeller (ed.), *Peasants and Lords in Modern Germany* (London, 1986) pp. 24–51 tackles the Anglo-Prussian comparison in an article translated from her piece in Puhle and Wehler (eds), *Preussen in Hinblick*. The question of the *Sonderweg* has aroused great controversy and a mountainous literature. The obvious place for the English-speaking reader to start is D. Blackbourn and G. Eley, *The Peculiarities of German History* (Oxford, 1984). The next step should be G. Eley's *Reshaping of the German Right. Radical Nationalism and Political Change after Bismarck* (Newhaven, 1980) and a collection of his essays entitled *From Unification to Nazism* (Boston, 1986). David Blackbourn's work on the Centre in Württemberg, where aristocracy counted for very little, is less relevant to a student of the German upper classes, but his collected essays in *Populists and Patricians* (London, 1987) well repay reading. So do those of R. J. Evans in *Rethinking German History* (London, 1987). In the other camp, in other words the one that emphasises elite manipulation, a seminal work is by H.-U. Wehler, translated into English as *The German Empire* (Leamington Spa, 1985). The classic statement of the case against the Junkers is by H.-J. Puhle, *Agrarische Interessenpolitik und preussischer Konservatismus im wilhelminischen Reich 1893–1914* (Bonn, 1975). The English reader can get a sense of Puhle's general position in 'Lords and Peasants in the Kasserreich', pp. 81–109 in Moeller (ed.), *Peasants and Lords*. Attacks on the Junkers are, of course, anything but monopolised by German historians. In his *The Social Origins of Dictatorship and Democracy* (London, 1966) Barrington Moore very much had them in mind in his argument that without the revolutionary destruction of traditional elites the journey to democratic modernity is impossible.

35. A. Offer, *The First World War: An Agrarian Interpretation* (Oxford, 1989) p. 95.

36. The quotes are from T. L. Crosby, *English Farmers and the Politics of Protection 1815–1852* (Hassocks, 1977), p. 97 and R. Stewart, *The Politics of Protection. Lord Derby and the Protectionist Party 1841–1852* (Cambridge, 1971) pp. 155–6.

37. G. D. Phillips. *The Diehards. Aristocratic Society and Politics in Edwardian England* (Cambridge, 1979) p. 155.

38. Offer, *The First World War*, pp. 332–3; S. B. Webb, 'Agricultural Protection in Wilhelminian Germany: Forging an Empire with Pork and

Rye', *Journal of Economic History*, vol. XLII (1982), pp. 324–5; D. Spring, 'Earl Fitzwilliam and the Corn Laws', *American Historical Review*, vol. LIX, no. 2 (1954) pp. 287–304, here p. 292. Offer attacks, in my view rather convincingly, the opposite point of view advanced by K. D. Barkin in *The Controversy over German Industrialisation 1890–1902* (Chicago, 1970).

39. The statistics come from p. 60 of W. O. Aydelotte, 'The Country Gentlemen and the Repeal of the Corn Laws', *English Historical Review*, vol. LXXX (1967) pp. 47–60.

40. My main source here was J. B. Conacher, *The Peelites and the Party System 1846–52* (Newton Abbot, 1972): see, for example, his comments on pp. 16–17. Among the vast literature on the famous Peelites, a new biography of the almost unknown Earl of Lincoln helped me considerably: see F. D. Munsell, *The Unfortunate Duke. Henry Pelham, Fifth Duke of Newcastle, 1811–1864 (Columbia, 1985)*. Derby's comment is quoted by R. Stewart, *The Politics of Protection. Lord Derby and the Protectionist Party 1841–1852* (Cambridge, 1971) pp. 182–3.

41. J. R. Rettalack, *Notables of the Right. The Conservative Party and Political Mobilisation in Germany 1876–1918* (London, 1988); the quote from the Bavarian Peasant League is on p. 102. Rettalack is, in my view, a little inconsistent in blaming the Conservatives both for old-fashioned prejudices about modern politics and for demagogic and selfish programmes. I share Eley's sense that a halfway-house between the two was not easily found given the attitudes of the Conservative electorate.

42. On Bethmann-Hollweg, see K. H. Jarausch, *The Enigmatic Chancellor* (Newhaven, 1972).

43. The quote is from p. 167 of A. B. Cooke and J. Vincent, *The Governing Passion* (Brighton, 1974).

44. Prince L. H. von Pückler-Muskau, *Tour in England, Ireland and France in the Years 1826, 1827, 1828 and 1829* (Zurich, 1940) p. 227; D. Southgate, *The Passing of the Whigs 1832–1886* (London, 1965) p. 76; on Russell, see J. Prest, *Lord John Russell* (London, 1972).

45. Southgate, *The Passing of the Whigs*, p. 417.

46. Cooke and Vincent, *The Governing Passion*, p. 92; D. Spring, 'Earl Fitzwilliam and the Corn Laws', *American Historical Review*, vol. LIX, no. 2 (1954), *passim*: the quote is from p. 289.

47. Lord Blake and Hugh Cecil (eds), *Salisbury, the Man and His Policies* (London, 1987); the quotes come from p. 99 and 112 of Robert Stewart's contribution, 'The Conservative Reaction's Lord Robert Cecil and Party Politics'. The whole book provides an exceptionally clear and comprehensive picture of an outstandingly intelligent man. For his comment on Milner, see p. 105 of Phillips, *Diehards*.

48. Stewart, *The Politics of Protection*, p. 220; D. C. B. Lieven, *Russia's Rulers*, pp. 158–9.

49. Quoted in Stewart, *The Politics of Protection*, p. 84.

50. E. Jordon, *Friedrich Wilhelm IV und der Preussischer Adel bei Umwandlung der ersten Kammer in das Herrenhaus* (Berlin, 1914): see, for example, pp. 80–5, 170.

51. Spitzemberg, *Tagebuch*, pp. 257, 329, 493; Oldenburg-Januschau,

Erinnergungen, p. 20; Siegfried von Kardorff writes of Wilhelm von Kardorff's mother that she was incapable of lying, had great willpower, a monumental sense of duty and was often frighteningly frank: *Wilhelm von Kardorff. Ein nationales Parliamentarien im Zeitalter Bismarcks und Wilhelm II. 1828–1907* (Berlin, 1936) pp. 11–12. These were authentic Junker traits. E. von Kleist, 'Adel und Preussentum', *Suddeutsche Monatshefte*, vol. 23, no. 5 (February 1926) pp. 378–84 is the authentic voice of political Junkerdom at its harshest, narrowest and most reactionary.

52. P. Anderson, *Lineages of the Absolutist State* (London, 1974).

53. M. Raeff, *The Well-Ordered Police State: Social and Institutional Change through Law in the Germanies and Russia 1600–1800* (Newhaven, 1983).

54. The most recent – and very interesting – attempt to understand the last Kaiser is J. C. G. Rohl and N. Sombart (eds), *Kaiser Wilhelm II. New Interpretations* (Cambridge, 1982).

55. This theme is tackled with great skill by F. Stern, *Gold and Iron. Bismarck, Bleichröder and the Building of the German Empire* (London, 1980).

CONCLUSION

1. A. J. Mayer, *The Persistence of the Old Regime. Europe to the Great War* (New York, 1981).

2. D. Calleo, *The German Problem Reconsidered* (Cambridge, 1978) questions some Anglo-American views and assumptions about old Germany in a thoughtful way. My comments about Japan are mostly based on my own experience of living in Japanese society, but for a recent scholarly study of modernisation theory and contemporary Japan see, for example, G. McCormack and Y. Sugimoto, *Modernization and Beyond. The Japanese Trajectory* (Cambridge, 1988).

3. M. Wiener, *English Culture and the Decline of the Industrial Spirit 1850–1980* (Cambridge, 1981).

4. W. Mommsen, *Max Weber and German Politics 1890–1920* (Chicago, 1990), pp. 91–100.

5. H. Perkin, *Origins of Modern English Society* (London, 1969) and *The Rise of Professional Society* (London, 1989).

6. G. D. Phillips, *The Diehards. Aristocratic Society and Politics in Edwardian England* (Cambridge, 1979) p. 107.

Bibliography

W. Abel, *Agrarkrisen und Agrarkonjuktor. Eine Geschichte der Land-und-Ernährungswirtschaft Mitteleuropas seit dem hohen Mittelalter* (Hamburg, 1966).

D. Abrikossow, *Revelations of a Russian Diplomat* (Seattle, 1964).

Akademiya Nauk CCCP, *Krizis samoderzhaviya v Rossii, 1895–1917* (Leningrad, 1984).

Almanach de Gotha, (Gotha, 1816–1914).

M. L. Anderson and K. Barkin, 'The Myth of the Puttkamer Purge and the Reality of the Kulturkampf: Some Reflections on the Historiography of Imperial Germany', *Journal of Modern History*, vol. 54, no. 4 (1982).

P. Anderson, *Lineages of the Absolutist State* (London, 1974).

A. M. Anfimov, 'Chastnovladel'cheskoe lesnoe khozyaystvo v Rossii v kontse XIX–nachale XXv', *Istoricheskie Zapiski*, vol. 63 (1958).

A. M. Anfimov, *Krupnoe pomeshchishchee khozyaystvo Evropeyskoy Rossii (Moscow, 1969)*.

Anonymous, *Am Hofe des Kaisers* (Berlin, 1986).

E. Freiherr von Aretin, 'Vom Adel in Bayern', *Suddeutsche Monatsheft*, vol. 23, no. 5 (February 1926).

J. A. Armstrong, *The European Administrative Elite* (Princeton, 1973).

H. Graf von Arnim-Muskau and W. A. Boelcke, *Muskau: Standesherrschaft zwischen Spree und Neisse* (Frankfurt, 1978).

F. von Arnold, *Russlands Wald* (Berlin, 1892).

M. Arnold, *Higher Schools and Universities in Germany* (London, 1892).

W. L. Arnstein, 'The Survival of the Victorian Aristocracy', in F. C. Jaher (ed.), *The Rich, the Well Born and the Powerful. Elites and Upper Classes in History* (Urbana, 1973).

K. K. Arsenev, 'Vospominaniya Konstantina Konstantinovicha Arseneva ob Uchilishche Pravovedeniya 1849–1856', *Russkaya Starina*, vol. 50 (1886).

W. R. Augustine, 'Notes towards a Portrait of the Eighteenth-Century Russian Nobility', *Canadian Slavic Studies*, vol. 4 (1970).

W. O. Aydelotte, 'The Country Gentlemen and the Repeal of the Corn Laws,' *English Historical Review*, vol. LXXX (1967).

S. Bader, 'Zur Lage und Haltung des schwäbischen Adels am Ende des alten Reiches', *Zeitschrift für württemburgische Landesgeschichte*, vol. V (1941).

K. D. Barkin, *The Controversy over German Industrialisation 1890–1902* (Chicago, 1970).

C. Barnett, *Britain and Her Army 1509–1970* (London, 1970).

C. Barnett, *The Collapse of British Power* (Gloucester, 1984).

J. Bateman, *The Acre-Ocracy of England* (London, 1876).

J. Bateman, *The Great Landowners of Great Britain and Ireland* (London, 1883).

S. Becker, *Nobility and Privilege in Late Imperial Russia* (De Kalb, 1985).

J. V. Beckett, *The Aristocracy in England 1660–1914* (Oxford, 1986).

R. Berdahl, 'Conservative Politics and Aristocratic Landowners in Bismarckian Germany', *Journal of Modern History*, vol. 44, no. 1 (1972).

R. Berdahl, 'Preussischer Adel: Paternalismus als Herrschaftssystem', in H.-J. Puhle and H.-U. Wehler (eds), *Preussen in Hinblick* (Göttingen, 1980).

R. Berdahl, *The Politics of the Prussian Nobility* (Princeton, NJ, 1988).

V. R. Berghahn, *Germany and the Approach of War in 1914* (London, 1973).

I. V. Bestuzhev, *Bor'ba v Rossii po voprosam vneshney politiki* (Moscow, 1961).

D. Beylau, *Militär und Gesellschaft im Vorrevolutionären Russland* (Cologne, 1984).

R. M. Bigler, *The Politics of German Protestantism The Rise of the Protestant Church Elite in Prussia 1815–1848* (Berkeley, Calif., 1972).

D. Blackbourn, *Populists and Patricians* (London, 1987).

W. L. Blackwell, *The Beginnings of Russian Industrialisation 1800–1860* (Princeton, NJ, 1968).

Lord Blake and H. Cecil (eds), *Salisbury. The Man and His Policies* (London, 1987).

I. Blanchard, *Russia's Age of Silver* (London, 1989).

P. Blickle, 'Katholizismus, Aristokratie und Bürokratie im Württemburg des Vormärz', *Historisches Jahrbuch*, vol. 88 (1968).

M. Blinkhorn (ed.), *Fascists and Conservatives* (London, 1990).

J. Blum, *Lord and Peasant in Russia from the Ninth to the Nineteenth Century* (Princeton, NJ, 1961).

J. Blum, *The End of the Old Order in Rural Europe* (Princeton, NJ, 1978).

G. Bonham, 'State Autonomy or Class Domination: Approaches to Administrative Politics in Wilhelmine Germany', *World Politics*, vol. 35 (1983).

S. D. Bowman, 'Antebellum Planters and *Vormärz* Junkers in Comparative Perspective', *American Historical Review*, vol. 85, no. 4 (1980).

Brockhaus & Efron, *Entsiklopedicheskiy slovar'*, 43 vols, SPB, 1890–1906.

J. C. Brown, *Forests and Forestry in Poland, Lithuania, the Ukraine and the Baltic Provinces of Russia* (Edinburgh, 1885).

O. Brunner, *Adeliges Landleben und Europäischer Geist* (Salzburg, 1949).

E. Burke, *Reflections on the Revolution in France* (London, 1790).

J. B. Burke, *A Genealogical and Heraldic Dictionary of the Peerage and Baronetage of the British Empire* (London, 1815–1914).

J. B. Burke, *A Genealogical and Heraldic History of the Landed Gentry* (London, 1815–1914).

M. L. Bush, *Noble Privilege, Volume 1, The European Nobility* (Manchester, 1983).

M. L. Bush, *Rich Noble: Poor Noble. Volume 2, The European Nobility* (Manchester, 1988).

M. L. Bush, *The English Aristocracy. A Comparative Synthesis* (Manchester, 1984).

J. Bushnell, *Mutiny and Repression. Russian Soldiers in the Revolution of 1905* (Bloomington, 1985).

D. Calleo, *The German Problem Reconsidered* (Cambridge, 1978).

D. Cannadine, 'Aristocratic Indebtedness in the Nineteenth Century: The Case Reopened', *Economic History Review*, vol. XXV, no. 30 (1977).

D. Cannadine, *Lords and Landlords. The Aristocracy and the Towns 1774–1967* (Leicester, 1980).

D. Cannadine, *The Decline and Fall of the British Aristocracy* (Newhaven, 1990).

D. Cannadine, 'The Landowner as Millionaire: the Finances of the Dukes of Devonshire', *Agricultural Review*, vol. 25 (1977).

J. Cannon, *The Peerage of Eighteenth-Century England* (Cambridge, 1984).

R. Carr, *English Fox-Hunting* (London, 1977).

R. Carr, *Spain, 1808–1975* (Oxford, 1989).

R. Carr and J. P. Fusi, *Spain. Dictatorship to Democracy* (London, 1979).

F. L. Carsten, *A History of the Prussian Junkers* (Aldershot, 1989).

L. Cecil, 'The Creation of Nobles in Prussia. 1871–1918', *American Historical Review*, vol. 75 (1970).

L. Cecil, *The German Diplomatic Service 1871–1914* (Princeton, NJ, 1976).

J. D. Chambers and G. E. Mingay, *The Agricultural Revolution 1750–1880* (London, 1966).

G. Chaussinand-Nogaret, *The French Nobility in the Eighteenth Century. From Feudalism to Enlightenment* (Cambridge, 1985).

J. C. D. Clark, *English Society 1688–1832* (Cambridge, 1985).

J. B. Conacher, *The Peelites and the Party System 1846–52* (Newton Abbot, 1972).

M. Confino, *Domaines et Seigneurs en Russie vers la fin du XVIIIe Siecle. Etude de Structures agraires et de mentalités economiques* (Paris, 1963).

M. Confino, *Systèmes Agraires et Progrès Agricole. L'Assolement Triennal en Russie aux XVIIIe–XIXe Siècles* (Paris, 1969).

A. B. Cooke and J. Vincent, *The Governing Passion* (Brighton, 1974).

G. A. Craig, *Germany 1866–1945* (Oxford, 1981).

G. Craig, *The Battle of Königgratz* (London, 1964).

G. Craig, *The Politics of the Prussian Army 1640–1945* (New York, 1964).

T. L. Crosby, *English Farmers and the Politics of Protection 1815–1852* (Hassocks, 1977).

T. Darlington, *Board of Education. Special Reports on Educational Subjects. Vol. 23. Education in Russia* (London, 1909).

L. Davidoff, *The Best Circles* (London, 1986).

W. Demel, 'Der bayerische Adel 1750–1871,' MS.

W. Demel, 'Die wirtschaftliche Lage des bayerischen Adels in den ersten Jahrzehnten des 19 Jahrhunderts', in A. von Reden-Dohna (ed.) *Der Adel an der Schwelle des burgerlichen Zeitalters* (Stuttgart, 1988).

K. Demeter, *The German Officer Corps in Society and State 1650–1945* (London, 1965).

V. I. Denisov, *Lesa Rossii, ikh eksploatatsiya i lesnaya torgovlya* (SPB, 1911).

C. Dipper, *Die Bauernbefreiung in Deutschland* (Stuttgart, 1980).

C. Dipper, 'La noblesse allemande à l'époque de la bourgeoisie. Adaptation et continuité', in *Les Noblesses Européennes au XIXe Siecle*, Collection de l'Ecole Francaise de Rome (Rome, 1988).

J. von Dissow, *Adel im Übergang* (Stuttgart, 1961).

G. Dobson, H. M. Grove and H. Stewart, *Russia* (London, 1913).

A. Doeberl, 'Graf Conrad Preysing und das Erwachen der Katholisch-Konservativen Partei in Bayern', *Gelbe Hefte*, vol. 2 (1926).

M. Gräfin Dönhoff, *Kindheit in Ostpreussen* (Berlin, 1988).

J. P. D. Dunbabin, 'Expectations of the New County Councils and their Realisation', *Historical Journal*, vol. VIII, no. 3 (1965).

O. Freiherr von Dungern, 'Der Aufbau des Adels in Deutschland', *Suddeutsche Monatshefte*, vol. 23, no. 5 (February 1926).

H. W. Eckhardt, *Herrschaftliche Jagd, baüerliche Not und bürgerliche Kritik* (Göttingen, 1976).

École Francaise de Rome, *Les Noblesses Européennes au XIXe Siecle* (Rome, 1988).

G. Eley, *From Unification to Nazism* (Boston, 1986).

G. Eley, *Reshaping of the German Right. Radical Nationalism and Political Change after Bismarck* (New Haven, 1980).

G. Eley and D. Blackbourn, *The Peculiarities of German History* (Oxford, 1984).

N. Elias, *The Court Society* (Oxford, 1983).

E. E. Eltz, *Die Modernisierung einer Standesherrschaft. Karl Egon III und das Haus Fürstenberg in den Jahren nach 1848/9* (Sigmaringen, 1980).

K. Epstein, *The Genesis of German Conservatism* (Princeton, NJ, 1966).

R. J. Evans, *Rethinking German History* (London, 1987).

E. Fehrenbach, 'Das Erbe des Rheinbundzeit: Macht und Priviligienschwund des badischen Adels zwischen Restauration und Vormärz', *Archiv für Sozialgeschichte*, vol. XXIII (1983).

E. J. Feuchtwanger, *Democracy and Empire. Britain 1865–1914* (London, 1985).

D. Field, *Rebels in the Name of the Tsar* (Boston, Mass., 1976).

J. Flemming, *Deutscher Konservatismus 1780–1980* (Frankfurt, 1985).

T. W. Fletcher, 'The Great Depression of English Agriculture 1873–1896', *Economic History Review*, vol. XIII (1960–1).

R. Floud and D. McCloskey (eds), *The Economic History of Britain since 1700*, vols 1 and 2 (Cambridge, 1981).

T. Fontane, *Wanderungen durch die Mark Brandenburg*, 5 vols (Frankfurt, 1984).

G. Franz, 'Landwirtschaft, 1800–1850', in H. Aubin and W. Zorn (eds), *Handbuch der deutschen Wirtschafts und Sozialgeschichte*, Band 2 (Stuttgart, 1976).

T. H. Friedgut, *Iuzovka and Revolution*, vol. 1 (Princeton, NJ, 1989).

K. Fuchs, *Von Dirigismus zum Liberalismus. Die Entwicklung Oberschlesiens als preussisches Berg und Hüttenrevier* (Wiesbaden, no date).

R. Fulford (ed.), *Darling Child. Private Correspondence between Queen Victoria and the Crown Princess of Prussia 1871–1878* (London, 1976).

R. Fulford (ed.), *Dearest Child. Letters between Queen Victoria and the Princess Royal 1858–1861* (London, 1964).

R. Fulford (ed.), *Dearest Mama. Letters between Queen Victoria and the Crown Princess of Prussia 1861–1864* (London, 1968).

R. Fulford (ed.), *Your Dear Letter. Private Correspondence between Queen Victoria and the Crown Princess of Prussia, 1865–1871* (London, 1971).

L. Gall, *Bismarck. The White Revolutionary*, 2 vols (London, 1986).

N. Gash, *Aristocracy and People, Britain 1815–1865* (London, 1979).

M. Ya. Gefter, 'Iz istorii monopolisticheskogo kapitalizma v Rossii', *Istoricheskie zapiski*, vol. 38 (1951).

E. Gellner, *Plough, Sword and Book* (London, 1988).

P. Gerbod, 'Le loisir aristocratique dans les villes d'eaux françaises et allemandes au XIXe Siecle (1840–1870)', in K. F. Werner (ed.), *Hof, Kultur und Politik im 19 Jahrhundert* (Bonn, 1985).

D. Gerhard, 'Der deutsche Adel bis zum achtzehnten Jahrhundert', in P. U. Hohendahl and P.M. Lützeler, *Legitimationskrisen des deutschen Adels 1200–1900* (Stuttgart, 1979).

M. von Gerlach, *Von Rechts nach Links* (Zurich, 1937).

I. F. Gindin, 'Pravitelstvennaya podderzhka ural'skikh magnatov vo vtoroy polovine XIX–nachale XXV', *Istoricheskie zapiski*, vol. 1, no. 82.

J. R. Gillis, *The Prussian Bureaucracy in Crisis. 1840–1860. Origins of an Administrative Ethos* (Stanford, Calif., 1971).

M. Girouard, *Life in the English Country House* (London, 1978).

H. Gollwitzer, 'Die politische Landschaft in der deutschen Geschichte des 19/20 Jahrhunderts. Eine Skizze zum deutschen Regionalismus', *Zeitschrift für Bayerische Landesgeschichte*, vol. 27 (1964).

H. Gollwitzer, *Die Standesherren. Die politische und gesellschaftliche Stellung der Mediatisierten 1815–1918* (Stuttgart, 1957).

W. Gorlitz, *Die Junker. Adel und Bauer im Deutschen Osten* (Limburg, 1964).

Gothaisches genealogisches Taschenbuch der gräflichen Haüser (Gotha, 1930–39).

Gothaisches genealogisches Taschenbuch der uradeligen Haüser (Gotha, 1930–39).

Genealogisches Handbuch der gräflichen Haüser (Marburg, 1981).

P. Grabbe, *Windows on the River Neva* (New York, 1977).

M. Greiffenhagen, *Das Dilemma das Konservatismus in Deutschland* (Frankfurt, 1985).

Gronow, *The Reminiscences and Recollections of Captain Gronow*, 2 vols (London, 1900).

H. M. Grove, *Moscow* (London, 1912).

W. L. Guttsman, 'Aristocracy and the Middle Class in the British Political Elite 1886–1916. A Study of Formative Influences and of the Attitude to Politics', *The British Journal of Sociology*, vol. V (1954).

T. Häbich, *Deutsche Latifundien* (Königsberg, 1930).

G. M. Hamburg, 'Portrait of an Elite: Russian Marshals of the Nobility 1881–1917', *Slavic Review*, vol. 40 (1981).

G. M. Hamburg, *The Politics of the Russian Nobility 1881–1905* (Rutgers, 1984).

T. S. Hamerow, *Restoration, Revolution, Reaction. Economics and Politics in Germany 1815–1871* (Princeton, NJ, 1958).

K. Hammer, 'Die preussischen Könige und Königinnen in 19 Jahrhundert und ihr Hof', in K. F. Werner (ed.), *Hof, Kultur und Politik im 19 Jahrhundert* (Bonn, 1985).

R. Hauf, 'Die Oberpräsidenten von Ost und Westpreussen 1871–1918', in K. Schwabe (ed.), *Die Preussische Oberpräsidenten* (Boppard, 1985).

A. V. von Hauxthausen, *The Russian Empire. Its People, Institutions and Resources*, translated by R. Faire, 2 vols (London, 1968).

E. Heier, *Religious Schism in the Russian Aristocracy 1860–1900* (The Hague, 1970).

H. J. Helmigk, *Märkische Herrenhäuser aus Alter Zeit* (Berlin, n.d.).

G. Herdt, *Der württemburgische Hof im 19 Jahrhundert. Studien über das Verhaltnis zwischen Königtum und Adel in der absoluten und konstitutionellen Monarchie* (Göttingen, 1970).

D. Higgs, *Nobles in Nineteenth Century France. The Practice of Inegalitarianism* (Baltimore, Md., 1987).

G. Hirschmann, *Das Nürnberger Patriziat im Konigreich Bayern 1806–1918* (Nuremberg, 1971).

S. Hoch, *Serfdom and Social Control in Russia* (Chicago, 1986).

H. H. Hofmann, *Adelige Herrschaft und Souveräner Staat* (Munich, 1962).

P. U. Hohendahl and P. M. Lützeler, *Legitimisationskrisen des deutschen Adels 1200–1900* (Stuttgart, 1979).

Prince C. von Hohenlohe-Schillingfürst, *Memoirs of Prince Chlodwig of Hohenlohe-Schillingfürst*, 2 vols (London, 1906).

M. Howard, *The Franco-Prussian War* (New York, 1969).

H. D. Hudson, *The Rise of the Demidov Family* (Newtonville, 1986).

G. Hueckel, 'Agriculture during Industrialisation', in R. Floud and D. McCloskey (eds), *The Economic History of England since 1700* (Cambridge, 1981), vol. 1.

I. Hull, *The Entourage of Kaiser Wilhelm II* (Cambridge, 1982).

S. P. Huntingdon, *Political Order in Changing Societies* (Newhaven, 1968).

A. A. Ignatiev, *A Subaltern in Old Russia* (London, 1944).

N. I. Ikonnikov, *La Noblesse de Russie*, 2nd edn, vols A1–Z2 (Paris, 1958–66).

H. James, *A German Identity 1770–1990* (London, 1989).

K. H. Jarausch, *Students, Society and Politics in Imperial Germany. The Rise of Academic Illiberalism* (Princeton, NJ, 1982).

K. H. Jarausch, *The Enigmatic Chancellor* (Newhaven, 1972).

A. Jones, *The Art of War in the Western World* (Oxford, 1987).

E. Jones, 'Agriculture 1700–80', in R. Floud and D. McCloskey (eds), *The Economic History of England since 1700* (Cambridge, 1981) vol. 1.

E. Jones, 'The Changing Basis of English Agricultural Prosperity, 1853–1873', in P. J. Perry (ed.), *British Agriculture 1875–1914* (London, 1973).

E. Jordan, *Die Entstehung der Konservativen partei und die preussischen Agrarverhältnissen von 1848* (Munich, 1914).

E. Jordan, *Friedrich Wilhelm IV und der Preussischer Adel bei Umwandlung der ersten Kammer in das Herrenhaus* (Berlin, 1914).

N. M. Karamzin, *Memoir on Ancient and Modern Russia*, edited by R. Pipes (Cambridge, 1981).

S. von Kardorff, *Wilhelm von Kardorff. Ein nationales Parliamentarier im Zeitalter Bismarcks und Wilhelm II. 1828–1907* (Berlin, 1936).

N. I. Kareev, 'Kratkiy ocherk istorii Litseya, sostavleniy professorom N. I. Kareevym', in *Pamyatnaya knizhka Imperatorskogo Aleksandrovskogo Litseya* (SPB, 1886).

E. P. Karnovich, *Zamechatel'nya bogatstva chastnykh lits v Rossii* (SPB, 1885).

J. Keegan, *The Face of Battle* (London, 1978).

J. L. H. Keep, *Soldiers of the Tsar. Army and Society in Russia 1462–1874* (Oxford, 1985).

J. L. H. Keep, 'The Muscovite Elite and the Approach to Pluralism', *Slavonic and East European Review*, vol. 48 (1970).

F. Keinemann, *Soziale und politische Geschichte des westfälischen Adels 1815–1945* (Hamm, 1975).

E. Kemp and R. Mührer, *Die volkswirtschaftliche Bedeutung von Gross und Kleinbetrieb in der Landwirtschaft* (Berlin, 1913).

P. Kenez, 'A Profile of the Pre-revolutionary Officer Corps', *California Slavic Studies*, vol. 7 (1973).

P. Kennedy and A. Nicholls (eds), *Nationalist and Racialist Movements in Britain and Germany before 1914* (London, 1981).

P. M. Kennedy, *The Rise of the Anglo-German Antagonism 1860–1914* (London, 1989).

J. J. Kenney, 'The Politics of Assassination', in H. Ragsdale (ed.), *Paul I: A Reassessment of His Life and Reign* (Pittsburg, Penn., 1979).

V. G. Kiernan, *The Duel in European History. Honour and the Reign of Aristocracy* (Oxford, 1988).

W. S. Kircher, *Adel, Kirche und Politik in Württemburg 1830–1851. Kirchliche Bewegung, katholische Standesherren und Demokratie* (Stuttgart, 1973).

M. Kitchen, *The German Officer Corps* (Oxford, 1968).

E. von Kleist, 'Adel und Preussentum', *Suddeutsche Monatshefte*, vol. 23 (February 1926).

E. H. Kneschke, *Neus allgemeines Deutsches Adelslexicon*, 9 vols (Leipzig, 1859).

J. Kocka, 'Entrepreneurs and Managers in German Industrialisation', in P. Mathias and M. M. Postan (eds) *The Cambridge Economic History of Europe*, vol. VII, part I (Cambridge, 1978).

A. P. Korelin, *Dvoryanstvo v poreformennoy Rossii, 1861–1914* (Moscow, 1979).

R. Koselleck, *Preussen zwischen Reform und Revolution* (Stuttgart, 1989).

J. Köstler, *Geschichte des Waldes in Bayern* (Munich, 1934).

I. D. Koval'chenko, N. B. Selunskaya and B. M. Litvakov, *Sotsial'noekonomicheskiy stroy pomeshchichego khozyaystva evropeyskoy Rossii v epokhu kapitalizma* (Moscow, 1982).

K. A. Krivoshein, *A. V. Krivoshein 1857–1921. Ego znachenie v istorii Rossii nachala xx veka* (Paris, 1973).

C. Graf von Krockow, *Die Reise nach Pommern* (Stuttgart, 1981).

C. Graf von Krockow, *Warnung vor Preussen* (Stuttgart, 1981).

A. N. Kulomzin, 'Dmitri Nikolaevich Zamyatin', *Zhurnal Ministerstva Yustitsii*, no. 9 (1914).

A. Lambert, *Unquiet Souls. The Indian Summer of the British Aristocracy* (London, 1984).

F. Lannon and P. Preston (eds), *Elites and Power in Twentieth-Century Spain* (Oxford, 1990).

V. Ya. Laverychev, *Krupnaya burzhuaziya v poreformennoy Rossii 1861–1900* (Moscow, 1974).

J. P. LeDonne, 'Ruling Families in the Russian Political Order 1689–1825', *Cahiers du Monde Russe et Sovietique*, vol. XXVIII (1987).

D. C. B. Lieven, *Russia and the Origins of the First World War* (London, 1984).

D. C. B. Lieven, *Russia's Rulers under the Old Regime* (New Haven, 1989).

Prince Paul Lieven, *Dela davno minuvshikh*, MS (1952).

W. B. Lincoln, *In the Vanguard of Reform, Russia's Enlightened Bureaucrats 1825–1861* (De Kalb, 1982).

P. Lindau, 'Unter den Linden', in R. H. Davies (ed.), *The Great Streets of the World* (London, 1892).

C. von Lorck, *Ostpreussische Gutshaüser* (Kitzingen, 1952).

W. Loth, *Katholiken in Kaiserreich* (Düsseldorf, 1984).

Yu. M. Lotman, 'The Decembrist in Daily Life (Everyday Behaviour as a Historical–Psychological Category), in A. D. and A. S. Nakhimovsky, *The Semiotics of Russian Cultural History*.

D. M. Lyovshin, *Pazheyskiy ego Imperatorskogo Velichestva korpus za sto let* (SPB, 1902).

C. E. McClelland, *State, Society and University in Germany 1700–1914* (Cambridge, 1980).

G. McCormack and Y. Sugimoto, *The Japanese trajectory: modernisation and beyond* (Cambridge, 1988).

E. C. Mack, *Public Schools and British Opinion 1780–1860* (London, 1938).

E. C. Mack, *Public Schools and British Opinion since 1860* (New York, 1941).

J. P. McKay, 'Elites in Conflict in Russia. The Briansk Company', in F. C. Jaher (ed.), *The Rich, the Well Born and the Powerful. Elites and Upper Classes in History* (Urbana, 1973).

D. Macey, *Government and Peasant in Russia, 1861–1906* (De Kalb, 1987).

L. de Madariaga, *Russia in the Age of Catherine the Great* (London, 1981).

M. Maksimovsky, *Istoricheskiy ocherk razvitiya glavnogo inzhenernego uchilishcha 1819–1869* (SPB, 1869).

R. Manning, *The Crisis of the Old Regime in Russia* (Princeton, NJ, 1982).

P. Mansel, *The Court of France 1789–1830* (Cambridge, 1988).

S. Margetson, *St. John's Wood* (London, 1988).

E. W. Maron, *Forst-Statistik der sämtlichen Wälder Deutschlands einschliesslich Preussen* (Berlin, 1862).

R. Martin, *Jahrbuch des Vermögens und Einkommens der Millionäre in Bayern* (Berlin, 1914).

R. Martin, *Jahrbuch des Vermögens und Einkommens der Millionäre in Preussen* (Berlin, 1912).

R. B. Martinez and T. M. Barker, *Armed Forces and Society in Spain. Past and Present* (Boulder, Col., 1988).

A. J. Mayer, *The Persistence of the Old Regime. Europe to the Great War* (New York, 1981).

M. Mayzel, 'The Formation of the Russian General Staff 1800–1917', *Cahiers du Monde Russe et Sovietique*, vol. xvi, (1975).

G. Mee, *Aristocratic Enterprise, the Fitzwilliam Industrial Undertakings, 1795–1857* (Glasgow, 1975).

A. Mendel, 'The Debate between Prussian Junkerdom and the Forces of Urban Industry 1897–1902', *Jahrbuch des Instituts für Deutsche Geschichte*, vol. 4 (1975).

M. Messerschmidt, 'Preussens Militar in seinem gesellschaftlichen Umfeld' in H.-J. Puhle and H.-U. Wehler (eds), *Preussen in Ruckblick* (Göttingen, 1980).

P. Mikliss, *Deutscher und pölnischer Adel im Vergleich* (Berlin, 1981).

A. R. Millett and W. Murray (eds), *Military Effectiveness, Vol. 1, The First World War* 3 vols (Boston, 1988).

L. P. Minarik, *Ekonomicheskaya kharakteristika krupneyshikh sobstvennikov Rossii kontsa XIX–nachala XX vek* (Moscow, 1971).

G. E. Mingay, *English Landed Society in the Eighteenth Century* (London, 1963).

G. E. Mingay (ed.), *The Agricultural Revolution. Changes in Agriculture 1650–1880* (London, 1977).

G. E. Mingay, *English Landed Society in the Eighteenth Century* (London, 1963).

K. Möckl, 'Hof und Hofgesellschaft im Bayern in der Prinzregentenzeit', in K. F. Werner (ed.), *Akten des 18 deutschfranzösischen Historikerkolloquiums Darmstadt von 27–30 September 1982* (Bonn, 1985).

R. G. Moeller (ed.), *Peasants and Lords in Modern Germany* (London, 1986).

W. Mommsen, *Max Weber and German Politics 1890–1920* (Chicago, 1990).

M. M. Montgomery, *Gilded Prostitution. Status, Money and Transatlantic Marriages 1870–1914* (London, 1989).

B. Moore, *The Social Origins of Dictatorship and Democracy* (London, 1966).

W. E. Mosse, 'Adel und Burgertum in Europa des 19 Jahrhunderts. Eine vergleichende Betrachtung', in J. Kocka (ed.), *Bürgertum in 19 Jahrhundert*, 3 vols (Munich, 1988).

W. E. Mosse, *Alexander II and the Modernisation of Russia* (New York, 1962).

C. A. Moser (ed.), *The Cambridge History of Russian Literature* (Cambridge, 1989).

L. W. Muncy, *The Junker in the Prussian Administration under William II* (Providence, RI, 1944).

F. D. Munsell, *The Unfortunate Duke. Henry Pelham, Fifth Duke of Newcastle, 1811–1864* (Columbia, 1985).

J. Murray, *A Hand-Book for Travellers on the Continent. Being a Guide through Holland, Belgium, Prussia and Northern Germany* (London, 1843).

J. Murray, *Handbook for Northern Europe including Denmark, Norway, Sweden, Finland and Russia* (London, 1848).

J. Murray, *Handbook for Travellers in Russia, Poland and Finland* (London, 1865).

S. Neumann, *Die Stufen des preussischen Konservatismus* (Berlin, 1930).

A. Offer, *The First World War: An Agrarian Interpretation* (Oxford, 1989).

R. M. Ogilvie, *Latin and Greek. A History of the Influence of the Classics on English Life from 1600 to 1918* (London, 1964).

F. O'Gorman, 'Electoral Deference in "Unreformed" England: 1760–1832', *Journal of Modern History*, vol. 56, no. 3 (1984).

C. O'Grada, 'Agricultural Decline 1860–1914', in R. Floud and D. McCloskey, *The Economic History of Modern Britain* (Cambridge, 1981).

E. von Oldenburg-Januschau, *Erinnerungen* (Leipzig, 1936).

R. J. Olney, *Lincolnshire Politics 1832–1885* (Oxford, 1973).

C. B. Otley, 'Militarism and the Social Affiliations of the British Army Elite,' in J. van Doorn (ed.), *Armed Forces and Society: Sociological Essays* (The Hague, 1960).

Pamyatniki arkhitektury Leningrada (Leningrad, 1976).

P. Paret (ed.), *Makers of Modern Strategy from Machiavelli to the Nuclear Age* (Princeton, NJ, 1986).

V. Pareto, *Sociological Writings*, selected and introduced by S. E. Finer (London, 1966).

V. Pareto, *The Rise and Fall of the Elites: An Application of Theoretical Sociology* (Bedminster, 1968).

G. Parry, *Political Elites* (London, 1969).

F. Paulsen, *The German Universities and University Study* (London, 1906).

G. Pavlovsky, *Agricultural Russia on the Eve of the Revolution* (London, 1930).

J. Pearson, *Stags and Serpents* (London, 1983).

G. W. Pedlow, *The Survival of the Hessian Nobility 1770–1870* (Princeton, NJ, 1988).

J. Pellew, *The Home Office 1848–1914* (London, 1982).

H. Perkin, *Origins of Modern English Society* (London, 1969).

H. Perkin, *The Rise of Professional Society* (London, 1989).

J. A. Perkins, 'The Agricultural Revolution in Germany 1850–1914', *Journal of European Economic History*, vol. 10 (1981).

A. Perlick, *Oberschlesische Berg und Hüttenleute* (Frankfurt, 1953).

R. Perren, 'The Landlord and Agricultural Transformation, 1870–1900', in P. J. Percy (ed.), *British Agriculture 1873–1914* (London, 1973).

H. von Petersdorff, *Kleist-Retzow, Ein Lebensbild* (Stuttgart, 1907).

F. Petri and G. Droege (eds), *Rheinische Geschichte*, 3 vols (Düsseldorf, 1976).

G. D. Phillips, *The Diehards. Aristocratic Society and Politics in Edwardian England* (Cambridge, 1979).

P. M. Pilbeam, *The Middle Classes in Europe 1789–1914* (London, 1990).

W. M. Pintner, *Russian Economic Policy Under Nicholas I* (Ithaca, NY, 1967).

W. M. Pintner and D. K. Rowney (eds), *Russian Officialdom: the Bureaucratization of Russian Society from the Seventeenth to the Twentieth Century* (Chapel Hill, 1980).

R. Pipes, *Struve. Liberal on the Right 1905–1944* (Cambridge, 1980).

Princess Daisy of Pless, *From My Private Diary* (London, 1931).

Princess Daisy of Pless, *Daisy Princess of Pless. By Herself* (London, 1928).

Polnaya entsiklopediya russkogo sel'skogo khozyaystva i soprikasayushchikhsya s nim nauk, 11 vols (SPB, 1900–12).

S. Pollard and C. Holmes, *Documents of European Economic History, Volume 1; The Process of Industrialization: 1750–1870* (London, 1968).

A. Ponsonby, *The Decline of Aristocracy* (London, 1912).

V. Potto, *Istoricheskiy ocherk Nikolaevskogo Kavaleriyskogo Uchilishcha 1827–1873* (SPB, 1873).

Predlozhenie k trudam redaktsionnoy kommissii (SPB, 1859).

N. von Preradovich, *Die Führungsschichten in Österreich und Preussen (1804–1918)* (Wiesbaden, 1955).

J. Prest, *Lord John Russell* (London, 1972).

K. Prewitt and A. Stone, *The Ruling Elites* (New York, 1973).

N. A. Proskuryakova, 'Razmeshchenie i struktura dvoryanskogo zemlevladeniya evropeyskoy Rossii v kontse XIX–nachale XX veka', *Istoriya CCCP*, vol. 1 (1973).

Prince L. H. von Pückler-Muskau, *Tour in England, Ireland and France in the Years 1826, 1827, 1828 and 1829* (Zurich, 1940).

H.-J. Puhle, *Agrarische Interessenpolitik und preussischer Konservatismus im wilhelminischen Reich 1893–1914* (Bonn, 1975).

M. Raeff, *Origins of the Russian Intelligentsia* (New York, 1966).

M. Raeff, *The Well-Ordered Police State: Social and Institutional Change through Law in the Germanies and Russia 1600–1800* (Newhaven, 1983).

T. Raikes, *A Visit to Saint Petersburg in the Winter of 1829–30* (London, 1938).

P. E. Razzell, 'Social Origins of Officers in the Indian and British Home Armies', *British Journal of Sociology*, vol. XIV (1963).

A. von Reden-Dohna and R. Melville (eds), *Der Adel an der Schwelle des bürgerlichen Zeitalters* (Stuttgart, 1988).

F. Redlich, *Der Unternehmer* (Göttingen, 1964).

H. Reif, *Westfälische Adel 1770–1860* (Göttingen, 1979).

J. R. Rettalack, *Notables of the Right. The Conservative Party and Political Mobilisation in Germany 1876–1918* (London, 1988).

A. J. Rieber, *Merchants and Entrepreneurs in Imperial Russia* (Chapel Hill, 1982).

G. Ritter, *The Sword and the Sceptre, Volume 1, The Prussian Tradition, 1740–1890; Volume 2, The European Powers and the Wilhelmine Empire* (London, 1972).

R. G. Robbins, *The Tsar's Viceroys* (Ithaca, NY, 1987).

J. C. G. Röhl, *Kaiser, Hof und Staat. Wilhelm II und die deutsche Politik* (Munich, 1987).

J. C. G. Röhl and N. Sombart (eds), *Kaiser Wilhelm II. New Interpretations* (Cambridge, 1982).

M. Rolfes, 'Landwirtschaft. 1850–1914' in H. Aubin and W. Zorn (eds), *Handbuch der deutschen Wirtschafts-und-Sozialgeschichte*, vol. 2 (Stuttgart, 1976).

A. Romanovich-Slavatinsky, *Dvoryanstvo v Rossii* (SPB, 1870).

H. Rosenberg, *Bureaucracy, Aristocracy and Autocracy. The Prussian Experience 1660–1815* (Cambridge, 1958).

H. Rosenberg, 'Die Pseudodemokratisierung der Rittergutsbesitzerklasse', in H.-U. Wehler (ed.), *Moderne deutsche Sozialgeschichte* (Düsseldorf, 1981).

H. Rosenberg, *Grosse Depression und Bismarckzeit* (Berlin, 1967).

R. J. Ross, *Beleaguered Tower: the Dilemma of Political Catholicism in Wilhelmine Germany* (Notre Dame, 1976).

V. R. Rubakhin, *Grafy Apraksiny i ikh Peterburgskaya votchina – Apraksin Dvor* (SPB, 1912).

W. D. Rubinstein, *Men of Property. The Very Wealthy in Britain Since the Industrial Revolution* (London, 1981).

W. D. Rubinstein, *Elites and the Wealthy in Modern British History* (Brighton, 1987).

H. Rubner, *Forstgeschichte im Zeitalter der industriellen Revolution* (Berlin, 1967).

H. Rumschöttel, *Das bayerische Offizierkorps 1866–1914* (Berlin, 1973).

J. J. Sack, 'The House of Lords and Parliamentary Patronage in Great Britain, 1802–1832', *Historical Journal*, vol. 23, no. 4 (1980).

K. Saul, 'Um die konservative Struktur Ostelbiens: Agrarische Interessen, Staatsverwaltung und ländliche "Arbeiternot". Zur konservativen Landarbeiterpolitik in Preussen-Deutschland 1889–1914', in D. Stegmann, B. J. Wendt and P. C. Witt (eds), *Deutscher Konservatismus im 19 and 20 Jahrhundert* (Bonn, 1983).

S. Schama, *Citizens. A Chronicle of the French Revolution* (London, 1989).

L. von Scharfenort, *Die Pagen am Brandenburg – Preussischen Hofe 1415–1895* (Berlin, 1985).

P. Scheibert, *Die russische Agrarreform von 1861* (Cologne, 1973).

H. Schissler, *Preussische Agrargesellschaft im Wandel* (Göttingen, 1978).

H. Schissler, 'The Junkers: Notes on the Social and Historical Significance of the Agrarian Elite in Prussia', in R. G. Moeller (ed.), *Peasants and Lords in Modern Germany* (London, 1986).

G. H. Schlingensiepen, *Der Strukturwandel des Baltischen Adels in der Zeit von den Ersten Weltkrieg* (Marburg, 1959).

P. Schnepp, 'Die Reichsritterschaft', *Deutsche Geschichtsblätter*, vol. XIV (1913).

R. Schutt, 'Partei wider Willen. Kalküle und Potentiale konservativer Parteigründer in Preussen zwischen Ersten Vereinigten Landtag und Nationalen Versammlung', in D. Stegmann, B. J. Wendt and P. C. Witt (eds), *Deutscher Konservatismus im 19 und 20 Jahrhundert* (Bonn, 1983).

K. Schwabe (ed.), *Die preussische Oberpräsidenten* (Boppard, 1985).

A. Schwappach, *Grundriss der Forst und Jagdgeschichte* (Berlin, 1883).

W. Schwentker, 'Die alte und die neue Aristokratie. Zum Problem von Adel und bürgerlicher Elite in den deutschen Sozialwissenschaften (1900–1930)', in *Les Noblesses Européennes au XIXe Siècle*, Collection de L'Ecole Francaise de Rome (Rome, 1988).

W. A. L. Seaman and J. R. Sewell, *Russian Journal of Lady Londonderry, 1836–37* (Bath, 1973).

H. Seffert, 'Die Entwicklung der Familie von Alvensleben zu Junker-industriellen', *Jahrbuch für Wirtschaftsgeschichte*, vol. IV (1963).

I. Seleznev, *Istoricheskiy ocherk Imperatorskogo byvshego Tsarskosel'skogo nyne Aleksandrovskogo Litseya za pervoe ego pyatidesyatiletie s 1811 do 1861 god* (SPB, 1861).

P. P. Semyonov, *Detstvo i yunost* (SPB, 1915).

V. I. Serov, *The Mighty Five. The Cradle of Russian National Music* (London, 1948).

J. J. Sheehan, *German History 1770–1866* (Oxford, 1989).

A. Shubert, *A Social History of Modern Spain* (London, 1990).

A. Sinel, *The Classroom and the Chancellery. State Educational Reform under Count Dmitry Tolstoy* (Cambridge, 1973).

Count V. A. Sollohub, *Vospominaniya* (SPB, 1877).

Yu. B. Solov'yov, *Samoderzhavie i dvoryanstvo v kontse XIX veka* (Leningrad, 1973).

Yu. B. Solov'yov, *Samoderzhavie i dvoryanstvo v 1902–1907* (Leningrad, 1981).

Yu. Ya. Solovyov, *Vospominaniya diplomata* (Moscow, 1959).

D. Southgate, *The Passings of the Whigs 1832–1886* (London, 1965).

M. Spindler, *Bayerische Geschichte im 19 und 20 Jahrhundert 1800 bis 1970*, 2 parts (Munich, 1978).

D. Spring, 'Earl Fitzwilliam and the Corn Laws', *American Historical Review*, vol. LIX, no. 2 (1954).

D. Spring, 'English Landowners and Nineteenth-Century Industrialism', in J. T. Ward and R. G. Wilson (eds), *Land and Industry, the Landed Estate and the Industrial Revolution* (London, 1971).

D. Spring (ed.), *European Landed Elites in the Nineteenth Century* (Baltimore, Md., 1977).

D. Spring, *The English Landed Estate in the Nineteenth Century: Its Administration* (Baltimore, 1963).

S. F. Starr, *Decentralisation and Self-Government in Russia 1830–1870* (Princeton, NJ, 1972).

Z. S. Steiner, *Britain and the Origins of the First World War* (London, 1977).

Z. S. Steiner, *The Foreign Office and Foreign Policy 1898–1914* (London, 1969).

H. Stekl, *Österreichs Aristokratie im Vormärz* (Munich, 1973).

F. Stern, *Gold and Iron. Bismarck, Bleichröder and the Building of the German Empire* (London, 1980).

R. Stewart, *The Politics of Protection. Lord Derby and the Protectionist Party 1841–1852* (Cambridge, 1971).

K. Stiefel (ed.), *Baden 1648–1952*, 2 vols (Karlsruhe, 1978–9).

O. Graf zu Stolberg-Wernigerode, *Deutschlands konservative Führungs schichten am Vorabend des ersten Weltkrieges* (Munich, 1968).

Stolitsa i Usad'ba (SPB, 1913–1917).

L. Stone and J. C. F. Stone, *An Open Elite? England 1540–1880* (Oxford, 1984).

N. Stone, *The Eastern Front 1914–1917* (London, 1975).

G. P. Strod, 'K voprosu o vremeni pobedy kapitilisticheskogo sposoba proizvodstva v sel'skom khozyaystve Latvii', *Ezhegodnik po agrarnoy istorii vostochnoy Evropy* (1963).

C. S. Sykes, *Private Palaces. Life in the Great London Houses* (London, 1985).

R. Symonds, *Oxford and Empire* (Basingstoke, 1986).

N. V. Tcharykow, *Glimpses of High Politics* (London, 1931).

F. G. Terner, *Vospominaniya zhizni*, 2 vols (SPB, 1910).

R. von Thadden, *Prussia: the History of a Lost State* (Cambridge, 1987).

R. von Thadden-Vahnerow, 'Der Adel in Norddeutschland', *Suddeutsche Monatshefte*, vol. 23 (February 1926).

F. M. L. Thompson, *English Landed Society in the Nineteenth Century* (London, 1963).

F. M. L. Thompson, 'The Second Agricultural Revolution', *Economic History Review*, vol. XXI (1968).

F. M. L. Thompson, 'Private Property and Public Policy' in Lord Blake and H. Cecil (eds), *Salisbury, The Man and His Policies* (London, 1987).

F. M. L. Thompson, 'The Landed Aristocracy and Business Elites in Victorian Britain', in *Les Noblesses Européennes au XIXe Siecle*, Collection de L'Ecole Francaise de Rome (Rome, 1988).

F. M. L. Thompson, 'Aristocracy, Gentry and the Middle Class in Britain 1750–1850', in A. M. Birke and L. Kettenacker, *Bürgertum, Adel und Monarchie* (Munich, 1989).

A. P. Thornton *The Habit of Authority. Paternalism in British History* (London, 1964).

F. Tönnies, 'Deutscher Adel im neunzehnten Jahrhundert', *Die Neue Rundschau*, vol. 23 (1912).

W. Tooke, *View of the Russian Empire during the Reign of Catherine the Second and to the Close of the Present Century*, 3 vols (London, 1799).

H.-J. Torke, 'Das russische Beamtentum in der ersten Hälfte des 19 Jahrhunderts', *Forschungen zur Geschichte Osteuropas*, vol. 13 (1967).

K. Tribe, 'Prussian Agriculture – German Politics: Max Weber 1892–7', *Economy and Society*, vol. 12, no. 2 (1983).

S. M. Troitsky, *Russkiy absolyutizm i dvoryanstvo v XVIIIv* (Moscow, 1974).

Prince E. N. Trubetskoy, *Vospominaniya* (Sofia, 1922).

Trudy Iogo (–IX ogo) s'ezda upol'nomochennykh dvoryanskikh obshchestv, 32 (–39) gubernii (SPB, 1906–13).

M. A. Tsvetkov, *Izmenenie lesisosti Evropeyskoy Rossii s kontsa XVII stoletiya po 1914 god* (Moscow, 1957).

M. I. Tugan-Baranovsky, *The Russian Factory in the Nineteenth Century* (Illinois, 1970).

A. S. Turberville, *The House of Lords in the Age of Reform 1784–1837* (Westport, 1974).

W. Vamplew, *A Social and Economic History of Horse Racing* (London, 1976).

Count P. Vasili, *Berlin Society* (New York, 1884).

Count P. Vasili, *La Sainte Russie* (Paris, 1890).

Count P. Vasili, *La Société de St. Petersbourg* (Paris, 1886).

Count P. Vasili, *The World of London* (London, 1895).

M. van Creveld, *Command in War* (Cambridge, 1985).

A. P. Vergunov and V. A. Gorokhov, *Russkie sady i parky* (Moscow, 1988).

R. Vierhaus (ed.), *Das Tagebuch der Baronin Spitzemberg* (Göttingen, 1960).

R. Vierhaus, 'Vom aufgeklärten Absolutismus zum monarchischen Konstitutionalismus. Der deutsche adel im Spannungsfeld von Revolution, Reform und Restauration', in P. U. Hohendahl and P. M. Lützeler (eds), *Legitimationskrisen des deutschen Adels 1200–1900* (Stuttgart, 1979).

R. Vierhaus, *Germany in the Age of Absolutism*, (Cambridge, 1988).

F. F. Vigel, *Vospominaniya*, 7 parts (Moscow, 1864).

H. Vizetelly, *Berlin under the New Empire*, 2 vols (London, 1979).

B. Vogel, 'Reformpolitik in Preussen 1807–1820', in H.-J. Puhle and H.-U. Wehler (eds), *Preussen in Hinblick* (Göttingen, 1980).

Prince S. Volkonsky, *My Reminiscences*, 2 vols (London, 1924).

J. T. Ward and R. G. Wilson, *Land and Industry. The Landed Estate and the Industrial Revolution* (London, 1971).

S. B. Webb, 'Agricultural Protection in Wilhelminian Germany: Forging an Empire with Pork and Rye', *Journal of Economic History*, vol. XLII (1982).

H. Weber, *Die Fürsten von Hohenlohe im Vormärz. Politische und soziale Verhaltensweisen württemburgischer Standesherren in der ersten Hälfte des 19 Jahrhunderts* (Stuttgart, 1977).

S. Wehking, 'Zum politischen und sozialen Selbstverständnis preussischer Junker 1871–1914', *Blätter für deutsche Landesgeschichte*, vol. 121 (1985).

H.-U. Wehler, *The German Empire* (Leamington Spa, 1985).

P. K. Weitz, *Der niederrheinische und westfälische Adel in ersten preussischen Verfassungskampf 1815–1823/4* (Bonn, 1970).

V. Wendt, *Kultur und Jagd*, 2 vols (Berlin, 1908).

K. F. Werner (ed.), *Hof, Kultur und Politik im 19 Jahrhundert* (Bonn, 1985).

L. Graf von Westphalen, *Aus dem Leben des Grafen Clemens August von Westphalen zu Fürstenberg (1805–1885)* (Munster, 1979).

C. H. Whittaker, *The Origins of Modern Russian Education. An Intellectual History of Count Serge Uvarov* (De Kalb, 1984).

M. Wiener, *English Culture and the Decline of the Industrial Spirit, 1850–1980* (Cambridge, 1981).

R. Wilkinson, *The Prefects. British Leadership and the Public School Tradition* (London, 1964).

S. R. Williamson, *Austria–Hungary and the Origins of the First World War* (London 1991).

H. Winkel, *Die Ablosungskapitalien aus der Bauernbefreiung im West und Suddeutschland* (Stuttgart, 1968).

A. Winson, 'The "Prussian road" of agrarian development: a reconsideration', *Economy and Society*, vol. 11, no. 4 (1982).

R. Wittram, *Baltische Geschichte* (Munich, 1954).

G. L. Yaney, *The Systematisation of Russian Government: Social Evolution in the Domestic Administration of Imperial Russia 1711–1905* (Urbana, 1973).

V. K. Yatsunsky, 'Geography of the Iron Market in Pre-Reform Russia', in W. L. Blackwell (ed.), *Russian Economic Development from Peter the Great to Stalin* (New York, 1974).

P. Young and J. P. Lawford (eds), *History of the British Army* (Wallop, 1970).

J. K. Zabel, *Das preussische Kadettenkorps* (Frankfurt, 1978).

P. A. Zayonchkovsky, *Pravitel'stvenniy apparat samoderzhavnoy Rossii v XIXv* (Moscow, 1978).

P. A. Zayonchkovsky, *Samoderzhavie i russkaya armiya na rubezhe XIX–XX stoletiy* (Moscow, 1973).

Index